MAYOR

An Inside View of San Antonio
Politics, 1981–1995

An Inside View of San Antonio
Politics, 1981–1995

by Nelson W. Wolff

foreword by Henry Cisneros

San Antonio Express-News

10 9 8 7 6 5 4 3 2 1

Permissions
San Antonio Express-News
Post Office Box 2171
San Antonio, Texas 78297-2171

The paper in this book meets the minimum requirements of
the American National Standard for Permanence of Paper for
Printed Library materials, z39.48.1984.

Library of Congress Cataloging-in-Publication Data

Wolff, Nelson W., 1940–
Mayor : an inside view of San Antonio politics, 1981–1995 /
by Nelson Wolff ; foreword by Henry Cisneros.
p.   cm.
Includes index.
ISBN 1-890346-00-4 (hardcover : alk. paper). —
ISBN 1-890346-01-2 (pbk. : alk. paper)
1. Mayors—Texas—San Antonio—Biography.   2. Wolff, Nelson W.,
1940–   .   3. Cisneros, Henry.   4. San Antonio (Tex.)—Politics and
government.   I. Cisneros, Henry.   II. Title.
F394.S353A2   1997
976.4'351063'0922—dc21   97-3280
                                                                    CIP

Design by Layton Graphics

On the cover — Left photo: Mayor Henry Cisneros campaigns for
re-election in 1987. (Joe Barrera Jr., Express-News)
Right photo: Nelson and Tracy Wolff raise their arms in victory the
night Nelson was elected mayor in May 1991. (Doug Sehres, Express-
News)

To my wife Tracy, my best friend and the love of my life.

Nelson and Tracy Wolff with Henry Cisneros at an event in 1991. (Wolff collection)

A Special Recognition

This book would have not been possible without six years of close collaboration with Tom Brereton. His knowledge and insight into city government and local politics are invaluable.

Tom earned a master's of regional planning and a doctorate in social sciences (metropolitan studies) from Syracuse University. He moved to San Antonio in 1972 and became a professor of urban studies at Trinity University.

He eventually formed his own business as a consultant in planning and urban affairs. He became active in Henry Cisneros' campaign for mayor, writing his position papers. Throughout Cisneros' term he was instrumental in formulating policies.

When I ran for City Council in 1987 and then mayor in 1991 Tom was a key adviser. During my time in office he led a team of academics who worked with me in developing my agenda. He wrote my yearly agendas as he had done for Cisneros.

Today Tom continues to play a major role in developing urban policies. His intellectual insights into local government continue to make a profound impact on public policy.

Acknowledgments

First, a thank-you to my wife, Tracy, for her careful reading of this manuscript, and the suggestions that have helped me write this story with sensitivity.

Cary Cardwell's knowledge of San Antonio was essential to the editing of this book. For 20 years, he has been a journalist covering events in the city. He also served as city editor of the San Antonio Light. I am appreciative of his dedication in fine-crafting this work.

Several friends helped provide research materials and reviewed drafts of this manuscript. I want to thank them for taking valuable time out of their busy schedules. Thanks to: Alex Briseño, Al Philippus, Ron Darner, Rolando Bono, Norma Rodriguez, Travis Bishop, Rebecca Waldman, Martin Rodriguez, Clinton Bolden, Beth Costello, Jose Luis Garcia, June Garcia, Niki Frances McDaniel, Amelia Ramirez, Jacky Bolds, Shirl Thomas, Carmen Gonzales, Evelyn Salinas, John German, Sergio Soto, Tom Frost, Elisa Bass, Cliff Morton, Joe Aceves, Rebecca Cedillo, Paul Roberson, Jude Valdez, Dave Pasley, Danielle Milam, Marie Swartz, Mary Rose Brown, Joe Krier, Russ Johnson and Marc Nourani.

Table of Contents

Foreword

San Antonio has always been a city of many facets and complexities. From its earliest days, it has been characterized by its contradictions and dualities. It was first a village of Native American hunter-gatherers but soon became an outpost of Spanish missionary colonization. The chaplain who accompanied the first Spanish military expedition to the verdant site nestled among tall cypress trees at the edge of the river described an oasis amidst the harsh brush country the group had crossed on the route from the Mexican interior. Yet within a few years, the missionaries would write with frustration of the "indolence" of the native inhabitants and of the place itself.

Throughout its history, San Antonio has never been simple. It was the site of the Battle of the Alamo, which established the moral imperative for Texas independence from Mexico. But among the defenders inside the Alamo were also Mexican citizens fighting against their government's dictatorial policies. By the turn of the century, San Antonio was one of the nation's most progressive cities, but also a city of crushing poverty in its barrios and colonias. It became home to some of America's most important military installations in the mobilization for World War II, but was itself governed by a city government disdained for its inefficiency and even corruption.

That complexity of personality carried forward into the second half of the 20th century. My earliest mental image of a political event is a memory of a shopping trip downtown with my mother in 1953, when I was 6 years old. From the bus, she pointed out the mayor in a Southern-style white suit, speaking at a civic event on Alamo Plaza. A few moments later, as we walked to the McCrory's Five and Dime store on the opposite side of Alamo Plaza, she noted the "whites-only" drinking fountains.

Always it seemed issues of race, origin, and class bedeviled San Antonio. The city had been long divided, its people resentful and harboring the anger that rigid class lines make inevitable. In the 1960s, when the city should have basked in the impressive accomplishments of its successful world's fair, HemisFair '68, instead bitter protests brought the national civil rights struggle home. Mayor Walter McAllister, who led the city to invest in its downtown and modernized the municipal government, could not overcome the legacy of injustice and exclusivity.

In the 1970s, people in the poor neighborhoods of San Antonio were certain that the political and economic powers who controlled the city had consciously kept them down, discouraging new industry in order to keep wages low, keep unions out, and keep progressive leaders away. While Mayor Lila Cockrell introduced a personal leadership of consensus and welcomed new levels of participation through single-member districts, at the end of the decade national publications still wrote of a city smoldering with divisions and as a result incapable of participating in the economic momentum that was propelling other Sun Belt cities forward.

It was clear at the beginning of the 1980s that untangling the brier patch of contradictions and antagonisms must be the most important agenda. Before the city could make lasting progress, San Antonians would have to find enough common ground to be able to work together, to overcome the divisions at the city's heart.

The 1980s and 1990s in San Antonio have been a time of identifying and acting upon common themes and the most important unifying themes have been the quest for better jobs and opportunities for families. On these hopes a workable coalition was built and on these ambitions forums were created so that antagonists could talk to each other respectfully as people who had to learn to live together because they don't intend to live anywhere else and who needed each other in order to advance their own interests and dreams.

My friend, Nelson Wolff, has done an admirable service in chronicling the last two decades in San Antonio's public life. Though he has been far too generous in his characterizations of my work, he has ably captured the key moments of confrontation and reconciliation, of debate and decision. No one has done it better.

Nelson has combined the knowledge that comes from his involvement in virtually every important decision of the period with his gift for writing and a rare discipline to have kept good notes with which to supplement his keen memory and powers of observation. Most important, Nelson Wolff cares deeply about San Antonio. His devotion to the public interest has been evident for years in his capable service. Such devotion to a city and its people is manifestly visible once again in the values that motivate this book.

Henry Cisneros

Introduction

After completing two terms as mayor of San Antonio in 1995, I struggled for several months deciding how best to tell of a time of historic transformation for our city. That period began with the election of Henry Cisneros as mayor in 1981.

During Henry's eight years as mayor, my relationship with him progressed from a political supporter to a key player in his coalition for progress, to a City Council colleague and, finally, to a close friendship. I was able to observe this remarkable natural politician as he provided the leadership that changed the economic and political structure of San Antonio.

I began to write an account of the transformation of both the city and its key leader after Henry left office in 1989. At the time, I was serving as a city councilman during the term of Mayor Lila Cockrell. When I decided to run for mayor myself two years later, I set aside the manuscript for more than four years.

When I re-read the draft after serving as mayor I found it incomplete in dealing with the long-term implications of Henry's tenure. So I decided to carry the book forward through the end of my term.

Henry took our city from the political elitism of a closed Anglo-dominated system to a political pluralism in which minorities gained parity with Anglos. He changed the ceremonial office of mayor into a powerhouse. He used the new power to build community consensus from diverse interests.

With his coalition for progress in place, he pushed the city forward with a clarion call for fast-paced economic development. His push began the process of lifting our city from an economic backwater driven by an economy dependent on the federal government to a city with rising incomes and a diversified economy. Henry passed massive public works projects to complement the city's private-sector development.

When I became mayor in 1991, I remained faithful to Henry's economic development agenda. But I shifted my primary message to what I call "growth with grace." I placed at the top of my agenda youth, public safety, parks and the environment.

As this book goes to press, 16 years have passed since Henry's election. During this time we have diversified our economy by pursuing international trade, developing a financial and telecommunications industry, growing our health-care industry and expanding tourism. Through substantial investments in infrastructure, we have begun to cure the decades of neglect that left a legacy of congested streets, outdated sewage facilities, inadequate convention accommodations, deteriorating parks and dangerous drainage.

The city has taken a number of important steps to improve the quality of life: working for safe and aesthetically pleasing neighborhoods, seeking a better environment, promoting libraries and the arts and maintaining community standards of conduct. Our dying downtown was resuscitated and continues to become more and more active.

The story you are about to read begins during Henry's campaign for mayor in 1981. It is about how Henry, and then I, developed these major initiatives to push our community forward. It's a story about how a mayor can join the public and private sectors in a partnership to build a stronger community. It is also the story of how our friendship evolved out of political confrontation.

This book is not a history, but rather a personal account of the major political issues, confrontations and solutions that helped shape our city. It is at once a story of San Antonio, and also of every city.

Now, on with the tale.

1

Henry Cisneros for Mayor

I first felt the stirring of mayoral aspirations while standing in a field on a beautiful day in April 1981. It may seem an odd place for political inspiration. But this was one of those perfect San Antonio days: sunny and cool, with a slight breeze and, best of all, no humidity. And the young man who was about to speak possessed a natural eloquence that made his listeners believe that great things were possible.

About 50 of us had gathered next to a small office building on Jackson-Keller Road in northwest San Antonio, just inside the Loop 410 beltway that circles the city. A few blocks away is Robert E. Lee High School, home of the 1971 state champion football team led by quarterback Tommy Kramer, who would go on to play for the Minnesota Vikings.

San Antonio's municipal political season was in full bloom like the Indian paintbrush and bluebonnets spread across the field. The mayoral and City Council election was just days away, and we were attending a rally for Henry Cisneros, a tall, urbane, 33-year-old city councilman who was a candidate for mayor.

My good friend and Henry's uncle, Ruben Munguia, had asked me to help on the city's North Side. To win, Henry needed to capture a significant percentage of that area's predominantly Anglo voters. He was going against historic odds. No Hispanic had been elected mayor of San Antonio since Texas had joined the Union.

Ruben Munguia had certainly picked the part of town that felt like home turf to me. Looking across the field and over a drainage ditch to nearby West Avenue, I could see the office building and lumber yard that once served as headquarters of Alamo Enterprises, the business built by my father, my brothers, George and Gary, and me in the 1960s.

Ten miles farther east along Loop 410, on Nacogdoches Road, is the original Sun Harvest Natural Foods Store, which my brothers and I opened in 1979 in partnership with the Herrmann brothers, Ron and Don.

Business was not my only connection to the North Side. I had represented the area in the state House of Representatives and then the state Senate during the first half of the 1970s. With business and political roots in the area, I knew I could help.

But until that morning, standing in that field, I had found little reason to pay attention to municipal politics. I thought City Hall was the junkyard of the political system, with City Council members at the bottom of the political food chain. Politically, City Hall was a dead end.

I also believed the mayor's office provided only a shaky platform rather than the "bully pulpit" needed to get things done. The city charter, adopted in 1951, had seen to that. It curtailed the mayor's powers in favor of a council-manager form of government that gave most authority to an unelected city manager. Council members selected the mayor from among their ranks for a largely ceremonial role. The mayor presided over a short weekly council meeting, and represented the city at ribbon-cuttings and the like. Even after the charter was amended in 1975 to allow for the direct election of the mayor by the people, there was still no evidence of any real power in the office.

But now the voice of a young councilman from the largely Hispanic West Side was articulating a new vision of progress and power flowing from the office of mayor. Henry Cisneros was saying that city government could be instrumental in the overall life of the community. He was telling everyone in 1981 that somehow he was going to redefine the mayor's office and strengthen its powers. And he pledged to use this new-found power to address the low incomes of the citizens of San Antonio.

"San Antonio is a poor city," he said during the campaign. "Its people on average are poor, and therefore its city government is poor. Low incomes mean low property values, low sales tax collections, and so on down the list of city revenues." He quoted statistics showing that San Antonio's revenues were running at less than half the average of all U.S. cities with populations exceeding 250,000.

All across the city Henry was rallying people around a comprehensive blueprint for change. He based his campaign on five position papers. He led with his long suit, economic development, which emphasized a plan to create more and better-paying jobs by diversifying San Antonio's economy and enhancing education. The other four included budget and fiscal policy, crime and neighborhood services, streets and drainage, and energy development. Although he did not say where he would garner the power to accomplish the plan, he promised that he would take personal responsibility to make it happen.

No other mayoral candidate in recent history had developed such a plan for the city. No candidate had ever pledged to seek the power to implement his plan. People were responding to Henry's message. I liked what I was hearing and wanted to get involved.

He was stirring the political winds of change, winds that had been calm too long.

The GGL, COPS and Single-member Districts

For eight years prior to the election of 1981, City Hall had been a political quagmire. Without a consensus on how to move our city forward, it had become impossible to accomplish anything significant.

Three major political events in the 1970s had created this instability. Things began to unravel in 1973, when Charles Becker challenged the Good Government League, a group of conservative, mostly Anglo businessmen who had imposed on the city a political consensus of sorts for two decades. They had begun their reign shortly after the city adopted the council-manager form of government. And the GGL's slates of candidates — chosen at secret meetings by an anonymous nomination committee — were almost always victorious.

The Good Government League candidates pledged to act in the civic interest of all of the city under the then at-large electoral system. They pledged not to seek higher political office. They were expected to act as a board of directors of a business, to keep "politics" to a minimum and their weekly meetings short, and to stay out of the day-to-day business of running the city government.

The system worked. The mayor and council stuck to fixing streets, picking up garbage, and keeping police on the streets. The really important issues were reserved for behind-the-scenes action by the key business leaders in the Good Government League who held the real reins of power. Not only did they pick the mayor and members of council, they were the real decision makers on the big issues that affected San Antonio.

As a member of the Texas Legislature in the early 1970s, I had dealt with the power structure of the Good Government League. I served on the Appropriations Committee in the House, and then as vice-chairman of the Finance Committee in the Senate. These two committees held the greatest power over major funding issues for cities. "Key" San Antonians including Pat Zachry, John Peace, "Pop" Gunn, Louis Stumberg and Wilbur Matthews called on me regarding financial issues affecting San Antonio. Yet I never met nor heard from the mayor or council members.

Though one may question the legitimacy of any consensus forged by such an exclusive club, the members of the Good Government League at least kept the wheels turning at City Hall and kept the city moving forward in what they defined as progress.

The GGL leaders also were primarily responsible for two historic events that decided the economic future of San Antonio. First, they organized a World's Fair in 1968 that served to clear nearly 100 acres of dilapidated barrio within three blocks of the Alamo. "HemisFair '68," as the fair was called, positioned the city for international trade and laid the foundation for San Antonio's second-largest economic generator today, the tourism industry. They decided that the convention center would be located on the fair-grounds, in the near east part of downtown. This would be the foundation for an emerging hotel and restaurant development.

Second, the GGL leaders were key players in persuading the state to locate a University of Texas Medical School in San Antonio. This would become the foundation of our third most important industry, health care. They decided the school would be on the North Side of San Antonio. This decision was one of the major reasons that economic and population growth shifted to the north.

During its 20-year reign, the GGL won 77 of 81 council races. With that kind of electoral power, it was easy to have a political consensus.

But things began to fall apart for the league in 1973, when GGL City Councilman Charles Becker decided he wanted to be mayor and the league turned him down. Instead it picked former Secretary of State Roy Barrera Sr. The mayor was chosen by the City Council, but the GGL traditionally assigned its choice for mayor to Place 2 on the ballot. Charles Becker filed for Place 2 and challenged the Good Government League head-on.

Charles and his family had moved to San Antonio in 1926, when his dad decided to pull up stakes in Florida after a hurricane destroyed his Handy Andy grocery store. The elder Becker opened the first Handy Andy grocery store in San Antonio on the North Side, on Broadway next to Fox Studios. That store was on the edge of the city then, as few houses existed north of Hildebrand Avenue. The city of Alamo Heights had incorporated just four years earlier, with a population of 300. Many of that city's residents took the streetcar to the Handy Andy store.

As the North Side grew, so did Handy Andy. When the expressway system was built in the 1950s, people got in their cars and took off for the North Side. The exodus from the inner city to the suburbs grew as each year passed. In the 1950s, eight new municipalities incorporated in the North Side.

When Charles built Wonderland Shopping Center (now known as Crossroads Mall) on the southwest corner of Interstate 10 and Loop 410 in 1960, growth had stretched all the way to Loop 410, the new interstate beltway around the city. But, Charles said, "You could still stand outside our store, look north, and see nothing but jack rabbits and hoot owls."

During the 1960s, growth continued, but not at a very fast pace. There were only 15 office buildings built along Loop 410 during the '60s and only one was taller than two stories. Although construction began on the University of Texas Medical School in 1966, there was still little activity north of Loop 410, except for those same jack rabbits and hoot owls.

As the 1970s opened, many North Side businessmen blamed San Antonio's conservative business and political leadership for stifling growth. Many of these outspoken pro-growth leaders were connected to the development industry. They had to go outside the city to get loans. They were excluded from the elite social clubs. These brash, headstrong, in-your-face businessmen felt it was time for a change. New leaders like Cliff Morton, Jim Dement, Phil Barshop, and Louis Pitluk were heading up the revolt.

Their first step was to form the North San Antonio Chamber of Commerce in 1971. Businessmen Morris Jaffe and Jim Dement organized the chamber. They now had an organization to make their voices heard. In that same year, Charles Becker, before his break with the Good Government League, was elected city councilman on the GGL ticket.

During his first term on council, Becker became politically associated with the new business leaders and developers. "I respected the guts of developers who were willing to take sizable risks in building their projects," Charles told me several years later. "I felt they were being held back by the more cautious traditional businessmen who dominated the Good Government League. Around the state, our city was considered peculiar and quaint. I was tired of San Antonio being a used-car town. I wanted our city to become progressive and enter the 21st century. So I decided I would run as an independent candidate for mayor in 1973."

The Good Government League had a real fight on its hands. From the family's small beginnings, Charles was now wealthy, the owner of what was then San Antonio's largest chain of grocery stores, taking in more than $200 million in annual revenues.

Recognizing the weakness of the Good Government League, other independent candidates filed for office. Several developer members of the new North Chamber supported Charles for mayor.

From my position in the Texas Senate, I followed the events that led to the breakup of the Good Government League. I knew some of the break-away business leaders. Many had supported me in my successful race for the state Senate. I, like them, felt some resentment against the old order. I knew first hand the difficulty of obtaining loans and being accepted by the blueblood leadership. My family and I were in business for almost 10 years before we could get a working-capital loan from a local bank.

Becker won the 1973 election. And enough independent candidates were elected to council along with him to assure his selection as mayor. Two years later, only three GGL candidates for Council would win. Soon after the 1975 election, the Good Government League was buried quietly in the graveyard of politically defunct institutions.

The new guys wasted no time grasping the reins of power. Pro-development appointees were made to the City Water Board and the City Planning Commission. A new city manager was hired who was more in tune with pro-growth forces. He fired the deputy director of the city Planning Department who had advocated that North Side growth be held within Loop 410.

As a result, growth along and outside Loop 410 exploded. During the 1970s, 15 times more office space was created along Loop 410 than in the 1960s. Growth also leaped beyond Loop 410. Within two decades of Charles' election, the population center of the city was closer to north Loop 410 than to the central business district. In fact, the arc of Loop 410 between IH-10 on the northwest and IH-35 on the northeast was fast becoming the city's real central business district.

The second political upheaval came from the inner city. Even as the developers and the North Side gained prominence, a new power center was forming to challenge them. Inner-city Hispanics thought it was time they had a piece of the power. Communities Organized for Public Service began organizing in 1973, the same year Charles Becker was elected mayor. Ernesto "Ernie"

Cortes Jr., a graduate of Texas A&M University, became COPS' executive director in January 1974. COPS' power base was the Catholic parishes of the South Side and West Side, areas of the city that under the GGL regime had been chronically neglected. Somehow the streets there never got paved, the drainage ditches never got cleared, and new projects never got built.

The leaders of the new organization had studied the grassroots organizing techniques of Saul Alinsky's Industrial Areas Foundation. These techniques included various forms of organized confrontation. COPS members intimidated politicians and business institutions through mass demonstrations. In one legendary incident, hundreds of COPS members tied up business at Frost Bank by lining up to ask the tellers to make change for small bills. Then they got right back in line to change the coins back into bills. Another day, they brought the downtown Joske's department store to its knees as they wandered around the store, trying on everything and buying nothing. They intimidated politicians into attending "Accountability Nights," during which candidates and officeholders were required to give yes or no answers to loaded questions. If the answer didn't please COPS' organizers, the crowd was signaled to boo.

COPS was, and still is, a unique minority power group. Its agenda did not include civil rights or social welfare issues. Members wanted hard goods delivered to their neighborhoods in the form of streets, drainage and good city services. They wanted a decent place to live. They clashed head-on with the developers and the North Side for resources. By the 1981 election, they were a major power.

The third major political change occurred when the U.S. Justice Department challenged the at-large election of City Council members. Even though Hispanics and African-Americans made up a majority of the city's population, they never had equal representation on council. The GGL played a skillful game of including a token black and a few Hispanics among its slate of nominees, while effectively playing off the black East Side against the Hispanic West Side to keep control in the hands of the city's Anglo minority. Financial resources for a citywide race were simply not available to most minority candidates.

The opening for this challenge occurred as a delayed fallout from a massive annexation the city undertook in 1972. The city added 66 square miles and 51,400 people, mostly Anglos living in North Side neighborhoods.

When the Voting Rights Act was extended to include Texas in 1975, the 1972 annexation was retroactively reviewed by the Justice Department, which ruled that the action diluted minority voting strength. Federal bureaucrats gave the city two choices: Undo the annexation, or change the structure of City Council from at-large representation to single-member districts.

Council chose the latter course, and in January 1977, voters narrowly approved the charter amendment that would forever change the power equation at City Hall. Council expanded from nine members to 11, with only the mayor elected at-large. Ten districts were drawn because this was the minimum number that would allow one district to be a more-or-less "safe" seat for the city's 7 percent African-American population.

The first city election under the new system took place just four months later, in May 1977. It provided proof of how radically things had changed. Anglos suddenly found themselves in a minority on council, occupying only the mayor's seat and four district seats. Hispanics represented five districts, and a black represented the district where African-Americans were a plurality of the population. For the first time since 1837, the year after Texas won its independence from Mexico, Mexican-Americans held real power on the council.

The death of the Good Government League, the birth of Communities Organized for Public Service, and the adoption of single-member districts diffused political power in the city. No person or institution on the local political scene could command a consensus to move the city forward.

Henry Comes Home

Henry Cisneros first stepped into San Antonio's political confusion when he came home from Washington in 1974 at the age of

26. In the 10 years since his graduation from Central Catholic High School, Henry had obtained a first-class education. He held master's degrees from Texas A&M and Harvard, and a doctorate in public administration from George Washington University. He had worked for the National League of Cities and was a White House Fellow during the Nixon Administration, working as an aide to Housing, Education and Welfare Secretary Elliott Richardson.

Henry came home with a burning ambition for politics. While Henry's political torch was flaming in 1974, mine had burned out. During my time in the Legislature, I had led an effort to write a new state constitution. A Constitutional Convention was held in 1974 — the first time in almost 100 years that Texas completely reconsidered its governing document. But, ultimately, the convention fell three votes shy of the two-thirds majority needed to adopt the new constitution. I had also entered a race for the U.S. Congress in the 21st Congressional District, but lost by a single percentage point.

When Henry arrived home in 1974, I was back in the private sector working with our family business, Alamo Enterprises Building Supplies. We were expanding our building materials stores to Corpus Christi, McAllen and Del Rio. I was still keeping up with politics by occasionally attending political meetings at Munguia Printing Company, close to one of our stores on West Commerce Street.

It was ritual for Democratic politicians to make their way to Munguia Printing for good prices, quality printing and credit. But the astute politicians also came for advice. They knew to arrive about 5 p.m., when Ruben Munguia would have a decent bottle of whiskey ready to share as political strategy was plotted. I had been a political student of Ruben starting in 1969, when at the age of 29 I first ran for political office. Henry had been enrolled in Ruben's tutorial much earlier. Every Sunday after dinner, Henry would follow his grandfather and uncle to the shop, where he would get an earful from the politicos who gathered there.

The Munguias were part of a large migration of Mexicans who arrived in San Antonio after the turn of the century. These migrants were pushed out of their native country by the turmoil

Ruben Munguia, Henry Cisneros' uncle and political godfather, stands in his West Side print shop in January 1983. The shop served as a center for Mexican-American political strategy sessions. (Joe Barrera Jr., Express-News)

and violence of a decades-long revolution. During the first 25 years of this century, more Mexicans migrated each year to Texas than in the previous 200 years. By 1930, a third of the population of San Antonio was Mexican-American.

Many of the educated, urban, middle-class Mexicans settled on the West Side, in the neighborhood of Prospect Hill. It was a prosperous neighborhood with a rich mix of ethnic groups, including Mexicans, Germans, Italians and Poles.

Along with the middle class, the poor also came in much greater numbers from the haciendas of Guanajuato, Jalisco, Nuevo Leon and the other states of northern Mexico. The poor Mexicans also settled on the West Side, but farther west of Alazan Creek, toward the stockyards.

The Munguias were part of the educated class that fled Mexico. Jose Romulo Munguia y Torres, Ruben's father, was in danger of his life for the critical articles he had written about the Obregon and Calles administrations. Jose Romulo Munguia, his wife, Carolina, and their children, Ruben, Ralph, Bill and Elvira, Henry Cisneros' mother, left Mexico in 1926 to come to San Antonio. Coincidentally, this was the same year that Charles Becker's family also came to San Antonio.

Romulo Munguia settled his family in Prospect Hill. Ruben and his brothers and sister grew up during the 1920s and 1930s in a neighborhood of mixed races, but where the old traditions of Mexico were preserved. They had their own churches, clubs, stores and schools, and their own newspaper, La Prensa, where Ruben's father worked.

The West Side was anchored by the Missouri Pacific Railroad station, which provided many jobs. The whole area west of San Pedro Creek and east of Alazan and Apache creeks once was the heart of an active business area. Lebanese, Italian, Chinese and Mexican businesses all thrived.

But the West Side slowly changed. Construction of the huge, 1,180-unit Alazan-Apache Courts public housing project in the late 1930s increased the concentration of the poor. The shoddily constructed "shotgun" houses that surrounded the project deteriorated into the barrios of Colonia San Alfonso, Colonia Amistad and Avenida Guadalupe.

When Henry was born to Elvira and George Cisneros in 1947, the neighborhood was still a good place to live, but the outer edges were increasingly occupied by the poor. Henry had friends all over the neighborhood, but almost all of his friends were Hispanic. The Germans, Poles and Italians had moved out, leaving the neighborhood predominantly Mexican-American.

While Henry was pursuing his education, he came home for two short stays. In the summer of 1968, he served in City Manager Jerry Henckel's office. From January 1969 to January 1970, he served as a city staff member and eventually became assistant director in the Model Cities department that had been set up to administer San Antonio's Model Cities grants.

Four years later, in 1974, Henry returned home to take a position as an assistant professor at the University of Texas at San Antonio. It was not long before he took his first political step.

Through Ruben, I had kept up with Henry's early moves into politics. Ruben helped pave the way for Henry to run for the City Council on the weak Good Government League ticket in 1975. At that time, council candidates still had to run citywide, and Ruben felt Henry needed the connection to the established power structure. The GGL also had the strongest candidate for mayor in the 1975 election. Charles Becker decided not to run for re-election, opening the way for the highly regarded Lila Cockrell. This election would be the first direct election of the mayor.

But even Lila Cockrell's victory was not enough to save the Good Government League. Henry Cisneros was one of only three GGL council nominees elected in 1975. Former GGL Councilman Cliff Morton had organized an independent slate of candidates, and the "Independent Team" won six of the nine council seats. They truly were "independent" in the sense that they had little in common with each other, except that they were the alternative to the GGL.

Henry the councilman wasted no time getting himself known around the city. He spoke out on controversial issues that he knew would generate headlines. He fought a rate increase by Southwestern Bell. He vociferously campaigned against an out-of-court settlement between City Public Service (the city-owned gas and electric utility) and its gas supplier, Coastal States. He pushed for controls over the recharge zone of the Edwards Aquifer, the area north of the city where water seeps into the limestone aquifer that is San Antonio's only source of water. All these issues endeared him to many blue-collar working folks.

But looking ahead to an eventual mayoral race, Henry knew he must have some support from the business community. First, he needed to assure them that he was not their enemy. He had become suspect in a spectacular fight that followed a split council vote to rezone a site at U.S. Highway 281 and Loop 1604 (the far outer beltway, outside Loop 410) for a regional shopping mall. Concern over possible pollution of San Antonio's water supply provoked a successful referendum to overturn the council's action. In response, council imposed a moratorium on all new development over the recharge zone. The developers sued the city for $1 billion in damages, and forced the city into a humiliating retreat. While Henry had opposed the original rezoning, he also refused to vote for the moratorium on all new recharge-zone development.

Henry also led the fight to create a city Department of Economic and Employment Development. He spearheaded the creation of a "Centro 21" task force to be a catalyst for downtown development.

After the approval of single-member districts in 1977, Henry ran and won in District 1, representing downtown and the near West Side. He was now a rising star on the first council in modern city history with non-Anglos in the majority.

Single-member districts threw City Hall politics into turmoil. After a year of tension, in early 1978 a major explosion finally occurred when the "minority majority" exercised its power a little too crudely. They caucused separately and agreed to redirect unspent Community Development Block Grant funds for their districts. They rammed their package through in a 6-to-5 vote. This was a routine minor issue, but the Anglo council members were outraged by the way they had been excluded from meaningful participation in the decision.

The Anglos retaliated with the political equivalent of a nuclear strike. They reversed a previous position, and suddenly came out in opposition to a $98.4 million bond issue that council had already placed on the May election ballot. They had supported the bond projects, but now they claimed that the council majority had proven itself to be fiscally irresponsible. A previously unremarkable bond package became the issue in a dangerously escalating political race war.

The divisiveness of the issue was starkly demonstrated in the results of the bond referendum. The bonds passed in every single voting precinct where Anglos were a minority of the population. They failed in every single precinct with an Anglo majority, except the one that would have benefited from the largest drainage project in the whole package. Citywide, the issue went down in flames. In this political environment, it was impossible to accomplish anything meaningful.

Henry learned an important lesson. The minorities were a comfortable majority of San Antonio's total population, and therefore they could control a majority of the district council seats. But Anglos were still a majority of the city's voters, and therefore they still controlled any issue that required a citywide vote. These issues included who would become mayor, whether a bond issue would pass, and whether the city charter could be amended. Henry's later record makes it clear that he learned this lesson well.

The turmoil of the 1977-79 City Council was eased a bit when the election in May 1979 restored the Anglos to a 6-to-5 majority. Since then (through the 1995 election), Hispanic and black council members have never again been a majority of San Antonio's City Council.

Within two years, the disaster of the 1978 bond issue was erased by a successful bond issue of $90.3 million in May 1980 for streets, drainage, libraries, and police and fire stations. Henry also nurtured an image as a peacemaker, and a leader on the council in forging compromise and consensus. Representing the downtown business district gave him a ready-made platform from which to address development issues of citywide interest, and put him in frequent contact with many citywide business leaders.

Another significant opportunity for Henry arose out of an ugly fight that broke out in 1978 between COPS and the business community. The Greater San Antonio Chamber of Commerce contracted with the Fantus Company for an advertising campaign intended to support the industrial recruitment program of the chamber's spin-off Economic Development Foundation. Fantus identified San Antonio's low labor costs as one of the city's major advantages. COPS was incensed that the business elite was continuing to sell San Antonio as a "cheap labor" town, instead of pursuing the high-wage jobs it wanted to see the city develop.

Out of this incident, retired General Robert McDermott, the head of USAA, an insurance and financial services company, and then chairman of the Greater Chamber, founded an organization called United San Antonio, to try to restore a consensus on economic development strategy. McDermott, Mayor Cockrell and Henry Cisneros became "tri-chairs" of the new organization. Although United San Antonio accomplished little, it gave Henry still greater visibility in the roles of citywide peacemaker and economic developer. Perhaps equally important, the tri-chair leadership arrangement also provided a model that was repeated in the design of Henry's Target '90 Commission in 1983. More about that, though, in the next chapter.

For six years, from 1975 to 1981, Mayor Lila Cockrell did an extraordinary job guiding the city through the turmoil of a political revolution. And even though Anglos remained a majority on the council after 1977-79, single-member districts did produce a real revolution in San Antonio politics. All parties are at the table now, and all viewpoints must be considered. This is not the way it was under the GGL, under whose banner both Lila Cockrell and Henry Cisneros were first elected to council.

Lila succeeded because she had a genuine commitment to the process of politics. She presided over a revolution that was imposed by forces outside the city government, and steered a steady course of mediation through the ensuing turmoil.

The Election of Henry Cisneros

Henry wanted to run for mayor in 1979. He thought he had an understanding with Lila that she would not run for a third term. When she decided to run after all, Henry was angry and disappointed. But he didn't challenge her, and that was the right decision. Lila helped groom Henry for mayor during the next two years. Even though she did not endorse anyone in the race, everyone felt she had made Henry her protégé and that Henry was her favorite. Henry returned the favor soon after the 1981 election, arranging to make Lila the paid executive director of United San Antonio.

When Mayor Cockrell did step down in 1981, the field was clear for Henry's battle with the old order. By this time, the business leaders no longer held all the cards. Henry had a lot of new players in his camp: unions, neighborhood activists, and poor, inner-city Hispanics and blacks. This election was between an Anglo and a Hispanic, a North Side candidate who represented middle- and upper-income Anglos and an inner-city candidate who represented poor minorities.

Henry's opponent was North Side Councilman John Steen Sr. Steen was a well-respected civic leader, a member of just about every civic organization worth joining. He represented the best of the establishment, a kind, steady and conservative leader. Henry presented a stark contrast, young at age 33, Hispanic, well educated and with a progressive agenda.

All this brings us back to the beginning of this story, on the grassy field off Jackson-Keller Road. That was to be the first time I would hear Henry give a speech. I had heard about his ability to move a crowd, to really connect, and I was about to judge for myself. I was not disappointed.

Henry gave an inspiring speech after I introduced him. His melodious voice was reassuring and pleasing. The rising and falling intonation of his articulate speech struck just the right cadence. The Munguia political passion showed in his face and in his voice as he spoke of his hopes and aspirations for San Antonio. He sprinkled his speech with powerful words: "my commitment to the people ... whose progress is my life's work ... I will focus my leadership skills."

He told us he had the leadership ability and a plan to move the city forward. He said his economic plan would bring together the poor and the rich, the Hispanic, black, and Anglo, the Southsider and Northsider, to bring prosperity to San Antonio.

Henry made it clear his economic plan was the focus of his campaign. It included 24 planks, everything from increasing daycare opportunities for working women to developing engineering programs at local universities to developing a "co-prosperity zone" with San Antonio's sister city of Monterrey, Mexico.

It was Henry's speech that caused my first flicker of thought that it would be exciting to be mayor of a major city. After the speech it was clear from the crowd's response that Henry had inspired them. The message came across: Forget ethnicity, forget youth, forget ambition. Henry had a program, one you could sub-scribe to, and his opponent did not.

Henry hammered at this theme throughout the campaign. He accused his opponent of not sharing his "enthusiasm about eco-nomic growth," and of differing with him on "the sense of urgency, the basic importance of economic development to the people of his city."

Henry had to balance his campaign carefully. First he had to have a large turnout in the inner-city Mexican-American boxes. This was the easier task, as this was his natural constituency. But then he also had to appeal to Anglo voters on the North Side who turned out to vote in greater numbers. To reach them he turned to the business leaders who had broken away from the Good Gov-ernment League in 1973.

After eight years of political turmoil, these business leaders felt Henry was the candidate who could best develop political consensus, heal racial tensions and push our city forward eco-nomically. Henry was preaching economic growth, and that was right up their alley. They also recognized in Henry the potential to take San Antonio to a new level of recognition around the coun-try. They felt he would be a great salesman for the city. This articulate, handsome mayor with unbounded energy could travel the country, actively soliciting companies to locate in San Anto-nio.

The New York Times, the Washington Post, the news maga-zines and the television networks were soon tripping over each other to showcase this handsome, urbane Hispanic politician. Henry became the national poster child in a campaign to eradi-cate old stereotypes of Hispanic politicians.

The progressive business leaders also knew that Henry would have a future political career beyond being mayor. Businessmen like automobile dealer Red McCombs and homebuilder Cliff Morton led the effort to rally North Side support for Henry.

Henry's campaign was orchestrated by George Shipley, a political consultant out of Austin. Shipley was just beginning to make a name for himself throughout the state as a tough, no-holds-barred political genius. His polling kept Henry informed on exactly what people were thinking.

Henry's brother, George, was in charge of the grassroots campaign. Volunteers block-walked all over the city, workers were at each polling place on election day, and telephones rang to get out the vote.

On that election day — Saturday, April 4, 1981 — 155,831 people voted in San Antonio, a record that still has not been eclipsed. Henry took 61.8 percent of the vote, carrying the Mexican-American boxes at a 90 percent rate and more than 40 percent of the North Side Anglo vote. Henry turned out the inner-city vote like no other politician before or since. San Antonio had its first Hispanic mayor since before Texas joined the Union. The entire nation had its first Hispanic mayor of a city of more than 500,000 people.

Henry Cisneros clasps hands with enthusiastic supporters after his historic election as San Antonio's first Mexican-American mayor on April 4, 1981. (Express-News)

So, in May 1981, Henry went to the mayor's office and I went back to my office at Sun Harvest Farms. I felt good about contributing in a small way to Henry's campaign.

While Henry had stirred some latent political passions in me, those feelings quickly faded after the campaign. There were too many painful reminders of my political defeats during the 1970s. While I had started out the decade with a promising career by winning a House seat at the age of 29 and then becoming the youngest member of the Texas Senate in 1972 at 31, things turned sour in the second half of the decade. After losing the congressional campaign in 1974, I lost again when I tried a second time in 1978. I won the primary, but then lost in a Republican landslide to Tom Loeffler. Loeffler, incidentally, turned out to be perhaps the best and most effective congressman from San Antonio in decades. In any case, I needed more time to heal my political wounds.

I also wanted to see the answers to a few more questions. Would Henry really instill power in the weak mayor's office? If so, how would he do it? Could he develop political consensus to take positive steps forward? How would he hold the Anglo, Hispanic and black communities together?

There are always days in one's life that prove to be more important than they seem at the time. That day in the field along Jackson-Keller Road would prove to be one for me. It would take a while for my political spark to flare back up. It would also take time for a strong friendship and working relationship to develop between Henry and me. Both events would eventually take place together, and would have a profound effect on both of us and on our city. In the interim, I would bide my time and observe before I took another step into local politics.

I tucked away in my pocket a few lessons I had learned about mayoral politics. Just in case.

★★★
Lessons from Henry's Mayoral Race

■ **Catch the wave of changing political institutions.**
Political institutions change, and a successful politician must recognize those changes and put them to use. Henry won his first council race as the candidate of the Good Government League. Six years later when Henry ran for mayor, that institution was dead. Henry recognized and plugged into the new power centers: inner-city political institutions such as COPS, the labor unions, newly formed Hispanic and black organizations, and neighborhood associations.

■ **A council member must become the Sorcerer's Apprentice.**
A term or two as a council member can be invaluable as a political apprenticeship. First, of course, it gives you name recognition. Councilman Cisneros' fights against high utility rates and his efforts to protect the recharge zone of the Edwards Aquifer generated news coverage and gave him a positive profile among many voters. Since 1975, all mayors of San Antonio have first served on the council. This tradition is likely to change only if one of the 10 council members fails to position himself or herself for mayor.

■ **Build bridges across the city.**
Henry won the mayor's race because he had built bridges to North Side Anglos while maintaining his established ties with the inner-city neighborhoods he represented as a councilman. He built those bridges by pushing for economic development as the rising tide that would lift all boats, and by restraining his rhetoric on issues that were racially divisive.

Just as Henry had built bridges to North Side voters, I would have to build corresponding bridges to the inner city if I were to run for mayor. I would have to find a way to remind voters that although I lived on the North Side now, I was really still a kid from the South Side at heart.

2

A Delicate Balance: Target '90 and the Reshaping of Power

More than three years passed, and it was November 1984 before Henry invited me to our first private get-together since becoming mayor.

"Meet me for lunch at the Plaza Club," he told me. His choice of location spoke volumes about his success. Sitting atop the Frost National Bank Building, the Plaza Club commands a wonderful view of downtown and, more important, a reputation among the city's "players" as the place to see and be seen.

It was here, just a quick block from City Hall, where Henry frequently lunched. As his standing had grown, business leaders, corporate lawyers and top city officials came in increasing numbers, wanting to be close to the man under whose leadership the city seemed to be coming alive.

As for me, I had been totally absorbed in expanding Sun Harvest, our family's natural foods business, during Henry's first term. We expanded into Austin and Corpus Christi. I was determined to stay away from any further involvement in local politics, and contented myself with observing City Hall through the media and occasional visits with Ruben Munguia.

But as I approached my lunch meeting with the mayor, I had to acknowledge a tingle in my political nerves. Henry greeted me in the foyer. Although he was clearly the dominant political figure in the nation's ninth largest city, it seemed natural to call him "Henry." Everyone did, and he liked it. When Henry greets you, he makes you feel you are the most important person in the world at that moment. As we walked through the crowd to his reserved table, people would nod or greet him warmly, and he returned the gestures. His table stood in the northeast corner of the club, the farthest from the entrance. He sat with his back to the wall, observing the whole room, gathering valuable intelligence by noting who was meeting with whom.

"Well, I'm glad you are back safe from Nicaragua," he said. "You'll have to tell me about their elections." I had just returned as a member of a team of international observers. In March, I had also made two trips to El Salvador to observe that country's elections. Henry shared my keen interest in Latin America's turmoil, having served as a presidential appointee to the bipartisan Kissinger Commission on Central America.

As we sat down to what I knew would be a business lunch rather than a social affair, I reflected on Henry's first three years in office.

Off and Running

Henry had hit the ground running at a sprinter's pace after his election. Each day, I watched as the city's media followed this whirlwind of activity. Henry was tossing out so many new ideas and position papers that people began wondering whether he would exhaust himself or them first.

His timing was perfect. An ambitious mayor with an aggressive agenda could hope for no better opening than a city with low debt, low taxes, and a healthy economy. Military spending, tourism, and health care — our No. 1, 2 and 3 industries — were all riding sustained growth curves. Local financial institutions followed national trends by opening their coffers to almost any building project proposed by developers. Economic growth poured additional money into city funds with little resistance from taxpayers.

But economic development, Henry's clarion call, couldn't occur with unpaved streets and an undersized airport. He desperately needed two things. First was an improved infrastructure, everything from streets and drainage and public buildings to the airport, water supply, sewage treatment and electric utility systems. Next, he needed to enhance education if San Antonio were to attract information technology firms and other high-tech companies seeking a skilled work force.

Henry had no lack of ideas. But he was having trouble delivering the hard goods. His "wish list" of projects grew endlessly, but without a coherent plan of action, Henry's boundless energy was taking the city nowhere fast.

Aware of the problem, Henry tried to focus on the economic development part of his agenda. In September 1982, he published a remarkable piece of scholarship on information and technology jobs and how San Antonio might plug into that new wave. But the report landed with a heavy, dull thud. The media didn't have a clue on how to report it, and people were left scratching their heads.

Next, Henry started an effort to link San Antonio to Austin, the emerging high-tech capital of Texas located 85 miles north on Interstate 35. The mayor of Austin signed on to the idea of creating a technology "corridor" along Interstate 35 to compete with California's Silicon Valley and Boston's Route 128. Some local wags suggested the "alleged corridor" existed more in imagination than reality.

Henry understood that he needed concrete accomplishments sooner rather than later. Looking around, he saw that San Antonio's only existing high-tech industry of any importance was biotechnology. He began advocating the development of a research park. It was to be consciously modeled on the Research Triangle Park in North Carolina.

As he approached the 1983 re-election campaign, Henry could boast of at least two major accomplishments. He had led a delegation that convinced the state's Higher Education Coordinating Board to approve an undergraduate program in engineering at the University of Texas at San Antonio. And he took the first step in addressing infrastructure needs by placing a $56 million drainage bond issue on the ballot in 1983. It passed with 83 percent of the vote.

Henry's favorable poll ratings were so high leading up to the 1983 election that it scared off any major opposition. Although other politicians might envy him this position, it actually presented a serious problem. Henry knew that merely being re-elected over token opposition would not give him the mandate he needed to accomplish his goals. It could actually leave him weaker in the long run than if he had to survive by beating a serious opponent.

Henry found a solution by looking south to Mexico. He borrowed a page from the strategic playbook that had kept Mexico's Institutional Revolutionary Party, the PRI, in power since the 1930s. Henry had learned these lessons through his working relationship with Mexico's president at the time, Jose Lopez Portillo, and during his time at Harvard, where he was a classmate of a future Mexican president, Carlos Salinas de Gortari.

The strategy, as explained to me later by Henry's political consultant Tom Brereton, was simple enough. The candidate — in this case, Henry, of course — engaged in a systematic round of "consultations" with the leaders of labor unions, industries and other significant interest groups to compile a consensus agenda that would carry the party's candidate from one election to the next.

To execute this play in San Antonio, Henry published a first-draft agenda and organized a series of public forums to gather feedback. The draft was called "San Antonio: Target '90 — Goals and Decisions for San Antonio's Future." It was a compilation of 148 specific projects or program initiatives that he wanted San Antonio to achieve by 1990.

The report led off with a fanciful "news story," datelined 1990, that described what a fantastic community San Antonio had become as a result of these initiatives. It was cast as a report on a conference of Western Hemisphere leaders who had assembled in San Antonio to chart new directions for the hemisphere in the 21st century, and it described how many of the initiatives had propelled San Antonio to its new status as a leading world city.

Henry unveiled this agenda at a big luncheon in the convention center. His re-election "campaign" then consisted primarily of the public forums on the "Target '90" agenda. Representatives of all the affected interest groups were personally solicited to attend these forums, and everyone was invited to critique, refine and propose additional items.

No one had any idea how to calculate the cost of the entire program. It didn't matter. Henry was re-elected with 91 percent of the vote.

Now Henry had a new problem: what to do with this new, up-to-date, all-purpose civic wish list. Since the mayor of San Antonio lacks the institutional powers of the president of Mexico, he stalled for several months, pondering his next step. Finally he brought the program to council and said he would personally raise private funds to monitor implementation.

Council was not pleased. Members felt excluded from the process. They were alarmed at Target '90's potential for developing into a cult of personality centered on Henry. And their unhappiness was reported by the media. They rejected the goals as Henry laid them out, and resolved to start the whole process all over again. They wanted to make Target '90 an official project of the city government, supported by a direct allocation from the municipal budget. Council mandated that the new process would be open, democratic, grassroots and participatory.

Henry was stunned by this rebuke, but he recovered quickly. He embraced the new idea, and became general chairman of the Target '90 Commission that was officially created in July 1983. He selected Bob Marbut, then chairman of Harte-Hanks Communications, to be the coordinating chairman. More than 500 volunteers from 145 organizations participated in the process, making Target '90 probably the biggest and most unwieldy commission in local government history.

In retrospect, the council's bold rejection of Henry's first plan benefited both him and the city as a whole. It saved Henry from a

Preparing for a 5-mile run in 1985 are (left to right): Nelson Wolff, then chairman of Target '90; Mayor Henry Cisneros; City Manager Lou Fox; and Bob Marbut, who had served as Target '90 coordinating chairman. (Wolff collection)

futile, Lone Ranger pursuit of impossibly ambitious campaign promises. Instead, representatives of powerful institutions and a wide range of grassroots leaders would develop the goals and then commit to making them happen. This process established a stronger and more powerful consensus than Henry could have ever imagined. It was also a useful reminder that however high his standing in the polls, he still needed six votes to get anything through council.

That council decision also had political implications for me. At the time Target '90 was created, I was chairman of the World Affairs Council that Doug Harlan and I had founded in 1981. I was asked to be one of the chairmen of the Task Force on Foreign Trade. Transportation issues were later added to this task force.

The other task forces dealt with basic municipal services, education, development, revitalization of the city's "Southern Sector," utilities, transition to technology, biosciences and a combination of the arts, human services and youth.

This was my first step into local government since Henry's election. This time the political bug would bite a little harder.

On May 15, 1984, we issued our final report. There were now 93 "goals" plus 353 specific "implementing mechanisms." Each goal was assigned to one or more of the 145 organizations that participated in the process. It was their job now to make them happen.

As the process moved along, I began to realize that setting goals was not really the major purpose of Target '90. Developing consensus and building coalitions were. It was an extraordinary process never before seen in San Antonio. This was the genius of Target '90.

It was the energy and excitement of the individual participants and their connections that became the engine that would drive home many of the goals. People who had known about each other, who had occasionally read about each other in the newspaper, now came to know each other. Business leaders sat next to tenants in housing projects, and neighborhood activists dealt directly with the leaders of the police and firefighters unions.

People of different professional, ethnic and cultural backgrounds began to understand each other better, and to appreciate each other's values. People in wealthier northern San Antonio began to appreciate the problems of the inner city and vice versa. We all felt good about working together in a common enterprise to better our city. It was our plan now, not just Henry's.

San Antonio had now defined itself as an emerging city that put on its agenda everything necessary for economic development, equal opportunity, and a high quality of life. After we finished our report, the Target '90 Commission made an important recommendation: that the commission become a non-profit organization and be merged with United San Antonio. The combined organization was to act as a catalyst.

Although it wasn't planned, this move also helped bury a scandal that was personally embarrassing to Henry. The controversy erupted when the San Antonio Light broke a series of stories reporting that a United San Antonio staffer participated in a theft of funds from a River Walk charity concert series. The staffer, Alice Trevino, had worked in Henry's mayoral campaigns. Henry quickly distanced himself from Trevino, and he delivered to the newspaper one of his more memorable quotes: "The landscape of politics is littered with the bones of broken friendships."

At the conclusion of the Target '90 goal-setting process, I now had the answers to the three questions that had stuck in my mind after Henry's election in 1981. Could Henry develop power in the mayor's office? Yes. Could he develop consensus to move the community forward? Yes. Could he pull the Hispanic, Anglo, and black communities together? Yes.

Target '90 showed me that the mayor's office could make a difference. Henry showed how power could be injected in the office by a strong personality using the media to communicate his agenda.

Now I realized that the real action was at the local level, not the state or national. I saw that you really could make a difference in the life of your city, right here at home.

Chairman of Target '90

The Target '90 report, an elaborate four-color document now entitled "Target '90: Goals for San Antonio — To Build a Greater City," was delivered to council on July 2, 1984. Again, Henry sat on the report as he pondered what to do next.

In the lull, I began to consider a race for the City Council in District 8, on San Antonio's northwest side. It was Henry himself who made me start thinking about the race when he answered a question at a meeting of the Wednesday Breakfast Club.

The Wednesday Breakfast Club had been established in the early 1970s by San Antonio Light publisher Frank A. Bennack Jr., who is now the president and chief executive officer of the Hearst Corporation. Its members were a roster of influential business and political leaders who took their name from a similar organization led by former Mayor Walter McAllister in the 1930s.

After Henry had finished his speech, he was asked who was capable of succeeding him as mayor. He responded with several names including mine. This was a mistake; Henry never should have answered the question. It is dangerous for an officeholder to create a possible successor. If people began to look to someone else as heir apparent, then that person begins to accrue a degree of power that he or she would not otherwise hold. Power players always like to be on the good side of the next officeholder.

After the meeting, some of the names leaked out, including mine. A few people encouraged me to run for council to position myself for an eventual mayor's race. The more people encouraged me, the more seriously I considered the race.

Henry did not realize the mistake he made until one evening after a council meeting. I went up to him and told him I was considering the council race in District 8. I also said that if I won, I would like someday to succeed him as mayor. The expression on his face matched the tone of displeasure in his voice as he said, "Let's talk about this later," and then walked away.

Henry did not like the idea of my running because incumbent District 8 Councilman Ed Harrington was one of the mayor's important allies. Ed was a homebuilder and represented Henry's link to the North Side developers. Ed teamed up with Councilman Frank Wing, who could deliver the inner-city vote. Henry liked things the way they were.

After my conversation with Henry, pressure began to develop behind the scenes to keep me out of the race. Former District 8 councilman and developer Gene Canavan called and said the business community was committing $250,000 to re-elect Ed. While Ed's supporters worked to scare me out of the race, Henry had other ideas on how to deal with the problem he had helped create.

All this brings us back to the lunch at the Plaza Club. I knew the luncheon would have important consequences for my political future. Word had clearly been conveyed to me that Henry did not want me in the council race. I knew he would have some inducement up his sleeve to keep me out.

After we chatted about Latin America, Henry got down to business. He said, "Nelson, I believe that you can best serve our city as chairman of Target '90. I do not want Target '90's work to end up on a shelf. We must do everything we can to see that the goals are implemented."

Well, here it was, the carrot to keep me out of the council race. And what a juicy carrot to chew on. I immediately recognized the opportunity to play a role that would be important to the development of our city. I also realized that I needed more time and visibility before I could launch a serious council race. This position would give me both.

I answered, "Be neutral in the District 8 council race two years from now, and I will take the chairmanship of Target '90."

"You have my word," he replied. Then we talked in more detail about the organization and its makeup.

It was as easy as that. Henry was relieved to have me out of the way politically. I had the opportunity to be closer to the center of power and to watch how Henry operated. But I also had a sick feeling about not running for City Council. I knew that Ed Harrington's backers felt they had cleverly maneuvered me out of the race and were snickering behind my back. They would find out how clever they were two years later. But for now I had to grin and bear it.

I went to work right away on effecting the merger and setting up the organizational structure for Target '90. We hired Maria Elena Torralva to become the executive director, and adopted a $350,000 annual budget. We were ready to hit the ground running by January 1, 1985.

Right off the bat, Henry and I had trouble. The issue was how active Target '90 should be. Henry preferred that the organization act behind the scenes. I felt Target '90 had to be "out front."

At a council meeting in February, Henry sided with Communities Organized for Public Service when it opposed funding for the new Target '90. As a compromise Henry agreed to fund us for only one year. Henry blindsided me on the issue. When he suggested this compromise at the council meeting I had little choice but to say it was OK with me. COPS celebrated this as a major victory.

After the council meeting, I met Maria Elena at Mi Tierra, a Mexican restaurant located in Market Square, two blocks from City Hall.

Maria Elena explained why Henry had dealt us such a stunning blow. "Henry believes it is necessary to keep all the major players and organizations in the city off balance," she said. "He wants Target '90 to play an important role in the city, but not to upset the balance of power. COPS saw Target '90 as upsetting that balance, and he rose to their defense. He wants our work to be done quietly, behind the scenes. He gave COPS a victory, knowing that you would not protest when you are just getting your feet on the ground. We lost today, but he will balance things out in the end."

We both found out later that Henry had met with COPS leaders before the council meeting. They expressed fear that Target '90 could become a "shadow government," and that it might even lead to a reincarnated Good Government League. This was nonsense and Henry knew it. But at that meeting, he agreed to cut future funding for Target '90 and helped set the scene before City Council.

On that day I saw first hand how Henry applied his political theory of "balanced forces." To achieve fairness and equity in the distribution of city funds, and to stop any one group from becoming dominant, he had to make the weak strong and the strong weak.

Henry's power was needed in bond issues to strengthen the hand of the inner-city poor. He knew a bond issue could not be won without the support of North Side Anglos. But he also knew a bond issue could not be won without strong support from the mayor.

He leveraged his power to ensure inner-city groups of funds for neighborhood streets. He fought off attempts by the North San Antonio Chamber of Commerce to restrict street funds to major arteries. He also insisted on funds for inner-city drainage.

Henry's extraordinary application of his "balance of forces" theory during eight years as mayor is what kept San Antonio on a pro-growth road. Henry's coalition was the first one in modern San Antonio history that established a true sharing of power among Anglos, Hispanics and blacks, and between the rich and the poor.

The Greater San Antonio Chamber of Commerce along with the North San Antonio Chamber became the principal representatives for the Anglo establishment. COPS, along with the Metropolitan Congregational Alliance, an affiliation of progressive churches, and the Eastside Alliance, became the organizations speaking for inner- city Hispanics and blacks.

Within the ranks of the Anglo establishment, other voices also demanded a hearing, among them the home builders of the Greater San Antonio Builders Association, the Southside Chamber, the hotel industry, and the Board of Realtors.

Other power groups within the Hispanic community included the Mexican-American Legal Defense and Educational Fund, the Hispanic Chamber of Commerce, the Mexican-American Unity Council, the League of United Latin American Citizens and the Mexican American Business and Professional Women.

Labor unions, public and private, became players along with the Coalition of Neighborhood Associations. The Alamo Chamber of Commerce and the Baptist Alliance were both important voices for the East Side black community.

This coalition of power groups became Henry's engine for progress. That engine, if it was to maintain top performance, needed a continuous fueling of encouragement, controlled conflicts, and victories.

I learned that day in the council session that Target '90 had no special claim on Henry for support. If Target '90 was his creation, then it was also his to sacrifice. Henry began privately to criticize Target '90 to many community leaders. He began to distance himself from the organization. He acted as though he did not need its help. I began to feel that I had been set up for failure.

A few weeks after the council meeting, I cornered Henry after a meeting of a Target '90 spin-off organization.

"If you are not going to be supportive of Target '90, then I will tell the volunteers right now that you do not need their help," I told him. If Henry's real intention was to remove me from the leadership of Target '90, he had to know I would not go quietly.

Henry responded by expressing all the concerns that COPS had shown. "I envisioned Target '90 being a catalyst behind the scenes, not out front on issues," he said. "Besides that, I do not know how I fit in." He felt that he was losing control and this bothered him terribly.

Henry had created an organization that was growing out of adolescence. He did not know what it was growing up to be. The only way he could feel comfortable with Target '90 was not to be threatened by it. He had to know that I would not betray his trust and use the organization to my political advantage.

"Henry, you know damn well where you fit in is at the top," I answered. "Stop listening to the voices that are trying to pit me against you. The conspiracy theories about Target '90 are nothing but garbage." I reassured him that I was loyal to him and his program, and I promised to keep him better informed.

Henry agreed to provide more support to the organization. Over time he would chase away the demons that had caused him to become paranoid about Target '90.

Meet Mister Stubbs

The first major issue that Target '90 got "out front" on was a controversial bond package that Henry put together for a vote in 1985. Henry had already passed two previous bond packages, the first installments of a planned 10-year package of drainage and street bond issues.

Neither of the votes on the first two street packages was controversial because no tax increase was required. But short of miraculous growth in new taxable improvements, there was no way to finance the succeeding years without a corresponding series of tax increases. The 10-year program of street bonds also left no room for other improvements such as police and fire stations, parks or libraries.

So in 1985, Henry convinced the council to depart from the 10-year plan. Instead, a pared-down street and drainage schedule would be submitted to voters with money also allocated for police stations, fire stations and branch libraries. The complete package of five separate propositions came to just over $100 million, and it would require a 14 percent property tax increase.

This more aggressive bond package with a tax increase gave a small organization that had just incorporated in 1983 a chance to assert itself. The Homeowner-Taxpayer Association of Bexar County, led by Clauis Alden ("C.A.") Stubbs, was ready for battle. Stubbs was in his own personal style the aesthetically perfect counterpoint to Henry's sophisticated, urbane image.

I saw Stubbs for the first time at a debate on the bonds arranged by the Greater San Antonio Chamber of Commerce. A retired civil service employee of the military, Stubbs spoke with an East Texas drawl through a gap between his upper front teeth. He adopted a string bow tie, boots and Stetson hat as his personal trademarks, to effect an image of simplicity, honesty and integrity. He liked to be compared to Howard Jarvis, leading the masses in California in the crusade to enact Proposition 13.

The bond issue was further complicated by the fact that it was being submitted in an election year. Unlike his re-election campaign in 1983, this time Henry had a respectable, if not formidable, opponent. This was Phil Pyndus, a conservative businessman who had represented City Council District 8 from 1977 to 1981. His candidacy defined the extent of conservative opposition to Henry's progressive agenda.

Stubbs and the HTA appealed to those who felt bypassed by the city's progress, who received no benefit from growth, who felt oppressed by the "big boys" in fancy suits who supposedly were making millions at their expense. Stubbs represented the views of many of the middle and lower-middle income Anglos, often retired and living on fixed incomes.

Early on, Stubbs displayed the style that would come to characterize all his campaigns. His speeches and campaign flyers misrepresented city tax rates and spending. His style mixed emotional outrage with analysis, all delivered with homespun sincerity.

Target '90 endorsed the bond package. We were part of the coalition that Henry stitched together to pass the package. The chambers provided the financial muscle and the grassroots organizations delivered the vote.

Both Stubbs and Pyndus lost, but not without an effect on the progressive agenda. The margin of victory for the bond package slipped from 83 percent in 1983 to an average of 63 percent for the five separate propositions on the April 1985 ballot. At the same time, Henry turned back Pyndus 94,002 (71 percent) to 32,998 (29 percent).

The 1985 election was a major victory for Henry and his progressive agenda. The consensus developed in the Target '90 process and the institutions supporting it had fostered a community mindset that favored the progressive agenda.

On the night of his dual victory, I was at Henry's campaign headquarters in a storefront on Broadway. I watched Henry and the huge crowd from the top of a table in the back of the room. Henry was really pumped up. I noticed that he repeatedly used the word "I" instead of "we" as he talked about the victory.

Years later, Henry would reflect back on that night as the point where he determined to become more aggressive in pursuing his agenda. The "I" indicated he no longer felt it necessary to go through the painful process of forming a consensus before taking action.

I was pleased with the part that Target '90 played in the campaign. I felt that now we would be recognized as a major player.

Stubbs was not ready to cry "uncle," though. He had other ideas in his Stetson. Soon after the bond victory, we would jump into another major fight with him, and this one we would lose.

The Trouble with Fluoridation

At the May 1985 quarterly meeting of Target '90, our health services task force recommended that Target '90 endorse a city ordinance providing for fluoridation of San Antonio's water supply. San Antonio had rejected fluoridation in a referendum in the 1960s. We were now one of the largest cities in the country where this basic preventive health measure was not taken for granted. Our surrounding military bases had fluoridated water. The dental records of our low-income children showed the significance of this omission.

The vote before City Council was coming up in June, just one month after Henry's bond victory. I persuaded the Target '90 board to support the issue.

After the meeting ended, as I was helping Maria Elena Torralva and the staff clean up, she said, "Nelson, we just made a big mistake. Hispanics will never support fluoridation." She explained that there was still a lack of trust of the medical profession among San Antonio's Hispanic population. There was also a strong belief in natural cures. Fluoridation of the water supply would introduce "forced medication" and change a basic natural resource.

I did not heed Maria Elena's warning. On the day of the council vote, as I walked into City Hall to testify in favor of fluoridation, I saw community activist Kay Turner perched like a little elf on the steps outside. Kay had been active politically in the Good Government League. I asked her what she was doing here today. She said she was going to speak against fluoridation. No one knew much about Kay at this point in her public life, but we would all come to know her better.

The council chamber was filled with pro- and anti-fluoridation voices. I spoke on behalf of Target '90. The issue passed 7 to 4. Henry fought against his cultural intuition and came down on the side of logic, voting for fluoridation.

While fluoridation had nothing to do with the anti-tax, anti-growth movement, C.A. Stubbs saw an opportunity to win a victory at the polls. He led his Homeowner-Taxpayer Association in the collection of signatures to call a referendum on the council vote. More than 70,000 signatures were collected, 30,000 more than were needed. The referendum was scheduled for November 5.

The extent of the wariness that Henry and Maria Elena sensed among Hispanics became clear when COPS refused to endorse the issue. They knew how the people in their parishes felt. The very children that would be helped the most lost their principal support group.

The medical profession, led by the University of Texas Dental School faculty, was in the forefront of the battle. They were knowledgeable about the issue but not about politics. Throughout the campaign Henry seemed detached, wishing the whole thing would just go away.

The issue was defeated by a citywide vote of 38,947 for and 42,213 against. The local media gave Stubbs and the Homeowner-Taxpayer Association credit for the defeat. In fact, the issue passed in Stubbs' stronghold, the conservative boxes on the North Side. It lost on the Hispanic West Side, where Stubbs' influence was minimal. But this reality did not matter. The perception was that Stubbs had won, and so now he had major stature in the community.

The Spending Cap

Henry had little time to lick his wounds from the defeat of fluoridation. Barely a month later, in December 1985, Stubbs announced that the Homeowner-Taxpayer Association would circulate a petition to amend the city charter to restrict the growth of the city budget.

The "Spending Cap," as it was dubbed by the press, was intended to kill Henry's entire progressive agenda. It was the political equivalent of thermonuclear war.

Stubbs proposed to limit total spending from all sources by a formula reflecting annual population growth and inflation. He called this proposal an "Ability to Pay Index," but quickly picked up the media's shorthand and called it "The Cap."

In the abstract, the proposal was disarmingly simple. By keying the limit to total city spending, Stubbs thought he had closed a loophole that made earlier limits like Proposition 13 in California ineffective. Limiting property taxes, for example, only encouraged a government to increase or institute other new taxes instead. Limiting total tax revenues only led to more user charges. Stubbs thought that limiting total spending without regard to the source of revenues would be the ultimate limit on the growth of local government.

Despite this superficial appeal, however, the cap was a harebrained idea. If the city was at the spending limit and a city building burned down, we would be unable to spend the money from an insurance settlement to rebuild it.

Of course, none of this mattered to Stubbs and the HTA. They knew exactly what they were doing: They were going for Henry's jugular.

By the first week of May 1986, Stubbs carted up the steps of City Hall two cardboard boxes containing 25,812 valid petition signatures, 5,812 more than he needed to place the issue on the ballot. Although council members opposed the initiative 11-0, they had no choice but to call the referendum for Saturday, August 9.

Henry was eager to battle Stubbs this time around. Unlike the fluoridation vote, this was essentially a referendum on Henry, on his leadership and his vision for San Antonio.

On June 10, Henry called together a cross-section of about 30 community leaders, including me, in the board room of the city's largest homebuilder, Ray Ellison. Henry's chief political consultant, George Shipley of Austin, told us what everyone already knew: If the vote were held that day, the cap would pass overwhelmingly. The data also showed, though, that opinions could be changed if the present level of city spending could be justified.

Henry sketched the plans for an all-out campaign. Over the next two months, he marshaled his troops in a grand coalition. One full division in his army was composed of the builders and developers, who saw the cap as a threat to improvements in the city's infrastructure.

Another division was raised from the general business community, commanded by the generals of the Greater Chamber. They saw the cap as a negative signal broadcast across the country that San Antonio was no longer interested in business relocations and economic development.

Campaign speakers and the working press were all armed with a 50-page "resource manual" that compiled all available data on city spending and debt, and comparisons with other cities showing how low our tax and debt burdens really were.

Inner-city neighborhood organizations foresaw an end to the improvement of local streets and drainage, and cutbacks in city services of all kinds. As a result, COPS enlisted a division of volunteers to walk its neighborhoods.

Even Archbishop Patrick Flores wrote a "pastoral reflection" against the cap.

Stubbs launched his campaign on a typically strident note. He claimed that if the cap were defeated, 60,000 homeowners in San Antonio would be forced out of their homes by rising taxes within the next seven-and-a-half years. This provoked a front-page editorial in the San Antonio Light telling him to "stick to the facts" instead of making such "absurd" claims.

Early in the campaign, Stubbs made an important strategic error. Claiming that as a simple fellow he was no match for the mayor's formidable persuasive talents, he consistently refused to debate Henry. The public didn't buy Stubbs' reason for ducking the debate. The ranks of the undecided soon began to swell.

Henry needed all the help he could get, and so he asked Target '90 to be out front in the battle. We helped recruit speakers and got representatives of the 170 civic organizations participating in Target '90 to take the message back to their members.

In the midst of the campaign, City Council accelerated the schedule for adopting the annual budget for the fiscal year starting October 1. Ordinarily, the budget is debated in August and September, but it was important to have the next budget adopted before the cap could take legal effect. This move benefited the anti-cap forces, because the new budget illustrated some of the flaws in Stubbs' proposal.

City budget staff calculated that the real impact of the cap would have been to severely reduce city capital spending, which had grown dramatically over the last six years. A new $100 million airport terminal and a federally mandated $400 million regional sewage treatment plant had coincided with more than $300 million in voter-approved bonds for streets, drainage, police stations, fire stations and libraries.

In minority neighborhoods, COPS reminded its constituents of the "legacy of neglect" they had suffered under the Good Government League, before the advent of single-member districts. They were alarmed that now that the barrio streets were beginning to be paved and the drainage improved, certain elements in the community found it convenient to restrict city spending. Stubbs added to their fears by admitting that the next step after the cap would be an attack on single-member districts.

The anti-cap campaign also received a major gift when an implausible ally to Stubbs surfaced unexpectedly in favor of the cap. This was former City Councilman Bernardo Eureste, who had been defeated for re-election in 1985. Eureste had been elected with the first council from single-member districts in 1977, and he had quickly become known for his outbursts and inflammatory rhetoric. He had survived a re-election challenge in 1983 after he and a female companion had been mugged in the early morning hours in Brackenridge Park. He had fled the scene on foot, leaving his companion to be assaulted by the attackers. In 1985, Eureste was finally brought down when it was revealed that he had been accepting campaign contributions from developers at the same time he was attacking them by name in the press.

During his tenure on City Council, Eureste had made the budget his principal specialty. He was the architect of much of the spending to which Stubbs objected, and he put together the majorities to amend the city manager's recommended budgets to accommodate the spending increases. Now, at his own expense, he published an eight-page broadsheet that rambled in a long diatribe against politicians in general, Henry in particular, the developers and COPS.

The idea that Eureste would support the HTA initiative was simply ludicrous. He was the biggest gift anyone ever gave to the anti-cap campaign.

When the polls finally closed on August 9, the result was clear from the very first returns. When all the votes were counted, the cap was crushed, 75,576 to 38,135, or just short of two to one. Even Stubbs' own home precinct rejected it.

The defeat of the spending cap represented the high-water mark of Henry Cisneros' power to dominate the political scene. He had mobilized what was probably the broadest coalition in the history of San Antonio, and he had personally worked extremely hard to win the victory. In the years ahead there would be other battles, leading to other hard-won victories. But never again would Henry command so vast and disparate a coalition of forces, or lead them in such an emotionally satisfying crusade. For now, the grand coalition had smashed the forces of reaction, and there could be no doubt about who ruled San Antonio.

A few days later, though, a detailed analysis of the vote detected a pattern that boded ill for Henry's coalition. Citywide, the cap referendum brought out 27 percent of the Anglo vote, 19 percent of the black vote, and only 16 percent of the Mexican-American vote.

Boiled down, what this really meant was that the cap lost because it had been decisively defeated on the Anglo North Side. Whispers started in the business community that COPS had failed to deliver, despite its strenuous blockwalking campaign. Some people began to question whether anybody could organize the West Side precincts to turn out a vote comparable to Henry's first mayoral race. If that were the case, then the Anglo power structure might be able to reassert itself and govern without the help of the inner-city minorities. This kind of talk dissipated after a while, but it would resurface in a dramatic way near the end of Henry's time as mayor.

Target '90's participation in the passage of the $100 million bond issue, the ill-fated fluoridation issue, and the spending cap campaign was the most visible work of our organization. But it was the behind-the-scenes work and the quiet building of consensus that was the core business of Target '90. We developed a leadership group of 100 young professionals called "Future San Antonio" who committed to work for our goals.

Target '90 became a national model for community goal-setting programs. Twenty-seven cities sought information about Target '90. It was great publicity for our city.

After unveiling a major report at the end of 1985, the steam went out of Target '90. My term as chairman ended in 1986, and after that, the organization slowly went out of business. It was, of course, replaced by other progressive groups with new players and new ideas. The organization's final report, published in 1989 and titled, "San Antonio: Destiny 2010," can be found in the public library.

Meanwhile, two-and-a-half years after the spending cap, the Homeowner-Taxpayer Association would suffer again from being associated with an implausible ally. This time it wouldn't be Bernardo Eureste, but the group that was closest to Henry ideologically in many voters' minds: COPS. But the Alamodome is another story.

★★★
Lessons on Reshaping Power

■ **You can't get across town without a road map.**
A community consensus must be developed to move a city forward. That consensus should be expressed in an agenda with specific goals that connect all areas of the city.

■ **Set plenty of places at the table.**
People must feel that they helped develop the ideas that become part of a community consensus. One will always fight harder for one's own idea than for another's.

■ **Watch out for the Bogeyman.**
Opposition groups can win by using tactics that appeal to people's fear of change. This strategy is difficult to fight. The Homeowner-Taxpayer Association won the campaign on fluoridation using this tactic.

■ **Use the media to sell the agenda.**
Henry was a master of this. He knew what news stories the media were looking for. He knew how to package them to make them interesting. He was great at sound bites. He got to know the key media people personally.

■ **Campaign for your ideas as you would campaign for office.**
Henry did this in the fight against the spending cap. Polling, money, grassroots organization, blockwalking, a media campaign and phone banking are all necessary. Consensus alone is not enough. You have to get the people who share the consensus to the polls.

3

A Freshman Councilman

In October 1986, the city of San Antonio dedicated a new building and plaza on the HemisFair grounds to house the Universidad Nacional Autonoma de Mexico. Because of our historically close ties, San Antonio was the only city in the United States to have a branch of Mexico's premier university system. Henry Cisneros' grandfather, Romulo Munguia, had been one of the founding fathers of the San Antonio branch. But the original building UNAM occupied had to be replaced to make room for expansion of the convention center.

It was a pleasant day as dignitaries from Mexico and San Antonio gathered on the temporary stage in front of the new building for the dedication ceremonies. This was an important day, as Henry had worked hard to foster closer economic and cultural ties with Mexico. The 350,000 students of the University of Mexico system were important in fostering those ties.

I sat in the audience listening to Henry give his speech. I had trouble concentrating because I was thinking about what I was going to tell him after the ceremony. It was important that I approach him right and that I get a favorable response from him.

It was always best to catch Henry when he was in a good mood if you had something important to talk about. And he had been in a good mood ever since the defeat of the spending cap. He had won a great victory. He faced an easy re-election next spring. No one on City Council was giving him a bad time. The day and the occasion were just right. On this day he should know that I was going to run for the council.

During the year, speculation had grown about my interest in running in order to position myself for a future race for mayor. In its March issue, San Antonio Monthly magazine carried a picture of me on the front cover with the headline, "Is this man SA's next mayor?" At the time Rick Casey, now a columnist for the San Antonio Express-News, was the editor of the magazine. He made the decision regarding the cover story.

When Casey met me for the photo session he said, "You know, I did one of these stories on Henry when he was a member of the council." He showed me the cover of a previous issue with a photo of Henry smiling and holding a trash can. "I could be right twice," he said.

The speculation about my political plans was minor, though, compared to the speculation about Henry's political future. As the 1987 campaign neared, many thought this would be Henry's last hurrah as mayor. He was destined for greater things.

Even though he had to fight off negative forces during his third term, he had accomplished many major projects over his six years as mayor. Three successful bond issues, a $42 million downtown improvement plan and the building of the VSLI computer chip manufacturing plant were just a few of his accomplishments.

Henry was also receiving attention nationwide. In January 1982, he was named one of the 10 Outstanding Young Men of America by the U.S. Jaycees. In 1983, he had been appointed by President Reagan to serve on the Kissinger Commission. In 1984, Democratic presidential candidate Walter Mondale had interviewed him as a potential vice presidential candidate. In December 1985, he was elected president of the National League of Cities. All over town there was speculation that Henry would make a statewide race for governor before his next term was finished.

As people began to mill around after the ceremonies, I approached Henry just as he turned from a conversation with Charles Kilpatrick, then the publisher of the Express-News. Out of earshot of Kilpatrick, I said, "Henry, I've decided to challenge Ed Harrington in next year's council election." I reminded him that I would complete two years as chairman of Target '90 in November, and told him I would announce for the race in December. I concluded, "I hope I can count on you being neutral."

At our lunch meeting in the Plaza Club almost two years earlier, Henry had promised to stay neutral if I decided to run in 1987. I hoped I would not have to remind him of that pledge. Henry has a near photographic memory. I knew he would remember, unless he chose to forget.

Seeming genuinely pleased, he said, "The next two years will be very exciting. We'll be completing a number of major projects such as HemisFair Park, the downtown shopping mall and Marriott Hotel, and Sea World. It will be a fun time to be on the council. I'll be neutral, as I said I would be two years ago. Good luck."

I thanked him, we concluded our conversation with some small talk and went our separate ways.

Walking to my car, I mulled over that short, upbeat conversation. I was glad I didn't have to remind him about his pledge of neutrality. Part of the reason for Henry's favorable response was the fact that I had remained loyal to his agenda during my two years at Target '90. But I did not believe this was the real reason he felt comfortable about the race.

Henry was seriously considering a race for governor. And looking ahead to such a statewide contest, he would not feel threatened by anyone on City Council with mayoral ambitions, as he knew I had. I walked away with confidence that Henry was on his way to the statehouse and that I had a clear field in the race for mayor.

I also knew that once I told Henry about the race, word would get out. I did not want to be put in a position of having to be coy about whether I would run if I were approached first by the media. So the next day I let the media know of my plans to run and told them I would make a formal announcement in December.

Preparing to Run

Through October and November I prepared for the race. Running against an incumbent who has traditional campaign donors tied up, a challenger has no choice but to reach into his own pockets or to seek funds from non-traditional sources. I loaned money to my campaign in order to hire a staff and a public relations consultant and secure a campaign office. Ironically, the office I rented was in the Canavan Center, which former Councilman Gene Canavan had developed. Canavan was the man who two years earlier said he would raise $250,000 for the incumbent. He still was committed to doing so.

A few days before my formal announcement on December 16, I received a call from Henry's office asking me to have lunch with him the day after that announcement. Henry was not going to waste one day before he assessed my chances.

We met in a small, private room on the second floor of the Shogun Japanese restaurant on the banks of the San Antonio River. As we settled down to eat a little cabbage and beef sukiyaki, he asked, "Well, how does the race look?"

"Well, we had over 150 people at our announcement yesterday," I responded. "I have strong neighborhood support because Ed (Harrington) has simply not been responsive to their concerns."

Earlier in the year I had spoken before the council on behalf of neighborhoods opposing a commercial rezoning case. Ed supported the developers, as he had in almost every case. After the meeting was over, 200 people were really steamed about the council's decision to grant the rezoning. They would provide the core of my neighborhood support.

"Do you think you'll get a lot of business community support?" Henry asked.

"Some," I answered. "Most of my financial support will come from business leaders who have been friends over the years and who have not participated in previous council campaigns."

"How much money do you think you'll have to raise?"

"I think the campaign will cost about $150,000. I will raise it or put it up myself."

"Do you think you'll get the endorsement of the newspapers?"

"I don't know."

"I think you may get one of them," Henry said. He had not wasted any time checking out his close newspaper sources.

If you think this sounded like an interrogation, you are right. If Henry decided to get involved in the race, he wanted to be sure he was on the winning side. There is nothing worse for a mayor than having someone elected to the council whom you openly tried to defeat. That does not make for a good relationship.

I knew the developers were pressuring Henry to back Harrington. Henry would interpret any doubts I might express as an indication of a weak candidacy. That would cause others to smell blood before the fight even began. To keep Henry neutral, I had to convince him I was going to win.

Once he was convinced I was going to be a serious candidate, he went on to ask, "Are you still interested in following me as mayor if you win the council race?"

"Yes," I answered.

He did not pursue the question further. Instead, he went on to give his analysis of the council race. He said that Harrington would make an issue out of the fact that I was a Democrat running in a two-to-one registered Republican district. He also said Harrington would charge that the only reason I was running was because I wanted to be mayor. After tipping me off on the campaign issues Ed would raise, he shifted the conversation to his consideration for a statewide race.

"Have you kept up your statewide contacts since you were in the Texas Senate?"

"Yes, I've kept up with several old colleagues."

"As you know, I'm considering a statewide race, possibly for governor or lieutenant governor," Henry said.

"I've heard that, and I'll be glad to help."

We talked at length about the two possible races. I encouraged him to run for governor. I told him I thought he would have the best of both worlds. He would be accepted by the liberal wing in the Democratic primary because he was Hispanic and had supported a number of their causes. He would also appeal to Republicans in the general election because of his pro-business record as mayor.

Interestingly, we did not talk about city issues. I thought it strange that he did not ask me to commit to any local issue. That really convinced me that Henry was ready to run for statewide office in 1990 and that he felt OK about my coming on the council. At the end of the meeting he said he would get back to me about his statewide race plans after he consulted further with George Shipley.

Somehow, Express-News columnist Roddy Stinson found out about our lunch, and had a great deal of fun describing Henry's "neutral" stance on the race. He explained that while Henry was having lunch with me, Shipley was meeting with Ed Harrington. Stinson wrote, "Cisneros is eating sukiyaki with Wolff, but his right-hand political man is sharing bacon and eggs with Harrington. Neutrality, San Antonio style. Don't you love it? Where else you gonna get this kind of entertainment free?"

When Henry said he was going to get back with Shipley, I thought he meant to talk with him about his own statewide race. Now I knew they would compare notes and jointly assess my strength and Ed's.

On December 27, two weeks after our lunch, I saw Henry at the United Negro College Fund telethon. Pulling me aside, he said, "George Shipley has heard that you may be considering hiring a former partner of his. If you do that, George may decide to work for Harrington."

I told him I was not hiring anyone out of Austin. I went away feeling this was just an excuse for Shipley to work for Harrington. If he did, everyone would know who Henry was for. Something had happened in the two weeks since our visit at the Shogun restaurant.

I found out later that Shipley had done a poll for Harrington in December that showed Harrington with a 2-to-1 lead over me. Contrary to what he told me, Henry began telling the press that he was not serious about a statewide race and that he wanted only to be mayor. I felt he made the statement to protect his power base as mayor. He was in a re-election campaign and did not want to get ahead of himself.

Early in January, though, Harrington pulled a boner. He announced that he would oppose Henry's public safety bond issue that would be part of the April ballot. Henry fired back, telling his staff to stay clear of the race between Harrington and me. George Shipley was quoted by the San Antonio Light on January 25 as saying he would no longer work for Harrington. But this would prove to be a temporary break.

Just when things appeared to be in good shape again with Henry, an article appeared in the San Antonio Light with a headline stating that City Council District 8 was "The Real Mayor's Race." The Light's story speculated that if I won, then I would be favored to succeed Henry. I knew Henry hated this thought and that the article would probably have consequences later on in the race.

While doing everything I could to keep Henry out of the race, I also had to concentrate on organizing my campaign.

District 8, my district, was by far the city's largest with a population of 140,000 people, 81 percent of whom were Anglos. Rapid growth in northwest San Antonio and annexation had expanded the district to twice the size of the inner-city districts.

It is also politically progressive, with a large number of professionals. The 600-acre South Texas Medical Center with more than 58 institutions and 20,000 employees is in the heart of the district, which stretches from just below Loop 410 to Loop 1604. Development had chased Charlie Becker's hoot owls and jack rabbits out to the hills beyond Loop 1604, and the district was now home to a full quarter of the city's total property value.

I knew the district well because it was part of the area I had represented when serving in the Texas Senate and House. While it was prosperous and progressive, economic growth had placed strains on neighborhoods and the quality of life. Easy money from savings and loan institutions allowed developers to throw up ugly strip centers on just about every corner. Huge apartment complexes were located next to single-family homes. Neighborhood leaders felt Ed Harrington was oblivious to the downside of this uncontrolled development.

Harrington made other mistakes, especially in the area of constituent service. Citizens want their council representative to be responsive to life's irritations, large and small; things like a pothole, or a neighbor violating a code, or a loose cat or dog, or traffic cutting through the neighborhood, or any of a host of other things. They also want their phone calls answered. Harrington too often let his calls go unanswered.

Neighborhood leaders like Bill and Elinor Fries, Dan and Ellie Bump, and Bennie Newman were looking for a candidate who would listen and respond. These folks were active beyond their own neighborhoods, too, by helping to expand the Coalition of Neighborhood Associations beyond its original inner-city base. They organized a political action committee called "Neighborhoods Now!" and endorsed me in the race. They became the core support of my campaign.

Tracy Hoag, who had organized the task forces of Target '90, became my campaign manager. She organized our campaign staff and volunteers. She quickly put together 900 volunteers from neighborhoods, many of whom she had met during the Target '90 process, to work on the campaign. They formed the "Wolff Pack" and developed a specially designed bandanna to wear to all political events.

Harriet Marmon, a long-time civic activist, became the cheerleader of the group, most of whom had never before participated in a political campaign. Joan Wolff, my sister-in-law, organized our fund-raisers.

At night, a phone bank run by my good friend Pat Clayworth, a teacher at Mark Twain Middle School, would identify voters as either undecided, for me, or for Harrington. Pat had helped me in my races for the Legislature in the 1970s and she had run the phone banks for Henry's campaign. The next morning, supporters would get a letter mailed to them thanking them for their support and reminding them to vote. Right before the election they would be called again. The undecided would be sent more information about my stands on the issues. We left the Harrington supporters alone because it's difficult to change a vote if someone has already decided.

While volunteers were sending out letters, answering phone calls and blockwalking, I had a team of academics developing positions for me. Some of these people were from campaigns dating back to the 1970s, but most were friends I had made during the Target '90 process. The core members of this group included Tom Brereton, a consultant and writer in city planning and public affairs; Dick Howe, a professor of engineering at UTSA; Tucker Gibson, the Trinity University political science professor who did our polling; Charles Cotrell, vice president at St. Mary's University and a long-time liberal activist; and Bob Ashcroft, a consultant and adjunct professor at UTSA.

We developed a number of position papers to address my constituents' concerns, which included recycling, police protection, landscaping and new branch libraries, among others.

Fifteen intersections in District 8 were on the city's "most dangerous" list. I said that District 8, because of its size and economic impact, could be the "change agent" for the city. If we worked together, we could determine how economic development and the quality of life could be balanced.

We got as much free media as we could by calling news conferences whenever we thought we had a chance to get coverage. Tony Gonzalez did a great job of handling our public relations and developing strong advertising messages. We drew a picture of Harrington as a captive of the developers. We scoffed at him for not returning constituents' phone calls and for not having a district office to handle day-to-day constituent concerns.

Two months before the election, I began campaigning full time. In the morning, I went to the office to get on the phone to raise money. Every afternoon I blockwalked. We had organized our grassroots campaign along neighborhood lines rather than voting precincts. When I walked, I had neighbors go with me. I made it to every precinct in the district. At night, we either worked at the office, attended a political or neighborhood meeting, or had a backyard "get acquainted" party at a supporter's home.

In order to win, I knew I had to spend at least as much money as the incumbent. I needed to overcome Harrington's name recognition and the tremendous amount of free media that an incumbent receives.

I was able to raise funds from business associates I had developed over a lifetime in the building materials business and then in the retail natural foods business. Car dealers Red McCombs and Ernesto Ancira, banker Edith McAllister and oilman Robert West helped me. John Steen and cigar manufacturer Bill Finck came aboard with "old money," and developer Dan Parman came as a supporter with "new money."

The San Antonio Board of Realtors endorsed me and provided funds. Ed Harrington was a builder, but builders and Realtors are not necessarily natural allies. Realtors are concerned about maintaining property values in existing neighborhoods, and are attuned to neighborhood issues. The homebuilder leaves a subdivision forever once it is "built out."

While we hammered away at Harrington, he proceeded as though he had no re-election problem. He held a large fund-raiser in the wealthy Elm Creek neighborhood that netted him several thousand dollars. As Henry predicted, he attacked me for having mayoral ambitions and for the fact that I was a Democrat in a heavily Republican district. He made a number of personally unkind remarks, calling me a two-time loser because I had lost two congressional races, and circulating a sketch of a four-legged "Wolff" panting from exhaustion with its tail between its legs. These personal attacks only increased my determination to win. I started walking longer hours in the neighborhoods and putting in 18-hour days.

Harrington lacked a grassroots campaign. He didn't make the number of personal appearances I did. He did little blockwalking. Instead, he relied heavily on media buys and the support of traditional business leaders.

Our polling showed that our charges were sticking while Ed's were not, and that people thought it was great that the next mayor might come from District 8. The charge that I was a Democrat did not hurt because everyone knew that San Antonio's council is elected on a nonpartisan basis. Political activists knew I had previously supported a number of Republicans. I endorsed Cyndi Taylor Krier when she ran successfully for state senator. I had also endorsed Roy Barrera Jr. when he ran for attorney general and Lamar Smith when he ran for the U.S. Congress, succeeding Tom Loeffler.

As election day neared, I found out why Harrington was feeling so confident. One of my supporters told me he was polled over the phone by the Harrington camp. He was asked, "If Mayor Cisneros came out for Harrington," would that change his mind about his vote?

George Shipley was doing the polling to see if Henry could save Harrington. Behind the scenes, Henry was helping Ed by giving him credit for a number of city projects. He staged a news conference to announce that Harrington was instrumental in getting USAA to donate land for a police substation in District 8. It did not seem to matter that Harrington was against the bond issue that would have provided funding to build that very substation. Many other public works projects for District 8 were also announced right before the election.

Paul Thompson, whose column for the Express-News then represented a major political force, wrote on March 22, only two weeks before election day, that the vote was too close to call. "The entire working dynamics of San Antonio's City Council will fall apart if Nelson Wolff whips Ed Harrington in the April 4 election," Thompson wrote, "and Henry Cisneros, poor guy, will suffer misery and pain for two whole years. Cisneros, though he can't afford to say so, or even admit privately, would accept with serene resignation a Wolff defeat at the poll next month .... Let's put it like this: If Cisneros thought for a moment that Councilman Harrington was a cinch, or a near cinch to win, he'd have jumped in behind him long ago with, as they say, both feet."

I called Henry to remind him of his pledge to be neutral. I knew he was getting pressure from Ed's supporters to help, and he did not want to give up any power at City Hall when he still had two more years to serve as mayor.

Henry was very friendly. He said, "You know, a mayoral endorsement would only add five points" to the race he endorsed. But he went on to say he would not endorse Harrington.

As a result of that conversation, I concluded that Shipley's poll must have shown Harrington more than five points behind; otherwise, Henry might have endorsed him. Our own polling showed us surging ahead. Until that moment I had believed Henry's endorsement of Ed would have meant my defeat. I now knew I had been overly concerned about it.

The newspapers split on the race. The Express-News endorsed me and the San Antonio Light endorsed Harrington. The split surprised me. The Light viewed itself as a check on the power of City Hall while the Express-News was viewed as pro-establishment. I thought it would have been the other way around. You just never know what goes through a newspaper's collective mind.

Two days before the election, my Republican friends jumped in to help me. State Senator Krier, Judge Roy Barrera Jr., former Congressman Tom Loeffler (my Republican opponent in 1978), County Commissioner Jeff Wentworth, and Republican party leaders Diane Rath and Doug Harlan sent out letters endorsing me. The fact that I was a Democrat who was willing to step beyond party lines paid off.

On election night the returns rolled in quickly. I won all 35 precincts in the district as well as the absentee vote. I polled 13,364 votes to Harrington's 6,837, or 64 percent of the votes. More people voted in our council race than in Districts 1 and 2 combined. I was the only challenger to beat an incumbent. In fact, in the history of single-member districts beginning in 1977, only three council members had been defeated and two of those losses were attributed to scandals.

Henry won re-election easily with 67 percent of the votes. The public safety bond issue that Harrington opposed passed overwhelmingly. The newspapers were delighted to compare me to Henry, making much of the fact that Henry's margin of victory and mine were close. Henry was sensitive about such comparisons, and I would keep finding out how much Henry disliked sharing the stage.

The strong victory helped position me well for the mayor's race two years ahead. It also galvanized North Side neighborhood organizations. They would become a power to be reckoned with, and this new-found power would lead to many neighborhood victories.

It was also a very satisfying victory for me personally. I had patiently waited two years for this day. I had taken on the political establishment and had won. I showed them.

The First Day

At noon on May 7, 1987, the new term of City Council began in the 18th century Spanish Governor's Palace, across the parking lot from City Hall. It always seemed strange to call this place a palace because the white caliche building constructed two-and-a-half centuries ago is actually very small and unassuming. Behind the Governor's Palace is a delightful walled-in patio, with a fountain surrounded by a pebble walkway and bordered with native flowers and trees.

As I walked into the patio, off to the left of the fountain, under a grape arbor, I saw Henry, the council members, City Manager Lou Fox and his key staff members, all seated at five large tables. Henry had arranged for lunch in this place to set the tone for the new council term. A beautiful spring day enhanced the tranquil setting in this symbol of historical power. Henry moved gracefully from table to table, greeting the members of his council just as the Spanish governors must have done when San Antonio was a frontier capital at the edge of the Spanish Empire.

At the conclusion of the meal, Henry touched briefly on some of the challenges facing us. He said our biggest challenge would be to solve San Antonio's water problem, including both quality and quantity. He talked about the need to add 100 police officers, to develop a bond package for streets and drainage, and to finish the development of downtown.

He also spoke of the need to build a major sports facility. That issue went right over our heads. We had no idea how serious he was when he mentioned it. We would soon find out.

It appeared that Henry had everything in place for a successful last term that would position him for a statewide race. It also looked as if I was in a great position to succeed him. The city's horizon seemed filled with positive projects. The economy was holding its own, Sea World and the Research Park would soon open, the budget appeared in good shape, three new police stations were being built and several other public projects were nearing completion. The sailing looked smooth.

After lunch, we walked across the parking lot to City Hall. The structure was built in 1885 during the term of Mayor Bryan Callaghan. A man of Irish and Hispanic ancestry, Callaghan had been elected at the same age as Henry, 33, and a hundred years before Henry. City Hall was clearly feeling its age — the limestone was stained and cracking, and pieces were literally falling off the exterior walls. Its condition did not say much for the city's commitment to historic preservation.

After we took our oaths of office, Henry passed out a 20-page agenda that went into greater detail than the broad outline he presented at lunch. He entitled this agenda: "The Year of Seeing Tough Jobs Through to Completion." These titles were sometimes the butt of jokes around City Hall because of the hyperbole. But his agenda — a list of specific projects meant to be accomplished within a year — was the key to Henry's power. His authority was not bestowed by the city charter. It arose from Henry's self-appointed role as the city's *agendameister*.

City Council had acquiesced in this assumption of power by the mayor. I believe the turbulence and gridlock of the 1977-79 term, the first with single-member districts, played a part in the unspoken agreement to let Henry set the agenda as mayor. Three of the sitting council members in 1987 had served through that earlier era of political stalemate. But the main reason was that Henry understood the power he was assuming and no one else really did. Certainly no previous mayor understood it, because none had ever set an agenda before.

Before my first day on council, Henry had sent numerous warnings to me through the media not to tamper with this power. Henry enjoyed communicating with me this way. It was a nice filtering process. If it came across too harsh, he would assure me that the press had misquoted him. It was also a way to let the city know he was in charge.

A *San Antonio Light* article on April 7 quoted him as warning me, "I don't, you know, take to being pushed around and I don't take to having runs on my office. This is a role (setting the agenda) that I have carved out for the mayor's office."

I got the message. I had no intention of challenging this prerogative of the mayor. At the time I did not truly understand the significance of this agenda-setting power. As time passed I would learn.

The first day of council was relatively free of controversy except for one item. The Encore Development Corporation was seeking an extension of a contract to arrange financing and build a Sheraton Hotel on a site in HemisFair Plaza. Henry was committed to extending the contract, while several council members felt Encore should not be granted additional time because of its failure to perform. I was one of them.

At the start of the meeting we moved quickly through the "consent agenda" of contracts and noncontroversial items. Rather than follow the agenda laid out by staff, Henry skipped over the Encore Development issue. He needed time for Councilman Frank Wing to line up his votes.

Frank Wing was a civil service employee at Kelly Air Force Base in 1973 when he helped his friend Ernie Cortes organize COPS. Two years later, Frank helped elect a young Henry Cisneros to City Council. In 1977, Frank became a candidate in District 4 on the South Side. Henry returned the favor by walking door-to-door for him.

From his first day on the council, Frank became the conciliator, the power behind Henry and his most loyal supporter. He became the arbiter of federal development funds, the negotiator of the budget, the liaison to the staff and the councilman who put the tough votes together.

I watched Frank work the council for votes that day. He used Councilmen Weir Labatt and Jimmy Hasslocher to work on me. They represented Districts 9 and 10, the north central and northeast suburban districts bordering my district on the east. Frank would walk up to Henry and whisper in his ear as he accumulated the votes. Henry kept a vote total on a scrap of paper as

Frank reported to him. Finally the vote was called and Henry prevailed 6 to 5 without my vote.

I thought this might make him mad at me but it didn't. As long as Henry got six votes he saw no reason to put heat on other members whose votes he did not need. He knew he would need me and the other council members who voted "no" on future issues. By doing this he was able to limit his requests for votes from each council member, and only press when he really needed to.

It did not take long for me to understand the working dynamics of the council. It was simple: "Watch Wing." If Wing was for an issue you knew it would pass; without his support it would most likely fail.

Before City Hall was built, the councils had met in a small building near the present site. It was called "the bat cave" because bats literally hung out in the building. The chamber where we met in the present City Hall wasn't much better. It was a small,

City Councilman Frank Wing, an expert on the budget and police issues, gestures during a council meeting where he regularly served as Mayor Cisneros' "point man." (Rick Hunter, Express-News)

dark, dingy room with a low ceiling. There were no bats as far as I could tell, but it certainly would have been an appropriate place for them.

The council and mayor sat around a horseshoe-shaped table facing about 200 uncomfortable seats for citizens. In the middle of the horseshoe at a lower level sat the City Clerk and her assistant facing the mayor. To my back was a small table with two chairs behind it. One of these chairs was occupied by City Manager Lou Fox and the other by the city attorney.

Prior to Henry's election, the city manager held the real power at City Hall. He is appointed by a majority vote of the council and serves at their pleasure. As long as he has six votes he has a job. Because the mayor has only one vote, the city manager is not beholden to him more than to any other council member. Unless ....

On February 5, 1982, less than a year after Henry became mayor, he led an effort to fire the last strong city manager, Tom Huebner. Tom had survived the turbulence of the late 1970s and strengthened the city staff as a professional bureaucracy. But he had gone through a painful divorce, and racked up a pair of minor accidents and driving-while-intoxicated charges.

Henry convinced the council to replace Huebner with the manager's assistant, Lou Fox. Lou quickly understood the shift in power. If a mayor was strong enough to deliver six votes against the city manager, that city manager had better pay attention to the mayor.

Lou was 39 years old when he became city manager. Six feet tall, an ex-Marine with a muscular build developed by running in marathons, Lou had the stamina and determination to keep up with Henry's pace. Lou also understood politics better than anyone on the council. He wouldn't draw a fictional line between politics and administration the way previous city managers, including Huebner, had done.

Lou also knew that Henry was not going to interfere in his domain. Henry understood that a leader needs to distinguish major policy issues from procedural and personnel issues. Henry wanted to be able to rely on the staff to carry out his programs in ways that were faithful to their substance. If Lou delivered this,

Henry would not challenge him on the budget or personnel issues.

They both understood they needed each other. For the council-manager form of government to be progressive and action oriented, the mayor and city manager must be "in sync." Henry and Lou were perfectly in sync: Lou, Mr. Inside; Henry, Mr. Outside.

In 1987, Lou was named to the "All Pro Management Team" by City and State magazine. In 1988, he was selected by the magazine again as the nation's outstanding city manager. He would go on to serve San Antonio longer than any previous manager.

Free of management responsibility, the mayor can do what he should do. He can lead rather than manage. An important support in this role was the increasing staff assigned to the office after Henry became mayor. Lila had difficulty even getting a graduate student intern assigned to her office in the mid-1970s. That intern, Shirl Thomas, now became the mayor's full-time administrative assistant, the gatekeeper and liaison to the community and the city's real director of protocol.

After the first meeting of council, at least I knew who the key power players were. Henry Cisneros, Councilman Frank Wing and City Manager Lou Fox were the people to watch. But as I would learn, there was much more to understanding how to harness power. It would take me four years to understand how to strap the policy-making body of the council onto the management body of the bureaucracy to create an engine that could move the city forward.

"Peacock Patrols" and Constituent Service

Rita O'Brien, a neighborhood leader and volunteer who worked in my District 8 office, received a call from a constituent complaining about a neighbor. This neighbor kept about 10 peacocks that let out loud shrieks from time to time, often at night. The constituent told Rita an arrest warrant had been issued charging her neighbor with violating a city code that prohibited keeping such creatures inside the city limits. Rita called the police and asked them to arrest the neighbor.

When officers arrested Dick Adams, they told him they were doing so on direct orders from Councilman Nelson Wolff. The poor man finally convinced the officers to call and check, saying he had paid a one-dollar fine and the warrant was no longer valid. After checking, the police apologized and took him home. Later, I received the angriest call I have ever received from a constituent, and rightfully so.

I immediately went to his home to apologize. We talked for several hours during which I was treated to a personal tour and a lecture on the beauty of peacocks. Dick was very understanding, and before the visit ended he forgave me. Today, he still has the peacocks and I am his customer at a local men's clothing store.

This case was a most unusual one for our district office. After my election, I moved quickly to set up a neighborhood office, as promised in my campaign. I leased space in an office park on the edge of the Oak Hills neighborhood, conveniently located in the middle of my district. It was just across Loop 410 from Charles Becker's Wonderland shopping mall. Fredericksburg Road had developed into a major artery bordering one side of the South Texas Medical Center. Its intersections with the access roads of Loop 410 were some of the most congested and dangerous in the city.

No council member had ever before organized a district office to provide comprehensive services to his constituents. At most, they maintained a personal office away from City Hall as an add-on to their pre-existing business office. I raised funds from private sources to staff the office full time.

Tracy Hoag, my campaign manager, became the office manager. The phones began ringing right away. In addition to the paid staff of two, Tracy developed a group of 50 neighborhood activists who donated their time working in the office. They became "caseworkers" who handled complaints and pushed the proper city department to respond. They kept a file on each case and followed up until the complaint was settled. This caused a little tension with the city staff because they had never had a council office demand action as often as we did.

We developed an early warning system to alert neighborhoods whenever a zoning case was coming up that might affect them. Today, the city's planning department maintains a registry of neighborhood organizations to provide the same service citywide. We asked city staffers to come to the office to meet with citizen groups, sparing them a trip downtown to City Hall. We organized crime prevention meetings with the police in attendance. We sent teams of volunteers into neighborhoods to help them organize. When we started there were 30 organized neighborhoods in District 8. By the end of my term there were 120.

Not only had the neighborhood leaders proved that they could be a major force in an election, they also showed they had the staying power to be effective after the election. They performed a valuable service for which I will be ever grateful. I am sure the citizens whose complaints were handled by them feel the same.

★★★

Lessons of a Freshman Councilman

■ **Handshakes work better than TV ads in a neighborhood campaign.**
It's a waste of money to use television, radio and newspaper ads because too much of the message (and your money with it) goes out beyond the council district. Our grassroots organization was made up of volunteers. Our phone bank was staffed by professionals. Volunteers did the hard work of addressing a lot of our direct mail but professionals developed the message.

■ **You need your own money to get in the game.**
It is difficult to raise money against an incumbent who has not offended his own major contributors. When I seeded the campaign with my own funds, contributors knew I was serious. That enabled me to raise funds that otherwise would have been hard to secure.

■ **Define your own political turf.**
Traditional campaigns for public office are organized by voting precincts. We organized by neighborhoods instead. Neighborhoods care more about local politics than state or national

issues. They organize around zoning issues, police protection, code compliance and other local concerns.

■ **In a political campaign, arm yourself with a single good issue.**
Polling with phone banks can help you recognize the key concerns of your neighborhoods. Pick a good one and ride it till it drops. I used the issue of my opponent's close ties to developers.

■ **Setting an agenda is your most powerful tool.**
On the first day, as I listened to Henry laying out the city's agenda, I knew I had observed an important power of the mayor. Council members were relegated to minor tinkering, to developing secondary issues that did not conflict with the mayor's agenda. Some local politicians would fail to learn this lesson.

■ **Keep your door open to constituents.**
The importance of "constituent service" is strongest in city government. My district office made constituents feel that the city and their councilman cared. People will always remember if you did something for them. They will not always remember your votes. You can vote wrong and serve right and get re-elected.

4

Water Wars — I

On a steamy night in May 1987, only two weeks after I had taken office, I watched a group of people surround Henry Cisneros as he walked to his car near San Antonio College. Ernie Cortes, the organizer and founder of Communities Organized for Public Service, was shaking a finger and gesturing angrily at Henry. We were all leaving a stormy City Council hearing on the Edwards Aquifer, held in the campus' McAllister Auditorium.

As I passed by, I heard Cortes say he was angry because Henry had refused to appoint Councilwoman Maria Berriozabal to the committee charged with writing new regulations protecting the Edwards Aquifer Recharge Zone. COPS wanted Maria on the committee because of her strong stand against development over the sensitive area. The development community felt she was strongly biased against North Side growth and would use this issue to stop it.

They argued a while longer, until Henry abruptly opened the front side door of the mayor's limousine, hopped in, and sped away, leaving Cortes and his followers in a literal cloud of dust. It was not the first — and far from the last — heated argument over water in San Antonio.

I had come on the council at a critical stage in the development of city policy concerning San Antonio's most fundamental long-running problem. It was a problem that preceded Henry's mayoral terms, and it would remain a problem after Henry and I left office. Water is a universal concern in the southwestern United States, but one that has taken some unique twists in San Antonio.

San Antonio is the largest city in the United States with absolutely no surface water supply. All of our water comes from the Edwards Aquifer, a porous limestone formation stretching 185 miles across six counties lying west to northeast of the city, including a band under the city's northern sector.

This aquifer recharges rapidly from rainfall runoff and flowing streams in a smaller area to the north and west of the city. In times of normal rainfall, it provides abundant pure water that needs little treatment before it is pumped directly into the city's water distribution system.

In times of drought, however, pumping for both agriculture and urban uses exceeds the amount of rainwater recharge. The aquifer is also vulnerable to the threat of pollution through the same sinkholes and cracks in stream beds that allow rainwater to enter the underground reservoir. The portion of this recharge zone under the city's burgeoning northern suburbs faces the most immediate threat because of the intensity of development there.

The hearing at San Antonio College resulted from an unexpectedly heated controversy over a zoning decision made on April 9, three weeks before I assumed my council seat. That decision, approved by an 8-to-2 vote of the council, had authorized the building of a large shopping mall over the aquifer's recharge zone.

Henry had voted against zoning for the mall, saying he was opposed because large-scale development over the recharge zone might pose a threat to the city's water supply. His opposition sent shock waves through the development community. Without warning, he had revived one of the most bitter controversies of the 1970s.

Back in December 1975, as a first-term councilman, Henry had joined COPS and the Aquifer Protection Association in campaigning for a referendum to overturn a similar zoning decision, one that would have allowed construction of a mall on another site over the recharge zone. Although that referendum passed overwhelmingly, it was ruled invalid in the courts, and the city was soon embroiled in a high-stakes lawsuit over an attempt to impose a moratorium on all development over the recharge zone. The issue died when the city spent $1.6 million for a consultant to identify "sensitive areas" of the recharge zone, and suggest measures needed to prevent pollution caused by development in those areas.

In the decade since that controversy, development had proceeded without the city implementing the consultant's recommendations. In the two years before the new controversy broke out, 36 zoning applications had been approved, clearing more than a thousand acres for development over the zone with hardly a murmur of dissent.

Now here was Henry, in 1987, suddenly reawakening the community to the danger of uncontrolled development. Pressure from COPS and environmentalists, along with public concern over the huge mall, had galvanized Henry into action.

The implications of Henry's "no" vote also sent shock waves into the offices of retired General Robert McDermott, chairman of the board of United Services Automobile Association, San Antonio's largest private employer. Some 8,500 people worked for USAA, one of the nation's largest insurance and financial services companies. Its headquarters was a three-story building situated on 286 acres in my council district in the northwest part of the city. The building was larger than the Pentagon — a fitting comparison for a firm run by former military officers that specialized in service to military families.

McDermott not only ranked first among equals in the hierarchy of the local business community, he was also an acknowledged mentor to Henry Cisneros. At the time the zoning controversy broke out, "McD," as he was nicknamed, was planning his own major development over the aquifer. "La Cantera," as it was to be known, was conceived as a 1,600-acre development that would consist of a shopping mall, offices, recreational facilities and homes on the site of an old limestone quarry. Hence, its name, Spanish for "the Quarry."

The development was to be located at the intersection of Loop 1604 and Interstate 10, less than five miles from the proposed mall Henry had opposed.

Henry had encouraged USAA to invest in San Antonio. McD had complied with Henry's wish by paying more than $35 million for the land and $3 million for planning and engineering. I was present when the project was announced in February 1986, and recalled Henry's speech praising it.

On the night of the City Council hearing at McAllister Auditorium, a thousand people filled the hall. Tensions ran high. The business community argued strenuously that no new regulations were needed, citing studies by the U.S. Geological Survey that showed no deterioration in water quality, despite all the recent development over the recharge zone. On the other side, COPS and its allies countered that development had only just begun, and reminded council members that the consultant's recommendations to protect the aquifer had never been implemented.

At the conclusion of the hearing, Henry named a five-member council committee to review the existing safeguards and make recommendations to council and the Texas Water Commission on the need for any new regulations. In addition to himself, he appointed Councilmen Weir Labatt, Joe Webb, Frank Wing and me to the committee.

We held our first meeting on May 28, and Henry laid out a comprehensive agenda with an ambitious schedule for completion. We set up a process whereby four organizations would be recognized as "intervenors." Representatives from these groups would be accorded five minutes at each meeting to state their views.

COPS, along with the Metropolitan Congregational Alliance and the Eastside Alliance, formed one group. Each organization was active in the inner city and strongly opposed to development over the recharge zone. Their ally was the Aquifer Protection Association, which had been organized by Fay Sinkin. Fay was the wife of banker Bill Sinkin, who had chaired the planning committee for HemisFair '68. She was also a former board member of the

Edwards Underground Water District. Together, COPS and the Aquifer Protection Association had led the campaign to overturn the "supermall" rezoning a decade earlier.

The Greater San Antonio Homebuilders Association and a coordinating committee formed by the local chambers of commerce formed an alliance on the other side. Strong advocates of property rights, they contended that government had no right to stop them from using their land in a safe manner.

Early in the process, the Builders Association circulated a position paper threatening to sue the city. Our committee gave them a clear choice: stay with the process as we developed new regulations, or leave now and file suit. They backed down, and the tensions eased noticeably.

As new regulations were proposed, I began to use them on zoning decisions in my district, where most of the applications involving the recharge zone originated. City Council almost always acted on the basis of "district courtesy" in considering zoning changes.

In some cases, I convinced the City Council to deny the change if it was close to a sensitive recharge area. An example was a proposed gasoline station at the corner of DeZavala Road and Military Highway, a site close to a crevice leading directly into the aquifer. For the first time, the council turned down a rezoning case over the aquifer solely for environmental reasons. This was a major reversal from the policy of my predecessor.

Our committee continued to meet weekly until the council adopted our report on September 28. Our report's fundamental principle was that the city should tolerate "no degradation" in the quality of the aquifer water supply. To implement this policy, we made 29 major recommendations to Bexar County, the Texas Water Commission and other agencies. We called for stricter standards for sewer lines, limits on septic tanks and a substantial increase in the budget of the city's Environmental Protection Office. We banned a number of business activities near sensitive recharge areas. The report was adopted by the council unanimously.

This was the first step in protecting the recharge area of the Edwards Aquifer. Another major step would be taken in a highly charged political atmosphere in 1995. We will review that step later.

The Revolt of the Farmers

In the early morning hours of May 30, 1988 — a year after Henry's argument with Ernie Cortes outside McAllister Auditorium — Councilman Weir Labatt and I drove into the parking lot of City Hall. It was Memorial Day, and the only other car in sight was the mayor's sleek, blue Lincoln Continental. (Ford Motor Company provides a new car to the city each year at a token fee for the mayor's use, although Henry had been loath to give up the Volkswagen "Beetle" that was his trademark vehicle as a councilman.) Beside the Lincoln stood one of the two police officers assigned to drive and protect the mayor.

Henry sat alone in his office behind a stack of papers, waiting for the two of us. He looked up, shoved the papers aside and stood to greet us before we walked out to his car. We sped through the deserted streets of downtown and headed west on U.S. Highway 90. We passed through the towns of Castroville and Hondo and entered the dry, flat ranch country, flanked by huge irrigation farms on each side of the highway. The farms draw an enormous amount of water out of the Edwards Aquifer. Irrigation farming was instituted in the 1960s, after a devastating drought that afflicted the entire region in the 1950s. By the late 1980s, farmers were pumping about as much water from the aquifer each year as the city of San Antonio.

Our destination was Uvalde, located 90 miles west of San Antonio. Uvalde is the last place with a significant natural water supply on the edge of the West Texas desert. It is a classically conservative area, the home of Dolph Briscoe, a rancher who was governor when I served in the Texas Legislature, as well as John Nance Garner, who served as President Franklin Roosevelt's vice president.

It is also the home of Rodney Reagan, an irrigator and an elected member of the Edwards Underground Water District. Reagan was also the dissenting member of a regional ad hoc committee Henry had formed to develop a water plan governing aquifer users in all five counties. We were on our way to Uvalde to try to reach a compromise with the western agricultural interests and bring them on board in support of a water plan.

To create this regional committee in 1986, Henry had selected members from both the San Antonio City Council and the board of the EUWD, which had been created by the Texas Legislature in 1959 in the wake of the drought. The district was charged with conserving and protecting the Edwards Aquifer in a five-county area from Uvalde to San Marcos, 50 miles northeast. The Legislature, dominated then by rural interests, had given the district little real power. It lacked the authority to limit pumping, or even to require the registration and metering of wells.

Weir and I had been appointed to the joint committee as representatives of the City Council. Henry shared the chairmanship with Bobby Hasslocher, who was also chairman of the EUWD board. Before I came on board, the committee had reached a breakthrough consensus on a policy to manage pumping so that the annual volume of water taken from the aquifer did not exceed the average annual recharge through rainfall and stream bed percolation.

This was a major philosophical breakthrough, since the farmers had always regarded as inviolable their right under traditional Texas water law to pump unlimited amounts of water from beneath their land.

But how could we implement this policy in the real world — out in the western fields, and in the homes and businesses of the cities and towns that relied on the aquifer? That was the problem the committee was wrestling with in the fall of 1987, after I had come on board.

The fundamental problem is this: The people who are bound intimately by the rock and water beneath their feet have no common interest once that water reaches the surface. The irrigation farms in Uvalde and Medina counties to the west want water for their crops. To the east, Comal and Hays counties do not want to see their artesian springs go dry. And, of course, in the middle sits San Antonio, the largest city for hundreds of miles in any direction, needing additional water for economic growth.

If you punch a hole in the ground in San Marcos, you will likely strike water that went underground in Uvalde and missed being pumped out in San Antonio. And if you ride a raft down the Guadalupe River, on an average day 30 to 40 percent of the water supporting you has burst forth from springs fed by the Edwards Aquifer.

The one thing nearly everyone in the region could agree on was that the demands on the aquifer were fast approaching its annual recharge.

Such were the concerns we touched on in those weekly meetings in the fall of 1987. Henry presided from behind the conference table, writing our proposals in black crayon on butcher paper strung along the wall behind him. Sheets of paper were torn off as ideas were discarded, only to be replaced with new sheets of ideas that prevailed.

By November the majority of the committee had confirmed the earlier conclusion that the amount of water coming out of the aquifer had to be limited. This was still an agreement in principle; we had yet to concur on the specifics of how it would be accomplished. The committee also agreed to a proposal, made by Weir Labatt and me, that the entire region should pay for the development of additional water supplies.

Week after week, we plowed through the issues. We agreed on a conservation plan, a plan for reuse of wastewater for nonpotable purposes, and the development of four lakes, one of which was the Applewhite Reservoir, over a period of 50 years.

After six months of work, on March 10, 1988, the committee adopted a rough draft of the complete plan by a vote of 11 to 0, with one abstention. That seems like strong support, but the one abstention, Rodney Reagan, represented the intractable irrigation farmers to the west, with their numerous allies in the Texas Legislature.

It is difficult to describe to someone who hasn't witnessed it the depth of the farmers' and ranchers' feelings. As one of them told the joint committee, "If you aren't going to fight for your water, then there ain't nothing worth fighting for."

So there we were, on our way to Uvalde on Memorial Day to see if there was a possibility of reaching a compromise to convince Rodney Reagan to support the plan. We had been to Uvalde

Henry Cisneros talks on the phone as he sits in the mayor's Lincoln, which we used for our trip to Uvalde to face the irrigation farmers in an effort to forge a regional water plan. (Morris Goen, Express-News)

once before to meet with a large gathering of ranchers and farmers. They made it clear that they were not going to allow anyone to restrict their "right of capture." They knew how other farming communities in other states had disappeared as urban users bought out their water rights. They were committed to preserving their way of life, and irrigation was essential to their community.

I was not sure our trip was worth the effort. We were talking compromise and the ranchers and farmers were talking principle. I did not believe they would compromise, but Henry felt we needed to make this last effort.

On the trip over, we talked about our offer. To demonstrate San Antonio's willingness to assume its share of responsibility, we would begin with a promise to persuade the City Council to support the long-delayed Applewhite Reservoir project.

Second, we would give up trying to limit how much water farmers would be allowed to pump for their crops if they would agree merely not to develop any additional irrigation farms.

We pulled into Uvalde and got out of the car, entering the side door of a modest building in the town's business district. Up a narrow flight of wooden stairs was Jack Ware's law office. It was the classic small town lawyer's office: glass-enclosed book cases, wooden floors and early American furnishings. Small town lawyers don't need the pretensions of big city law firms to impress their clients.

We laid on the table our plan for Jack Ware, Rodney Reagan and three other citizens to consider. They appeared receptive. They did not commit, but they said they would talk with their citizens to see if they could garner support for the compromise.

As we left, four Uvalde citizens were waiting outside for our meeting to end to talk to their representatives. It was clear these folks did not entirely trust their negotiators. We would find out later just how much distrust there was.

Within two weeks, it appeared that our trip and plan had paid off. In June, our committee adopted the new compromise plan with support from the west. The farmers could use whatever amount of water they needed for their crops, but restrictions would apply to irrigation of "new" acreage. All aquifer water users, including the city of San Antonio, would have five years to establish their "historic" water rights. During years of abundant rain, no restrictions would apply on pumping. Water rights transfers would be permitted under a system of registration and control administered by the Edwards District.

Rodney Reagan voted for the plan. He said he was afraid that if we didn't come up with a plan soon, lawsuits would begin to be filed — tying everything and everybody up in the courts for years. Reagan said he would try to convince his people to support the plan, too.

After the joint committee approved the plan, we moved ahead with City Council action to approve the Applewhite Reservoir — a key provision of the compromise with the western interests.

We scheduled a public hearing on Applewhite for July 16. More than 400 people attended what became a nasty hearing. Angry voices condemned the building of Applewhite. COPS and the Metro Alliance spoke out against the plan, as did the Sierra Club. More opposition was voiced than support.

Like the dispute concerning development over the aquifer, the argument over surface water was not new. In the 1950s, the Army Corps of Engineers and the Guadalupe-Blanco River Authority began planning Canyon Lake as a flood control and water supply project in Comal County, north of San Antonio. While the Texas Supreme Court established that the city had the right to buy water from Canyon Lake, San Antonio never exercised that option.

Back in May 1976, as a first-term councilman, Henry had participated in the debate over a City Water Board recommendation to purchase 50,000 acre feet of water from Canyon Lake. Henry argued with John Schaefer, then chairman of the water board, over when San Antonio's pumping from the aquifer might be restricted. Schaefer warned that once we pumped the aquifer down to the point that the springs in New Braunfels and San Marcos went dry, then there would be pressure for controls.

Council turned down the Canyon Lake contract on a 5-to-4 vote, with Henry in the majority. He would later acknowledge this as the worst vote he ever made in his tenure on the council.

So now we found ourselves in a flare-up about the Applewhite Reservoir, which had been a controversial project from the start. It was designed to produce an average yield of 48,000 acre feet, but much less in a severe drought. Moreover, it would have little scenic or recreational value.

Opposition to Applewhite came from several directions. Many felt there was no limit on the potential water supply in the aquifer, either legally or physically, and therefore we should rely solely on aquifer water forever. Some felt the Medina River would not be sufficient to keep the lake full. Some of them and others also thought the water would be polluted, either from upstream sources or from a few old capped oil wells under the lake bed. Some thought the $180 million price was too high. Environmental organizations, like the Sierra Club, simply do not like *any* surface water project. And many simply did not want San Antonio to grow.

The opponents chose to ignore all the engineering studies that said the project would provide a dependable source of water.

After the public hearing, we proceeded with a July 21 council vote on Applewhite. The chamber was jammed again with an overflow crowd. Tempers flared. After a prolonged debate, we voted 8 to 3 to approve the project. The Homeowner-Taxpayer Association and the Sierra Club immediately vowed to launch a petition drive for a referendum to overturn the council's action.

One week later, the 238-page regional water plan was set for a council vote. The plan included conservation, wastewater reuse, aquifer water allocation, and the development of surface lakes. Council approved the plan by a 9-to-1 vote.

Next to approve the plan was the Edwards board, by a vote of 9 to 6. Contrary to Rodney Reagan's assurances, all six of the western representatives voted against it. The board also voted to hire a lobbyist to work for the regional plan in the upcoming session of the Legislature, which would convene in January 1989.

As the council and the Edwards board took action on the water plan, a storm began to brew in the west. Maurice Rimkus from Uvalde and former State Representative John Poerner from Medina County began a petition drive calling for the two western counties to withdraw from the Edwards Underground Water District. Enough petitions were collected to force a vote on January 21, 1989.

Former Governor Dolph Briscoe led the campaign against the plan and for withdrawal from the Edwards. He was the biggest landowner and irrigator in Uvalde County. The vote to withdraw was overwhelming in both Uvalde and Medina counties. The farmers had risen in revolt against any attempt to regulate their withdrawal of water.

Rodney had compromised on a principle when he initially supported the plan and he now found out that his people did not like it. The result of this revolt was to maim the Edwards District, leaving only Hays, Comal and Bexar counties under the agency's regional umbrella. These three counties accounted for a minority of the aquifer's annual recharge.

We would fight in the 1989 legislative session for approval of the plan, but the rural interests defeated it. For now the plan and the Edwards Underground Water District had both been destroyed. Rodney Reagan was right about one thing. We would be in the courts for years to come.

By the end of Henry's term, the construction of the Applewhite reservoir had begun. The petition drive to force a referendum failed miserably, gathering less than half the required signatures by the deadline imposed by the city charter. The petition circulators would be back, however, and next time the result would be different.

★★★

Lessons from Water Wars — I

■ **You don't miss your water till your well runs dry.**
We failed to convince people that unrestricted pumping from the Edwards Aquifer would eventually damage the underground water supply and dry up the springs in Comal and Hays counties. People simply could not envision this happening. Hence the battle to regulate withdrawals from the aquifer would carry over into my term as mayor.

■ **Don't let the developers pave Paradise.**
Developers backed off their threat to file suit when they recognized that Mayor Cisneros had built public support for protecting the aquifer recharge zone.

■ **Some principles cannot be compromised.**
The farmers were unyielding in their belief that it is their right to pump water from underneath their own land. This "property right" principle held an almost sacred status in the western counties. We tried compromise but it did not work and may never work.

5

"The Dracula Bill" and The Dome

The airplane was packed from cockpit to galley with 150 of San Antonio's most influential citizens. We were flying a mission that could finally push San Antonio into the "big leagues," if one believed Mayor Henry Cisneros, who stood up front playing cheerleader. It was Saturday, May 30, 1987, just three weeks since my first council meeting.

Our destination was Colorado Springs, where we intended to demonstrate San Antonio's "can do" spirit in a bid for the 1991 Olympic Festival. As the nation's largest and most prestigious pre-Olympic event, the festival matches 4,000 athletes in 34 sports.

We arrived at the compound of the U.S. Olympic Committee and proceeded to a large auditorium to make our presentation. We put on a great show, complete with mariachis and a video of San Antonio, and all accompanied by Henry's persuasive eloquence. The site selection committee was impressed.

But the showmanship was really smoke and mirrors, intended to distract from some serious shortcomings. We lacked sites for a number of important events. We had no Olympic swimming pool, no ice skating rink and no facility for the opening ceremonies, which in previous festivals had attracted 65,000 people. As alternatives, we promised to build a skating rink, hold the swimming events in Austin, and hold the opening ceremonies in front of the Alamo.

On the flight home, we celebrated because we had reached for a difficult goal, entering the sweepstakes for one of the nation's premier athletic events. We realized our chances were slim, but we felt the committee needed to know we were serious. If not this time, perhaps next time we would be chosen. By then, we could correct our lack of facilities.

With perfect timing, Henry broke into our festivities over the plane's intercom. Frank Tejeda, at the time one of San Antonio's state senators and later a congressman until his death in early 1997, had radioed Henry on the plane with important news. Tejeda said the Senate had just passed the bill to provide a funding source for construction of a domed stadium in San Antonio. The solution to one of our major shortcomings was a step closer to reality. Cheers erupted.

At the first meeting of the new council, when Henry had laid out his plans for the Alamodome, as it was later named, most of us thought he was engaged in wishful thinking. Henry had pursued this goal for at least four years without success.

But the plan he presented to the new council was real, and astonishing in its novel simplicity. He proposed to build a "pay-as-you-go" stadium, using a temporary half-cent increase in the sales tax throughout the VIA Metropolitan Transit Authority — essentially all of Bexar County.

VIA had the authority to levy a one-cent tax for its operations, but the rate had always been held at half a cent. A rough calculation showed that if the tax were increased for five years, the additional half-cent would raise between $160 and $170 million — enough to build the stadium without any long-term debt.

Henry got the idea from Robert Marbut Jr., who headed the "Committee for Progress," Henry's political fund-raising committee. Robert is the son of Bob Marbut, who was the coordinating chairman of the Target '90 Commission. Robert is an intense young man and, like Henry, a crafty political animal who would also learn his lessons well as a White House Fellow. He would eventually be elected to City Council from my own District 8 in 1995.

There was, of course, one "minor" problem to overcome — the Texas Legislature. It would have to amend the statute that created VIA to allow the agency's tax revenues to be used for a purpose other than operating a municipal bus system. Only after the Legislature approved could the city call a referendum on imposing the tax for a stadium. By the time Henry revealed the plan to council in early May, only a month was left in the legislative session. He would have to work quickly.

First, Henry persuaded the leadership of VIA to climb aboard with an offer the agency couldn't refuse. Pressure had been building in the city to strip VIA of its unused taxing authority and dedicate the half-cent tax to street maintenance. Giving up the tax temporarily would ensure that it would still be available five years later, when the agency might really need it.

Then he turned to the legislative delegation. State Senators Cyndi Krier and Frank Tejeda signed on right away. But there was trouble in the House. The delegation was split and wanted to know if Henry had the support of a majority of his council.

On May 26, Henry briefed the council again and circulated a memorandum of support for the legislation. A bare majority signed: Henry, and council members Yolanda Vera, Joe Webb, Frank Wing, Bob Thompson and me. Vera drove to Austin to personally deliver the letter to the delegation.

The clock was ticking; only five days left in the legislative session.

With two days left, the Senate was first to act. It approved the bill as we were flying home from Colorado. Upon arrival, we received word that Los Angeles had been selected as the site of the Olympic Festival. This setback added emphasis to Henry's drive to pass the legislation.

Although the bill had passed the Senate, it seemed dead in the House. Parliamentary rules prohibited the House at this late hour from voting on any bill that had not already passed on a preliminary vote. The VIA tax bill fell into this category.

But Henry would not be denied. In a brilliant maneuver, the language of the VIA bill was inserted into an unrelated House measure concerning the Corpus Christi transit authority. The Corpus bill had passed the House on a first reading, but was no longer needed since its Senate companion had already been enacted into law. The House bill thus became a perfect vehicle for this sleight-of-hand substitution. The "Dracula bill" — so dubbed by the media because it refused to die — passed on the last night of the session at 11:35 p.m., just 25 minutes before the final gavel. It was an amazing feat.

The Chamber, COPS, and The Dome

Henry lost little time setting up a stadium committee to hammer out the specifics of the referendum, which would now have to be approved by the voters. I served on the committee along with Councilman Bob Thompson, and members of a host of other governmental entities.

One of our major tasks was to pick a site for the stadium, which the media had quickly nicknamed "the Dome." By early August we had narrowed the choices to three: the Alamo Iron Works site, the Coliseum grounds on the East Side, and a site by Mitchell Lake on the South Side.

It was well known that Henry wanted the Alamodome to be located close to the convention center. At the Alamo Iron Works site, he saw an opportunity for convention-related events in the stadium, as well as sporting and entertainment events. The Henry B. Gonzalez Convention Center had given birth to the industry that had grown to become San Antonio's second largest. Still, there was untapped potential in the tourism and convention trade. Although San Antonio ranked ninth in the nation in the number of registered conventions, it could not compete for the larger ones. Even after two expansions in the 1970s and 1980s, the convention center was still woefully short on exhibit space for lucrative trade shows.

The site Henry favored was a tract of about 55 acres, sandwiched between a freeway and a railroad track, and located just east of the convention center. This aging industrial area became known as the Alamo Iron Works site because that was the name of its major occupant, a large supplier of industrial equipment founded in San Antonio a century ago.

On Monday, August 23, our task force presented its recommendations to a joint meeting of City Council and the VIA board. We proposed a 65,000-seat multi-use facility, to be operated by VIA. We recommended the Alamo Iron Works site, adding a walkway over Interstate 37 to connect the Dome to the convention center. The rationale that a site close to the convention center would increase the facility's number of "event days" was undeniable.

Another good reason to locate the Dome at the Alamo Iron Works site was to alleviate the psychological barrier formed by the interstate highway between downtown and the East Side.

Our plan included a VIA transit station at the Southern Pacific Sunset Depot, located between the Dome site and the St. Paul Square urban renewal area. We projected a total cost of $158.8 million, including land acquisition. Because there would be no debt to amortize, we projected the facility would break even by the third year.

Our report was followed by a September 2 public hearing. Five hundred supporters of the Dome jammed the meeting, a display of support orchestrated by Robert Marbut Jr. Nevertheless, I knew from the phone calls I was getting that there was great skepticism concerning the Dome. While the opposition was unorganized at this point, the rumblings couldn't be ignored.

Although most of the grousing came from anti-tax, anti-growth groups, some of it emanated from an unexpected source. Initially, the business community had been badly split on the merits of Henry's proposal. Many business leaders agreed with community dissenters who argued that a domed stadium should be a low priority in a poor city with so many other needs. Revenues from any tax increases, they believed, should go to education, infrastructure or other basic purposes.

So the Greater Chamber set up its own task force to study the issue independently. It was carefully balanced between avowed supporters of the Dome, avowed opponents, and those who were neutral. Jim Reed was chairman, while much of the research was coordinated by Dan Bump, the telephone company executive and neighborhood activist who was among my earliest supporters. Former Mayor Lila Cockrell was also on the task force, listed as a "neutral."

The group did an extensive analysis, collecting budgets and economic impact studies from every domed stadium in North America. It concluded that our projections were reasonable.

Three weeks after the public hearing, the Greater Chamber came out in support of building the Dome. Members adopted a unanimous but conditional report. The Dome must be built close to the convention center, and should be managed and marketed jointly with the center.

The support of the chamber added a critical element to Henry's emerging coalition. His original goal was to build a major sports stadium, not necessarily one with a roof. The effort was targeted to enlist the support of an organization called San Antonians for a Major Sports Complex, which wanted a stadium to entice major-league professional sports to the city.

But conventions and trade shows would require a domed stadium. The way had been cleared for this refinement in 1985, when Henry asked Ralph Bender, a flamboyant local architect with an uncanny resemblance to Mark Twain, to chair a committee to develop San Antonio's potential in *amateur* sports. Bender was a leader of the U.S. Pentathlon Association. Pentathlon is an Olympic sport of five events, and at the time, its American team members trained at Fort Sam Houston, an Army base in San Antonio. Bender's committee evolved into the San Antonio Amateur Sports Foundation, which put together San Antonio's bid for the 1991 Olympic Festival. The Sports Foundation became convinced that San Antonio needed a *domed* stadium, so the facility could be truly multi-purpose. The other pro-sports group had little choice but to go along.

With a domed stadium now in play, the chamber broadened Henry's coalition by pointing out that the Dome could be adapted to convention assemblies and trade shows. The chamber leadership knew San Antonio was in no position to win either a National Football League franchise or a Major League Baseball team. The city had neither the income level nor the television market to support one. But a multi-purpose stadium could add a new dimension to a booming industry that was constrained more by the city's present lack of facilities than by its economic weakness.

Henry knew that "economic development" could sell many uncommitted voters on the Dome, while a single-purpose sports stadium would not. But if the manpower and enthusiasm of the pro-sports supporters could be merged with the campaign money and organizational strength of the Greater Chamber ... I was watching a master politician in action.

To make the coalition truly unbeatable, Henry needed a missing element: support from a grassroots community organization with no direct interest in the issue. This support eluded him.

On a Sunday afternoon in late October, Henry and I joined several other council members in attending the annual meeting of COPS. A favorite feature of these COPS meetings with politicians is an "accountability" session. The candidate or public official is asked to respond with an unqualified yes or no answer to a series of questions that reflects the organization's position on its key issues. COPS had zero influence in my district. But I went knowing I would need to better understand this organization if I was going to run for mayor some day.

The meeting was held at a church hall on the near South Side. COPS leaders and public officials were jammed together on a small stage. Five hundred members sat in the audience, holding signs that identified their respective parishes.

Contrary to its carefully nurtured image, COPS is not an organization in which decisions flow from the bottom up. Its leaders are responsible for researching and developing issues, and they in turn communicate these issues to the group. In this meeting, COPS was in the process of reorganizing, with a single nominal leader giving way to five co-chairs. This would broaden the leadership and, it was hoped, revitalize the organization's lagging political clout.

The question that hung in the air was whether COPS would support or oppose the Dome.

The meeting proceeded quietly, with questions about the upcoming street and drainage bond issue and the city's commitment to better housing. Then Father Rosendo Urrabazo, one of the five new co-chairs, rose to speak.

Urrabazo was young but tough, a street-smart priest who had come to San Antonio from Los Angeles a few years earlier. He delivered an impassioned speech, saying that San Antonio was in the third world of nations with respect to housing, education and public safety. He charged that the only benefit from the Dome would be a few part-time jobs selling peanuts, for wages that amounted to peanuts.

"It turns my stomach when I hear that the stadium will make us a big-league city," Urrabazo said. "We will not settle for stadium peanuts!" Swept up in the emotion of the moment, the delegates resoundingly shouted down the Dome.

I watched Henry while Urrabazo spoke. His face revealed no emotion. I wondered if he had known in advance that COPS was going to oppose the stadium.

After the meeting, we talked. Henry was visibly upset and said COPS leaders had assured him they would pass over the issue. He said he was "betrayed."

Henry was so upset he could not contain his feelings. He told reporters after the meeting that COPS would no longer receive any "preferential treatment" from him. The regularly scheduled conferences that they enjoyed in his office would be terminated immediately.

This turned a relatively minor setback into front-page headlines. Henry embarrassed himself badly. His threat to cut off COPS was also an unintended admission that he had been giving the group "preferential treatment" in the first place.

But that embarrassment soon became the least of his worries. With COPS and the Greater Chamber directly at odds, the fight for the Dome was now guaranteed to become a battle royal.

The Dome Campaign

Early in February 1988, I asked my friend Jeff Wentworth, a former county commissioner and then a candidate for state representative, to include a single question for me in one of his campaign polls: How do people feel about increasing the sales tax to pay for the Dome?

The legislative district where Jeff was campaigning roughly overlaid my own council district. A few days later I received the results. Three out of four people said they would vote *against* the

Dome tax. Within the hour I shared the results with Henry. He said his own polls also showed support for the Dome eroding. COPS, HTA and a host of other organizations and people were organizing opposition. Their work was showing up in the polls.

Henry had planned to submit the Dome referendum to voters in May. I suggested he appoint a citizens' task force to study every aspect of the Dome proposal, and delay the election.

"Give me 30 days," he responded. "I'll find a solution."

It didn't take that long. On February 18, at a joint meeting of the VIA board and the City Council, Henry announced that he was shelving the sales tax idea. He said he would work to put together a public-private joint venture in its place. If for some reason that plan would not work, he would return to the sales tax idea, and submit the original proposal to voters in January 1989.

Investors weren't going to throw down $150 million for a domed stadium just to house conventions. The Dome needed a big draw. It needed an NFL team.

Over the next several months, Henry pursued the joint venture with all of his persuasive talents. He attended the NFL owners meeting in Phoenix on March 13, visiting individually with half the 28 owners.

Tex Schramm, the Dallas Cowboys' president and general manager, was impressed, as were several other owners. Schramm added to Henry's stature by telling the owners they might be talking to a future president. The incident gave San Antonio national attention, as the media surrounded Henry and asked about his city.

It was a good show, but the hard facts remained: San Antonio was the 47th largest television market with a per capita income below other NFL cities. The owners were cordial, and they mouthed words that made them appear receptive to Henry's pleas, but nothing came of the effort. I would find out for myself a few years later just how duplicitous the NFL owners can be. Meanwhile, the dream of an NFL team — someday, somehow — was kept alive by well-placed whispers just loud enough to help sell the Dome to sports fans.

On July 15, the financing choices were reduced to one when the public-private venture fizzled. Nevertheless, the effort was

Harriet Marmon, Tom Brereton and future Mayor Bill Thornton debate the pros and cons of building the Alamodome in January 1989. (Dennis Dunleavy, Express-News)

worth it. Henry could argue that he had tried his best and that the only way to build the Dome now was through the proposed sales tax increase.

The signatures needed to call the referendum had been ready and waiting since February. Robert Marbut Jr. had led 2,000 volunteers in collecting 76,000 signatures — more than enough.

In early September, the council reviewed a working agreement between the city and VIA to finance and operate the Dome. The election was called for January 21, 1989.

Not just the Dome was at stake. The vote would also be another referendum on the policies of Henry Cisneros. Opposition was strong, fueled by an unusual alliance: the conservative Homeowner-Taxpayer Association, and the inner- city's Communities Organized for Public Service.

The "Holy War"

Henry entered the campaign publicly wounded. His personal problems were exposed. (We will talk about those in the next chapter.) On top of that, he was a lame duck. Many of the Dome's backers questioned whether he had the political power to successfully lead the campaign.

Perhaps no one else in those circumstances could have. But Henry was, after all, Henry. And his personal problems had not dented his popularity as mayor. This became clear when a poll by George Shipley showed that Henry could have won re-election easily against any opponent, including Lila Cockrell or me.

The Dome campaign kicked off with a giant rally at Villita Assembly Hall. I spotted Henry and former Governor John Connally as they walked out of City Hall to attend the rally. When I was first elected to the Legislature in 1970, Connally had just completed his term as governor. He was one of Texas' best, and also a great friend to San Antonio. Henry invited me to accompany them.

Connally's support on this issue was a mixed blessing. His real estate empire had collapsed with the savings and loan industry, forcing him into an embarrassing personal bankruptcy. Opponents of the Dome mocked the notion of Connally supporting a project on economic development grounds. This was only the first of many cheap shots fired in the campaign.

Henry named five people to lead the campaign for the Dome: the Reverend Claude Black, a community activist; Valero CEO Bill Greehey; Mexican-food magnate Raul Jimenez; civic leader Edith McAllister; and developer Cliff Morton. Mary Rose Brown, with the Atkins Agency, devised a terrific public relations campaign. Chairman Bill Thornton led the Greater Chamber into action. Teams of volunteers armed with comprehensive "factbooks" and elaborate slide shows took the message to more than 30,000 people. I publicly endorsed the Dome and worked for its passage in my district.

The petition signers provided a pool of ready workers, most of them sports enthusiasts and especially football fans dreaming of a future NFL team for the Dome. Others were baseball fans, who apparently failed to notice that baseball was *not* considered for the Dome. Major League Baseball preferred open-air stadiums. The league would consider a domed stadium only if it had a retractable roof, which would have added major costs to the

Alamodome. Adding baseball would also make it difficult to book other events because teams play 82 home games. Consequently, baseball had been ruled out long before the campaign began.

The Dome debate — conducted over the television airwaves, on radio talk shows, in the newspapers, and at community meetings — was fundamentally about the city's priorities. Proponents argued that the Dome would generate economic growth to help fund education, social services and basic community infrastructure.

The opponents attacked what they considered to be a vulnerable link in our campaign: A city staff report predicting that the Dome would be profitable within three years. In one televised debate, former city councilman and HTA spokesman Van Henry Archer said his opponent, oral surgeon Bill Thornton, "knows more about pulling teeth than he does economics." San Antonio *Light* columnist Rick Casey denounced an HTA accounting expert as a "crackpot."

By contrast, the Reverend Rosendo Urrabazo, a COPS spokesman, seemed almost a model of self-restraint by denouncing the Dome only as "an empty, elegant monument in the midst of ruined and wasted lives."

At one point in the campaign, Henry called the developing battle a "holy war" for San Antonio's future. He soon regretted the comment, which gave local editorial cartoonists a month's worth of free material.

At a breakfast rally January 5, only 16 days before the election, we unveiled an economic impact study commissioned by the Greater Chamber and authored by Dr. M. Ray Perryman, a Baylor University economist. The report predicted that the Dome would create 858 permanent jobs, with another 5,050 jobs produced by the accompanying expansion of tourist-related industries. These permanent jobs would produce an economic impact worth $245 million a year.

The opponents produced their own experts who said the economic impact was exaggerated. But their arguments were buried beneath the daily onslaught of news and advertising orchestrated by the well-financed effort of the pro-Dome faction.

An exuberant Mayor Cisneros, flanked by San Antonio Spurs owner B.J. "Red" McCombs, talks about the future of the Alamodome after voters approved a tax to build the facility on January 21, 1989. (Rick McFarland, Express-News)

To close out the campaign, an eight-page tabloid entitled the "Dome Examiner" was mailed to 150,000 people targeted as likely voters. Television ads featured endorsements from an array of prominent, sometimes unexpected, supporters.

January 21 was election day. I spent a good part of that Saturday at the Greater Chamber's office — campaign headquarters. Fresh polling data indicated the election would be close. Express-News columnist Paul Thompson came by to quiz some supporters. As he left, he told me, "Henry's won the fight."

That night we crowded into a ballroom at the Riverwalk Holiday Inn. As the returns rolled in it became clear we were going to win. The final result was 93,091, or 53 percent, in favor; and 82,612, or 47 percent, opposed.

Henry entered the room to thunderous applause. He was high, real high, on an emotional peak higher than the one reached after the 1985 election. He could not thank everyone enough: Thanks for sticking with me despite my personal problems, for supporting me even though I'm a lame duck, for working hard to overcome strong odds, for helping me carry the day.

He was so exuberant, in fact, he said he might reconsider his decision to forego another run for the mayor's office. There was still time to file for the May election. As had happened before, Henry allowed his enthusiasm to get ahead of his judgment.

"The Bones of Broken Friendships"

The following Monday, I walked into Henry's office knowing his bubble had burst. That morning, in big headlines on the front page of the San Antonio Light, some of his closest business contributors said they would stick with Lila Cockrell even if Henry decided to run.

What really hit him hard in the article were some gratuitous shots from his friends about Henry's personal problems. It was a clear message to stay out of the mayor's race.

When I entered his office, Henry was holding the newspaper. He looked up.

"I can't believe they would do this to me."

"Henry, we both know that political supporters are not always loyal. Don't let something like this bother you. If you want to run, you don't need their money."

"But these are my friends!" he proclaimed. It seemed an odd comment from the man who had once said, "The landscape of politics is littered with the bones of broken friendships." Adding to his injury later in the day, Councilwoman Helen Dutmer, an Alamodome opponent, said, "I told you they would do this to you ... use you and then throw you away."

Henry told me he hadn't really been all that serious about running. The Dome victory had recharged his political juices and he got carried away on election night. He had planned to meet with Lila Cockrell the following Wednesday, and if she objected, he would stay out of the race. But the meeting never came about.

Henry believed Lila was behind the news story, and her name was added to the list of people who should pay for turning against him.

Publicly, Henry announced he would stick to his decision not to run. But he would exact a price from the business leaders who had dishonored him in print.

His opportunity came over the makeup of the Dome Advisory Committee. On the night of the Dome victory, Henry and the business leaders had agreed on a number of names to serve as committee members. None would survive.

When the chamber formally submitted a slate of 11 individuals, Henry went on the attack. He accused the business community of attempting to "roll over" the groups defeated in the referendum. Discarding the chamber's list, he convinced the council to appoint others to the Dome Advisory Committee.

Henry's power in matters involving the Dome grew after the council, determined that an ambivalent Henry must serve on the Dome Advisory Committee, appointed him when he was away from the city on business. He was later named committee chairman.

Keeping faith with his project, Henry continued to serve as chairman of the Dome Advisory Committee after he left the mayor's office. Getting the Dome built would ultimately prove as difficult as the campaign for voter approval had been. But that's another story.

★★★

Lessons from the Dome Campaign

■ **Build political networks that reach beyond your office.**
Henry had relationships with the speaker of the Texas House, the lieutenant governor and key state legislative leaders. That enabled him to succeed in pushing them to pass the Dome legislation.

■ **If at first you don't succeed, keep trying.**
Our first attempt to attract the Olympic Festival failed, but two years later, we won the prize.

■ **There are no permanent enemies or friends in politics.**
Political friends must not be mistaken for true friends. Two of Henry's organizational allies blindsided him during this period — COPS, by opposing the Dome, and the business community, by threatening to support Lila Cockrell if Henry ran for another term. Politicians cannot take for granted support from other politicians or from political organizations.

Once in Saltillo, Mexico, I asked a businessman during lunch who he thought would be the next president of Mexico. He replied, "I do not know, but I know that he will be my best friend." When you are in power, everyone is your friend. When you are out of power, you discover who your real friends are.

■ **Identify your political resources and use them all.**
The Dome campaign, which started out so far behind in the opinion polls, needed all the help it could get. That aid came from the Greater San Antonio Chamber of Commerce in the form of money, power and volunteers. The campaign recruited its core supporters from the 70,000 petition signers.

■ **In politics, timing is everything.**
Henry delayed the submission of the Dome vote, first from January 1988 to May 1988, and then to January 1989. Had he called the vote on either of the earlier dates he probably would have lost. He needed time to build the case for the Dome.

6

Private Lives; Public Repercussions

On June 12, 1987, as I made my way to the maternity ward at Southwest Texas Methodist Hospital, I was flooded with memories of the births of my three sons, Kevin, Scott and Matthew. All were born at Methodist; three happy occasions as each came screaming into the world to join their sister, Lynnie, in our family. As I reached the door to the maternity ward, the memories faded and the sad reality of why I was there began to hit me.

The stars seemed perfectly aligned for Henry Cisneros as we began the 1987-89 term of council. Henry quickly learned that I had not run to cause him trouble, but rather to work hard for my district and prepare myself for an eventual race for mayor. The council was off to a good start; we were working well together. Henry also seemed happy in his personal life. He and Mary Alice eagerly awaited the birth of their first son.

On June 9, Henry was in the delivery room with his daughters, Mercedes and Teresa, when Mary Alice gave birth through a Cesarean to their son, John Paul Anthony Cisneros. He was named

John Paul in honor of the pope, who had said Mass in San Antonio less than a year before. The name Anthony honored the city that Henry loves so much.

Born prematurely, John Paul weighed 5 pounds, 14 ounces and was 20 inches long. Henry had said, "What a wonderful thing to see the baby born. I'm very proud. The baby is early, but healthy."

But it did not take long for happiness to turn to fear. Within an hour of John Paul's birth, problems became evident. The baby turned blue and a heart murmur was detected. John Paul was in very serious condition.

As I passed the glass windows of the newborn nursery, I kept thinking, "What should I say to Henry?" How do you respond to the great blessing of a newborn son tempered by the fear of life-threatening complications? I turned down the hallway and saw Henry standing alone several doors down.

As I walked up he smiled, embraced me and said, "I'm glad you came by. It means a lot to me." Together we walked into Mary Alice's private room.

The curtains were drawn, and several colorful bouquets were displayed on the window ledge. We stood quietly in the dimly lit room as a priest, standing by the end of Mary Alice's bed, prayed for her, John Paul Anthony, and the family. Mary Alice was lying in the bed with her eyes closed.

The priest looked up at the conclusion of his prayer and Mary Alice opened her eyes. Henry said, "Honey, Nelson is here." Her face was drawn and pale as she turned toward me, and there was sorrow in her brown eyes and blank stare. I touched her hand, smiled, and said nothing. Henry said, "I'll be back in a little while. I want to show Nelson our son."

We walked down the hall to the infant nursery and stood in front of the viewing window. Inside, a nurse spotted Henry and carried John Paul Anthony to the window.

I don't know what Henry was feeling before I arrived, but as we stood before his son, he was in control, intellectually and emotionally. He outlined a path for John Paul's recovery, and explained in detail how it would be accomplished.

He explained that his son was born with a heart that consisted of two chambers instead of four, and three valves rather than four. The baby's circulation was affected, with less oxygen than is needed feeding the tissues. He said as his son grew older, the additional pumping requirements on the heart might cause congestive heart failure. Henry continued, mentioning other problems with John Paul's liver, stomach and spleen. He said he was going to contact the best doctors in the country to help his son. A series of operations would begin probably in about a year.

He smiled at the baby as he told me his plans. Never once did he express any doubt about the ability of the medical profession to cure his baby boy.

I thought of my son Matthew as Henry talked. When Matthew was two years old, he had aspirated peanuts into a lung. High fever came and went for a month as he fought a serious case of pneumonia. He underwent three operations. My friend, Dr. Fred Grover, spent five hours on the third operation and succeeded in removing the peanut fragments from the lung. During that month, I spent almost all my time at the hospital. I couldn't think clearly and was pessimistic about Matthew's chance of recovery. But here was Henry, optimistic and ready with a plan for his son. I must tell you, I really admired his determination.

I left the hospital feeling much better than when I arrived. Henry convinced me that his son was going to be OK. He had fixed so many problems before, and he was going to fix this one, too.

As the days and weeks passed, I visited with friends in the medical community. John Paul had a rare and complex form of congenital heart disease. The doctors also discovered that he had no spleen. Without one, he was susceptible to a constant threat of infection.

Today, as this book goes to publication, John Paul Anthony is alive and well. He overcame the odds with a determined father and an extraordinarily strong mother who was by his side every step of the way. I believe Mary Alice's prayers and love saved John Paul.

The day after John Paul's birth, the baby's pediatric cardiologist, Dr. James Rogers, told a news conference, "I think the public

Henry Cisneros shares a playful moment with his wife, Mary Alice, his son, John Paul Anthony, and some family cats in July 1991. (Doug Sehres, Express-News)

should know that this will drastically affect the mayor's life and his activities." Dr. Rogers proved prophetic.

During the next two years Henry would wrestle with the decision of whether to undertake a statewide race, run for re-election or enter private life. John Paul would weigh heavily in his decision. As Henry reviewed his options, my political future twisted and turned with the ups and downs of Henry's emotions and indecisiveness.

A Conversation on a Bus

The tremendous challenges Henry and his family faced because of John Paul did not slow the pace of his mayoral responsibilities. In August, two months after John Paul's birth, I joined Henry on a chartered bus to look at potential sites for the Dome.

As I sat down on the bus, Henry slipped into the seat beside me. As we pulled away from the convention center, Henry spoke about the importance of the recently completed second expansion of the convention center. He pointed out the link between the convention center and, nearby, the Rivercenter Mall and 1,000-room Marriott Rivercenter Hotel. He spoke about the improvements to HemisFair Plaza that were nearing completion. He left unsaid the need for the Dome to be connected to this activity, but it was clear what he was driving at.

As we drove through downtown he talked about the turmoil that would erupt as soon as the contract was let for the $40 million TriParty street and walkway improvement project. He predicted everyone would fight and complain during construction, and then praise the project after completion.

As we headed south toward Mitchell Lake, he pulled a piece of paper out of his billfold. Written on it was a short list of the major projects he was working on. This was not "the big list" he kept on a yellow pad and updated every week. It was a list of strategic projects that stretched beyond weekly consideration.

He laid the list on his knee and said, "I'd like to go over a few items with you that I want to complete during this term, since it will probably be my last."

It seemed as the summer months passed that Henry had reconciled the time he would need to devote to John Paul's illness and the time necessary for a statewide campaign. He had traveled around the state and all signs were favorable. Roy Spence, Walter Mondale's media adviser and a consultant to numerous successful statewide candidates, held a fund-raiser for Henry in Austin that netted $30,000. Popular and powerful Lieutenant Governor Bill Hobby announced in July that he would not run for re-election or for governor.

Henry was now ready to talk about the future of San Antonio without him as mayor. He ticked off items on his list: a plan to protect the aquifer, a regional water plan with Applewhite revived, another street and drainage bond issue, and redeveloping the last nine acres of HemisFair Plaza, which would be renamed HemisFair Park.

"And, I'm determined to get the Dome issue submitted to the voters and approved before I leave office." I told him I supported all those projects.

Then he caught me totally by surprise.

"What do you think the next mayor should be planning to do?" he asked.

Here we were, only three months into his term. I hadn't given a thought to what I would do if I were to be elected some two years in the future. It struck me as curious how "the next mayor" seemed such an abstract concept to him.

I said something about consolidating the gains he had made, about the need for more efficient government, and the need for a new planning process such as Target '90.

He mused, "I doubt that he will be able to have any new initiatives in his first term. But after the first term, he will need to create a new set of initiatives for the next century. I hope the next mayor will share my vision. But if not, then he must make it clear where he wants the city to go."

We went on to talk about important issues the next mayor would face: annexation, open spaces, housing.

As we neared the South Side location, Henry rose and began to address the group about the proposed site. I remained in my seat to reflect on our conversation.

My first thought was that I had better get my act together! I was excited about the discussion, and felt as though Henry was trying to be helpful by forcing me to think ahead. It sounded good to me: Henry was going to be governor and I would become mayor!

But I had read the signs wrong *again*. On August 17, two weeks after the bus ride, Henry stunned everyone by releasing this statement: "Today, I wish to state that I will not be a candidate for the office of governor, senator, or any other statewide position in 1990."

I was reminded of Dr. Rogers' prophetic remark when Henry's statement continued. "The family stresses associated with John Paul's care require attention that is not compatible with gearing up for a major statewide effort." He also offered a second reason.

By giving up a statewide race, he said, "It will allow me to tackle some very challenging public issues in San Antonio — a stadium referendum, and a bond election — without opponents damaging those efforts for reasons of wanting to cripple a campaign for higher office."

The decision Henry now faced was this: run for re-election as mayor or enter private life. His decision was critical to my own. While it made great political theater, I was tied to the end of a yo-yo. I didn't like it, but there wasn't much I could do about it, either.

There was one other titillating factor in this conundrum about Henry's political fate. Before he announced he would not run for statewide office, the rumor mill had been churning about a purported "problem" in Henry's private life. Texas Attorney General Jim Mattox, who had his own plans to run for governor, reportedly had threatened to "go public" unless Henry withdrew. Months would pass before the public learned the nature of Henry's dilemma.

Dual Withdrawals, "Cold Turkey"

Summer turned to fall, and the day after Thanksgiving, I walked up to City Hall and punched in the number combination that would open the locked door to the mayor's office suite. Henry didn't like being locked in. For years, the mayor's door had been open, allowing reporters, politicians and city staff to walk in and out of the suite at will. But death threats against Henry and the general increase in societal violence had ended such casual hospitality.

Henry liked to come to City Hall on days like this, when no one else was around. It is the only time to find peace and tranquillity in the place. It's also a great time, in the darkened halls of the building, to commune with the political ghosts of San Antonio's past — Mayors Brian Callaghan, Maury Maverick, Walter McAllister — and ponder your next move.

Henry had asked me to come by. I knew he wanted to talk politics. Since announcing in August that he would not run for statewide office, he was feeling uneasy that I aspired to his seat.

"What do you have to say?" he asked abruptly.

I knew exactly what he meant. "I hope you decide to run again. I'm in no hurry to move up."

Henry relaxed and leaned back in his chair. He said, "Since I've withdrawn from a statewide race, people seem to think I've made up my mind not to run for re-election. I feel like I'm losing control. I don't like that." He said he needed to reassert his authority if he was to have any chance of completing his agenda before leaving office — *if* he did leave at the end of this term. He would decide whether to seek re-election by next summer, and visit with me again before then.

I said that was fine with me.

I knew the withdrawal pains were really starting to hit him. With no statewide race to look forward to, leaving public office "cold turkey" would be hard.

I saw Henry again later that evening. A large crowd gathered in front of the Alamo for the traditional lighting of the city's Christmas tree. Henry gave me a warm "abrazo" — an embrace — as I stepped onto the ceremonial platform. He was jubilant and hugging everybody, his face beaming like a child's as he pulled the switch to light the tree. Then, he led everyone in singing Christmas carols.

As I watched him that night, I realized how much Henry loved his job. With all the traumas in his personal life, the job of mayor provided his security and purpose. I thought that night that he would never leave office, and perhaps that would be best for everyone concerned.

A joyous holiday season spun us into 1988, a year that would bring major life changes to us both. Our political lives were affected by changes in our personal lives. And with city elections coming the following year, each of us had to determine the best way to manage our conflicts.

In February 1988, I told Henry before a council meeting that my marriage was breaking up and that I had been living alone in an apartment. Over the years Melinda and I had simply grown apart in our marriage. I told Henry that Express-News columnist Paul Thompson would break the story in the next day's paper. He asked me to stop by the office after the council meeting was over.

That evening, we talked about our personal lives until way past midnight. The anguish in Henry's face and the contriteness of his voice conveyed the conflict of the strong emotions coursing through him. There was another woman in his life, Linda Medlar.

It seemed as though the whole town was obsessed with "the Medlar affair" in 1988. Everyone at City Hall and in the media knew about it already, but Paul Thompson revealed it to the rest of the world in a front-page Express-News story, complete with a headline quoting Henry professing his "deep love" for Medlar, a local political consultant. The affair became the stuff of soap operas, as Henry's spouse, Mary Alice, filed for divorce but then reconciled with the mayor.

The story continues to play out as this book goes to press. Henry has left his Cabinet post as housing secretary in President Clinton's first term to become president and COO of Univision, a Spanish-language broadcast network.

Meanwhile, an independent counsel is studying Henry's payments to Linda for support after they split, and the issue of whether Henry lied about the amount of those payments in an FBI background check.

These reverberations were still years ahead at this point. In the meantime, it was clear to those who read between the lines that Henry's affair with Linda Medlar was the *real* reason for his withdrawal from the statewide race a year earlier. Now, it would become a major factor in Henry's decision concerning whether to seek re-election as mayor. Giving himself plenty of time, he announced in the spring that he would decide by September 15, 1988.

On September 12, Henry announced he would not run for re-election. This was what I was waiting for. The next day, I announced my intention to run for mayor. I actually prepared in advance two versions of an announcement speech. One version would have announced my candidacy for re-election as District 8 councilman, and endorsed Henry for re-election as mayor. It was in the trash can.

I filed my campaign statement with City Clerk Norma Rodriguez and named a campaign treasurer, Ernesto Ancira, as required by law. We began organizing and sent out letters asking for financial contributions.

Despite the excitement, like Henry I struggled with conflicting emotions. I wanted to be mayor; I had prepared myself. Yet I knew that my success might prevent me from solving the difficulties in my personal life. My divorce had been granted. And now there was a wonderful woman in my life, and we had decisions to make about our future. I had watched Henry put his political life first, and had seen the price he paid in his personal life. As we said in my boyhood neighborhood, the pay-out was "above the South Side price limit."

In early November, Henry and I had breakfast at the Holiday Inn on Loop 410. In our earlier meetings, he had been the penitent and I the priest. Now, I was pouring out my problems to him. I told him my divorce was complete and I intended to marry Tracy Hoag the following summer.

After listening to my anguish, Henry gave me what I believe to be the best advice of my life. He said, "Don't wait to get married. Get out of the race and get your personal life in order. If you don't, the press will be following every move you make and speculating about your personal relationships. If you love her, get married right away. There will be another time for you to run for mayor. The price of office is not worth an unhappy personal life."

At a crowded, tense news conference on November 9, I withdrew from the mayor's race and re-filed for the District 8 council seat. I cited the problems in my private life as the reason for withdrawing.

"You have to have the right spirit and everything needs to be right for you," I told reporters. "I recognize the time is not right for me to run for mayor." I apologized for not seeing these problems clearly when I had announced two months earlier. I went on to encourage Henry to run again for re-election. Questions about my personal life poured from the reporters, but I refused to answer any of them. They continued to shout questions at me as I left the room.

I was emotionally drained after that news conference. I knew that by withdrawing I had probably written my own political obituary. I had disappointed my supporters, who had put their names on the line for me and helped bankroll my campaign.

I didn't have to worry about writing a political obituary. The media did it for me. They said the real reason I withdrew was because former Mayor Lila Cockrell had decided to enter the race. She had released a poll showing she was favored over me by a margin of 50 to 37 percent. The media also cited my difficulties working with some members of the council. Councilman Jimmy Hasslocher was quoted saying, "Nelson has not paid his dues. He is certainly not a team player by any means."

Looking back today, I see that Jimmy was pretty close to being right. I did not get along with some members of the council. And he was right about the implication that serving on council for less than two years was not a great deal of experience.

I might add there was one dissenting voice in the media who viewed things similarly to Hasslocher but in a more positive light. San Antonio Light columnist Rick Casey said that two more years on the council would give me the time to reach out to the southern sector of the city. He said, "Another term on the council could enable him to run a better campaign — and to be a better mayor." That was great foresight.

But no one else in the media was buying into Casey's analysis. Ironically, the fact that my divorce had been a one-day story contributed to the perception that the real reason for my withdrawal must have been Lila's poll. It was the only available alternative for public speculation.

Again, as in 1985 when I accepted the chairmanship of Target '90 instead of running against Ed Harrington for council, I had to eat crow. Only this time it was much worse. In 1985, I had not already launched an actual campaign.

After withdrawing, I went about getting my personal life in order. Right after I talked with Henry I called Tracy and said, "Let's not wait. Let's get married January 1, and start the new year right."

After asking, "Have you lost your mind?" she agreed, and on January 1, 1989, Tracy Hoag and I were married. As of this writing we have been married for eight years. She has made my life whole. She is my partner, the love of my life, and the source of my happiness.

I went on to win re-election to the council in 1989. Henry kept to his decision not to run again and Lila was duly elected mayor.

Lessons from Private Lives; Public Repercussions

■ **A politician has no private life.**
There was a time when a politician's personal life was, indeed, private. For better or worse, that is not the case today. Settle any personal problems *before* you enter public life or seek elective office.

On June 17, 1994, I sat next to my friend, Secretary of the Treasury Lloyd Bentsen, as we signed a NAFTA agreement. We talked about the probe of Henry arising from the Medlar affair. Bentsen said, "Henry should have never come to Washington until he had settled his problem. The Washington media and partisan politics are vicious. If they smell blood they will attack and try to destroy you."

■ **Act decisively on personal problems.**
I was "out front" about my divorce and it was a one-day story. Henry had to endure the agony of daily news stories because he discussed his situation with too many people and could not make a decision about his personal life.

■ **Avoid tying your political life to someone else's.**
I now understand how Henry felt when his initial race for mayor was contingent on whether Lila Cockrell would run. In a similar manner, I was left dangling in the wind because of Henry's indecision about a statewide race. His personal problems became mine. I was determined that in the future I would never put myself in that position again.

■ **Think ahead and set goals for governing.**
Henry's question to me about what the next mayor should do took me off guard. A candidate for office always thinks first about how to get elected, not about what to do once in office. But the candidate should have both a strategy for winning, and a program for governing.

7

Henry's Finale

The early libraries in San Antonio were clubs that women formed for reading enjoyment. Their meager financial support came from fees charged to those who used the books and the reading rooms. In 1899, the clubs formed an organization aimed at attracting the attention of Andrew Carnegie, hoping he would build in San Antonio one of the more than 2,000 libraries he envisioned would spread literacy throughout the United States.

Those early library advocates were successful in obtaining $50,000 from the Carnegie Foundation. The city of San Antonio provided land, furniture and maintenance for the building. The library opened in 1903 on the corner of Presa and Market streets.

Funding was a struggle from the start. The library received a small amount of financial help from a special city tax, but individual donations of funds and books were critical to its operation.

Five decades passed before the city provided direct funding from general revenues to the library system. The new city charter of 1951 created a Library Board of Trustees and provided operating money.

In 1968, spurred by HemisFair and the realization that visitors from throughout the world would see San Antonio for the first time, the city built a new downtown library on the corner of Market and South St. Mary's streets. The 100,000-square-foot building was a major step toward a modern, comprehensive facility. The old Carnegie Library became the home of the Hertzberg Circus Museum.

Although the city took responsibility for funding, the struggle for resources continued. For various reasons, the library system never enjoyed strong City Council support. For one thing, library board appointees were not influential community leaders. Council members usually picked a librarian or public school teacher, or a neighborhood person who was interested in the local branch library. The board members simply lacked the political and financial muscle to make things happen.

The director of the library system was required to be a professional librarian. While this was entirely appropriate, librarians usually are not steeped in political skills. So library directors found themselves eating from the far end of the trough when the budget was drawn up for council consideration.

Many council members felt that the library system's only purpose was to provide reading pleasure and enjoyment to a small portion of the population. They didn't consider the library important to the educational system or to the economic development of our city. As a result, our library system stayed in the Dark Ages with respect to buildings, technology, information resources, research material, number of books and trained personnel.

Henry Cisneros studied in the library as a youngster and was aware of its shortcomings. In 1985 he began to breathe a little life into the antiquated system. He created the San Antonio Library Foundation, run by a separate board of directors, and the city provided funding for the foundation to hire an executive director. Evelyn Cooper was the first, succeeded by Maria Cossio in 1988. Maria had been director of the San Antonio branch of the University of Mexico, and was well connected in the community. Under her leadership, the foundation began to attract strong community leaders who eventually would provide effective muscle.

When I was elected to City Council in 1987, I became an advocate for the library system. Rapid changes were on the horizon regarding information sharing. I believed our library system could become a leader in sharing the rapid transmission of information with schools as well as businesses.

During my first year on council, I worked closely with library board Chairwoman Joan Mellard, now Voigt, in successfully lobbying the council for an increase of $1 million in funding. I closely followed the work of the library board as its members drew up a new master plan.

On February 17, 1988, the library board approved a five-year master plan calling for $48.35 million in capital expenditures. It included the rebuilding of all the library branches and, to cap things off, advocated construction of a new central library.

It was a good formula, but it lacked a financing mechanism. Henry declared his support, especially for a new downtown library, but felt that constructing a new building would prove politically impossible. Instead he suggested developers renovate an existing building and lease it to the city. He suggested a vacant Sears store on the northern edge of downtown or a failed indoor shopping mall known as Fiesta Plaza, just west of downtown, for renovation.

The library board received six proposals for renovations to create a new central library. The proposals included both the Sears building and Fiesta Plaza. Unfortunately, each proposal seemed more a cure for the problem of an empty building than a plan to meet the need for a state-of-the-art library. The process was in total confusion.

The solution came as Henry, who was coming up on his last months in office, thought about which issues to place on the May ballot. Although he would not be running for re-election, he wanted one last opportunity to add a notch to his record. He wanted his presence felt to the very end.

So Henry met with each council member to ask for input. A charter amendment to increase council salaries, fluoridation of the water supply and a quality-of-life bond issue were the main topics of consideration.

During the Dome campaign, Henry had promised COPS to put a "quality of life" bond issue on the May ballot. It was a vague promise without agreement as to just what that issue might be. I felt our library system should be in the mix.

Yolanda Vera, who represented District 7, southwest of my district, was a strong proponent of literacy services. She had led the effort to create a San Antonio Literacy Commission and to open literacy centers around the city.

Yolanda and I met with Henry in early February to present our ideas jointly. "Henry, let's go with the library issue," I said. "If we don't do it now, it will never be accomplished. The economy is continuing to slow down. We need to pass the bond issue before it gets worse. We also don't know how the next council and mayor will work together. You have the momentum with the Dome victory. Quite frankly, you are the only one who can win this issue for us."

Yolanda argued that education and libraries should go together. Building literacy centers next to the branch libraries would strengthen the appeal of a library bond issue.

I added, "Remember, Henry, I made a promise to build a new library in the Great Northwest area." This was a promise I had made to the homeowners association in an area the city annexed into my district in 1988. "You need to help me deliver on it."

"I want to do this," Henry said. "We need to bring our library system into a new era. I'll work on a package to submit. Help me build support for the issue."

On February 27, 1989, in a special work session, City Council approved a $46.4 million bond package that earmarked $28 million to build a new downtown library, with the rest going to eight literacy centers, expansion or replacement of 17 existing branches, and the construction of one new branch in the Great Northwest neighborhood.

The package offered something for everyone. Each council district had at least one branch library. The fact that eight literacy centers were programmed for eight council districts simply reflected political reality. Certainly, the need was greatest in the inner city, but the votes were predominantly on the North Side.

Mayor Cisneros pledges support for a new library at a rally of
Communities Organized for Public Service in April 1989. (Joe Barrera
Jr., Express-News)

Henry followed the rule that you must divide the spoils equally
across the city if you expect a bond issue to pass.

The final council vote on the bond issue came on March 9,
only five weeks before absentee voting would begin. Some were
concerned that we had moved too fast without proper planning.

The business community said it would be hard to raise funds
because of the costly Dome vote and the fund-raising activities of
candidates for their own elections. To make matters worse, Henry
was fighting with the business community over the makeup of
the Dome Advisory Committee and the choice of architects.

The fact that the bond issue carried a property tax increase
automatically made it harder to pass, even though the increase

amounted to less than two cents per $100 of value. Confusion over the location of the central library concerned many people. The voters would have to trust that council would pick the right site. Finally, the bond issue by law could not include operating funds. So, with budgets tight, people feared we might end up with a Cadillac building but no money for gasoline.

In spite of all those concerns, there was one overriding factor in favor of the bond issue: Henry. He had led our community to numerous public referendum victories. He had passed bond issues for streets, drainage, police and fire substations, and a handful of earlier branch libraries. He had defeated the spending cap initiative. He had won the Dome victory. He had lost only once — the referendum on fluoridation. He would be out of office after May and no one knew what would happen after his exit.

The campaign had a bit of good luck. HTA decided not to fight the bond issue, and no other organized opposition formed. I suppose part of the reason was that everybody was exhausted after the January Dome campaign. Another reason was that most people knew how antiquated our library system was. If opposition had been strong, I doubt the issue would have passed.

The business community, because of concerns about funding for future operations, supported the issue reluctantly. I met with Bill Thornton, who was then chairman of the Greater Chamber. He was personally supportive but said the chamber would have to study the issue.

The chamber waited until March 30 to endorse the issue, two weeks before absentee voting started. The business community would have looked bad supporting a domed stadium and then refusing to support a library project. In the end, they had to go along with Henry.

Councilman Frank Wing played a key role in the library campaign. Henry's relationship with General Robert McDermott, head of USAA, had deteriorated to the point they were no longer speaking. The fallout over regulations to protect the Edwards Aquifer Recharge Zone was the first problem they had. The fact that McD said he would support Lila Cockrell even if Henry ran for mayor again added to their mutual distrust.

But Henry needed funding for the library campaign. He also knew McD was concerned about funding the infrastructure needed for the Texas Research Park. Perhaps a deal of mutual interest might be made.

The Research Park was a crown jewel of Henry's "high tech" economic development strategy, dating back to his first term as mayor. McD was a key player in this strategy, having persuaded billionaire H. Ross Perot to donate $10 million to a non-profit foundation devoted to establishing biotechnology in San Antonio. The foundation had acquired 1,500 acres in the far western suburbs of San Antonio, but implementation of the project was painfully slow. The University of Texas Board of Regents approved creation of an Institute of Biotechnology at UTSA, which would be the park's first "anchor tenant," and the Texas Highway Department had agreed to build a new access road, called Research Parkway. But more funds were needed for development.

So Henry turned to Frank Wing for help. He asked Frank to meet with McD. Frank gave his word to McD that he and Henry somehow would secure $7 million for streets and drainage in the research park. General McDermott in turn agreed to lead the effort to raise funds for the library campaign.

In mid-March, George Shipley polled voters and found only 52 percent supported the bond issue. Even that support was soft. The library branches were more important to most voters than a central library. Crime and education ranked above the library in importance.

Henry made good use of this information. If people supported education, they needed to understand the link between education and the library. Henry was soon organizing Educators for the Library, and he got the regional chapter of the Texas State Teachers Association to endorse the issue. Education became the central theme throughout the campaign.

As in past bond issues, Henry campaigned hard. He blockwalked with COPS and Metro Alliance. He held six "town hall meetings" to mobilize support, and he got the AFL-CIO to endorse the bonds. He also put to work a strong phone bank of professionals and volunteers who urged people to vote.

The mayor and council races on the same ballot were lackluster. This was both good and bad. The good part was that it enabled all of us to use our time to campaign for the bond issue. The bad part, Henry feared, was that voter apathy might defeat the bonds.

On election night, May 6, when the absentee vote came in, it looked at first as though we might lose. The bonds trailed in that vote by 10 percent. But on election day, enough supporters came out to overcome the negative absentee vote.

The voter turnout of only 78,921 showed how little interest there was in the election in contrast to the 155,871 people who voted when Henry first was elected mayor. The library issue passed with 55 percent of the vote. Lila Cockrell was elected mayor once again, with 59 percent of the vote over a weak opponent. All incumbent council members won easy re-election. I received 81 percent of the vote in my district.

In the short period from January to May 1989, Henry had won two major issues, the Dome and the library. It was an extraordinary effort that would pay lasting dividends for the city.

A Farewell

After the election on May 6, Henry would remain mayor until June 1. He continued to work 18-hour days and kept a full agenda before the council. His last days were filled with controversy as the fight with the business community over the selection of the Dome design team dragged on until near the end of May.

On Thursday, May 25, during his last City Council meeting, we all had our chance to say goodbye. I praised him on his vision for the city and the skill he exhibited to realize that vision. I said he had the courage to make the weak strong and the strong weak in his effort to balance community forces for the common good.

"I would love to stay," he said after we all concluded our remarks. He added that it is not healthy for anyone to stay at the center of things as he did for eight years. But he admitted it was difficult for him to go back to private life.

Henry had begun to plan his transition by organizing a new business during his last few months in office. It would be an investment banking firm called the Cisneros Group. He would seek to manage investment funds held by public and private pension plans.

Looking at him that day, I knew he was wishing for some miracle that would allow him to stay. He had sat at this table for 14 years, six as a councilman and eight as mayor. It was hard to let go. I understood this had to be one of the saddest days of his life.

Although he had won two great victories in his last five months in office, he was leaving office right after a split with several of his friends over the Dome issue. The public display of difficulties in his personal life played out during the last seven months of his term. Just four months prior to his departure, he had considered running again, only to be pushed aside by people he thought were his friends. Now he was leaving the office he loved for a new life that seemed to hold little excitement or promise.

The following Sunday as I drove by City Hall, I saw a large crowd of mostly older Hispanics waiting to get inside the building. The crowd, estimated by police to number 5,000, sweated under a sweltering sun as they waited patiently for a chance to go inside. This would be their last opportunity to shake the hand of the mayor they so proudly elected to office eight years earlier.

A Mexican string band played while Henry stood for hours shaking hands and signing autographs. His wife, Mary Alice, his children and his mother and father were by his side. It was an emotional farewell as people called out to him "Viva Cisneros."

I had intended to pay my respects to Henry, too, but after seeing that large crowd I decided to pass up the opportunity. Besides, I thought, this is the people's — not the politicians' — day to say goodbye.

Three days later, at midnight on May 31, Henry jumped into his brother's pickup and left City Hall for the last time as mayor of San Antonio. On that last day, he still put in his usual 18-hour effort.

Henry left an extraordinary record of achievement. He promised in his first campaign in 1981 that economic development would be the centerpiece of his work in office. He delivered. When he took office, 421,100 people had jobs in San Antonio. When he left, there were 576,800 people working, a 37 percent increase. When he took office, per capita income was $8,561. When he left, it was $13,244, a 54.7 percent increase.

He also said in the 1981 campaign he would invest in infrastructure that had been so badly neglected prior to his election. He won six bond elections totaling $526.8 million, for streets, drainage and public buildings. In three of those elections, the people imposed additional taxes on themselves. There was also the Dome, and the airport and sewer projects financed by revenue bonds.

The list of specific projects Henry accomplished during his term was as long as the laundry list he kept on a daily basis.

But Henry left the city with more than a compilation of projects. He showed us that as a city we were better than we thought. He elevated minorities to the status of equal partners with the Anglo establishment. He changed the office of mayor into an office of substance. He became a national leader and an idol to thousands of people. For eight years, Henry *was* the city. And he was my friend.

★★★

Lessons from Henry's Finale

■ **Balance your public and private lives.**
During 14 years in office, Henry had allowed his public life to consume him. After seeing the pain that accompanied Henry's departure, I was determined that if I ever served as mayor I would not let the office devour me.

■ **Weave individual interests into a rope of community support.**
To win passage of the library bonds, which in the beginning lacked strong public support, Henry appealed to a variety of interests. He combined literacy centers with the branch library expansions. When polling proved that education had appeal as an issue, Henry focused entirely on the educational value of libraries as the campaign's theme.

■ **Horse trading greases the wheels of politics.**
Councilman Frank Wing's meeting with General McDermott was critical to the library campaign. Trading streets and drainage in the Texas Research Park for financial support for the library campaign helped push the bond issue over the top. Later, McDermott would donate $1 million through USAA to the new downtown library.

8

The Return of Lila Cockrell

When Lila Cockrell was sworn in on June 1, 1989, I had put all my aspirations to be mayor on the back burner. Tracy and I were still in the honeymoon stage of our six-month-old marriage. I was content to enjoy my private life, spend some time in my business and continue my work as a councilman. With Lila at the helm again, I thought we were in for a period of smooth sailing.

At age 67, Lila was an experienced leader. During World War II she had served as a WAVE officer and a company commander. She developed her taste for politics as president of the League of Women Voters and, in 1963, she was tapped by the Good Government League to run for City Council, where she served until 1970. She split with the GGL that year when it refused to support her for mayor. But the rift proved temporary, and after yet another stint on council, she became the GGL candidate for mayor in 1975. Her election earns a special place in San Antonio history — as the first mayor directly elected by the voters.

Lila served until 1981. She was an effective voice for the establishment, and a mediator among warring council factions in a time of intense change. The Good Government League had broken up, single-member districts were instituted in 1977, and for the first time a majority of the council was non-Anglo. Lila offered no substantial agenda of her own, but she did an outstanding job guiding the city through the difficult transition to an ethnically diverse political system.

But upon her return to the office in 1989, her strengths were no longer seen as such. Lila became a victim of heightened expectations. Henry Cisneros had transformed the mayor's office. Over the eight years of his tenure, people became accustomed to strong, forceful leadership. For the first time, the mayor had become the real leader of the city and was held accountable for the good and bad that occurred. As it would turn out, Lila was re-entering the office of mayor at an unlucky time. Events would quickly spin out of control.

For starters, Lila came into office during an economic slowdown. In the wake of the savings-and-loan collapse, property values were declining, unemployment had risen to 7.9 percent and, inevitably, the city was facing budget difficulties.

To complicate matters, Lila would soon be confronted with some mistakes from the Cisneros years that required strong leadership to correct. Henry made this task more difficult by critiquing her publicly, perhaps as payback for what he still perceived as Lila's slap when he had mused about running for re-election after the Dome victory.

At our first council meeting, as expected, Lila did not lay out an agenda. By that simple omission, she abandoned the most important power Henry had instilled in the office of mayor. The members of City Council, who all had served under Henry, were used to following the mayor's agenda. Now there was none.

Events, however, would quickly set one. First out of the box on June 12 was a projection by City Manager Lou Fox that we faced a $25 million to $30 million shortfall for the budget year beginning October 1, 1989. Along with this bad news came a revelation that the staff had made serious errors in estimating the cost of the police union contract the council had adopted in November 1988.

"The .44-caliber Mouthpiece"

You might not expect to find a routine police-labor contract among the major issues to impact the city during the period from 1981 to 1995. But the approval by council of that contract in 1988 would do more to damage the credibility of city government than any other event. Ultimately it would produce a complete turnover of City Council within five years.

To understand why, one must first meet Sergeant Harold Flammia of the San Antonio Police Department. Harold was the provocative, tough-negotiating president of the San Antonio Police Officers Association, the police union. The San Antonio Light once profiled him with the headline, "The .44-caliber mouthpiece." Harold had told me over breakfast one time about the incident that had changed his life, propelling him into the leadership of the police union and, subsequently, the negotiation of the most lucrative contract in the department's history.

Harold began the story by telling me how the call for "burglars in action" had crackled over the radio on the night of January 7, 1982, as he and his rookie partner were driving down Zarzamora Street on the West Side. The call was no big deal; it was common in any major city and Flammia had handled many such calls during his 13 years on the force.

When he arrived at the scene, he saw a man dressed in black crash through the window of a store. He drew his gun and chased him across the street, down a driveway and around a garage. As he ran around the corner, the suspect turned and fired. They crashed into each other, both of them firing away. Flammia blew five holes through the burglar, starting at the top of his chest and going down. The suspect shot Flammia three times. "I had the better gun," Flammia told me. "He died; I lived. If it had happened today, I would also be dead because the crooks now have greater firepower than we do."

Flammia spent five and a half months in the hospital, going under the knife 10 times and twice receiving the Last Rites. Mayor Cisneros and Councilman Wing visited him in the hospital. Councilman Wing hung his personal rosary beads on the corner post of Flammia's hospital bed, saying, "These will help. Keep them; you will get well."

During those months in the hospital, anger consumed him — anger at the lack of equipment, the old cars, the outdated communications equipment, the cramped offices, inadequate manpower, sorry training, low pay and low standards for acceptance into the force.

"We were being asked to do more and more with less and less. I was pissed off at City Hall because it did not provide the resources we needed," he told me.

After he got out of the hospital, Harold began to plan to win the presidency of the San Antonio Police Officers Association. He knew he wanted a part in changing the department for the better. "All talk and no action was going to come to a halt," he told me. "I felt we had a right to the fruits of our labor just as any other working person did."

Four years after the shoot-out, Harold was elected president. During his first two years in office, he consolidated his power. He convinced association members to create a political action committee to raise funds for friendly City Council candidates. He got to know key leaders in the business community and persuaded them to support additional resources for the police department. He banged down the door of City Manager Lou Fox demanding more. He was threatening, obnoxious and vociferous in his demands.

By the time the existing police contract came up for renewal in 1988, the SAPD had come a long way, but it still had a long way to go. The police union became one of the mainstays of a statewide organization, the Combined Law Enforcement Associations of Texas, or CLEAT. Members became expert at getting from the state Legislature whatever they could not get from City Council at the bargaining table. Perhaps the most questionable legislative victory was an exemption from our City Charter prohibition that forbade employee participation in political campaigns.

The new contract took the union where its leadership really wanted to be. It made our police officers the highest paid in the state. It short-circuited the normal budget process by specifying major new expenditures for equipment, including "take home" cars for certain officers and a portable radio for every officer. It established a pre-funded medical plan for current and retired police officers, with contributions from both the officers and the city. It provided triple-time-and-a-half pay for work on holidays and added a sixth holiday to the overtime schedule. It included longevity pay increases, a generous incentive program for officers to pursue higher education and a pay differential for assignment to undesirable shifts. It gave the union a monopoly on opportunities for "moonlighting" in private security work at city facilities.

The contract even provided for the union president to be relieved from active duty in order to attend to union business full time while remaining on the city payroll at full pay and benefits. The new contract also carried a four-year term in place of the one or two years of previous contracts.

The negotiations leading up to this contract were long and difficult, but all of Harold's work finally paid off on October 6, 1988, when City Council adopted the contract with only one negative vote. The lone opponent, Weir Labatt, my colleague from District 9, said his only objection was that he felt it was wrong in principle for the city to keep the union president on the payroll while his full-time job put him in an adversarial relationship to city government. There was little debate. Both Mayor Cisneros and Flammia praised the contract. City Manager Lou Fox recommended approval. The contract seemed almost as thick as a book. Council members looked to a staff summary that calculated the cost of the contract at $17 million.

I had mixed emotions on the vote. I did not like Harold's heavy-handed approach and the use of campaign contributions to get votes. I never accepted contributions from the police union. But with crime on the rise, I believed our police officers should be paid the best and furnished with the best equipment. So I voted for the contract.

The contract was the crowning achievement of Harold's career and the death knell for that City Council. But the repercussions were slow in coming. Over the next seven months, the contract did not even come up again for discussion.

Then Lou Fox delivered a bombshell: The total cumulative cost over the life of the contract would be $44.6 million. The earlier estimate of $17 million was only the additional annual cost in the fourth year of the contract, not the cumulative cost of the increases phased in over four years. The council was stunned. Pulling an unexpected $27 million out of the city's hat over three years would require taking some serious financial steps. Fox, feeling defensive, said there was no chicanery by the staff to hide the true cost.

Council members had differing recollections as to what staff actually had told us. I clearly remembered asking in executive session if the $17 million was the total cost of the contract. I was told yes. Memory was all we could go on, since executive sessions were not taped. But Jimmy Hasslocher remembered it the same way I did. He was outraged, charging, "We got duped by the staff."

C.A. Stubbs jumped on the issue right away. He went on the radio and encouraged people to call us and express their outrage over this stupid error. Our phone lines were jammed for days. Lila called for a staff report to the council explaining how an error of this magnitude could have been made.

Two weeks later, a report by Assistant City Manager Marcus Jahns confirmed that the estimates were incremental annual costs. He admitted the contract had been negotiated without input from the legal, budget or finance offices. He said the estimates had been done in a hurry and that some costs, including much of the additional equipment, were not calculated. Council was put in the position of having to admit that we had not understood the true cost of the contract.

Later it was also revealed that the projected contributions to the pre-funded medical plan may have created a monstrous unfunded future liability for the city. The city's long-time finance director, Carl White, was fired when he released an estimate of the full cost to columnist Rick Casey. White contended he was required to release it under the state's Open Records Act, but Lou Fox said it was an inaccurate preliminary estimate. Councilman Frank Wing also came under attack for the behind-the-scenes role he had played in negotiating these contract provisions. It was common knowledge around City Hall that Frank had a continuing romantic relationship with a policewoman, which created at minimum an appearance of a conflict of interest.

In the wake of Marcus Jahns' report, Councilmen Jimmy Hasslocher, Weir Labatt and I thought it was time for Lou Fox to go. He had successfully served as city manager for eight years, longer than any of his predecessors. Teaming up with Mayor Cisneros, Lou had made things happen. But the police contract was a major blunder, and Lou's excuses were undermining public confidence in the city. It seemed to me he was also getting burned out, and that his heart was no longer really in the job.

Jimmy arranged for the three of us to meet with Lila. This fiasco was not of her doing; she had inherited it along with the associated budget problems. But she was mayor now, and the public expected her to deal with it. We told Lila we felt she needed to ask Lou to resign voluntarily. We told her it would be better for her to get a fresh start with a new city manager. We argued that this was the only action she could take to regain public confidence. We assured her that the call was hers, and that she had our votes if she decided to act.

Lila decided not to ask for Fox's resignation. While Weir, Jimmy and I did not go public with our views, each of us privately advised Lou to resign. We told him it was in both his and the city's best interests. Overall, he had done an outstanding job. But regardless of how good a job you have done, there is always a right time to leave.

The Budget and the Rollback

Before Lila's election, everyone knew the 1989-90 budget would be a difficult one. Property values had cratered in the wake of the savings and loan collapse, and unemployment was rising. In her typical prudent style, Lila had appointed a committee during her campaign to advise her with recommendations on the budget, but the committee was instructed not to complete its report until after the election. The committee was led by Carroll Jackson, a stockbroker who had been my own campaign finance chairman when I first ran for council in 1987. Tom Brereton, who had taught urban fiscal management in the Urban Studies pro-

C.A. Stubbs, president of the Homeowner-Taxpayer Association, files petitions for a referendum vote to roll back city taxes on December 14, 1989. (Charles Barksdale, Express-News)

gram at Trinity, was vice chairman. Most members were accountants from local offices of what were then the "Big Eight" accounting firms, and were associated with the Greater Chamber. The timing of the committee's report coincided with the release of the city manager's proposed budget, which would reveal for the first time the precise magnitude of the projected red ink.

I had been on City Council through two budget cycles. It was clear to me after my first budget battle, in the summer of 1987, that serious financial problems for the city were just around the corner. In that first year, within a month of being elected, I called for the consolidation of city departments from 32 to 20, elimination of two of the four assistant city managers, pay cuts for reassigned department heads and enough layoffs to enable the city to hire 100 new police officers. I won no support from the council. The next year, Councilman Weir Labatt and I tried a tag-team approach. Again, the proposals were thrown out of the ring.

It was no surprise to me in 1989 to find a $25 million to $30 million shortfall thrown in the council's collective face. But if the budget shortfall were not trouble enough, along came Lila's budget committee report. The committee's recommendations were published on June 23, nine days after Lou Fox's proposed budget was submitted.

The committee report started out by saying that the city was well managed and there were no blatant examples of waste, but it then criticized the city's financial management in detail. The committee identified four main reasons for the city's budget problem: reduced property values, "mandates" imposed by higher-level governments and previous councils, repeated use of one-time funds to plug budget shortfalls and the city's rapidly rising debt.

The most explosive item in the report was a suggestion to increase property taxes by 22 to 34 percent. It was just one of the report's 74 recommendations, but it was the one that made the document a political hot potato. The city looked woefully incompetent. The city was not responsible for falling property value or mandates from federal and state government, but the other factors were the fruits of poor policy decisions by councils and staff, past and present.

Lou Fox took the report in stride. "We've been walking a tightrope," he said. "At some point in time we have to get off. This may be the year." What he should have said is that all of us were likely to be pushed off that tightrope. The citizens were ready to shove. C.A. Stubbs would be the first to lend them a hand.

In this politically unhealthy atmosphere, we now began to address the budget. The credibility of both the council and city staff were under attack. Rather than have council develop priorities for cutting the budget, Lila felt it would be better for the staff to do so. This was the approach she had always used before.

As the budget battle got under way, Lila kept her own counsel. Seven City Council members, including me, said we would vote for a tax hike of up to 15 percent if a good, sound budget were presented. Finally, in early September just days before the budget deadline, Lila said she could support a 12 percent tax increase. She did not say what budget cuts she would support to achieve this figure.

As Lila formulated her position, council members were engaged in a knockdown, drag-out fight on taxes as well as spending priorities. Lila was hearing echoes of the council wars of 1978, and said she feared an ethnic impasse on the budget.

The news media speculated as to when Lila would step in and put a stop to the infighting. News reports talked about her caution and her wait-and-see attitude. Finally, on the Sunday night before the Thursday council vote, Frank Wing and I met with her. The three of us reached an agreement and garnered council support for it.

On Thursday, September 14, the council in a 9-to-2 vote adopted a tax increase of 12 percent. We made $15 million in cuts and eliminated 500 jobs from the budget.

Tax increases and real service reductions are both hard for the public to digest. A budget that combines the two is a formula for political disaster if not handled right. We did not handle it right. The weeks of public feuding over the budget only added to public disenchantment with City Council.

During the budget debate, C.A. Stubbs warned the council that if we went over an eight-percent increase in property taxes he would start a campaign for a "rollback" referendum.

Initially, we did not take Stubbs' threat seriously. We rationalized that the amount of increase over eight percent was too small to concern taxpayers. The extra spending above eight percent would cost the average taxpayer just 71 cents a month. We felt it was well justified. The $3.9 million to be raised by the additional four percent tax increase would pay for 50 additional police officers, additional books for the library and school crossing guards. With a $60,000 homestead exemption for the elderly, the majority of Stubbs' core constituency already paid not a penny in city property taxes. Stubbs' own taxes had gone down 54 percent over the past five years because of this exemption, so his city property tax bill for 1989 was $13 a month.

On "D-Day" for the budget vote, Stubbs carted up to City Hall a red wheelbarrow containing 20,000 petition forms. He said his supporters were ready to hit the streets if we supported more than an eight percent hike. He was true to his word. As soon as we adopted the budget, the referendum petition drive was on.

Stubbs and the Homeowner-Taxpayer Association had until December 13, three months, to collect almost 44,000 valid signatures. We thought this was impossible. But our warning lights should have flashed in mid-October when the San Antonio Board of Realtors came out in support of Stubbs. The board mailed 4,000 petitions to its members. The apartment association also helped in the effort to collect signatures.

On October 23, COPS came in on the city's side, threatening to tear up the rollback petitions if anyone brought them into its neighborhoods.

But while COPS took this early stand, the business community remained silent through September, October and November. The Greater Chamber had originally recommended that the council not go over the eight percent limit exempted from rollbacks by state law. Chamber leadership had not reviewed its position since the council vote.

On October 25, Lou Fox gave notice of his resignation, effective June 1, 1990. The media said he left under pressure from some council members, which was true. By the time of Fox's resignation, public outrage over the police contract had grown to bonfire proportions. Stubbs' petition process was well on its way to success. If Lou had tendered his resignation in June, I believe confidence in the staff could have been restored. It was too late now. All over town people were talking about how incompetent the city staff was for negotiating the contract, and how inept the City Council was for approving it "without reading it."

In early December, Stubbs announced he had enough signatures. After that, Lila said that she might ask council to roll back four percent of the increase voluntarily. I was quoted in the Express-News as saying I would wait for Mayor Cockrell's recommendation. Other council members said they would not roll back the tax increase.

On December 12, Lila said she would stand and fight. In a news conference with Greater Chamber Chairman Bill Thornton and Hispanic Chamber Chairman Al Aleman, Lila said she would not ask City Council to voluntarily roll back the tax increase. Thornton and Aleman would join forces with Robert Hilliard, a former council member, to lead an anti-rollback campaign. A San Antonio Light editorial supported the mayor's decision.

Events began to gather speed. On December 13, Stubbs brought to City Hall 71,158 signatures, of which only 43,480 needed to be valid. He accused the city of embracing only the rich and powerful and turning its back on residents.

The next day the Greater Chamber threw its support to the anti-rollback effort. Lila formed the political action committee. The anti-rollback forces were late coming to the game. Stubbs already had a potential 70,000 votes in his pocket. Working overtime as the holidays approached, City Clerk Norma Rodriguez soon determined that the petitions met the signature requirement. At the December 21 council meeting we set February 3 as election day for the rollback.

Two days later political consultant George Shipley gave us a lump of coal for Christmas — a poll showing the rollback would win 2 to 1. This was only 10 days before absentee voting started. Lila asked citizens not to vent their rage against City Council by voting for the rollback.

Stubbs knew he was on the verge of a major victory, and he unloaded on the council. He accused us of "blackmailing" the voters by holding hostage the increases in police manpower, library books and school crossing guards. In fact, we had identified these programs as the ones to be funded by the additional four percent tax increase for valid reasons. Most important was that they all required new expenditures in the budget, and therefore represented the real-world choices voters faced in the rollback: Did they want more cops, books and crossing guards or not?

Unlike Stubbs' previous campaigns, this one was a sophisticated effort. Stubbs didn't have to depend on "talk radio" alone. With victory in the wind, he was able to raise money to air his message commercially on five local radio stations. He contacted more than 200,000 people over the phone via pre-recorded messages. He sent out 55,000 "truth fliers" to residents.

Stubbs delivered a low blow featuring comic elements reminiscent of Johnny Carson's mind-reading skits. He announced he had a *secret* plan, kept in a sealed envelope, for balancing the city budget. He said he would open it and reveal his solution during a televised debate on the rollback.

When Stubbs was finally shamed into revealing his plan beforehand, it turned out he actually had several plans. One would close various parks and tourist attractions, including the Tower of the Americas at HemisFair and the historic Spanish Governor's Palace, while still counting all the revenues generated from those facilities. Another was to stop granting tax abatements for new investments in the city's economy. This policy was an important economic development tool, but it annoyed many of Stubbs' followers. Obviously, Stubbs knew perfectly well that ending this policy would neither cut city expenditures nor increase city revenues by a single cent in the current fiscal year. Playing to his fans, Stubbs had delivered the cheapest shot of his entire political career. It even angered Lila.

Lost in the campaign rhetoric was the fact that of America's 50 largest cities, San Antonio ranked 49th in revenue per capita, 44th in city employees per capita and 38th in property taxes per capita. Stubbs told the voters to "send a message" to City Hall. And Henry was not around to counter his strident rhetoric.

Stubbs was so confident that even before election day he began to talk about future initiatives. He wanted to change the way council was elected, saying again that single-member districts gave rise to "ward politics." He wanted to set a limit on council terms. He wanted to take collective bargaining away from police and firefighters.

On January 26, 1990, only a week before election day, the San Antonio Light carried the headline, "Cockrell blasts past spending." A subhead said, "Mayor takes aim at fiscal policies during the Cisneros administration." This was the first time that Lila had openly criticized Henry Cisneros' tenure. The break with Henry clearly measured her desperation in a losing battle.

Campaign ads asked people to trust Lila. She was the only elected city official besides Weir Labatt not tainted by the police contract. In the ads she said she was surprised at how bad things were when she got to City Hall. But while her message absolved her from blame, it increased voter anger at city government.

All of us on City Council fought hard to stop the rollback, but it was a lost cause. On February 3, voters rolled back their taxes to an 8 percent increase by a vote of 76,167 to 42,673, a 64 percent majority. Only one council district, District 5 on the West Side, voted against the rollback. It was an overwhelming victory for Stubbs.

In accord with the rollback results, City Council instructed the staff to issue checks totaling $4.1 million back to the taxpayers. Contrary to Stubbs' assertions during the campaign that the small people were getting hurt, the largest property-tax refunds went to large businesses. For example, USAA and Southwestern Bell together received more than $80,000 in refunds. Single-family homeowners received only $1.8 million in refunds — an average of $8.30 each.

Lila asked citizens who received refunds to donate them to the Library Foundation to make up for the $600,000 in lost funding. Taxpayers sent in more than $102,000. Balous Miller, president of Bill Miller Bar-B-Q, picked up the cost of the crossing guards. We did not hire the additional 50 police officers.

Bourbon, Cigars and Making the Hard Choices

The walls of my small office at home are covered with lightly stained pine. Books of history, biography and politics line the walls on two sides of the room. My oak desk, which has served me for more than 30 years, faces a large window with wooden shutters.

As I write this book, I occasionally look outside for the cardinals that fly into a small courtyard where I keep my bird feeder. It's a pleasant place to write. It is also a quiet and private place away from City Hall to visit about important decisions affecting the city.

In my office on the night of March 20, 1990, I asked Assistant City Manager Alex Briseño to kick his shoes off and relax as I handed him a Makers Mark bourbon on the rocks. I chomped on a good Travis Club cigar made by my friend and former state Representative Bill Finck, and took a sip of whiskey. I asked Alex how he would handle the mess at City Hall if he were selected as city manager.

Before Alex and I visited, we had gone through a long selection process for the next city manager. After Lou Fox gave notice, with his resignation to be effective six-and-a-half months later, the council decided to employ a professional search team.

Before the search could begin, Henry Cisneros said in a newspaper interview on December 7 that the search should be called off and that we should hire Alex. He said that Lou Fox was a "lame duck" and that because of the rollback campaign we could not afford to wait.

Mayor Cockrell and most of us on council felt it was inappropriate for Henry to be speaking out on this issue. In effect, he pulled the rug out from under Lila by pre-empting her.

We carried an important lesson away from the police contract fiasco — that public process is vital in making major decisions. We felt we needed a thorough search to identify the best candidates for city manager.

We may have been right about the desirability of a search, but Henry was on target when he said the times demanded a quick decision. By late January, there was no doubt that the rollback forces were going to win. Lou Fox had been unable to hold his staff together. A key budget staff member had resigned. The tax rollback would add to our problem of managing the deficit we faced in next year's budget. On January 27, I said that an experienced local candidate with good fiscal management skills could address the pressing problems with more expediency than someone from outside the city. I said Alex Briseño had the edge over everyone else.

Alex had a solid record as an assistant city manager. A graduate of Central Catholic High School, he had attended Texas A&M University, then earned a bachelor's degree in economics and a master's in urban studies from Trinity University in San Antonio, one of the nation's best private schools. He had served as a captain and a general's aide during four years in the Army. During his 13-year career with the city, he had handled every job professionally. He did not carry the scars of the police contract because he had not been included by Lou Fox in the negotiations.

While Alex was my favorite candidate, I was determined to keep my mind open. By the time Alex and I visited at my home, I had read the resumes of all the finalists. Although their verbal

Alex Briseño is sworn in as San Antonio city manager by City Clerk Norma Rodriguez on April 26, 1990. (Bob Owen, Express-News)

presentations were yet to be heard, I saw nothing in their resumes that showed any to be a better candidate than Alex.

Alex told me he had a plan and was ready to implement it if selected. It featured immediate changes in key personnel, a lean budget for the next year that would cut the fat out of City Hall and, the real kicker, the elimination of several hundred jobs.

After the rollback, we were facing a budget shortfall of $24 million for the next fiscal year. Alex said he could balance the budget with a tax increase that would be less than the eight percent rollback level.

I liked what I was hearing. If the public were to regain confidence in City Hall, the new city manager must take decisive action. Alex said he was ready. At the end of the evening, I toasted him and said, "You have my support. I will work for your appointment."

The council interviewed six finalists during the morning of March 31. We then went into executive session. Lila and some other council members wanted to extend the interview process. They were not ready to vote. Lila felt a decision now would be made in haste. I argued that I had heard all I wanted to hear and had made up my mind. Dragging out the process would only add to the confusion. Frank Wing and Yolanda Vera made similar arguments. In a vote of 6 to 5, we prevailed.

We went back into open session at about 5 p.m. and in a 10-to-1 vote we selected Alex to be city manager. He was the first Hispanic to serve in that position in San Antonio.

Alex quickly went about doing the things he told me he would do. Within a month, he proposed eliminating 323 jobs, including his now vacant post of assistant city manager. He fired another assistant city manager and two department heads. When yet another assistant city manager left to take a new job, Alex was able to point to a consolidation of power and responsibility within the manager's office. He was the man, and the responsibility rested on his shoulders. Even C.A. Stubbs complimented Briseño's actions.

★★★

Lessons from the Return of Lila Cockrell

■ **Lead, follow or get out of the way.**
Lila Cockrell did not realize how radically the mayor's role had changed under Henry Cisneros. By assuming her former role of mediator, and by not asserting control, she allowed City Council to drift and bicker. She failed to clean house in the wake of the police contract fiasco. She allowed her budget committee to recommend an explosive 22 to 34 percent tax hike. Ultimately, by not making the hard choices herself, she opened City Hall's doors to public anger and the success of the tax rollback.

■ **One mistake can lead to a public lynching.**
A single mistake that leaves public officials looking careless or inept can lead to public outrage. Sloppy staff work and shortcuts in the public process on the police contract destroyed confidence in city government.

■ **A Lone Ranger can crack City Hall.**
One determined individual can make a real difference. Harold Flammia proved that by his leadership of the police union. Today we have a well-paid police department, with high standards of training and some of the best equipment available.

■ **Never borrow from Peter to pay Paul.**
City Council for years had used one-time financial windfalls to plug budget shortfalls. This "kiting" of funds is bound to crash in the long run.

■ **Strong progressive leadership can create resentment.**
Henry Cisneros pushed this community forward at a rapid pace. In the process, he ran over a number of people and organizations. I believe the tax rollback had as much to do with this resentment, especially over the Alamodome vote, as it did with lack of confidence in local government.

9

A New Mayor

The Plaza San Antonio Hotel sits on Alamo Street across from the entrance to HemisFair Park. The elegant stucco building trimmed in brick is one of the city's premier hotels. Inside, adjacent to the hotel restaurant, is a private dining room.

On the morning of March 17, 1990, a little more than a month after the rollback, Tom Brereton and I joined Henry Cisneros for breakfast in the private dining room. We had asked Henry to meet us to talk about the book Tom and I began working on when I joined City Council.

Henry wasn't interested in talking composition. He was still smarting from Mayor Cockrell's casting blame on his administration for the budget shortfall during the heat of the rollback campaign. "Henry, don't worry about it," I told him. "We may be having budget problems now, but it's mostly due to the economic downturn. History will prove you right once we pass this difficult stage. The projects you started will pay great economic benefits for the future."

Henry went on to talk about the consequences of the rollback election. "The loss of the rollback has hurt Lila," he said. "She's like a person teetering on a cliff — a little shove and she's over. Bill Thornton has made it worse for her because of his efforts to position himself for next year's mayoral race. What are you waiting for?"

"Henry, I had pretty much made up my mind to forget about running for mayor in the near future. But I admit Thornton's maneuvering has made me reconsider. If Lila steps aside, then Bill will have an open field and I'll be out of the picture for good." I told him that Tracy and I were planning a series of breakfasts to ask people not to commit to a candidate until the field became clear.

Henry was blunt. "The city needs you to run. You need to start thinking offense and pick some issues you can stand up for. You'll have to demagogue a little, hammer away at Lila and hold your nose while you're doing it if you expect to win. If you decide to run, come by and see me."

I told him I'd seriously consider his ideas and call him when I made up my mind. We talked about some other issues. When we got up to leave, Henry said, "I'd be proud to have you as mayor when the Dome opens in 1993."

Immediately after the February 3 rollback, Bill Thornton began asking for commitments based on an understanding that he would run only if Lila decided not to seek re-election. At the same time, Al Aleman began meeting with Hispanic groups, offering himself as a candidate whether Lila ran or not.

While Al and Bill were lining up support, C.A. Stubbs was working on plans for a new round of voter initiatives: term limits, elimination of police and fire union bargaining, and challenging single-member district elections.

Meanwhile, a more significant "grassroots rebellion" was reorganizing. People opposed to the Applewhite Reservoir began to organize another petition drive to overturn the council's decision to build the dam. We were barely a third of the way into Lila's term, and the city's political pot already was at full boil.

When I left that breakfast with Henry, my political juices really started to flow. Henry had given me the best advice of my life in November 1988 when he told me to put my private life first and not run for mayor. The result was my happy marriage. Now he was advising me to jump into the next mayor's race. Could he be right again?

Tracy and I talked at length about whether I should run. I knew I would need her total support. She had run my council campaign and now she would have to run the mayoral campaign. We would have to take a large financial risk because most of the business community would stick with Lila. Despite her political vulnerabilities, Lila was formidable. She had run in nine campaigns, five for City Council and four for mayor. She had never lost. We also knew it would be hard to establish credibility after the way I pulled out of the mayor's race in 1988. The odds were against us.

But we also feared we would live to regret it if we passed up the chance. I was haunted by the fact that I had pulled out of the earlier mayoral contest. Tracy knew I really wanted to run. Coming home one day in late March, I laughed happily when she said, "Let's do it." *Yes!*

After our decision I visited Henry's office. Cisneros Asset Management was in a historic building on Presa Street in downtown San Antonio. To reach it, you went through a courtyard to a small alley between two buildings, and down the alley to an elevator. As you walked into his office, you were faced by a bookcase reaching to the ceiling on one wall. Memorabilia from his years as mayor filled the office.

Henry greeted me and said, "Let's get George Shipley on the phone." Shipley was Henry's political consultant for all his campaigns as well as for every referendum Henry won. He also had conducted the polling for Mayor Cockrell in her campaign.

Henry put George on the speaker phone, and said, "Nelson Wolff is in the office, and I believe he's ready to run for mayor. You should help him."

George said he thought Lila could be beaten, but it would take an expensive and hard-hitting campaign. He said he wanted to visit with me further about the possibility. Then he suggested that we plug Jack Martin into the conversation. Jack had worked for me as a young man when I was in the Texas Senate. He had gone on to become chief of staff for U.S. Senator Lloyd Bentsen, and he was now a successful political consultant.

When Jack got on the phone, Henry started to promote my candidacy. Jack said, "Henry, you don't need to sell me on Nelson. I'm ready to help."

When I got ready to leave, Henry said, "I believe they'll both work for you. Follow up with a visit to George."

I thanked him and said I was almost certain I would run.

In early April, Tracy began a series of breakfasts in our home, located in the Oak Hills neighborhood. As you enter, to the left of the Saltillo-tile foyer is a large, recessed living room with 20-foot-high ceilings. Three sides of the room are lined with brick and plate-glass windows. A large fireplace flanked by bookshelves covers the remaining wall. The room can accommodate up to 100 people.

Once a week, Tracy got up at 5:30 a.m. to begin preparations to accommodate 30 to 50 people for breakfast. Guests could choose from a traditional trail driver's repast of eggs, bacon, and biscuits; or a Sun Harvest healthy breakfast of cereal, oatmeal and fruit more suited to the influx of young professionals to the city, many of them in the medical field. I addressed these gatherings on issues facing the city and asked them to keep their minds open as to whom they would support for mayor in 1991.

While all this behind-the-scenes political activity was going on, Lila told the press in April she was planning to run again. Potential candidate Thornton pledged his support, saying, "If she chooses to run again, I am confident people will recognize her ability to lead and keep her in office."

On April 15, 1990, the San Antonio Light published an article written by Henry Cisneros in which he listed several people he thought could be mayor. Councilman Frank Wing was his favorite, and Henry said he had tried unsuccessfully to get him to run in 1989. Frank has never wanted to be mayor, though. Henry said that I had a sense of history, I was a genuinely decent person and I had a "big picture" sense of the future of San Antonio. He went on to say he did not understand why a large segment of the business community opposed me. It was clear to everybody that Henry preferred several people over Lila Cockrell.

In June, the San Antonio Light printed an analysis of Lila's first year in office. It included some quotes that hurt her politically. The Rev. Claude Black, a former city councilman who served with Lila, said, "She hasn't taken charge. If you don't take charge, someone will fill the vacuum." C.A. Stubbs was quoted as saying, "If you play too low key, there's the appearance that no one's in charge."

These two articles were a clear signal that the editorial leadership at the Light was ready to stir up a mayor's race. They wanted progress, and were signaling that a good challenger would have full coverage in the news pages as well as editorial support.

As the breakfasts progressed throughout April and May, Tracy and I met with George Shipley and began putting the campaign together.

One of the first tasks was to conduct a detailed poll. My good friend and former County Commissioner John Steen Jr., son of the John Steen whom Henry had defeated in the 1981 mayor's race, raised the funds to pay for this poll. Shipley conducted it in June and we got the results in early July. It showed that while Lila had an overall favorable rating of 59 percent, fully two-thirds of the voters felt San Antonio needed new leadership in the mayor's office with a new vision for the city.

The purpose of the poll was to gain financial support for my campaign by showing that Lila could be beaten. We shared the results with several people in the business community. The San Antonio Light got hold of it somehow, through either Henry or George Shipley. Both of them wanted to make sure the pressure stayed on me to run.

Neither the poll nor the public criticisms fazed Lila. She did not scare easily. She announced she would hold a fund-raiser July 17. Eighty sponsors signed up at $350 apiece. Lila was letting everyone know she was in the race for real and she expected to win.

While the mayor's race was shaping up, C.A. Stubbs launched not one, but two petition drives at the quarterly meeting of his tax-watchdog organization in May. One was a charter amendment to limit City Council members to a lifetime total of two two-year terms. The other was a reprise of the failed referendum campaign against the Applewhite Reservoir. Stubbs was lending his organization's weight and petition power to the other anti-Applewhite activists. Lila promised to campaign against term limits as well as the attempt to halt construction of the Applewhite Reservoir.

Our mayoral campaign — led by Ramiro Cavazos, who had recently resigned as executive director of the Hispanic Chamber — spent the summer preparing for a September 18 kickoff. More than 200 people crowded into a conference room at the historic Menger Hotel next to the Alamo for our announcement. The campaign staff was ready, and there were bumper stickers, buttons and signs all over the room. I gave a 15-minute speech outlining the three major themes of my campaign: better jobs, safer neighborhoods and quality education. I pledged to develop a new agenda to carry San Antonio through the 1990s.

Businessman Jose Medellin became my treasurer. Glynn Dyess, my best friend of 42 years, made the first large contribution to the campaign.

While the kickoff was a great success and received favorable news coverage, the shape of the race was changing rapidly. The day I announced, Al Aleman pulled out and Councilwoman Maria Berriozabal said she might run. Henry Cisneros gave a boost to her campaign by saying she was "like a sister" to him and that he had great respect for her.

On October 27, my 50th birthday, Maria announced she would run for mayor at a well-attended event in the back yard of her Beacon Hill home, just north of downtown. I knew she would run a first-class campaign. The talented Lionel Sosa would direct her media campaign, and trial lawyer Frank Herrera would raise a huge amount of money for her. They would make her look great.

Now we had a three-way race with the addition of a major inner-city candidate. The Express-News ran a story saying Henry would support Maria. The next day, Henry repudiated the report. I had to remind him that he was the one who had gotten me into the race in the first place. While Henry's endorsement would not make a lot of difference if I were running for a City Council seat, it could prove to be the determining factor in a close mayor's race.

On October 23 the Light published a poll showing a virtual three-way tie among Lila, Maria and me. Our internal polling was showing the same.

Lila kicked off her campaign November 17 with a rally in Market Square, the downtown ethnic "mall" where tourists mingle with native San Antonians. Four days later, former city councilman and former Republican Chairman Van Henry Archer announced that he would run. Archer had represented District 9, the near North Side, between the terms of Glen Hartman and Weir Labatt. He is conservative and anti-establishment, and seems to relish creating controversy with his outspoken, often outlandish remarks. He uttered his most memorable line in 1988, when he dismissed the delegates to a national women's convention in San Antonio as "a bunch of hairy-legged women." Now, new spice was added to the campaign.

By the February filing deadline, Councilman Jimmy Hasslocher and anti-Applewhite activist Kay Turner also joined the race. With San Antonio's usual crop of minor candidates, a total of 11 names appeared on the ballot. We knew Maria was a cinch for the runoff because she was the only strong Hispanic candidate. The North Side vote would splinter among several strong Anglo candidates. It was imperative I do well on the South Side where I grew up. I went back to my roots to build a winning base of support.

My father, Nelson, was 13 when he moved to San Antonio with his parents Adolph and Emma Wolff in 1932. Both my grandparents were immigrants from Germany who settled on a farm in Pflugerville, where my dad was born. Forced off the farm by the Depression, they moved in with Dad's sister Augusta, her husband, Fritz Schwartz, and their six children in a white frame house at 1303 South St. Mary's Street.

Dad went to school one year at Page Junior High School and then dropped out and went to work at the Majestic Oil Company, in the 4900 block of South Flores Street. A cafe called the Red Top Inn was located in the same block. One day in 1936, Dad met my mother, Marie Williams, who was waiting tables in that cafe. The cafe was owned by her cousins, Billie Jo and Myrtle Williams, who declared it was love at first sight. My parents were married in 1939.

On October 27, 1940, I was born in our home on McKinley Street on the South Side. My father held my mother's shoulders and my grandmother held her feet as I emerged wailing into Mom and Dad's bedroom. The doctor charged Dad $10 for assisting at the birth. Thereafter, whenever Dad was questioned about my value, he said, "Well, I know he's worth at least ten dollars."

The South Side was a great place to grow up during the 1940s and '50s. The neighborhoods contained neat little white frame houses occupied mostly by blue-collar and working-class families like ours. Dad drove a truck for Texas Consolidated Transportation Company. My mother stayed home and did the work of raising me and my two brothers.

Everyone knew each other in those neighborhoods. Without air-conditioning, neighbors sat on the curbs or their front porches to catch the early evening breeze. As the adults visited, we kids had the run of the streets. Neighbors watched out for each other's kids. No one locked their doors.

We went to baseball games at Richter Field and Mission Stadium, swam at Hot Wells, had picnics at Roosevelt Park, and went with Mother and Dad to dance to Western music at the local honky-tonks. We played baseball at Kite Field (now a shopping center), went to nine-cent Saturday matinees and traded comics at the neighborhood food store. I walked to school at Riverside Elementary and then to Page Junior High.

During my last year of junior high, in 1955, my father was transferred to Houston. I graduated from Bellaire High School there. We returned to San Antonio in 1961 after the company my dad worked for went bankrupt. My father, my brothers George and Gary, and I started selling roofing materials out of an abandoned filling station at 919 Roosevelt Avenue on the South Side, a site now covered by a freeway. The business, Alamo Enterprises, eventually grew to eight stores in South Texas.

My roots were deep on the South Side and I had kept up my contacts there. But the neighborhoods I returned to campaign in were different from those I grew up in. As the city had pushed north, the South Side stagnated. While the homes were still well kept in some neighborhoods, such as Highland Park and High-land Hills, most of the other areas had deteriorated. Incomes dropped; crime increased.

But new leaders were emerging to combat that trend. The South Side Chamber of Commerce had formed in the early 1980s to promote economic development. Political leaders including State Representatives Robert Puente, Ciro Rodriguez and Frank Madla fought to bring major projects to the South Side, such as Palo Alto College. They all supported me in the election. When Ciro was asked why, he said, "Nelson knows the dead-end streets of the South Side." Every week I walked the old neighborhoods where I had grown up.

In January, the mayoral campaign was overshadowed by the impending Gulf War against the Iraqi forces that had invaded Kuwait. Almost all press coverage, even hometown, focused on the war. Local political campaigns were a low priority. Many experts thought this helped Lila. But, fortunately for the "Allies" (not for Lila's advisers), the war ended too quickly for the scar-city of campaign coverage to have any real impact, and the media soon focused again on the mayoral race.

While we waited, our campaign put out an array of position papers — more than all other campaigns combined. I had strate-gies on everything from ethics to solid-waste disposal. I also formed the "San Antonio Tomorrow" commission — 105 citizens working from the bottom up to develop an agenda for the 1990s.

Position papers are a necessary evil. Like campaign money, you need them to prove you're "a serious candidate." But they're ignored by the media for three reasons: too long, too hard to ana-lyze, and they don't translate into 10-second sound bites. Voters remember at most two or three things about a candidate when they cast their ballots, and those things rarely come from position papers. Human nature being what it is, voters are more likely to remember the negative than the positive. The best-conceived position papers in the world would do nothing to help me win this race.

It was clear that if I expected to be in a runoff with Maria, I had to overshadow the other Anglo candidates and make the race between Lila and myself. I had to begin challenging Lila directly or I'd be lost in the crowded field and the race would be over for me.

There were risks in attacking Lila. She was a well-respected woman who had served in public office for 30 years. When you run against an incumbent, you have to attack the incumbent's record and show how you would handle the office differently. If you cannot, why should voters remove the incumbent? All your great plans for change mean nothing unless you get elected.

We began with a news conference on January 29. Lila's leadership style was outdated, I charged — "window dressing" and "ribbon cutting." I satirized her call for "an economic summit."

Lila punched back. In a jab based on the police contract controversy, she said what really was outdated was my lack of fiscal responsibility. She said she was "shocked, angry and disgusted," charging that my attacks revealed a desperate candidate with a badly faltering campaign.

In early March I followed up with another assault, saying Lila had no plans for the future, no jobs agenda and no plan for education. She responded with a beautifully delivered line, "Nelson, where have you been?" She said it was all contained in the city's master plan and that I should read it.

Our thrust-and-parry tactics, which had little to do with the clash of ideas, did achieve our real objective. We raised my profile and created the public impression that the race was between Lila and me. While the news stories we generated were important, they were good only for one day. But the give-and-take with Lila had established the basis for television ads. We narrowed the attacks to three issues, and our paid media ads kept them in front of the public.

While Lila and I verbally slugged it out, Maria Berriozabal sailed serenely above the fray. She announced she would hold three national fund-raisers. New York Mayor David Dinkins and Manhattan Borough President Percy Sutton, whose family was an East Side San Antonio political dynasty, endorsed her. Governor Ann Richards contributed $2,500 to her campaign. Between January and March, she raised more money than any other candidate — $199,415 — of which more than half was lent by Frank Herrera and Lionel Sosa.

As election day neared, various organizations with political clout began to announce their endorsements. Lila won those of the police and firefighter associations, and the San Antonio Express-News. Various local unions endorsed Maria. I received the endorsement of the San Antonio Light, the San Antonio Builders Association, the San Antonio Apartment Association and, most important of all, the San Antonio Board of Realtors. President Charley Williams led an organization of more than 5,000 brokers and agents in San Antonio who were active throughout the city.

We closed out the campaign with positive TV ads — clips of me jogging, the story of how my family and I started a small business on the South Side, and ads saying I had a job plan, an education plan and a neighborhood plan for the city. Three things we wanted people to remember were that I was vigorous, I would lead and I had a plan for San Antonio.

In the midst of running hard campaigns, four of us had to sit down with each other every Thursday at City Council meetings. Jimmy Hasslocher, Maria, Lila and I kept politics out of the council meetings. We managed to treat each other fairly and respectfully during the meetings. We even managed to kid each other about the campaign. Three days before election day, Lila showed up for a debate at WOAI Radio wearing a cast on her arm. She had a hairline break in her wrist. I said, "I hope you don't use that on us." She playfully raised her hand and gently swung at me, saying, "Whack!"

Collectively, Maria, Lila, Jimmy and I had put in more than 55 years of public service. We had managed to develop some pretty tough hides over that period of time. We all knew politics was rough and expected to receive our share of the bumps.

Finally, the May 4 election day arrived. Voters numbered 131,751 — the largest turnout since Henry's election as mayor a decade ago.

The results were: Maria, 30.5 percent; Wolff, 26.15 percent; Lila, 20.68 percent; Van Archer, 16.11 percent; Kay Turner, 3.85 percent;

and Jimmy Hasslocher, 1.64 percent. The balance was divided among the five other candidates.

Our strategy had worked. I had differentiated myself from Lila. Now, the voters would choose between Maria and me in a runoff election.

Lila was gracious in defeat. How a person handles himself or herself after a political loss says a lot. I had lost two previous campaigns and knew the pain associated with defeat. Lila continued to serve as mayor during the runoff, and never complained about losing.

As for the issues on the May 4 ballot, the term-limit amendment passed with 65.26 percent of the vote. The vote to stop Applewhite prevailed with 51.39 percent of the vote. These would radically impact our city's political system, which we will take up in later chapters.

With three incumbent City Council members leaving their positions to run for mayor, there also had been three council seats open for the May 4 vote. Oral surgeon and Greater Chamber chief Bill Thornton had declared for my District 8 seat as soon as it was official that both Lila and I were in the race for mayor. Thornton won easily. Roger Perez, a young lawyer who just happened to be Henry Cisneros' brother-in-law, replaced Maria in an easy race in District 1. And Lyle Larson, a businessman with a record as a partisan Republican, replaced Jimmy Hasslocher in District 10. Lyle was tall, young and handsome, and was quickly tagged as the "hunk" of City Hall — a role that seemed alternately to amuse and embarrass him.

Only one incumbent council member was turned out of office involuntarily: Joe Webb, the black East Side grocery store owner who had been on City Council since the first elections by district in 1977. He was unseated by a young African-American lawyer named Frank Pierce.

Timing is so important to a politician's chances for success, both as candidate and as officeholder. Lila's timing in 1989 was great for winning the mayoral race, but not for holding office. The lesson from Thomas Wolfe's novel "You Can't Go Home Again" would be an appropriate one for many politicians to understand. Lila came home to a totally different mayor's house in 1989, one that demanded political skills different from those that brought her success in her first terms.

Lila will be remembered as one of the great political leaders of San Antonio because of her effectiveness as a council person, the success of her first terms as mayor, and the continuing leadership she provides in civic affairs.

On the night of the May 4 primary, while in a state of jubilation, I was asked by reporters what I thought of the rejection of the Applewhite Reservoir. I said I thought the people didn't want to drink water from the Applewhite, and therefore we might finish the reservoir and use it for non-drinking purposes, or perhaps sell it to another entity to develop.

What a colossal mistake to make only three weeks away from a runoff election with Maria! All hell broke loose. San Antonio Light columnist Rick Casey wrote that I had badly misinterpreted the vote. He wrote that the people had said, "Stop the dam project this minute."

Over the weekend, I agonized over the issue. I felt strongly that the project was needed in order to secure a supply of water that would reduce our complete dependence on the Edwards Aquifer. I knew the Applewhite opponents had totally misrepresented the facts about the project. But, regardless of why people voted to reject it, the results were overwhelmingly clear. The ballot read, "an ordinance abandoning the Applewhite Reservoir project."

I finally realized that the question I faced was not whether the project was needed, but whether I would respect the democratic process. That process doesn't always provide the right answers. But I realized that even if the voters had made a bad decision, it was one I must nevertheless respect.

Four days later, I held a press conference to say I would make the motion to stop construction and abandon the project at the next City Council meeting. Acknowledging the voter mandate, council abandoned the project. The issue was effectively removed from the runoff campaign.

The runoff election lasted only 21 days. Maria had come through the first election unscathed while Lila and I were busy tussling with each other. Maria had the opportunity to capitalize on this by appealing to Lila's former supporters.

Absentee voting started 11 days after the first election. We had been presumptuous enough to plan ahead for the runoff campaign. Our television ads were running in the first week. Maria didn't get her TV ads up until the second.

In my ads, I cast the issue as one of which candidate could best help create more jobs and control taxes. I stressed my entrepreneurial background and my pro-growth position. An American Airlines subsidiary was considering locating in San Antonio and was requesting a tax phase-in. I committed to support it if elected. Maria would not commit her support. I pledged to hold taxes within the rate of inflation in my first year, and ruled out any tax increase in my second. Maria would not make such a commitment. I was controlling the issues that would dominate this short campaign.

Maria and I participated in San Antonio's first Spanish-language-media debate between mayoral candidates. We debated on KCOR Radio and on KWEX-TV. I made my opening and closing remarks in Spanish but answered questions in English.

On May 13, we appeared before Communities Organized for Public Service. Maria pledged $5 million for job training. I said I would work with them but would not pledge $5 million. This strengthened my standing with most voters because I refused to bow to COPS' well-known pressure tactics.

I continued to work hard in the inner city. I didn't want to be elected just by North Side voters. I blockwalked the South Side again. Councilwoman Helen Dutmer, who represented District 3 in southeast San Antonio, endorsed me.

Forty Hispanic leaders endorsed me in Mi Tierra restaurant, a traditional hangout for Hispanic politicians and liberal political junkies.

I also worked hard on the East Side. Isaac and Katie Jones, the parents of State Representative Karyne Conley, gave a party for me in their home. A number of African-American ministers endorsed me. My good friend Joe Scott, a businessman, ran my campaign on the East Side.

Unlike the first election, the runoff lacked any real controversy. Neither Maria nor I employed negative advertising.

As we neared election day, the total spending by all the candidates had exceeded $1 million, making this the first million-dollar mayoral campaign in San Antonio's history.

Election night, May 25: Tracy and I, some family members and some key supporters sat in our room at the Menger Hotel as the absentee vote came in. Our early start in the runoff paid off when we won 60 percent of the absentee vote. The number of people voting absentee had dropped only 12 percent from the first round of voting — just a smidgen.

This high absentee turnout indicated that the election day vote also would be high. We had worked hard to get our supporters to vote absentee. We knew the election day vote would bring the totals much closer.

Maria did carry the vote on election day, but not by enough to overcome our early lead. When the final results came in, I had 52.65 percent of the total, winning by 6,367 votes. I was pleased to see I had also carried two of the inner-city City Council districts, on the South Side and the East Side. It was an exceptionally large turnout for a runoff election: 120,567 people, compared to the 131,751 who had voted in the first election.

When we were assured the win was solid, Tracy and I went downstairs to a roaring crowd of supporters. With Tracy at my side, I told them they were getting two for the price of one. I said that Tracy and I would both work hard to make our city better. The audience knew it was true and welcomed the prospect.

From the day we announced in September to the May election, nine months had passed. Now we were witnessing the birth of a "new" city. I was full of energy, hope, and determination to make my term of office meaningful.

"Creating Camelot"

Tracy and I slept only three hours the night of my election. My first day as mayor-elect was a Sunday, and at 9 a.m. we were on the South Side at St. Peter's and St. Joseph's Children's Home. Archbishop Patrick Flores was saying Mass to celebrate the 100th anniversary of the foster-care facility. Tracy, a good Catholic, had received a call inviting us.

During the Mass, Archbishop Flores asked Tracy and me and my two sons, Scott and Matthew, to come forward. As we stood before him, he said, "Bless him abundantly with the wisdom and the courage to be able to discern your divine will in what is best for the people of this city." Archbishop Flores' blessing was a powerful message to me and our community to work together. It set the right tone for the start of my term.

Tracy and I shared a late breakfast with State Representative Ciro Rodriguez, Councilwoman Yolanda Vera and other supporters at Mi Tierra. Then we joined my friend Joe Scott and attended services at the Reverend J.J. Rector's Antioch Baptist Church and the Reverend J.S. Smith's New Light Baptist Church on the East Side. I promised the congregations they would have a place at the table of "equity and decision." Later in the day I met with City Manager Alex Briseño and Mayor Cockrell to plan the transition.

During that first week, Tracy and I ran into Henry after a function at the Marriott Rivercenter. Standing outside on the sidewalk waiting for his car, Henry looked at Tracy and said, "Together you can create Camelot." Henry knew I had a powerful political attribute in Tracy, who is vivacious, beautiful and politically astute. I would tell people throughout my term that her job was to make two friends for every enemy I made. She would do even better than that.

I wanted a unique swearing-in ceremony for City Council on Saturday, June 1. Historic La Villita — "the Little Village" — would be our setting, to capture the history and diversity of San Antonio. The public would be invited. City Clerk Norma Rodriguez handled the arrangements expertly.

Our stage was at La Villita's Arneson River Theater, built during the Depression as part of the public works project that gave the city its renowned River Walk. The outdoor theater sits at a point where the San Antonio River makes one of many sharp bends, and a ribbon of water separates the audience and the stage.

On the appointed day, the council and I boarded a decorated barge to head upriver. As we neared the river bend, we saw hundreds of cheering people jammed onto the grassy tiers of seats across from the stage. La Rondalla del Mercado Mariachis band was playing. We disembarked, passed through the crowd shaking hands, and crossed the river over the bridge to the stage.

It must have been Archbishop Flores' earlier blessing that caused the sun to pop out and whisk away the threat of rain as we stood on the stage. The archbishop provided the opening prayer and the children of the Healy Murphy school led the Pledge of Allegiance. The 1991 Citywide Revival Choir sang several gospel songs and then we were sworn in. I made a few remarks, and then the Reverend J.J. Rector closed the ceremonies with a prayer. A public reception followed in Juarez Plaza.

Monday was my first official day at the office. I arrived early, sitting in the front seat of the mayor's limo, rather than in the back. I invited the media into the office and told them they would have open access. I showed them the desk and chair I would use. The desk belonged to former Mayor Maury Maverick, who renovated and revived La Villita in 1935. I brought to the office the chair of former state Senator Red Berry. Berry was a controversial senator during the 1960s who advocated splitting Texas into two parts so the people of South Texas could enact legislation to allow horse racing, a sport to which Berry, an inveterate gambler, was deeply attached. He was a hero to the South Side, and I sit in his chair today as I write this book.

Throughout the week, I met with my team of urban experts, led by Tom Brereton, to fine tune the agenda. We worked from the document developed during the campaign by the "San Antonio Tomorrow" task forces. I met with Mexican Consul General Humberto Hernandez Haddad, Police Chief Bill Gibson, other city department heads, and labor and business leaders. My staff, Shirl Thomas, Amelia Ramirez and Jackie Bolds, helped me get my feet on the ground from the beginning.

I met with each council member to get input. Four of the 10 were new. I wanted to get to know each of the new members personally and to strengthen my ties with the veterans. I needed to make sure that we got off to the right start by creating a team approach to solving the city's problems. Together, we identified issues in which each member could take a leadership position.

After all the meetings, I had to determine what the core of my message would be when I laid out my agenda. Throughout Henry's eight years as mayor, he focused almost all his energies on economic development. It was his clarion call. Only at the end of his term did he begin to change his message — almost imperceptibly. In his last five months, he rushed to the table the library bond issue, which passed. He mentioned his concerns about child care, job training and the arts. But it was too late.

I remembered Henry's advice on the bus trip in 1987, when he expressed his hope that the next mayor would share his vision. But if not, Henry continued, his successor should make clear where he wants the city to go. I was totally committed to Henry's vision of job growth and would work hard to establish San Antonio as an international city to help accomplish this. But I wanted to emphasize a message that transcended economic development.

I wanted a message that would speak to the everyday concerns of the often-forgotten people of the city, the people who walked and drove on the poured concrete and asphalt, who worked in the newly constructed buildings and who lived with their children in our expanding neighborhoods. I wanted at the top of the agenda the *issues of human development*: youth, child care, job training, public safety and economic opportunities for small-business people.

As part of the message of human development, I wanted to convey a corresponding message that our city should grow with grace. I would push hard for economic development, but I wanted it tempered with the need to protect and enhance our environment. I wanted issues such as recycling, open spaces, landscaping, water quality and beautification of our city to come to the forefront.

I also wanted to adopt a policy that would isolate the Homeowner-Taxpayer Association. I knew if I could get the budget in good shape and avoid any increase in the property tax I would diminish HTA's cause.

On the opening day of City Council, I laid out a 15-page agenda to deliver the message I would articulate over the next four years.

In the introduction, I said the voters had installed a "shot clock" for us by approving term limits. If we were to have an impact, we must move fast or give up the ball. That offhand analogy caught people's imagination and became the most enduring quote of my entire term.

I listed 37 specific objectives to accomplish the aims of human development and "growth with grace." I called for a new master plan to address the city's physical development, new job training initiatives, a youth commission, better child care, an education alliance, recycling, scenic corridors, landscaping and sign ordinances, impact fees to encourage growth within Loop 410, and the development of more parks. I also called for holding any tax increases to the rate of inflation. I wanted to settle this issue early, before we began to build the budget.

It's one thing to lay out an agenda and another to accomplish it. I came to office with strong North Side support and weak inner-city support. I needed to build bridges to the inner city to accomplish my agenda. I needed very much to have the support of COPS. I knew their specific agenda coincided with mine. I wanted to be the champion of their agenda.

Henry came to office with strong inner-city support. His bridge to the North Side was the business community. He had to push an agenda of unimpeded economic growth to keep that support.

Henry was strong enough in the inner city that he could afford to offend his base of support there, as he did when he opposed COPS over the Dome. For me to be successful in my agenda, I would have to be strong enough on the North Side to oppose my base of support, the business community, on growth-related issues.

I also knew that I did not have — nor would I ever have — Henry's political strength. I was elected under a two-term limit and could serve only four years, as opposed to Henry's eight. Besides, Henry's destiny lay beyond the office of mayor, so his political power would hold through the end of his term. I had no desire to seek another political office, thus my political power would wane as my time in office neared its end.

To bolster my power, I needed to develop close ties with the city staff and the council. I would devote a huge amount of effort to accomplish these close working relationships.

I wanted people to know I had a plan, an open door to discuss that plan, and a pledge to work hard to see it enacted. This was a major step toward restoring the power in the mayor's office that had been lost during Lila Cockrell's term.

I must tell you that something magical happens when you become mayor. There is an aura about the office that gives you a feeling you can accomplish just about anything. I felt as though I had picked up King Arthur's sword and Sir Lancelot's armor and no one could do me harm.

I also know that power is a potent mistress and must be used sparingly. To establish real authority, I needed to pick a fight on the right side of a controversial issue, and I definitely needed to win. I needed to go about this task quickly because my time was so short due to term limits. I needed an issue.

The one I chose was job training. My agenda included a reorganization of the federal Job Training Partnership Act program in San Antonio. The agenda also called for the creation of a new job training program, an idea being pushed by COPS and the Metro Alliance. It was perfect. It built those bridges I needed to the inner city while addressing the business community's need for more skilled workers.

But it was impossible to proceed with any new job training program without first addressing the existing problems with the JTPA.

The program was a mess. Its large board included people working for agencies that received job training contracts. The average job training stint lasted only four months, not long enough to accomplish much. The two staffs that administered the $20 million program, one from the city and the other employed by the board, were constantly feuding.

I met with Alex Briseño to plan our assault. Our formula called for reducing the board from 30 members to 19, prohibiting conflicts of interest, providing for a single staff and reducing the number of separate training programs. I had to convince, in addition to the City Council, Bexar County and the county judges in the 11 rural counties around San Antonio who are partners with us in the regional program.

I began by asking all members of the existing board to resign. Some did; others resisted. I negotiated the support of the Greater Chamber, then I went after labor. To get the unions on board, I met with Bob Salvatore and Jesse Bielefeld. They were against the change until I assured them of fair representation on the new board. The momentum was building for my side.

I met with each council member to go over their concerns. On June 27, City Council adopted the plan. Bexar County Judge John Longoria gave his support. Bexar County and the rural county judges adopted the change in July.

San Antonio Light columnist Rick Casey wrote that he had not seen power exercised like this since the days of Henry Cisneros. Winning this first battle was absolutely critical. It's like the first touchdown of a football game. It boosts your confidence and gives you momentum. The office of mayor is about winning, and there is no better way to win than to score on the first play.

★★★

Lessons from a New Mayor

■ **In politics as in boxing, a tie goes to the champion.**
A challenger must move aggressively against an incumbent. That means differentiating yourself and throwing hard shots. I would not have won had I not gone after the shortfalls in Lila's record. As much as voters say they don't like negative campaigns, they do respond to the messages and vote accordingly.

■ **A political campaign is like a military campaign.**
To win, you need the best general and the latest intelligence. I could not have won without George Shipley's help. He would call me every night to ask, "Do you think we won the day?" Each day was a separate battle, based partly on the numbers coming from our ongoing polling.

■ **Find your issues and hammer them home.**
Just as in the council race, my team for the mayor's race identified key issues, this time with the help of polling. In the council race, we focused on one. Voters give the mayor's race more
attention, so in the runoff we chose two: jobs and taxes. We
hammered home those issues and convinced voters I was the
best candidate to deliver more jobs and fewer taxes.

■ **Momentum counts in politics as in sports.**
The "Big Mo," as some sportswriters call it, can make you or
break you. I broke first out of the gate with my advertising
during the runoff election against Maria, and that momentum helped carry me to a win. Likewise, my first victory in
fixing the job training mess set me up for further wins as mayor.

■ **Never second-guess voter intentions.**
The mistake I made trying to interpret the voters' intentions
on Applewhite could have cost me the runoff election.

■ **Learn to understand the media.**
Get to know the individual reporters and the editorial boards
of the newspapers. Of the two, the reporters count most. Their
coverage can make or break you on the front page or at the
top of the evening news. Editorial endorsements run inside
the paper. Learn to read the signals. The San Antonio Light
was sending clear signals that the city needed someone to run
against Mayor Cockrell. I was the first challenger to pick up
on those signals, and received excellent coverage for several
months before any other candidate entered the race. I also
eventually received the paper's endorsement.

■ **Once in office, open the doors wide.**
Seek widespread input into your agenda. You don't need to
focus on one or two issues as in the campaign; you need a
bundle from which to govern.

■ **City Council can be a half-circle of friends, or of enemies.**
The best way to form a team is to seek input from every member. I met for hours with each council member. I promised I would never blindside them or leave them out of the decision-making process.

■ **Pick an early fight and win it.**
I picked the battle over the Job Training Partnership Act. It is a risk, but it is one worth taking. If you win, you have established power early.

■ **Creating a good mayor takes time.**
A two-year term on City Council isn't enough time to prepare for the job of mayor. In San Antonio, the mayor is responsible for a city with more than 10,000 employees and a budget in excess of $750 million. Unlike the CEOs of major corporations, a new mayor has never served in a comparable job. A mayoral candidate needs at least four years' experience on council before running. Unless term limits are changed, this will become the *most* experience any potential candidate can ever have.

10

A Long, Hot Summer: Saving Our Youth

On August 27, 1991, I visited and spoke with a group of constituents I had never met before. I spent the day in three of San Antonio's public housing projects — Villa Veramendi Homes, Cassiano Homes, and San Juan Homes — talking with young gang members.

Some of those I encountered gazed back with blank, hollow eyes. It felt like looking into an empty room. Others seemed like normal kids as they played basketball on the worn-out asphalt courts. I invited some to my office to talk more.

Five of them came. It was the first time a mayor had met with gang members at City Hall. As we sat down, I said, "Thanks for coming by. Tell me what I can do to help." One responded, "Hey, man, you don't give a damn about us. You send your tough-guy cops after us."

"I sent the police to break up the gangs," I said. "Being in a gang is only going to get you in trouble."

Another broke in: "You don't know about gangs, living in your big house on the North Side. We need our gangs to help protect each other. The police are not going to bust us up. My gang is *mi familia* (my family)."

He was right, that I lived in the big house and knew little about gangs. "We want to help you get out of the gangs. We want to give you a job, recreation and educational opportunities."

"Man, that's bullshit. All you want to do is send your goons after us."

They left as they had come in, distrustful, angry and frustrated with the establishment. They did not buy into anything I had to say. Some of this was my fault. Earlier in the summer I had declared war on the gangs without understanding much about them. Now I was willing to learn.

The war on the gangs was not something I expected to be doing only a few weeks into my term. But the city was suffering record homicide rates and a sudden explosion of youth violence. Aggravated assaults by youths had increased 122 percent and attempted murders by 100 percent in the first six months of 1991. Kids as young as 12 were killing people. No other civilized country in the world had such an epidemic of kids killing kids and also killing adults. Much of the youth violence was driven by gangs, and San Antonio was seeing an increase in gang indicators, such as drive-by shootings and graffiti.

In June, during my second weekend in office, there had been a rash of six murders. I awoke Monday to the headlines about these murders, and a sickening feeling that things would get worse before they got better. I needed solutions and I needed them quickly.

My immediate problem was what to do with 300,000 kids beginning their summer vacation. With the tremendous jump in youth violence we were faced with a long, hot, dangerous summer. In a deadly irony, we had closed parks and cut back existing youth programs in order to hire more police officers.

I called a news conference to say I was going to light a fire under the bureaucracy to spur activities to help youth. Alex Briseño juggled the budget to find some additional funding. We launched "Operation Cool It" and established 35 sites for Night Owl recreation programs. We extended swimming pool hours and offered part-time city jobs. I called on parents to watch their kids and for the kids to "cool it."

But this was only a Band-Aid. I began to meet with community groups for input on how to deal with escalating youth violence. The early consensus was that the serious violence could only be addressed by focusing on the gangs. Break up the gangs, punish the gang members and violence would stop, I thought.

So I got tough. I told the media we were declaring war on the gangs. The headlines screamed this threat to every gang member across the city. I continued my hard-line verbal assaults, calling the gang members "punks." I said we were coming after them.

We developed a Juvenile Serious Habitual Offender Action Plan to target the "Teen Crime Kingpins." We learned that four to seven percent of juvenile offenders are responsible for 70 percent of the serious crime. We created a special unit within the police department to track gang activity. We made TV commercials showing kids being locked up, with the tag line, "Don't join gangs."

We set up a Juvenile Restitution Program. Juvenile offenders of the least serious misdemeanor crimes were required to "work off" rather than "pay off" their fines. They were usually assigned to clean-up crews at various government and non-profit agencies.

Many of the gang members lived in public housing projects. With 60 such projects in San Antonio, more than 15,000 people live in the 12 largest. The remaining 45 are small, including 23 senior-citizen projects. The largest is Alazan-Apache Courts, with 3,500 residents.

I began working with Apolonio Flores, executive director of the San Antonio Housing Authority, to develop a plan to combat violence in the 12 largest projects. We developed a "Park and Walk" plan to get police officers out of their cars and walking the sidewalks of the projects. We assigned extra patrols to the more dangerous projects.

Flores agreed to institute a drug- and gun-free environment. He announced a plan to evict tenants who had guns in their units or brought alcohol or drugs onto the premises.

It was while checking on the success of these programs in public housing that I had begun to talk to gang members, both current and former. I also talked with professionals, and began to understand the nature of gangs and the differences among the types of gangs. I learned to differentiate between the really bad kids and ones who were simply lost and had joined a gang seeking a family.

With a few exceptions such as the "Mexican Mafia" (created within the Texas and California prison systems), San Antonio really does not have many gangs whose members are hard-core, young-adult criminals. In Chicago, New York and Los Angeles, gangs consist mostly of young adults conducting serious criminal enterprises.

Most of the gangs in San Antonio are not criminal, profit-driven organizations. They are groups of young kids caught up with killing and hurting each other over the most minor infractions — graffiti, turf, hand "flashes" signaling gang initials.

I began to realize the threats I was making to gang members only made matters worse. Instead of targeting my remarks at the hard-core young criminal, I made a scattershot statement that threatened the manhood of every kid who was a member of a gang.

The vast majority of gang members come from dysfunctional families. Many are one-parent families living in the housing projects. Government policies have helped foster childbearing out of wedlock by providing benefits and separate living quarters to teen-age girls who have children. They are youngsters who often cannot take care of themselves, let alone their children.

More than half the recipients of Aid to Families with Dependent Children are mothers who have never married. About 80 percent of the children born to unwed, teen-age dropouts will live in poverty. Many grow up not even knowing who their fathers are. Nationwide, the number of children born to unwed teen-agers rose sharply from about 250,000 in 1980 to 357,000 in 1990.

Some gang members were born to drug-addicted mothers. Many are abused at home. Out of these dysfunctional families come kids with no discipline, no love, and no hope.

The wave of these kids is like a tide rolling up on a beach. There will always be a new set of 14-, 15-, and 16-year-old kids coming at you. The cycle of violence increases with each new wave. We have to stop it or we will continue to suffer at the hands of ever-more-hardened criminal adults.

Local governments don't have a boxful of cures for kids from dysfunctional families. Municipal resources are limited. At best, we can offer programs that will help save the marginal kids who can be offered some hope before they slip into a life of crime. And we can try to protect the good kids from harm.

Out of the meetings I had with superintendents, religious leaders, law enforcement officers and other citizens, I created the "Mayor's Task Force on Juveniles" to present a comprehensive plan by the first of 1992. It was agreed that while we were developing the comprehensive plan we would begin to implement ideas as they were adopted by the group.

One of the early ideas was a youth curfew. Many of us felt that if we could get kids off the streets late at night, we could cut down on the level of violence when it's at its worst. We could save some kids if we could just keep them home during these dangerous hours.

The Curfew

In the early morning hours of July 12, 1991, the police picked up my son Scott, then 14 years old, and three of his friends. He and his friend Ryan had met their girlfriends on the grounds of Colonies North Elementary School. They were not doing anything wrong except for meeting on school property. The police escorted them all home.

The media would not have made much of the incident except for the fact that through the first two months of my term I vociferously advocated a nighttime curfew for youth. The proposed ordinance included parental fines for those parents whose kids were out on the streets after midnight. My son and I did not set a very good example, but we certainly called attention to the issue.

Bob Thompson was the first City Council member to advocate a curfew. He wanted one implemented in his district because it was experiencing the largest outbreak of youth violence.

I liked the idea and asked Bob to help develop an ordinance to apply citywide. He agreed to take the lead. Bob and I also felt that the curfew ordinance should hold parents responsible for keeping their kids home late at night. The curfew would be our first attempt at trying to instill parental responsibility.

Working with Bob, the city staff and members of the mayor's task force, we developed a proposed curfew ordinance and began to hold public hearings. The curfew was designed not to punish the kids who violated it, but their parents. On the first offense, a warning would be given to the youth and parents. On the second, a personal visit would be made by city juvenile case-workers. On the third, the parents and the youth would be fined. We made exceptions for youngsters who worked or were under adult supervision. The success of the plan depended on parental cooperation.

The debate on the curfew raged through the months of June and July. I stepped up my efforts to gain support from the public. At every opportunity, I said that nothing good could happen to kids under 16 who were on the streets between midnight and 6 a.m. They belonged at home.

On the same day my son Scott was picked up, the City Council began debate on the curfew ordinance. I asked Scott if he wanted to come to City Hall and answer reporters' questions. He did. We held a joint news conference while the council met.

Scott answered all the media's questions, adding, "I would like to apologize to my father and mother and to urge all other teen-agers not to be out that late because you can get into really deep trouble." Asked whether he supported the proposed curfew he said, "I think it is a pretty good idea." After the news conference, he stayed to watch the debate.

Council was deeply divided over the merits of the curfew. On July 25, the day of our vote on the ordinance, strong objections had been raised by civil libertarians, a vocal group of students and the head of the police union. Constitutional questions were posed about holding parents accountable for the acts of their children and taking away the rights of young people to be on the streets late at night.

But I think government has the right to set reasonable restrictions on the rights of children. Government forces them to go to school, prohibits them from buying alcohol and cigarettes, and subjects them to the control of their parents. I felt that requiring them to stay off the streets at night did not violate their constitutional rights.

I knew I had six solid votes going in. After an acrimonious debate, Councilman Roger Perez, who was undecided, cast his vote for the curfew and it passed 7 to 4. This was not only San Antonio's first curfew but also the first time a San Antonio ordinance was passed to pin responsibility on parents — not a criminal sanction, but a fine.

At the same council meeting, we also created San Antonio's first Youth Commission. It consisted of 22 students in grades 10 through 12. They were asked to make recommendations on issues dealing with youth. We also asked them to work with the city staff in monitoring the curfew and report back with recommendations in six months.

In the first six months, 481 youths were caught violating the curfew. About half were turned over to our Department of Community Initiatives for help, usually with problems at home. The curfew was turning out to be a warning signal that brought the intervention of social service agencies. The Youth Commission, after studying the results, recommended continuing the curfew.

During its first two years, the curfew showed overwhelmingly positive results. Overall juvenile crime victimization was down by 53 percent. And during curfew hours, the drop hit 77 percent.

Of the 2,984 youths cited for curfew violations, only 3.5 percent were written up more than twice. The Department of Community Initiatives did a home assessment of 883 youths who violated the curfew more than once. They showed what we expected: Only a quarter had a stable home environment, even fewer had two parents at home, and three of every four did not attend school on a regular basis.

These findings highlighted the problem with dysfunctional families. Our Community Initiatives Department increased its child and family counseling services and its crisis intervention program to approximately 700 families. Our Health Department increased services in family planning, in prevention of maternal substance abuse, and in the Women, Infants and Children program.

The threatened fine led to greater parental responsibility. Municipal Court imposed fines in only 12 cases. The curfew gave parents a reason to tell their kids to be home by midnight. The empty streets allowed police to concentrate on serious crimes.

We followed up with a daytime curfew. In December 1993, the City Council passed an ordinance prohibiting school-age children from public areas during school hours without an authorized excuse.

We also passed an anti-graffiti ordinance. Graffiti is how gangs speak to each other and set the perimeters of their territory. Many cities across the nation have given up trying to control graffiti. We were determined to combat it. The ordinance provided sanctions against youths arrested for graffiti violations, requiring them to clean graffiti across the city. The ordinance also held parents responsible.

Today all three ordinances remain in force. The curfews and the anti-graffiti ordinance were effective in waking up a lot of parents — including me — to their responsibilities.

"The COalition"

On January 6, 1992, at 4:30 p.m., Henry Cisneros escorted Hillary Clinton, wife of then-presidential candidate Bill Clinton, into his office of eight years and now mine for the past six months. As we sat down to visit I said, "Thank you for coming by. I met your husband last August. I must tell you that at the time of our visit I did not know he was going to be a candidate for president, much less a serious one."

I had met then-Governor Clinton on August 8, 1991. His staff had called my office to set the appointment. There was talk about his candidacy but he was considered a long shot. When he came by, I was in a council meeting. I excused myself to meet with him.

As I walked into my office, he was sitting alone in the upright wooden armchair I had used during the Constitutional Convention of 1974. The first thing I noticed is that he had a good front porch pushing out the button of his coat. He stood, the porch receded, and we shook hands.

He seemed a little tired and a bit detached. He talked about some national issues, little that I remember because I wasn't tuned in. While we were visiting I wondered why I was wasting my time talking to a governor of Arkansas when I should be patching potholes, picking up stray dogs and fighting crime. After our visit, I asked him to say a few words to the council, which he did, and then left. I never gave the visit a second thought until my meeting with Hillary and Henry.

Henry's involvement in the Clinton campaign alerted me that it was a serious effort. I tuned in when he brought Hillary by. As she sat down, she responded to my remarks about her husband.

"He may not have been a serious candidate five months ago, but he is now. We are going to win," she said simply. "Henry tells me that both of you have been working on youth issues, and that your wife is leading an effort for better child care. Those are issues I am most concerned about."

During the time my committee on juveniles had been meeting, Henry and USAA's General Robert McDermott had been quietly holding parallel meetings with a group of business leaders. I had attended both as we tried to develop a youth values and alternatives report. Henry and McDermott's group had the financial and political muscle to help implement any or all of our recommendations.

I said, "Henry has told me about your work with children. It's too bad that violence had to get out of control before all the rest of us tuned in. Youth violence and crime have moved to the top of my agenda. I believe they will be major issues in the presidential race."

"Youth violence is on the rise because of how we, as a society, have treated our children," she said. "They are growing up in a very violent society without the security of a strong family." She explained that we had to try to make up for their lack of a family. Good prenatal care, nutritional meals, quality child care, more Head Start programs, recreational programs and after-school care are just a few of the necessities. "But most important," she added, "they must know that we care, and you have to find a way to show them that."

Now, after having met them both, I thought that if Bill Clinton did win it would be in large part due to Hillary. She was focused and passionate about children. I was impressed that she talked only about that issue and not about her husband's campaign.

It was unfortunate that early in President Clinton's term Hillary got bogged down in the quagmire of health care reform rather than pursuing children's issues. Her excellent book on child rearing, "It Takes a Village," written in 1996, got her back on track.

One week after Hillary's visit, my task force on juveniles issued its recommendations. The report had three major aspects: It recommended tougher punishment for violent youths and additional facilities to hold them away from society. It addressed parental responsibility by making parents accountable financially for their children's actions. It also called for increased mentoring, and educational and recreational programs.

After Hillary left, the words that stuck in my mind were, "Find a way to show them that you care." I would not let them go unaddressed.

On May 6, as I pulled up to the Claude Black Eastside Service Center, Mary Rose Brown of the Atkins Agency greeted me and escorted me to a side door. I went inside to a small room where people were changing into black T-shirts with the logo of "The CO" on the front. Spurs players Terry Cummings and Antoine Carr, several radio personalities, and members of the Youth Commission were putting on the T-shirts. I slipped one on, too.

We walked out into the assembly hall to a room filled with kids and rock music. Members of the Youth Commission held up black and orange posters with trendy graphics that announced the formation of "The CO" — short for "The COalition." Slick posters with MTV-style graphics urged kids to "Improve your hang time," "Join The CO" and "Kick it."

We had been planning this day for many months. Atkins Advertising went to high schools and middle schools to research what programs young people were looking for, what community leaders they listened to, what language they used and what appealed to them in colors and graphics.

After the research was completed, the city's parks and recreation director, Ron Darner, together with Carol Kelly, now

Nelson Wolff wears a T-shirt with "The CO" logo as he scoots down a water slide at a Sea World event promoting the youth organization. (John Davenport, Express-News)

O'Malley, began organizing an array of recreation and education programs. Ron also worked with outside agencies that served young people to plan thousands of hours of year-round recreation programs, special events, and field trips.

The day we launched "The CO" we had only $1 million in private contributions to augment public funds to bring an exciting and unique program to the youth of San Antonio. "The CO" was a partnership among the city, numerous public- and private-sector youth agencies, local media, the business community, and the Youth Commission.

VIA Metropolitan Transit provided 641,000 free bus rides to the recreational sites. Fiesta Texas and Sea World provided free passes. Businesses gave discount prices to members of "The CO" and the billboard industry gave us signs around town to advertise.

We knew youth would respond to celebrities — from radio and TV personalities to sports and music stars. Popular radio personality Sonny Melendrez became principal spokesman for the program, while the media gave us free time to advertise "The CO" with rock music and radio spots.

Several of the San Antonio Spurs helped, and we brought in former heavyweight champion George Foreman, featherweight champion Jesse James Leija, and then-Houston Oilers quarterback Warren Moon for special events.

"The CO" helped double registration for city-sponsored summer recreational programs with more than 30,000 signing up the first summer and membership doubling the second.

The launching of "The CO" inspired council to take an unprecedented step and rank youth at the top of our funding priorities. Previously, public safety was always ranked first. The result was an increase of more than $10 million in programs reaching youth, bringing our budget to $50 million for youth-related programs.

City Council approved a plan by Alex Briseño to create a Youth Initiatives Office, making us the first city in the nation to create a department to coordinate, plan, and provide oversight to all programs dealing with youth.

The day we launched "The CO" was one of my most exciting as mayor. During succeeding months, I visited with hundreds of kids who wanted love and attention, someone to care about them, someone to give them a sense of direction and, yes, some discipline.

"The CO" is still going strong today with more than 85,000 members.

After-school Care

On July 2, 1991, I met with two men who would refine my thinking about the problems of youth and crime: Ernie Cortes Jr., founder of Communities Organized for Public Service, of course;

and the Reverend David Semrad, a leader of the Metropolitan Congregational Alliance. By 1991, Cortes no longer served as the nominal leader of the local COPS organization. He had moved to Austin to head the Texas Industrial Areas Foundation, a state-wide coalition of activist groups similar to COPS and the Metro Alliance. He still kept a close watch on the organization he founded, and continued to serve as a behind-the-curtains strategist.

Ernie is generally a step ahead of everyone else when it comes to community-based initiatives. "Contrary to what most people believe, it's the hours between 3 p.m. and 6 p.m. when most young kids are vulnerable," he said. "The older kids may get into trouble late at night, but elementary and middle-school kids get in trouble during the afternoon." Mothers and fathers are out working, and there's no supervision for the kids. "I have an idea to help latch-key kids. Reverend Semrad will work with you to make it happen."

After Ernie gave me his idea in July, I supported a pilot program of after-school care. Ron Darner took the lead in setting up three pilot sites. We entered a partnership with COPS and Metro Alliance, the PTA, school administrators and teachers. From 3 p.m. until 6 p.m., we provided recreation and educational programs fueled by snacks for the kids at the three pilot schools.

In the fall of 1991, I went to Beacon Hill Elementary School to see how Ernie's idea was working. Kids were spread out across the front yard of the school. They were sitting on the lawn in small groups eating snacks with teachers and PTA members. Several members of COPS and Metro were on the front porch along with school officials. It was 4 p.m., an hour after school had let out.

The purpose of my visit to Beacon Hill Elementary was to show off the pilot program to the media. I needed to build community support in order to expand the program. I was determined to gain council support to increase the number of sites.

The partnership we formed was a non-bureaucratic venture and very cost effective. PTA members volunteered and teachers worked for less than their usual salary. The schools provided the facilities. The city paid for the snacks and the teachers.

The program not only provided a safe haven for kids but many of them also made better grades in school. The program also gave many parents a meaningful way to help the school.

The COPS and Metro Alliance leaders worked with Ron Darner to select 20 sites for the next year. I worked with them as we successfully lobbied each member of the council to support funding for the 20 sites.

They were all successful, so the next year COPS and Metro challenged me to seek funding for 60 schools. We rose to the challenge and funded the 60 schools in 1993. In 1994, COPS and Metro wanted to see programs in every inner-city elementary and middle school. I accepted that challenge, too, and today we are in 136 schools, which is almost every one in the inner city.

The program is free to the kids. More than 30,000 are now enrolled in the after-school program. The City Council appropriates $2 million a year toward the program.

But the funding is delicate. As a partnership, the program could fall apart at any time. During my last year in office, it was threatened because of internal feuding among the board members of the San Antonio School District.

I wasn't going to let petty politics scuttle the program and hurt the kids. I met with Connie Rocha, president of the school district's board, and board member Gene Garcia on July 8, 1994. Garcia demanded an assessment of each student in the program to see if grades were improving. Otherwise, he threatened to eliminate the program's funds.

My anger exploded. "If you want to endanger thousands of kids by not providing a safe, wholesome environment, then say that and quit giving lame excuses," I said. "We have plenty of schools who want this program. If the board does not support it, we will take it elsewhere." Then I escorted him out of the office.

A little righteous anger can be a good thing. Different interest groups from the business community to the newspaper to COPS and the Metro Alliance came together to support after-school care. Not only did Garcia fail to kill the program, he also lost his re-election bid in 1996.

Meanwhile, the city of San Antonio received three national and state awards for our youth programs. In 1992, the U.S. Conference of Mayors recognized us for the best partnership for vulnerable youth in cities over 100,000 population. We received the Texas Coalition for Juvenile Justice Advocate for Children Award in 1992. In 1994, we received the Texas Attorney General's Criminal Justice Award.

It is nice to be recognized for the youth programs we instituted, but awards only reflect a brief moment in time. Perseverance and tenacity will be required to build on the accomplishments our city achieved. Any letup will unleash an escalation of violence in years to come.

★★★

Lessons on Youth Issues

■ **Prevention works better than apprehension.**
My conversation with Hillary Clinton and my meetings with gang leaders were turning points in my understanding of youth violence. Society must shore up dysfunctional families to save the kids. The COalition and the after-school programs were major initiatives with positive results.

■ **"Talk the talk" when reaching out to young people.**
I don't believe "The CO" would have succeeded so well if we had not used the symbols, jargon, and music of youth.

■ **"Macho" is not a message that works.**
My declaration of war on the gangs was way off base. Threats against at-risk kids, especially males, only isolate them more from society. Threats also give recognition and status to anti-social behavior. On the other hand, many at-risk kids will respond to positive messages and programs.

■ **Parents can be held accountable for their kids.**
The curfew ordinance showed that parents will respond when threatened with sanctions for not preventing their children from violating the law.

■ **Adding police while closing swimming pools does not make for a cool summer.**
Our response to the outbreak of crime during the late 1980s was simply to add more police. Adding police with no new strategy to combat crime is wasted money. Youth crime continued to increase until we developed serious alternative programs.

11

Crime and Punishment

Crouched in right field at Rosedale Park, I was ready for the crack of the bat to send a baseball my way. I was on the "field of dreams" this May night in 1994 because of a love of baseball that had begun in my youth.

Now 53, I was pitching and playing outfield for Jack Lee's Fun Time Black Sox, a hardball team of men 30 years and older in the National Adult Baseball Association. We played on the baseball fields of Kennedy High School, Olmos Park and Rosedale. It was a great stress reliever. But not this night.

The crack I heard was the sound of gunfire behind me. I turned and saw kids on the adjacent soccer field and T-ball field hit the ground. Others were running down the street.

My stress level was anything but low this night. Police Chief Bill Gibson had warned me to take care because of a death threat from a gang. I never made the threat public nor did I think much about it until I heard the gunshots.

After a short pause, we continued the game as if nothing had happened. As the inning ended, I saw three older youths by the right field fence motioning for me to come over. My first reaction was, "They are here to do me in." But then I thought if I did not go over I would be showing fear and that would be a bad message. I went over and they asked me for my autograph. I was ashamed of my first thought.

The police arrived on the scene quickly. It turned out that the shooting was unrelated to me or to any of the men playing baseball. But I realized with certainty that I was right two years earlier when I first took a stand on trying to stop the flow of guns in our city.

Guns seemed to be everywhere. On New Year's Eve and the Fourth of July, you could hear gunshots resounding throughout the city. A young girl had been killed when one of these stray bullets came to rest, and others had been injured. The city had to start a campaign to warn residents about the dangers of firing pistols and rifles into the air.

More worrisome was the use of firearms in crime. In 1990 the city experienced what was then a record number of homicides, 218. The first six months of 1991 had been no better, showing an upward trend at a rate of 10 homicides more than the previous year. Guns were used in most of the murders.

Weapons were falling into the hands of ever-younger kids. Drive-by shootings were on the increase. We had to install metal detectors in some of our government buildings. Young people could buy firearms at flea markets and gun shows, and from thousands of adults licensed to sell guns out of their homes. Kids were carrying assault weapons, sawed-off shotguns and a dizzying array of handguns.

I wasn't interested in taking guns away from lawfully armed citizens. In fact, I keep a shotgun under my bed. But I knew that anything I said about restricting access to guns — even to help save our kids — would immediately draw fire from the National Rifle Association. Even on the local level, the NRA can retaliate with a vengeance. But after some thought, I decided to do the right thing.

I first spoke out on the subject at a news conference on February 18, 1992. I called on parents to search their kids' rooms for hidden guns. No questions would be asked of parents who turned in guns. The police department set up a special phone line for parents to call to arrange to turn in the weapons at one of the police substations.

My office was soon flooded with angry calls. The radio talk shows misrepresented my views, saying I wanted all citizens to turn in their guns. They fanned the flames of the gun advocates. But I did not back away from the "turn in your guns" program. Instead, I advocated it more strongly. More than 20 guns were turned in during the first 12 days. It wasn't a large number, but it was a symbolic start.

On December 16, 1993, the City Council passed a weapons ordinance with a fine of between $100 and $500 for violations. It prohibits any person from discharging a firearm within the city limits or carrying a firearm on public property. Youngsters 17 or younger are prohibited from carrying a firearm on a public right-of-way. The ordinance also forbids an adult from allowing a person under 17 to have unsupervised access to a firearm. The police are granted the right to seize weapons from violators.

Undercover work by the police found that many of the kids were getting their guns at the many flea markets around the city. We stationed undercover agents at the markets to identify purchasers. When the youth left the private premises, a policeman would arrest him when he got into his car.

The gun shows had become something like a free-fire zone. Anybody could sell a gun to anyone in a gun show. You did not need a license. They were self-policed by the operators, so weapons of all sorts purportedly could be purchased at some of the shows. This began during the Reagan administration, when an agreement was reached to prevent the Bureau of Alcohol, Tobacco and Firearms from attending and monitoring gun shows. The shows became a ready source of guns for youthful criminals, as well as more dangerous individuals. David Koresh, leader of the Branch Davidian compound outside Waco, and his "Mighty Men" disciples obtained many of the weapons used in the fatal firefight with ATF agents at shows in other parts of the state and nation.

In San Antonio, police undercover work proved how dangerous the shows could be. In February 1994, an undercover officer caught two former gang members buying assault weapons at one of the gun shows in the convention center. On other occasions, we caught older gang members distributing guns to younger kids outside the gun shows.

What upset me most about the gun shows here was that the city of San Antonio was providing space for them at our convention center. The city was a party to allowing easy access to guns. During the 1980s, there had been one or two shows a year. By the early 1990s, there was a gun show every month.

Working with Councilwoman Lynda Billa Burke, I sought support from the City Council to stop the city from hosting the gun shows on city property. This action brought out officials of the NRA. They appeared at City Hall saying we would be violating the constitutional rights of the gun show operators by denying them a place to hold their shows.

Nevertheless, after weeks of debate, council on April 14, 1994, banned gun shows on city property. One of the representatives of the NRA said the ordinance was probably more restrictive than any enacted in other states to regulate gun shows. The NRA ran ads soliciting support to file a lawsuit against the city, and the gun show operators also threatened legal action. They never filed the suit.

Guns will continue to be a divisive issue in our country. The NRA has drawn a line in the dirt that prohibits any rational discussion of the issue. While the majority of people support reasonable restrictions on the transfer of guns, the gun lobby showers funds in huge amounts to members of Congress to stop legislation.

The easy availability of guns has contributed to the level of violence. Let every law-abiding citizen have access to a hunting gun, but let us stop the transfer of guns to those who will do us harm.

Criminal Neglect

On February 16, 1992, six members of a gang burst into the home of 14-year-old Blanca Garcia, while she celebrated her birthday with friends, and began firing wildly. Blanca was killed. It was little comfort to the family to discover that the gang members actually were looking for the home of a rival gang member and had come to the wrong address. The family was outraged even more when judges reduced the bond from the amounts recommended by the grand jury on four of the gang members charged with the murder.

San Antonians were sick to death of crime. Criminal activity had been on a steady rise since 1978, and the increase really began to spike in the late 1980s. In response, we had added 200 police officers, increasing the force from 1,406 to 1,606 during my four years as a councilman.

But increasing the number of police officers wouldn't solve the problem if lenient judges and overcrowded prison officials kept putting violent offenders back on the street. Blanca Garcia's case was just one in which this had occurred.

Another was the case of Raul Meza. From his pictures in the newspaper, the 32-year-old Meza looked like a clean-cut young man who would not harm anybody. But Meza's looks were deceiving. Meza had been released from prison after serving 11 years of a 30-year sentence. He had raped and strangled an 8-year-old girl in Austin in January 1982.

Why then, had Meza arrived in San Antonio in July 1993, almost two decades before the presumed end of his sentence? Because he had been released under the "mandatory release" rules of the Texas Department of Corrections, and had returned to his mother's home on the East Side.

These rules combined the actual time he served with make-believe time awarded through "good behavior" points. Meza had received good-behavior points even though he had stabbed a person while he was in prison. The truth was that the state's overcrowded prisons were forced to release people out the back door because of the overwhelming numbers coming in the front doors.

While public pressure eventually forced Meza out of San Antonio, these lenient judges and the state's irresponsible release of violent prisoners were incredibly frustrating to most of us working in public service at the local level.

Out of this frustration, I called a news conference in August 1992 to attack a particular local judge for reducing the bonds of violent criminals. I said that too often the criminal justice system favored the criminal. I called for the defeat of local judges who were too lenient.

The San Antonio Bar Association immediately jumped down my throat. They reprimanded me for criticizing judges. Others in the judicial system quickly piled on in attacking me for my remarks.

Shoot-from-the-hip approaches wouldn't work to fight crime, I realized. While we could continue to build on local initiatives, such as the weapons ordinances, we needed to get active at the federal and state levels. There had to be a coordinated attack against crime, and I was going to see what I could do to make that happen.

MUSCLE and the State

My first steps in that direction took place shortly after my election as mayor. At the same time I was campaigning to become mayor, Bruce Todd was running for the same post in Austin, the state capital located 85 miles north on Interstate 35. Two months after our dual victories, Tracy and I invited Bruce to dinner at Aldo's restaurant on Fredericksburg Road in San Antonio.

Bruce is tall and full bodied, with black hair. He has an easygoing manner in his dark business suit, and is personable the way most politicians are. He is a CPA by profession.

Bruce and I took a quick liking to each other and became good friends. Over the years, we worked on several projects together. But on the night of our dinner, the conversation centered on only one major issue, crime.

"Unless the next session of the Legislature addresses the rising crime rate, we will never get crime under control. Let's team up, work with the governor, and lobby the Legislature for anti-crime legislation."

"Great," I said. "I still have a lot of friends in Austin since the days I served in the House and Senate." We went on to talk about what legislation was needed and how we could share resources and information.

Dallas Mayor Steve Bartlett also had some ideas about lobbying the Texas Legislature. The Dallas Crime Commission, an independent non-profit organization, had been advocating tougher legislation to fight crime. Bartlett, a former congressman, saw the need for joint efforts by the mayors of large Texas cities. I told him of the work that Bruce Todd and I were planning to do.

Out of our joint concerns evolved Mayors United on Safety, Crime and Law Enforcement (MUSCLE). The mayors of the state's eight largest cities — Houston, Dallas, San Antonio, Arlington, Austin, Fort Worth, Corpus Christi and El Paso — made up MUSCLE. While only 35 percent of the people of Texas lived in our cities, we had 60 percent of the state's crimes. Each mayor won council support for funding MUSCLE based on the size of each city. The money was used to hire staff and fund operations.

Our first meeting had been held December 16, 1991, in Dallas. We began work on our proposed legislative package. We agreed that for any item to be included in the package it would have to have unanimous approval. We sought input from district attorneys and police chiefs in our cities. We were free to lobby individually for other anti-crime issues. Over the next 11 months, we put together a 12-point program to control crime.

On November 13, 1992, two months before the Legislature went into session and three months after my ill-fated public attack on lenient local judges, we presented our plan to Governor Ann Richards. Our top priority was the building of additional prison cells and the development of a priority system that would hold violent offenders in prison longer.

During the 1993 legislative session, nine of our 12 proposals passed. Legislation passed allowing prior bad acts of the defendant to be admitted in the punishment stage of trials. We also increased penalties for guns discharged in populated areas, and revised the family code to allow sharing of information on juveniles among police, courts and other agencies.

After our success in the 1993 Legislature, we started work immediately preparing for the next session, which would open in January 1995. We did even better in 1995, as the Legislature passed 11 of the 12 bills we supported. They included parental accountability, prohibition against possession of handguns by juveniles and several prevention programs.

While working with MUSCLE, I also supported other issues not on the mutual agenda. State Representative Bill Siebert and

State Senator Jeff Wentworth introduced a bill to clarify that judges had a right to set higher bails if they thought the accused was a threat to the general public.

The judges I had criticized said the Constitution prohibited them from taking into consideration the safety of the general public when setting a bond. They were wrong, because the law Siebert and Wentworth sponsored has held up under constitutional challenge.

Governor Ann Richards was super in "working" many of the anti-crime bills. She was a leader in advocating the additional prison beds Texas desperately needed. I supported her by campaigning for the passage of a bond issue that provided funding for the building of 34,003 prison beds, a bond issue approved by voters.

MUSCLE did not take a position on the new penal code, although I supported it. It was controversial because it lowered the penalties for non-violent crime. It set up a system of state jails to hold what became fourth-degree felonies. But the bill also included a major provision addressing violent offenders. Every convicted serious felony offender sentenced to a life term would have to serve 30 years before being eligible for parole. "Good time" provisions had pushed the number of years served much lower under existing law. This provision would have a major impact on reducing violent crime in Texas.

During the legislative sessions I developed a close working relationship with Alan Polunsky, a San Antonio lawyer and a member of the Texas Board of Criminal Justice. Alan was instrumental in changing the Department of Corrections rules regarding the release of prisoners. The change made it harder for prisoners convicted of violent crimes to be released.

More than 1,500 prisoners are members of adult prison gangs. Many of these gangs' activities spill out onto the streets of Texas cities, directed by state prisoners from their cells and carried out by released inmates. Our police chief, Bill Gibson, met with state prison Director James Collins to set up a flow of information about the gangs and the release of gang members from San Antonio. This exchange kept us out in front of actions planned by prison gang members and their outside associates.

MUSCLE continues in operation today in the 1997 session of the Legislature. The organization has been successful because it concentrated on one issue, crime. The organization also has served as an excellent clearinghouse, allowing good ideas that have succeeded in one city to be implemented in others.

The Crime Prevention Commission

I first met Lyle Larson when he was a teen-ager campaigning for his father in San Angelo, Texas, in 1978. His father and I were both candidates for Congress in the 21st Congressional District. We both lost — his father in the Republican primary, and I as the Democratic nominee in the general election. I would not meet up with Lyle again until 13 years later, the year he was elected to council and I was elected mayor.

Lyle quickly became a local political star and a darling of the media. He had developed a good working relationship with key members of the police department. As a freshman councilman, he fit the bill for a very important role I wanted him to play.

As I met with my colleagues in MUSCLE, we shared information on how to get citizens involved in crime fighting. Everyone agreed it takes a joint effort of police and citizens to make our streets safe.

Each city had a different way of doing it. Some cities had task forces on crime that came and went. Others had non-profit organizations, such as the Dallas Crime Commission, with no connection to city government. I wanted something more than what I had heard about.

I felt San Antonio needed to develop a crime commission that directly reported to the City Council. I wanted it to include council members, police officers and citizens. If good people were going to serve, they must know that action would be taken on their recommendations. With key players at the table, they would know the commission would be taken seriously. When an issue dealing with crime came to council, I wanted everybody on board.

On November 20, 1992, just a week after MUSCLE presented its legislative program to Governor Richards, the City Council passed an ordinance creating the Greater San Antonio Crime Prevention Commission. We became the first city in the nation to establish such a commission through legislation.

I appointed the commission's 29 members and designated Lyle Larson chairman. I felt Lyle had the ability to pull divergent forces together. Captain Al Philippus, who would become police chief in 1995, led the staff.

We now were organized to fight the crime problem at both the state and local level.

We had also begun other initiatives. Councilman Bill Thornton took the lead in early 1992 to develop a police staffing plan that would increase the number of police officers by putting civilians in some clerical positions.

We created a downtown foot and bike patrol, and the Police Athletic League to work with kids. We began foot patrols in housing projects. We intensified efforts to teach children about the dangers of drug use through the DARE program, and a rock'n'roll band of uniformed police officers kids loved. The Crime Prevention Unit expanded its outreach to more than 300 homeowner associations.

The city had also formed a close working relationship with the county. Bexar County Judge Cyndi Taylor Krier and I worked together on many crime-related issues, along with District Attorney Steve Hilbig and Sheriff Ralph Lopez. Krier was a leader in building additional local jail beds, and County Commissioner Bobby Tejeda was key in building additional juvenile detention facilities.

As a result of these initiatives, in 1992 we experienced our first overall decline in crime since 1978 — 7.1 percent fewer crimes than the previous year's totals. Rape, robbery, aggravated assault, burglary, and larceny all went down. Unfortunately, murders increased in 1992, hitting a high of 219. Although we had a reduction in overall violent crime, the numbers were still too high.

Breaking Records

I called Police Chief Bill Gibson to my office in late May 1993. The news from the streets was still bad. We were moving toward yet another record year for murders!

I said, "Chief, we have got to do something dramatically different to control violent crime. I know the Police Department has
a wide range of responsibilities. But I must tell you, right this
moment I don't give a damn about anything other than controlling violent crime. People are scared, and we have got to do something about it! If we don't act now, 1993 will be another record-
breaking murder year. I want you to concentrate your forces and
go after the really bad guys."

After listening to my ranting, he said calmly, "I will come up
with a plan of attack."

On June 4, 1993, Councilman Larson, Chief Gibson and I
announced at a press conference the formation of a 102-member
violent crimes task force backed by a 141-member investigative
task force. Captain Gilbert Sandoval headed up the task force. Its
officers would concentrate on high crime areas of the city and
work during the hours when most crime was committed.

It began to have an effect. Arrests for violent crimes increased
during the last six months of 1993, while the murder rate began
to slow. Police recorded 840 felony arrests with the seizure of 295
weapons and 5,000 rounds of ammunition.

I believe that the formation of the violent crime task force was
the most important step we took in controlling violent crime. Our
timing was good because the state had begun to add more prison
beds and had set a priority on holding violent criminals. The guys
we were arresting were going to do some serious time.

Overall crime went down in 1993 for the second year in a row.
It dropped by 10.5 percent compared to 1992. In September 1994,
my usual critic, Roddy Stinson, said something complimentary
in his column in the Express-News: "Attention, everyone, getting
tough works." He wrote that the turning point came when I said
we were going to "stop the madness" and create a violent crimes
task force.

After conducting public hearings in early 1993, the Crime Prevention Commission swung into action, developing the daytime
curfew ordinance, the anti-graffiti ordinance and the weapons
ordinance I wrote about in previous sections. They all made an
impact on youth crime.

The commission recommended a Cellular On Patrol program, in which civilians were issued cellular phones programmed with a direct line to the police department. They patrolled their neighborhoods as volunteers, prepared to call in suspicious activity. We started the first program on the East Side, in the area represented by Councilwoman Ruth Jones McClendon. Ruth and I handed out certificates to the first graduating class of 50 adult volunteers on October 30, 1993. A year later we had 400 people on patrol with the phones.

The commission recommended a Civilian Police Academy to teach citizens how to work with the police department in crime prevention. The first class of 50 citizens graduated on March 3, 1994.

In May 1994 the commission supported the public safety portion of a bond package we submitted to the voters. The bonds provided $8.1 million to be matched with $9 million in other funds to build a police technology center. The center is home to the hostage-negotiation team, the gang unit, the bomb squad, and special operations of the SWAT team, all buttressed by a state-of-the-art fingerprint identification system and communications equipment.

We brought our police department up to a historic high of 1,812 officers in the 1994-95 budget year. In May 1995, council and the police union agreed to a new contract that corrected many of the excesses of the controversial pact Harold Flammia had won in 1988. The new agreement reduced the city's liability under the union medical plan, reduced some of the overtime pay excesses, and continued placing some civilians in clerical jobs. It also put civilians alongside police officers on the disciplinary review board for the first time.

The Crime Prevention Commission supported a plan to control domestic violence developed by City Manager Alex Briseño. We created a domestic violence unit within the police department.

The commission recommended extending parental responsibility to all Class C misdemeanor violations by children. On February 1, 1995, the City Council passed an ordinance subjecting parents to fines, community service or parenting classes at the judge's discretion if one of their children committed any class C misdemeanor. Our success with the daytime and nighttime curfew provided the basis for enlarging the scope of parental responsibility.

The Crime Prevention Commission continues its work today.

The Feds

As I pulled out my chair to join President George Bush and eight other guests at his table, he said, "Hey, fellas. Let's not talk serious business tonight. Keep it light." As I sat down, I slipped the file card with notes for my conversation back into my pocket. Crime, the Weed and Seed program and drug rehabilitation centers were hardly the topics that met the president's criteria for conversation that night.

The occasion was a state dinner on the stage of the Majestic Theater on February 27, 1992. President Bush and Secretary of State James Baker were hosts to the presidents of Mexico, Colombia, Peru, Ecuador, and Bolivia, and the foreign minister of Venezuela, for an international conference. While a number of topics would be discussed at the conference, drug trafficking was the major one.

When Tracy and I greeted President Bush and his wife, Barbara, at Kelly Air Force Base, I handed him a white paper on San Antonio's perspective on the drug problem. The paper was developed over the previous month by a broad-based group of law enforcement officials and representatives of social service agencies.

The essence of the paper was that the fight against drugs should be fought by dividing resources evenly between law enforcement and prevention and treatment. The current ratio was 70 percent law enforcement to 30 percent prevention and treatment.

We picked the federal program called Weed and Seed to implement and fund in San Antonio. Its purpose is to "weed" the bad guys out of a selected geographic area of a city and then "seed" the area with good programs.

On the night of the dinner, I hoped to press home the points in our paper. I said, "Mr. President, I believe the Weed and Seed program your administration started is the right road to controlling crime and drugs."

"I received your paper and referred it to our people. You will get a response." Then he turned his head to Peruvian President Alberto Fujimori, who sat between us, and started another conversation.

I tried a couple of other times to engage the president in a conversation about serious urban problems. I was surprised he never once asked me about an urban issue.

If I could not carry on a conversation with President Bush, I thought I might as well try another president. President Fujimori of Peru was elected in 1990 when he upset the candidate of the Spanish elite who had ruled the country since the Spanish conquest. He was of Japanese descent. I asked him, "Are we really going to stop the flow of drugs by burning fields of marijuana, coca plants, and poppy seeds?"

He answered, "No. In my country the farmers will always grow coca instead of coffee because coca can be harvested four times a year instead of once for coffee. It is a cash crop. Our people have chewed the coca leaf for centuries. But if you pay the farmer the difference between the two crops, he will plant mostly coffee."

Coca leaves can be legally used in Peru for teas and chewing. It is illegal in Peru to sell the leaf to be chemically transformed into cocaine. But it is sold illegally by many farmers to drug lords from Colombia who do transform it into cocaine. The major port of entry into the United States is now overland from Mexico instead of through Miami by boat.

I said, "As long as there is demand, will drugs always make it into our country?"

He responded, "As long as the price is high enough to cover the risk, it will always make it into your country. It is the demand of Americans that drives the trade. Stop the demand and there would be no need for us to meet."

President Fujimori reassured me that our strategy in San Antonio of emphasizing drug prevention was correct. I was pleased that the white paper on drugs that we presented to President Bush was on target.

Curiously, Barbara Bush did seem very interested in drugs and youth problems. She and Tracy visited a local Boys and Girls Club and met with young people. They also went to a Center for Health Care Services to meet with drug addicts who were being treated in a methadone program that substituted a legal drug for their addiction to street drugs. Tracy said Barbara was very knowledgeable and interested in these programs. In fact she personally gave funds to Avance, a program that teaches better parenting.

Despite my disappointment in not engaging President Bush on my index-card of issues, I was elated two months later when we received a $1.5 million grant for the Weed and Seed program.

We designated an area on the East Side to "weed and seed." We began an expanded outreach program from the Barbara Jordan Center, the city's East Side "multi-service center." A local drug prevention organization — San Antonio Fighting Back — led the way in reaching out to young people. The COalition provided recreational programs.

We built a new baseball field at the Springview housing project, started a kids' garden and encouraged parents to get involved. We cleaned the area of debris and graffiti and tore down crack houses using city codes as a tool.

Our balanced attack worked. An equal effort between law enforcement and prevention, as we outlined in the white paper presented to President Bush, was the key to success. From September 1992 until May 1994, police service calls declined by 13 percent *each month*. We used the lessons learned in other sections of the city.

As a member of the U.S. Conference of Mayors, I supported raising the issue of crime to the top of the agenda after the Gulf War ended. While the people were concerned about the economy, they were equally concerned about the high level of crime. The Conference of Mayors pounded the presidential candidates hard to address crime issues. President Bush didn't seem to get the message. Bill Clinton did.

On August 27, 1992, two months before the election, Clinton spoke at the Hyatt Regency Hotel here. He talked about his plan to create jobs and fight crime. He was fully tuned to domestic issues.

At the close of his speech, I gave him a photo book of Texas and said, "Remember our friend Henry Cisneros when you win. He knows the problems we face in major cities. I hope you carry Texas as you carry this book of Texas around."

After Clinton's election in November, he brought a new perspective to the federal fight against crime. He was willing to take on the NRA and support reasonable gun control. He understood the need for crime prevention programs. He was for capital punishment and for long sentences for hardened criminals.

President Clinton also supported the hiring of more police officers. On December 20, 1993, I participated in a telephone conference call with President Clinton and several other mayors as the president awarded grants for additional police. The grants were given to cities that had implemented effective community policing programs. San Antonio received funds for 40 officers. His election moved crime to the top of the congressional agenda.

President Clinton appointed a strong attorney general. Janet Reno had been a tough prosecutor in Florida. I first met her when she came to San Antonio on June 7, 1994, to visit our Weed and Seed program.

As I walked alongside this gangly, soft-spoken lady, I found out just how sharp and tough she was. It was a hot day as we walked through a garden the kids had cultivated across from the Eastside Multiservice Center. Hecklers were following us with placards branding her a killer for her decision to forcibly enter the Branch Davidians' compound on April 19, 1993, in an action that resulted in the deaths of almost all the occupants. As they hollered, she calmly kept talking to me as we walked along.

As she looked at kids trading police cards rather than baseball cards she said, "This is great that you are building a close relationship between the kids and the police. Too often the kids think the police are the enemy. Good idea on making the cards.

"We need all the help we can get in passing the crime bill," she added. Congress was engaged in a major debate over a $30.2 billion crime bill that included $6.9 billion for crime prevention programs. Senator Phil Gramm of Texas and other congressmen were calling crime prevention a boondoggle. They apparently

U.S. Attorney General Janet Reno (left to right) discusses the Weed and Seed anti-drug program with City Councilwoman Ruth Jones McClendon, Police Chief Bill Gibson, and Mayor Nelson Wolff. (Wolff collection)

never bothered to see what was happening in poor and crime-plagued areas of their towns.

The NRA was trying to kill the bill because it had a ban on 19 different assault weapons. "I will do my part in supporting the bill," I told Reno. "Our council passed a resolution in support of the bill that we are sending to the Texas delegation."

I thanked her for her leadership in speaking out against the violent messages that infested the media and for supporting joint programs between federal and local law enforcement personnel.

When we parted she said, "Looks like your city has really got it together. We will continue to do our part. Keep up your work."

In late August, the bill passed both houses of Congress. The vote was close in the House because of the NRA opposition. President Clinton gave credit to the bipartisan effort of mayors. It was a major victory in the fight against crime. Many recognized it as the smartest, toughest crime bill in America's history.

In January 1997, the Treasury Department reported that the number of gun dealer licenses had fallen more than 57 percent since the passage of the bill, which required higher fees, fingerprinting and face-to-face interviews with federal inspectors.

A New Chief

I had called Chief Bill Gibson on the carpet in 1993 because of our skyrocketing murder rate. But the truth was that he had taken a department in turmoil in the mid-1980s and restored its sense of pride and integrity. He was a man who had risen from the ranks and had the support of the rank-and-file. His eight-year tenure in the top job coincided with the eight years that I served on the council and as mayor.

Prior to Gibson's promotion, the police department had been rocked by a major scandal in 1985 involving a vigilante patrolman, Stephen Smith, who had killed at least three criminal suspects and wounded others. The story had been the subject of a made-for-TV movie. Gibson took over the troubled department during the highest crime period in the city's history. His leadership was instrumental in bringing crime down.

When Gibson retired, City Manager Alex Briseño appointed Deputy Police Chief Al Philippus to replace him. Philippus had been the chief architect of community policing. He was the key liaison for MUSCLE, the Greater San Antonio Crime Prevention Commission, the police department, the City Council and citizens. He was the perfect choice to lead the police department into the 21st century.

The combined force of the federal, state and city governments, along with local citizens, had a dramatic effect on crime in San Antonio. Beginning in 1992, overall crime dropped each year: 7 percent in 1992, 10 percent in 1993, another 10 percent in 1994, and 9 percent in 1995. Violent crime took the biggest drop in the four years. It declined an unbelievable 45 percent. Murders fell from a high of 229 in 1993 to 140 in 1995. Other cities that took similar measures saw reductions in crime, but most were nowhere near the decreases achieved in San Antonio.

But experts warn of trouble down the road. The number of teen-agers is expected to grow by 20 percent in the next decade. Young males are the most likely to commit crimes. It is going to take an intense effort of positive programs for youth, community policing, strong law enforcement, instilling community values, and a strong working relationship with the state and federal governments to keep crime rates falling.

★★★

Lessons on Crime and Punishment

■ **A posse can fight crime better than one man.**
By working with the mayors of the state's eight largest cities
we were able to forge a strong alliance to influence anti-crime
legislation. MUSCLE became a potent force in the Legislature,
passing 20 of 24 proposed bills.

■ **More people die from handgun violence than in war.**
President Clinton understood the danger we were facing in
urban areas. The passage of the Brady handgun control bill,
the banning of 19 assault weapons, and the $30.2 billion crime
bill — all under Clinton — had a major impact in the fight
against crime. Clinton also recognized the importance of community policing.

■ **A prison cell waiting makes the best deterrent.**
The best deterrent against adult criminals is a police force that
will apprehend, a jury that will quickly convict, and a prison
bed waiting. The state's decision to add prison beds and to
put a priority on holding violent prisoners provided a key
missing link that was needed to control violent crime.

■ **As the bumper-sticker says, each city must "Support the
Blue."**
It is impossible to control crime without a strong bond
between the police and citizens. That bond has broken in
major cities such as Los Angeles and New Orleans. The Greater
San Antonio Crime Prevention Commission provided the
essential citizen link to our police department.

■ **Prevention and enforcement should be equal partners.**
The implementation of the Weed and Seed program on the
East Side of San Antonio showed that a balanced approach
between drug prevention and law enforcement is effective.

Stopping demand for drugs is as important as apprehending drug sellers.

■ **Kids keep coming at us like waves on a beach.**
Any letup in our efforts and crime will increase again. The youth population will grow in the future, and unless prevention programs continue to grow, then youth crime will soar higher than we experienced even in the late 1980s and 1990s.

12

A Question of Values

In a curtained-off area of the Alamodome, Tracy and I stood waiting to meet Paul McCartney. We had both grown up listening to the music of the Beatles. It was liberating, exciting and part of a youthful rebellion. I can remember my grandmother telling me how evil their music was. "It's going to make you kids wild and unruly," she said.

Now it was 30 years later, May 1993, and after a few minutes McCartney came through the curtain smiling and sticking out a hand to shake. I said, "Thanks for coming to San Antonio. I really appreciate your accepting my invitation." San Antonio was not originally on Paul's concert tour. I had written and called, asking his agents to add us to the itinerary.

"Glad to be here," McCartney said. "I hear you're in the health food business."

Tracy replied, "Yes. We're selling your wife's book in our Sun Harvest stores." Paul and Linda were both vegetarians, and Linda's book, "Home Cooking," included recipes for vegetarian dishes.

We gave Paul a cowboy hat that he put on, and had a picture taken of us together. He was extremely charming, talkative and

Music legend Paul McCartney wears a Western hat given to him by
Nelson and Tracy Wolff prior to his performance at the Alamodome in
May 1993. (Wolff collection)

younger looking than his 50 years. His people had to pull him
away to get ready for his concert.

On a similar night, on October 3, 1992, I had visited heavy-
metal rocker Ozzy Osbourne. At one time a heavy drug user,
Osbourne was notorious locally for an incident a decade earlier
when he was arrested for urinating against the Cenotaph in front
of the Alamo.

As I walked into his dressing room, Osbourne stood, short,
emaciated, aged beyond his years, his hand shaking as he held a
cigarette to his lips. He smiled and extended his other quivering
hand. Years of drug use had obviously taken a toll. "How did you
like the concert?" he asked.

"A little loud, but I liked your beat."

On October 1, 1994, I also met Steve Tyler, lead singer for the
rock group Aerosmith. He was in town for the ground-breaking
of the Hard Rock Cafe. Like Ozzy Osbourne, Tyler had once been
a drug user.

Steve was a nice-looking man in his 40s, but very thin with hollow cheeks. As we rode in a boat down the river to the ground-breaking, I said, "I bet it was exciting during the Seventies, when your band had a string of hits."

"I don't remember a thing about the Seventies," he replied.

From the Beatles to Ozzy Osbourne and Aerosmith was a distance measured in cultural decline. We went from experimental but life-affirming rock stars to Satan-worshipping, heavy metal, drug-user stars. By the 1980s, San Antonio had a reputation as a prime venue for the heaviest of "heavy metal" concerts, and ugly incidents were often reported at these events in our convention center.

By the 1990s, "gangsta" rap and heavy metal had added guns, violence and misogyny alongside the drugs. One gangsta rap song included the lyrics: "They wonder why they label me insane, because I loaded the clip and took the nine to the copper's brain." If my Grandma were alive and heard today's rock and rap, she would rank the Beatles with gospel singers.

Rock had become Big Business that earned its money from culturally destructive messages. It was not just rock music, but many other entertainment messages that were acclimating young people to the acceptability of violence.

By January 1994, I had decided to take on the entertainment industry for promoting this climate. I wanted to use the mayor's office as a bully pulpit. I knew it might seem a futile battle, one city's mayor against a worldwide, multibillion-dollar industry. But I believe a mayor should be a voice in support of a community's values. Other voices in other quarters were also speaking out. Perhaps in concert we would be heard.

I didn't want to jump on the "religious right" bandwagon, but I knew they were articulating some moral issues that society could support. While I did not agree with all their views, I felt they were on the right track in their anger at the entertainment industry. They voiced other concerns that I also thought were appropriate — the need for anti-pornography laws and opposition to the spread of casino gambling.

When a politician begins to talk values and morals, he preaches on a slippery slope. When you advocate protecting youth from harmful messages and actions, you bump smack into free speech and individual liberties. I knew my message would not be universally well received, but I decided to go ahead anyway.

I fired the first salvo in my address at the opening session of City Council in 1994. I said that as citizens we should take a stand against the entertainment industry that was selling depictions of violence, drug use and casual sex to our youth.

"It is beyond question that the messages of violence that they continually purvey play a major role in desensitizing our youth to violence as a casual and routine fact of life," I said.

I followed up with rallies on the steps of City Hall, attended by religious leaders who spoke out against gratuitous violence in films aimed at young people. The San Antonio Community of Churches, led by the Reverend Dr. Kenneth R. Thompson, took the lead in rallying support for community values.

I urged citizens to boycott retail stores that sold cassettes, CD's and video games that used violence and the denigration of women as amusement. I said we should refuse to buy products advertised on television programs that contained violence and casual sex during prime time.

I joined a coalition of churches that opposed the showing of "NYPD Blue" during prime time. Many ABC affiliates declined to show the drama until its content was toned down as a result of the complaints.

I wrote U.S. Senator Ernest Hollings supporting his legislation to curb the airing of violent shows during a time that children were still awake. I met with Attorney General Janet Reno when she was in San Antonio and asked her to keep pressure on the industry. The threat of legislation eventually brought industry leaders together with President Clinton in March 1996, when they agreed to establish a television rating system similar to that used in movies, and to push for the use of a V-chip that would allow parents to block adult material from their cable television.

Locally, I chastised the television news stations for leading with violence on their newscasts. San Antonio had always suffered from its reputation as a market where "if it bleeds, it leads" the newscast. Now that we were the nation's ninth largest city, I asked, "Is it really necessary to dwell breathlessly on all of the gory details, with blue and red lights flashing in the background, to catalog every bullet hole, and to make celebrities of the punks who committed the outrage?"

The Rocky Mountain Media Watch analyzed the tapes of 100 local news programs in 58 cities on a single night. They found that the average local news broadcast ran about 12 minutes of actual news, and that about 40 percent of those stories involved violence or disasters. Fifty-two of the 100 broadcasts led with violence or disasters.

In 1994, 11 local news stations in cities from Seattle to Albuquerque began to play down graphic crime and accident-scene videos. They still reported bad news, but they sought to make their newscasts more sensitive to family concerns. They recognized that the time they devoted to covering crime was disproportionate to the other events in their communities.

I convened a meeting of all the local television news directors to encourage them to follow the news stations that were not playing up violence. I received a surprisingly good reception. The level of TV violence did decline — at least for a while.

The battle against exploitive entertainment is one that must be fought every day. A public official has a right just as does any other citizen to participate, even take the lead, in those efforts.

Casino Gambling

Merv Griffin rolled up to City Hall in a chauffeur-driven white limousine on January 19, 1994. He emerged with his trademark smile to greet the waiting media, which followed him into my office. Griffin, the successful television game show host and producer, was now capitalizing on the gambling industry. He wanted to talk with me about the merits of casino gambling on the San Antonio River.

With his white hair and chubby cheeks, Griffin is a charming guy. We spoke for about half an hour as he pitched the merits of casino gambling. "Put the casino on the river and the tourists will flock to San Antonio," he said. "Let the tourists do the gambling and help your tax base. Only 20 percent of the gambling is done by locals in Las Vegas."

"I'm one of those tourists who go to Las Vegas occasionally to deposit my funds," I said, laughing. I could laugh about it because I was not a serious gambler and could afford to lose. Many others aren't so lucky.

"If Texas passes casino gambling, my company can put a great operation here," he said.

I thanked him for coming by, but told him I had not made up my mind about the merits of gambling in our community. After the meeting, I told the media I was unsure about his proposal.

By 1994, many states had legalized gambling. The $30 billion industry thought Texas would be another prime market. The industry really liked San Antonio because of our huge tourism industry. They liked the River Walk because that was where the action was.

I knew that San Antonio's future was bound symbolically to the River Walk. For decades, it had been a quiet, family-oriented stretch of restaurants, a few bars and some gift shops for tourists along a narrow ribbon of the San Antonio River that cut through downtown. But the nature of the River Walk was already beginning to change, with louder bars and restaurants that appealed to a younger crowd. Plans were in the works for millions of dollars worth of new development. How we encouraged that growth would in many ways reflect the kind of city we wished to become.

Although my public statements were cautious, I knew that I would oppose casinos. I had strong moral and religious reasons to do so. Compulsive gamblers harm their families, their children and others with their addiction to gambling. Slot machines were especially attractive to older gamblers, so much so that they had acquired the nickname "granny grinders." Studies have shown gambling-related increases in white-collar crime. Gambling usually brings other bad elements with it, including prostitution and organized crime.

While I knew the moral and religious issues would appeal to a large portion of our population, I also knew that I needed to articulate economic reasons to reach our key business leaders who were being tempted to promote casinos. So I started meeting with the owners of businesses located on the River Walk.

We talked about the economic consequences to small businesses in Atlantic City when gambling was legalized. Within a year, the number of restaurants there dropped from 250 to 150. The casinos were like giant sucking tubes that pulled people out of other restaurants with inexpensive food so people would gamble. Room rates were kept low to entice customers, but the hotels not affiliated with casinos suffered.

The casinos in Atlantic City did not lead to downtown development. When you step out the back of the casinos you could think you're in a Third World country.

We also talked about how San Antonio had worked hard to create a family atmosphere for visitors on the river. A poll of the River Walk merchants showed a large majority opposed casinos and gambling. I needed to do little to persuade them to come out against casinos on the river.

With the merchants' support in hand, I persuaded the City Council to take a public stand against gambling on the river. Then I decided to take the next step. I began to speak out against casino gambling, not just in San Antonio but elsewhere in the state.

I said it would not help tourism in cities trying to provide a family atmosphere. I said if tourists wanted sleazy joints, pornography and gambling, they could visit New Orleans.

Michael Allen of the Wall Street Journal interviewed me. I was the only mayor of a major city in Texas opposed to casinos. The others were already making plans on how to spend the money. The interview gave me statewide publicity and strengthened my hand in lobbying against gambling at the Legislature.

I knew that if the Legislature allowed a local referendum on gambling, the war to stop it would eventually be lost. The industry's firepower was overwhelming. I said that if you want to kill a snake you must do it before it grows up. If the Legislature allowed a referendum, that snake would grow too big to kill.

We were successful during the 1995 session. Representative Frank Corte Jr. took the lead in our delegation. But the 1997 session, under way as this book goes to press, is another battle.

As of this writing, 24 states have legalized casino gambling. The spread started in 1988, when Congress allowed Indian reservations to set up casinos. It is estimated that more money is spent in casinos than on movie tickets, theater, opera and concerts combined.

I hope the spread of gambling stops, and I believe San Antonio and our River Walk can prosper without it.

Pornography

During the late 1980s and early 1990s the number of adult movie stores, tanning parlors offering sex, and old-fashioned strip clubs began to increase again in San Antonio.

Dozens of "massage parlors" offering sex had caused problems for the city and county in the 1970s until new ordinances forced them to close. Now these sexually oriented businesses were making a comeback under new commercial guises. Concern began to grow as they encroached on our neighborhoods, and, thus, came closer to our children.

Teresa Weaver, a local religious activist, began a movement to rally the community against pornography and its connection to sexual exploitation. Weaver was soon joined by a coalition of churches. She asked me to help persuade City Council to adopt a strong anti-pornography ordinance, and I agreed.

Teresa brought youth groups to City Council for the "Citizens to be Heard" segment we schedule at every council meeting.

They would speak in support of a strong ordinance. But while theses advocates appeared in public, lobbyists for the "smut" industry were working with First Amendment supporters behind the scenes to rally council members and city staff to kill the ordinance.

Some of the more degenerate disciples began to work on me. All my neighbors were sent a picture of my head superimposed over a lewd guy. Some of my neighbors called my wife expressing indignation about receiving the picture. It had embarrassed them and upset their families. The police could never track down who sent the picture.

I kept pressure on the city staff to develop the ordinance, and on my council colleagues to pass it. We scheduled the vote for April 27, 1995. On the morning of the vote, I found out that some council members were prepared to support an amendment to gut the ordinance. It's such a dishonest game — a politician comes out strongly for an issue publicly, and then quietly supports a killer amendment that usually goes unnoticed by most citizens.

The industry tried an old political trick — divide and conquer. They told inner-city representatives that the sexually oriented businesses and adult video shops would relocate from the North Side to their neighborhoods if the regulations passed. The amendment that lobbyists said would prevent such a result was the "killer." The industry was playing on false fears.

On the "Mayor's Forum," a live cable TV show hosted by T.J. Connolly that was broadcast right before each council meeting, I exposed this plot. It fell apart in the light of public revelation.

We passed the ordinance as written. It prohibited the opening of an adult video store or other sexually oriented business within 1,000 feet of a neighborhood, school, place of worship, or public park. It also banned them in the downtown area. The ordinance required such businesses to register and pay a $575 fee.

The effect of the ordinance was to identify only 30 potential sites in the city in which these businesses could locate. The existing 30 businesses were given time to recoup their investments before having to move. The ordinance will make it difficult to open new sex shops in San Antonio, although pornography sellers always try to find loopholes and often succeed.

The ordinance passed unanimously, to resounding cheers from the people who had worked so hard for its passage. The hard work of Teresa Weaver and her coalition of churches, the Downtown Residents Association, the San Antonio Conservation Society and others paid off. San Antonio had stopped a growing but undesirable industry.

In January 1997, I was named a defendant along with the city in a lawsuit filed by the owners of the Cabaret Club on the San Antonio River. The suit asked for damages, alleging I had vowed to close the club. The suit is still pending as this book goes to press.

The ordinance we passed in 1995 came at the same time that postal authorities were investigating the pornography business nationally and internationally. In May 1996, the authorities illustrated how insidious the pornography industry had become.

Postal inspectors arrested 45 people in a child pornography "sting." The company set up by postal authorities had a mailing list of 2,000 people. Investigators said videotapes confiscated in the sting showed criminal acts — images of children as young as 7 having sex with each other or with adults.

I was proud of the action we as a city took against the smut industry in 1995.

The anti-pornography ordinance and the pressure on the entertainment industry will help protect families and children from harmful messages. The stopping of casino gambling will prevent one more harmful social ill from destroying families.

My years as mayor convinced me that a community can defend its values, and even make its voice heard in the national debate on these issues.

★★★

Lessons from A Question of Values

■ **One voice can make a difference.**
In rock music, pornography and gambling, national interests were attempting to impose negative values on our community. Yet, reverse pressure from that community worked against them. I was just one mayor, yet my views made a splash when reported in the Wall Street Journal.

■ **Boycotts can work.**
Everyone, including public officeholders, has the right to refuse to buy from a company, to boycott products, to ask a company to change policies, and to object to television shows or movies that promote violence. The new television ratings came about because of public pressure.

■ **Local governments can use some of their regulations to help maintain community values.**
The location of these businesses can be regulated, as can their noise levels and the placement of visible signs, even though the businesses can probably never be eliminated.

13

Championship Fights: John Sununu, Don King, and Julio Cesar Chavez

U.S. Representative Lamar Smith was on the telephone with some bad news. It was the week before Thanksgiving 1991, and Lamar, one of San Antonio's three congressmen, almost ruined the holiday. If what he was telling me came true, it would set us back badly in our effort to position San Antonio as a center of international trade.

"Nelson, ease up on your efforts to bring the inter-American drug summit to San Antonio," Lamar told me. "I just talked to John Sununu (President Bush's chief of staff). He told me the summit will be held in Miami, Florida."

I was stunned. "Lamar, the State Department has already said it wants to have the summit in San Antonio. Why is the White House changing that decision?"

"Well, the president is receiving political pressure from Florida. Sununu thinks it should go to Miami."

The topic of our conversation was the summit meeting mentioned in an earlier chapter that would bring President Bush together with leaders of Latin America to discuss economic issues and the fight against the multibillion-dollar illegal drug trade.

The presidents of Mexico, Peru, Bolivia, Colombia and Ecuador, as well as the foreign minister of Venezuela, had all agreed to attend.

An international conference turns a world spotlight on the community where it is held. Hundreds of reporters attend and the host city's name shows up in datelines to stories in newspapers around the world. A summit bestows on that community the stature and the visibility it needs for future international investment, trade and tourism.

Among ourselves, we liked to talk about San Antonio becoming an international trade center, an "economic gateway" between Latin America and the United States. But if this vision was ever to be more than talk, we had to work hard to make it happen. We had to take chances. We had to make ourselves visible in the world arena.

The San Antonio Summit was a perfect chance. And it was critically important to do it now. Mexico's President Carlos Salinas de Gortari had proposed a trade agreement among Canada, Mexico and the United States. The North American Free Trade Agreement would slowly and systematically eliminate tariffs and trade barriers among the three countries. With proper positioning, San Antonio could finally make its "gateway" dream come true.

But with the drug summit almost in reach, Lamar was hearing we might lose it. I was furious! Just two years before, we lost out to Houston as host of the "G-7" summit of industrial nations. It was the same old story: We played the game fairly, with a gentle lobbying effort, and we fell short, as we always had in the past. "Good old San Antonio," I could hear them smirking in Houston. "It's a nice town, but it's just not in the same league."

This time, I decided, we would play the game differently. If we were to lose this time, it would not be because we didn't fight, and fight hard.

After getting off the phone with Lamar, I fired off a letter to John Sununu: "I am bitterly disappointed to learn that the decision to locate the summit is being made for what I consider purely political reasons, rather than on the merits of demonstrated support for the administration's goals and the logic of geographic proximity."

Then I called the news media to my office and gave reporters a copy of the letter. I told them that if the president was facing a political cost for bypassing Miami, then he would also pay a political price for not coming to San Antonio. I said I was going to do everything I could to get the decision changed.

That same day, the White House put out a news release saying the administration was considering California and Florida as well as Texas as sites for the summit. Lamar was more circumspect in his remarks to the media than he had been with me. He told reporters simply, "Sununu did not say anything that would encourage me. He mentioned three sites, but he did not say he had a preference for San Antonio." He didn't criticize Sununu at all.

The next day, the San Antonio Express-News carried the headline "S.A.'s drug summit chances fade" and "Wolff rips politics." The story said that California and Florida would also be considered as sites. The media thought the decision had not been made. I knew it had, and I had nothing to lose by playing hardball.

On the Attack

Four days later, with Thanksgiving near, I went on a WOAI radio show with Congressman Smith. I blasted Sununu again for politicizing the decision of where to hold the conference. In an angry voice I said, "Lamar, you should not accept 'no' for an answer. It's your job to fight for the summit to come to San Antonio." Lamar said he would continue to try.

I kept up the pressure daily. Some members of the media warned that I was overplaying my hand. Others felt my harsh remarks would hurt future relations with the White House. I thought differently. When you're in a tough political battle, being the nice guy generally gets you short shrift.

On December 3, I got a break. John Sununu resigned. His arrogant, smarter-than-you attitude had finally caught up with him. He had made enemies for President Bush within the Republican Party as well as among Democrats. I publicly applauded his forced resignation.

With Sununu out of the way, I tempered my remarks, but I still kept the pressure on Congressman Smith and the White House. Many of the president's close friends in San Antonio, people such as Joci Strauss, helped tremendously.

On January 22, 1992, President Bush announced that the drug summit would be held in San Antonio after all. I congratulated the president on his decision and Congressman Smith for working hard to win the summit for San Antonio.

Now we were faced with the fact that we had only one month to prepare for San Antonio's first international summit and an accompanying state dinner. Two days after the announcement I flew to Washington to meet with White House officials to begin preparations. More than 1,400 officials and twice as many media representatives were expected to attend. Councilwoman Yolanda Vera and the city's director of international relations, Jose Luis Garcia, handled planning for the event.

Yolanda recruited hundreds of citizens as volunteers to aid in preparations. We called them the "I-team" for "international." The structure of the organization we created was used by the State Department for future international events held in other cities.

We developed a logo for the summit with White House approval. We named it the "San Antonio Summit" because the participants had decided that the summit would encompass economic as well as drug issues. We set up a media operations center to accommodate 800 to 1,000 reporters, photographers, and producers from 65 news organizations around the world.

Finally the day came. Tracy and I met each leader as he arrived at various hours at Kelly Air Force Base. It was exciting to watch the presidential planes land and their leaders emerge.

A Majestic Dinner

On the night of February 26, Tracy and I attended the most elaborate state dinner ever held in San Antonio. The setting was elegant — the recently restored Majestic Theater in downtown San Antonio with its faux-Moorish architecture and a ceiling resembling a twilight sky with stars twinkling and clouds drifting by.

Dishes and flowers flown in from the White House were placed on the tables set on the theater's stage. Tracy hosted the table of Secretary of State James Baker. Looking at the waiter pouring a fine wine, the Texas lawyer and rancher turned to Tracy and said, "Do you think I could get a good cold beer?"

Tracy smiled and told him, "I am sure you can." Baker got his beer. It was a stellar evening, as Van Cliburn played the piano at Barbara Bush's request.

The summit discussions were held in the McNay Art Museum, a Spanish Colonial-style mansion on several acres of beautifully landscaped hillside in northeast San Antonio. It was the first museum in Texas devoted to modern art. The secluded site provided ample space for security.

While the presidents met, Tracy hosted a first lady's luncheon for Mrs. Bush. Tracy had clashed with some members of the White House staff who wanted the luncheon to be an elite little affair. But Tracy had convinced them to have a large luncheon with a broad cross-section of women. It was a big success, and the first lady was impressed.

Although my attempted conversations with President Bush did not go over well, everything else about the summit went perfectly. Even the weather was beautiful.

San Antonio was finally on the international map.

Julio Cesar Chavez, Don King and NAFTA

I was surprised to see the tall, heavy-set black man walking across the green field. As he drew near the group of mourners gathered around my father's casket, I could see sweat rolling down his face and his trademark steel-white hair standing straight up. It was the hot summer day of July 16, 1993.

I was touched that international boxing promoter Don King had made a special trip to San Antonio to be at my father's funeral. I knew that Dad, if he could see him, would have been

Boxing promoter Don King (left) discusses the championship boxing match he was staging in the Alamodome with Express-News Publisher and Chief Executive Officer Larry Walker and Mayor Nelson Wolff. (Wolff collection)

glad. They both enjoyed boxing and cold beer. They liked to roll dice, play a little poker and bet on sports.

Dad had died after several years of slowly slipping away as Alzheimer's disease shut down his brain. He followed my mother, who had passed away two years before I was elected mayor. Even though Dad was alive at the time, I'm not sure he understood I was mayor.

Like my father, I enjoyed boxing and was a fan of two great local fighters, Robert Quiroga and Jesse James Leija. But it was not just my love of boxing that had first brought me together with Don King.

The world's greatest promoter wanted to use the Alamodome for an international match between Mexican champion Julio Cesar Chavez and Pernell Whitaker of the United States.

I knew the match would attract media from all over the world. Just like the San Antonio Summit, the fight would be another opportunity to showcase San Antonio, only this time, two years after the summit, we were in the middle of the national debate about adopting the North American Free Trade Agreement.

People whispered that King only came to my father's funeral to cement my support for the upcoming Chavez-Whitaker fight. Friends had warned me that Don would take advantage of San Antonio and me; that he would take us to the cleaners.

There were many reasons why people did not trust Don King. He grew up in the ghettos of Cleveland, Ohio, running numbers. He went to prison after kicking a man to death over a gambling debt.

Boxing promoters and managers are as mean and tough as the boxers in the ring. And King rose to be the world's top promoter. He managed several great fighters, including heavyweights Muhammad Ali and Mike Tyson. When Tyson went to prison for rape, Julio Cesar Chavez became Don's top fighter.

I first met Don only five months before my father's funeral. In early March 1993, I received a phone call from Carol Darby, manager of the Alamodome. She said, "Mayor, how would you like to host the fight between Julio Cesar Chavez and Pernell Whitaker?"

"You bet I would. When?"

"Don King would like to do it in September."

"Great. Tell me what to do."

Carol said she would get back to me.

With an 87-0 record and 74 knockouts, Julio Cesar Chavez was the world's best in the lightweight divisions. He held the WBC Super Lightweight and IBC Junior Welterweight championships.

Not only was Chavez a great boxer, he was worshipped by the poor people of Mexico. He had grown up poor in Culiacan. After he became wealthy, he stayed true to his roots and remained in Culiacan, close to the people. Often he would donate his share of the boxing purse to poor people. In one fight, he donated his purse to the victims of the Mexico City earthquake. He always had time for people — signing autographs, taking pictures, shaking hands.

Chavez's opponent, Pernell Whitaker, was the WBC Welterweight champion, with a 32-1 record. Pound for pound, the two fighters were considered the best in the world.

We arranged a visit by King to San Antonio on March 23. After meeting at Mi Tierra restaurant, Don and I went to the fights.

As Jesse James Leija delivered sharp jabs to his opponent, Louie Espinoza, we talked about the potential match between Chavez and Whitaker.

Don first thought of bringing the fight to San Antonio when Chavez defeated Greg Haugen in February in Mexico City before 136,244 people at Aztec Stadium. This was the largest crowd in boxing history.

Almost all of the important boxing matches in recent history in the United States had been held in Las Vegas. The casinos pay big bucks to get the fights because they draw gamblers.

Heavyweight fights are the largest draw. But Don thought that because of Julio Cesar Chavez's popularity in Mexico, he could draw a large crowd in the Alamodome in San Antonio.

Don said, "If I bring the fight to San Antonio, I want you to be personally committed to promoting the fight in the Alamodome. I will need help with the business community and the newspaper."

I replied, "Be square with me and I will do all I can to make it a success."

He smiled and said, "Man, you are all right."

As Jesse landed a great punch, I said, "You need to put Jesse on your card."

"I'll work on it," he said.

After the fight, on the way home I felt good about Don. Growing up on the South Side, I had developed a few street smarts myself. I thought we had connected and understood each other. He was also a hell of a lot of fun. He is bigger than life, with better skills than any politician. He can talk, slap backs, cite quotes, and deliver the best one liners. I liked him right off the bat.

After Don's visit, the media speculated he was just using San Antonio to get a better deal with the Las Vegas casinos. We thought otherwise. We felt if we could get the numbers to work, Don would come to San Antonio. We also knew that Chavez wanted to fight in San Antonio.

Carol Darby met with some insiders from Las Vegas and learned what would be necessary to bring the fight to San Antonio. With this inside information, Carol was ready to negotiate with Don King's people. At a news conference in April, we announced that we had a signed deal.

On April 19, Don and I rode together in the Texas Cavaliers' Fiesta River Parade. As we began our trek down the river, I was worried how the crowd would react when they saw Don. No need. They recognized him right away. They shouted, clapped, and hollered. Don drew as much media and crowd attention as the fighters.

Don said, "I need to have the total support of the Express-News. Can you arrange a meeting?"

I called publisher Larry Walker. I said, "Larry, can Don and I come over and meet with you about the fight?"

"Come on over," Larry said.

Larry is a former minor-league baseball pitcher, a motorcycle rider and a cigar smoker. He likes to have fun, and can smell a good deal when it gets close to him. He knew that Chavez would sell newspapers. He was ready to talk.

As we sat down at a long conference table in the Express-News building, Don said, "This is going to be greatest fight ever and a big international event. I need you to be my partner in promoting this fight. I need you to be a sponsor. I need front-page coverage leading up to the fight."

"I'll have a team of reporters on the fight," Larry responded. "What's the deal on the sponsorship?"

Don and Larry hammered out a sponsorship package. The Express-News gave great coverage to the fight. Larry also liked Don personally.

Don arrived back in San Antonio 10 days before the fight and stayed. Every day he had a media event, most of which I participated in. Chavez did not have professional trainers. I thought this was an ominous sign for Chavez.

Most of the business leaders did not want anything to do with Don or the fight. They decided to stay at the country club. It's much safer there. It was too bad that most of them could not see the international significance of the fight. Don criticized the business community for the lack of support he was getting from them. I was asked to defend the business community but instead I defended Don. Among those who did help were Red McCombs, Ernesto Ancira and Bill Greehey.

On September 9, the day before the fight, I ran with Chavez. He ran at a quicker pace than I was used to. After the first mile, I was struggling to keep up. He looked over at me and said, "Breathe easier." Breathe easier? I was having a hard time breathing at all!

Still, I could tell Chavez was sluggish. As we ran, the group of Chavez supporters that traveled with him laughed and talked about the great time they were having in San Antonio. Chavez was enjoying the adulation. He was partying a little too late. He liked his beer a little too much.

I was getting worried because, if Chavez lost, I was afraid the crowd might explode. Boxing fans are a lot tougher than fans at other sporting events.

I saw Don later in the day. I said, "Don, I'm worried about Chavez. He doesn't look ready to me. Is he going to win?"

"I don't know who is going to win," Don said, "but I know who is not going to lose."

I hesitated a moment, then smiled, and walked off.

On the night of the fight, I made my way to a ringside seat. Excitement was in the air as Chavez entered the ring with his trademark red bandanna. As he stood next to Arturo Vegas singing Mexico's national anthem, a tremendous roar went up from the crowd.

During the fight the supporters of Pernell Whitaker remained silent. They knew they were in Chavez country. From the start, Whitaker landed the most punches.

The fight was called a draw, but everyone thought Whitaker had out-boxed Chavez. They were boxing for Whitaker's title, so whether it was a draw or a win for Whitaker, he retained it. The crowd went quietly home with few incidents.

Was it worth it? Yes. The crowd was the 10th largest in the history of boxing. More than a thousand media members came to San Antonio. Millions of people throughout the world watched the fight. The hotels, retail shops and restaurants had the best weekend in memory. For the week prior to the fight San Antonio was mentioned every day on CNN Headline News and Cable

News Network. The boxing match raised San Antonio's profile as the fight in Congress for NAFTA intensified.

★★★
Lessons on Championship Fights

- **A howling "Wolff" at the White House door gets what he wants.**
  San Antonio never would have been selected for the summit had I not mounted a forceful public campaign. I had to criticize the White House for playing politics when Sununu suggested the site should be changed to Miami.

- **Take the lead or the White House will.**
  We organized our events quickly and assumed control rather than let the White House arrange everything. The state and civic dinners, a correspondents' party in front of the Alamo, and Tracy's luncheon for the first lady were all successful because we took the lead and pushed our own interests rather than letting the White House staff focus everything on the presidents.

- **Visiting reporters are always looking for another story.**
  We took advantage of the international media that came for the summit to present our city in a favorable light. By entertaining the reporters, we managed to generate some positive stories about San Antonio as well as the business of the conference.

- **An international fight throws a bright light on your city.**
  The Chavez-Whitaker fight drew more attention from more people than the San Antonio Summit, and was more profitable to our tourist industries.

14

The Battle for NAFTA

"**P**resident Salinas wants you to be in Mexico City next Tuesday," Humberto Hernandez Haddad said. "He did not say why, but it must be important."

When a president summons, one responds. "Tell him I'll be there," I told Humberto, Mexico's consul general to San Antonio. It was Friday, September 18, 1992.

Humberto was a former senator from the state of Tabasco. His political career hit a short-circuit in Mexico after Carlos Salinas de Gortari was elected president. Humberto had made the mistake of getting into a political conflict with President Salinas' father while both had served in Mexico's Senate. When Salinas took office as president, he assigned Humberto to San Antonio, far from the center of power.

Humberto had become a good friend. He was astute about the labyrinth of Mexican politics.

In April 1991, just before my election, Mayor Lila Cockrell was host to a visit to San Antonio by President Salinas. He had attended the opening of "Mexico: Splendors of Thirty Centuries," a major exhibition of the country's art. While here, Salinas had announced his proposal for a North American Free Trade Agreement among Canada, the United States and Mexico.

NAFTA would create the largest trading bloc in the world, with a combined economic output of more than $6 trillion and 360 million people from the Arctic atop Canada to the tropical jungles of southern Mexico. The proposed treaty would dismantle tariffs and trade barriers over a 15-year period. It would enhance the ability of the Western Hemisphere to compete with the European and Asian trading blocs. A bold step forward, the proposal was embraced by President Bush and Canadian Prime Minister Brian Mulroney. Besides being bold, it was also controversial.

I supported NAFTA. Many large American corporations had been shipping American jobs to Asia. I thought it made a lot more sense to work with Mexico. Although we might lose some jobs in the short run, overall it would produce a net job gain for both countries. Mexico imported more goods produced in the United States than any country except Japan.

My family set an example of how trade would benefit both countries. My brothers, George and Gary, had a manufacturing plant in Mexico that assembled wooden window frames. All the components for the windows were made in the United States.

Within a month of being elected, however, I found out how difficult the trade pact would be to sell in the United States. I went to San Diego, California, to attend a meeting of the U.S. Conference of Mayors. A vote on the NAFTA agreement ended in a tie. I was surprised. But many of the big-city mayors opposed the pact, fearful of losing jobs to Mexico, or worried about Mexico's lax environmental regulations.

Knowing the battle would be difficult, I was determined to position San Antonio to take advantage of the trade pact. Trade with Mexico was increasing and our city needed to capitalize on it. I wanted to build on the solid groundwork that Lila Cockrell and Henry Cisneros had laid.

After my election, I quickly moved to strengthen our trade opportunities. Mexico's second largest city is Guadalajara, in the state of Jalisco in western Mexico. We are sister cities. Jalisco Governor Guillermo Cosio Vidaurri came to San Antonio on June 10,

1991, to make a gift of a kiosk for Milam Park. During the visit, I told him we would open a trade office in Guadalajara.

Mexico is a country of many small businesses. Similarly, the economy of San Antonio is fueled mostly by small business. While large corporations wouldn't need a trade office, it was a necessity for small businesses. Once established, the trade office would provide advice and link companies.

City Council approved funding, and in October, Tracy and I led a delegation to Guadalajara during that city's annual festival, and used the opportunity to open our trade office. Governor Vidaurri praised us for being the first major city in the United States to open a trade office in Mexico.

Under Councilman Bill Thornton's leadership, the city also created an organization known as Medical Destination San Antonio to promote our $6 billion health care industry in Mexico. In a related effort, UT Health Science Center President John Howe has successfully used public funds to attract private investment for biosciences research.

Long before Humberto called me to meet with the president, Salinas and I had established close ties. I had first met President Salinas when he was secretary of budget and planning under President Miguel De La Madrid. I had picked up Salinas at the airport in 1983 when he came to San Antonio to address the World Affairs Council.

Fluent in English, Salinas chose to deliver his remarks in Spanish, as did most of Mexico's government officials when speaking in the United States. We were photographed together, and I kept that picture in my office during my four years as mayor. Speculation as early as 1983 was suggesting he might be Mexico's next president.

Physically, President Salinas does not cut much of a figure. Small, prematurely bald, he looked like any of the nondescript technocrats transforming Mexico into a modern nation. He was educated in the United States, and was a classmate of Henry Cisneros at Harvard University.

I did not see Salinas again until he visited San Antonio in April 1991 as president. I sat with members of his Cabinet at a dinner hosted by Mayor Cockrell. Secretary of Commerce and Industrial Development Jaime Serra Puche sat next to me. He would become Mexico's chief negotiator on NAFTA.

All the Cabinet members were up to date on the local mayoral race I was engaged in at the time. "Henry Cisneros has said some nice things about you," Jaime said. "My friends tell me you are going to win."

"I hope you're right. If I do, I look forward to working on several initiatives with Mexico." They knew more about the mayor's race than many of our leading citizens.

I next encountered President Salinas at the San Antonio Summit in February 1992. I met with him privately at La Mansion Hotel. La Mansion was built in the late 1960s on the San Antonio River, and the structure incorporated a portion of the historical building that housed St. Mary's University's first law school. The Spanish stucco architecture and elegant rooms made it a favorite hotel for visiting Mexican and U.S. dignitaries. Former CBS News President Fred Friendly, an in-law of the Munguia family and more distantly of Cisneros, insisted on staying there whenever he visited San Antonio. The hotel is owned and managed by my friend Pat Kennedy.

I asked my sister-in-law, Margarita Miska, to join me in the meeting with Salinas. Margarita, recently married to Tracy's brother Larry Miska, had known Carlos since they were children. Her parents, Eduardo and Margarita Galindo, were friends of Carlos' parents.

As we entered the room, Margarita cried out, "Carlos!" and they embraced. Speaking in Spanish for a few minutes, President Salinas told her he had great respect for her family and appreciated her parents coming to his mother's recent funeral.

Margarita's presence was important in establishing a close relationship with President Salinas. Friends and family are the ties that bind both political and business relationships in Mexico.

President Salinas was interested in the depth of support for NAFTA, and I told him it was strong in San Antonio and Texas. At the end of our conversation, I said, "Mr. President, I hope you will support San Antonio as the place to host the initialing of the free trade agreement."

He smiled, but didn't answer the question.

So when Humberto called seven months later and asked me to be in Mexico the following week, I knew President Salinas had something important to tell me. The date was approaching when the three leaders would attend ceremonies to initial the trade agreement. I hoped that was what the call was about. I told the media I was going on a trade mission.

I quickly assembled a delegation. It included Humberto; Bill Greehey, chairman of Valero Energy; Dr. James Leininger, chairman of Kinetic Concepts; Dennis Nixon, president of the International Bank of Commerce; and Jorge Verdusco, chairman of the Texas-Mexico Authority.

We arrived at Los Piños, the presidential mansion in Mexico City, on September 23, and were escorted into a small meeting room to await President Salinas. He startled us by entering from a side door to the patio, but we quickly stood to greet him.

During our meeting, we brought the president up to date on the initiatives our city had taken in promoting trade. I said, "The trade office we opened in Guadalajara in October of 1991 has been a big success. We plan to open another one next month in Monterrey."

He told us he appreciated the aid San Antonio had provided after a sewer line filled with petroleum fumes had exploded with devastating results in the middle of Guadalajara on April 22, 1992. Along with my son, Matthew, I had flown aboard businessman Morris Jaffe's plane to bring needed emergency supplies to our sister city.

When anything of this magnitude goes wrong in Mexico, someone is singled out to pay the price. In this case, Mayor Enrique Dau Flores was jailed. I had met him in San Antonio only a couple of weeks before the accident. He had been in office only one month. Jalisco Governor Cossio Vidaurri was asked to resign. Carlos Rivera Aceves was appointed interim governor by Salinas.

During the meeting with President Salinas, Greehey, Leininger, Nixon and Verdusco briefed the president on their business investments in Mexico. President Salinas had been privatizing many Mexican businesses and was seeking foreign investment. He said he appreciated their interest.

"We really appreciate the work that Humberto Hernandez Haddad is doing in San Antonio," Greehey said. "We hope you will continue to post him in San Antonio."

Salinas smiled and replied, "Don't worry. He will stay there." Few people in San Antonio were aware of the rift between them. I believe I was the only one in the room beside the two principal parties who knew about it. I realized that Salinas had just delivered a message to Humberto.

At the close of the meeting, I said, "We're working hard for the free trade agreement. We hope that the initialing ceremony will be held in San Antonio." Back home, we had been lobbying hard with the White House to support San Antonio as the site.

President Salinas replied, "I will be seeing you soon, and more often than you think."

Initialing the Future

At times, it's a challenge to interpret the subtleties of Mexican political discourse. But when President Salinas said, "I will be seeing you soon," the message could not have been clearer. The Free Trade Agreement would be initialed in San Antonio.

The Bush administration had apparently given President Salinas his choice of U.S. cities, and he picked San Antonio. I had to contain my excitement and not let the cat out of the bag for fear I might lose the cat.

On September 28, the White House announced that the signing would take place in San Antonio on October 7. One of the most important trade pacts in the history of the United States would be signed in San Antonio.

I knew the White House had been impressed with our handling of the San Antonio Summit, which laid a foundation for our selection as the site for the signing of the NAFTA agreement.

Once again I turned to Councilwoman Yolanda Vera to handle the event. The site for the ceremony would be the Plaza San Antonio Hotel Conference Center, a renovated 19th-century German-English school building now adjacent to the contemporary hotel. Between the two wings of the old school lies an open, landscaped patio where the signing would take place.

Mayor Nelson Wolff stands (left to right) with President George Bush, Mexican President Carlos Salinas de Gortari, Canadian Prime Minister Brian Mulroney, and Tracy Wolff. (White House)

The initialing of the 2,000-page treaty after 14 months of negotiation was an important milestone. I took the opportunity to give President Bush a six-page paper that outlined the roles San Antonio and South Texas could play under NAFTA. Our city was a logical site for manufacturing and distribution, located at the nexus of two interstate highways; one running north and south, the other east and west.

Business leaders from all three countries attended the signing ceremony. I greeted each Mexican business leader personally. The powerful families of Ortiz Mena, Clarion, Zambrano, Azcarraga, Garza Sada, Losada, Ancira and others attended. As Salinas led Mexico toward privatization, many of these business leaders had purchased the previously state-owned industries. Mexico now had 12 billionaires, more than any other country.

At 3:40 p.m. on October 7, the three leaders stood in the overcrowded courtyard watching as their representatives initialed the agreement. Then each gave a short speech.

After the initialing ceremony, the leaders held a reception in the courtyard. I had greeted each one as he had arrived at Kelly

Air Force Base. Tracy had previously met President Bush and President Salinas, but not Prime Minister Brian Mulroney of Canada. When I introduced her, he said, "Mr. Mayor, I appreciate the fact that you greeted me at the airport, but why didn't you send your wife?" He was a great guy. He later wrote us a personal note thanking us for the city's hospitality.

In less than a year, San Antonio had been host to two major international meetings. Each gave San Antonio visibility throughout the world and positioned us as the lead city in the United States supporting NAFTA.

Houston and Dallas, our large and rich cousins to the east and north, now looked at us with a little envy. Because trade was increasing, both cities were making greater efforts to forge closer ties with Mexico.

When Dallas tried to position itself as the gateway to Mexico, I commented, "The only thing Dallas knows about Mexico is where Cancun and Acapulco are."

Henry, Lloyd, Bill and NAFTA

After the pomp and circumstance of the signing ended, the real battle for NAFTA began in Congress. There was no doubt that Mexico and Canada would ratify the treaty. But the United States was an uncertain prospect. Those who supported the treaty faced a tough challenge.

The presidential election a month after the signing added to the complications. President-elect Bill Clinton had said he supported the treaty but wanted some changes. No one knew for sure how committed he really was. Many representatives on the Democrat side of the aisle were strongly opposed. Labor unions who were among Clinton's staunchest supporters were opposed. The strength of White House support would depend on whom Clinton appointed to his Cabinet.

We were elated when Clinton appointed U.S. Senator Lloyd Bentsen of Texas as treasury secretary. Bentsen had grown up in the Rio Grande Valley. He understood Mexico perhaps better than any other elected official in Washington. He understood the benefits of free trade. He would be a strong advocate pushing President Clinton to work hard for the pact.

But the appointment of Bentsen threw Texas politics into turmoil. Governor Richards now had the task of appointing a replacement who would then have to run in a special election. Many of us urged the governor to appoint Henry Cisneros. We thought he was the only candidate who could beat the Republicans.

Actually, we had more of a problem than just convincing Governor Richards. We also had to convince Henry to take the appointment if it were offered. That was not an easy task. He had already received feelers concerning a possible Cabinet appointment.

George Shipley met with Governor Richards and Henry for a preliminary discussion on the appointment. Henry expressed his concern over his son John Paul's upcoming operation as well as the lingering problem of his previous relationship with Linda Medlar. Governor Richards made no offer at this meeting.

On November 24, 1992, I spoke with Henry after a ceremony at Hidden Cove Elementary School. He said, "Who would have thought that a Hispanic boy from the West Side of San Antonio may be faced with a choice between being appointed United States senator or a Cabinet member? I believe I may be offered secretary of housing and urban development."

I replied, "Henry, what great choices! But I hope you'll run for the Senate. We're ready to help you."

A few days later, I left for a trade mission to the Far East. Henry had been the first San Antonio mayor to forge a relationship with the Far East. He had led a trade mission to Korea and Japan in June 1985. He consummated the sister-city relationship with Kumamoto, Japan, in December 1987.

In Tokyo, we met with Akio Morita, chairman and co-founder of Sony, a $43-billion company launched in 1946 in a bombed-out Tokyo department store. Sony has a manufacturing plant in San Antonio and was interested in expanding.

Morita was a close friend of our trade representative, Mrs. Naoko Shirane. He was also friends with Secretaries Bentsen and Cisneros. He spent almost an hour with our delegation.

Many Japanese business leaders feared that NAFTA would become a tool used to slow the import of Japanese goods into the United States, but Morita told us he strongly supported NAFTA.

"Free trade is what made our company strong," he said. "I believe our government should do more to eliminate governmental red tape that makes it hard for us to import." Morita was always a step ahead of other Japanese business leaders.

At the close of our meeting, Morita accepted my invitation to visit San Antonio. He would arrive on October 11, 1993, and approve the expansion of the Sony plant in San Antonio.

We spent two days in our sister city, Kumamoto, on Kyushu, the southernmost island of Japan. The city of 300,000 is clean, free of crime and very friendly. Mayor Yasumoto Tajiri and our Japanese hosts were extraordinarily kind to us. We stayed in a hotel across the street from a 16th-century castle.

I called Henry from Kumamoto on December 2 because I could no longer stand not knowing what was happening. We had last talked eight days earlier. When he answered the phone, I asked for the latest news.

"Mary Alice wants me to run for the Senate. I believe I'm ready to do it."

"Great! Tracy and I are ready to help. Tracy has agreed to help you organize the campaign." We talked for a while longer about the upcoming race.

Ten days later, I arrived in Dallas on my return from the trade mission. I received a message to call George Shipley.

"Get hold of Henry," he told me over the telephone. "I believe he is going to cop out of the Senate race. Try to change his mind."

I tried to reach Henry, but it was too late. He had left the previous day for Little Rock amid speculation that he would be appointed to President Clinton's Cabinet. He told the media he thought Governor Richards had moved beyond his name in selecting a replacement for Senator Bentsen.

As it turned out, her appointment of former Congressman Bob Krueger, who defeated me for the U.S. Congress in 1974, was a disaster. Krueger lost in the special election by a wide margin to Kay Bailey Hutchison.

Henry had again come full circle on a statewide race. He appeared ready to run in 1992, as he did in 1988, when he almost ran for governor. The personal considerations were the same as they had been four years earlier: the fragile health of his son John Paul and the possible scandal of his affair with Linda Medlar.

During our December 12 meeting, the City Council paused to watch the televised announcement as President Clinton nominated Henry Cisneros to be secretary of housing and urban development. We broke into applause, as Henry became the first citizen in the history of San Antonio nominated to serve as a Cabinet member.

Five days later, Henry came home to a hero's welcome; home to City Hall, where he had begun his career 17 years earlier; and home to old friends and colleagues. We held a reception at the Spanish Governor's Palace. As he pulled up and stepped out of his car, he was greeted by the music of mariachis and warm embraces. It was an emotional evening for everyone.

Tracy and I attended President Clinton's inauguration. It was the first time for either of us. I wanted to get in some early lobbying for the NAFTA agreement.

Then on February 5, 1993, I returned to Washington at Henry's invitation. He had invited the mayors of several large cities to meet with him at the offices of HUD, and later to meet with President Clinton at the White House.

We gathered in an elongated room at HUD with an extended table down the middle. We sat around the table with HUD staff members lined up on the wall behind us. Henry wanted to know our priorities as mayors of the nation's large cities, and we gave him a list.

Then we visited with the president and Vice President Al Gore in the East Room. After the president concluded his remarks, he stayed to visit. Clinton loves to make small talk as well as debate issues. It's hard to resist him; like Henry, he's so good at making you feel important.

Standing in a small group surrounding the president, I said, "Mr. President, I'm sending you three Columbia bowling balls made in San Antonio, one each for Hillary, Chelsea and you." My friend, Columbia President Ron Herrmann, had come up with the idea. President Clinton liked to bowl and was in the process of renovating the White House bowling lanes.

He paused, then smiled as he said, "What about the holes?"

"Now that is thinking ahead," I replied. "The letter accompanying the balls contains the name of a person here in Washington who can come over and drill the holes."

With that opening, I made a pitch for San Antonio and South Texas, telling him, "Mr. President, thank you for appointing Henry Cisneros and Lloyd Bentsen to the Cabinet. They both understand Mexico and our part of the country. I hope you will listen to their advice on the NAFTA treaty."

He said he would.

As time passed, both Henry Cisneros and Lloyd Bentsen would play major roles in the administration. Secretary Bentsen would be the key leader in setting economic policy and pushing for the passage of NAFTA. Henry Cisneros would become an innovative reformer of HUD and a catalyst in gaining Hispanic support for the treaty. Henry and President Clinton had bonded early. They became close friends as well as colleagues.

Trouble on the Hill

It's a rare event to find yourself in the same room with four presidents of the United States. As I sat in the second row of seats, looking at one Democrat and three Republican presidents, I thought how fortunate we were that these four leaders from the two major parties could come together when it counted.

We were at the White House and the date was September 14, 1993. President Clinton had invited Jimmy Carter, George Bush, Ronald Reagan and Gerald Ford to attend a "kickoff" event for the effort to push NAFTA through Congress. President Reagan could not attend, but sent a letter of support.

Until this date, there had been speculation that President Clinton would not exert every effort to pass the trade agreement. Doubts would linger even after this "kickoff."

All the presidents spoke out on the need for free trade. They all supported NAFTA. President Clinton used the occasion to sign an amendment that set sanctions for violating environmental and labor standards.

Coming away from that meeting, I wondered how we could lose. It turned out we could lose very easily unless the president made a major effort. The initial burst of enthusiasm faded. Congressional tallies showed the treaty losing.

Less than a month after the White House kickoff, I staged a commemorative ceremony of the initialing of the NAFTA agreement on the grounds of the Plaza Hotel. I tried to get a White House representative, but the staff didn't respond, so I prevailed on my friend, Housing Secretary Henry Cisneros, to come.

The ceremony was more like a wake. We unveiled a stone monument commemorating the signing. Some of the media dubbed it a tombstone for NAFTA. Henry tried to pick up everyone's spirit with his speech.

After the speech Henry and I talked a while. I said, "Henry, are we going to lose this battle?"

"The president is really having a lot of trouble with our party members," Henry replied. "Dick Gephardt (the House majority leader) is not only going to vote against the treaty, he is also working against it. There's real doubt about its passage."

"Is the president going to make an all-out effort?" An all-out effort means the president puts this issue on the line and is willing to trade to get votes.

"Yes, but I don't know if it will be enough."

I could not believe the vote would be lost. All the work we had done to get this far might now go up in smoke.

We had worked hard to position San Antonio to take advantage of the trade pact, and we had worked hard to strengthen our ties with Mexico.

For example, Tracy assumed a major role helping an organization called D.I.F., Internal Development of the Family. She visited orphanages, raised funds, and arranged for donations of medical supplies. She also assisted a Mexican organization to preserve historic structures. She went on trade missions and hosted numerous Mexican delegations that came to San Antonio, all with the support of her close friend, Cristina Rodriguez Weiss.

I worked with several Mexican states encouraging them to open trade offices in San Antonio. By 1993 the states of Durango, Tamaulipas, Jalisco, Morelos and Nuevo Leon had opened trade offices in San Antonio.

We opened another San Antonio trade office in Monterrey. Nuevo Leon Governor Socrates Rizzo and Monterrey Mayor Benjamin Clarion Reyes joined us for the opening. Both the trade office in Guadalajara and the one in Monterrey were funded partially by the San Antonio International Affairs Foundation. I appointed Ernesto Ancira to head up a committee to work with the airport and custom agents to ease the entry of foreign visitors. Tracy led the effort to raise $300,000 for the international foundation at a gala at the estate of Bill and Darolyn Worth.

We had worked hard to build support for the treaty. In April 1993, I hosted an international crossroads meeting of 20 mayors from Canada, Mexico and South Texas to discuss the impact of the trade agreement on our cities.

At that meeting, Lynda Y. de la Vina, director of the Institute for Studies in Business at the University of Texas at San Antonio, presented a paper advocating the creation of a bilateral bank funded by the United States and Mexico to provide funding for infrastructure needs. At the time we did not realize how important an idea this would become.

At the end of the conference, we unanimously adopted a resolution supporting NAFTA. The conference received good media coverage in all three countries.

In July, we hosted a bilateral meeting between Mexico and the United States on financing infrastructure needs along the border. I watched the conference as U.S. Representative Esteban Torres of California, then an opponent of the pact, discussed the need for a bilateral bank to finance infrastructure needs. He said his support of the NAFTA treaty depended on creation of such a bank. He had introduced legislation to create it.

Twelve days after our sad commemoration of the signing of NAFTA at the Plaza Hotel, my hopes for the passage of the treaty rose a little. On the night of October 19, I watched Vice President Al Gore breathe life back into NAFTA when he clearly won a nationally televised debate with Ross Perot. He made Perot look foolish in his arguments against the pact. The debate began to change public opinion.

I returned to Washington on November 15, just days before the House vote, accompanied by a large delegation of Hispanics representing the Texas Association of Mexican-American Chambers of Commerce. We spent three days lobbying.

While I was in Washington, the New York Times printed a story about my support of NAFTA. The story quoted me as saying that the only picture I have of a president in my office is that of President Salinas. When I saw Henry later in the day, he laughed and said, "Are you looking for a presidential appointment in Mexico after you finish your term?"

Later, I saw President Clinton at a gathering at the Smithsonian to rally support for the treaty. A large crowd of lobbyists and supporters of NAFTA stood in front of a roped-off area not far from where he spoke. After delivering his remarks, he stopped briefly

Mexico Consul General Humberto Hernandez Haddad cracks a *cascaron* (confetti egg) over the head of a smiling Mayor Nelson Wolff after Congress approved the North American Free Trade Agreement. (Morris Goen, Express-News)

in front of a few of us. I said, "Mr. President, we're working hard. Are we going to win?"

He smiled and said, "Yes, we are going to win."

On the eve of the NAFTA vote, I was interviewed by CBS. The network ran parts of the interview on the "CBS Evening News" and on "CBS This Morning." The stories depicted San Antonio as "the Hong Kong to Mexico's China." They said we were the most pro-NAFTA city in the United States. I think they were right in that assessment.

The president's prediction was also correct. Two days later, at 10:30 p.m. on November 17, 1993, the House of Representatives passed House Resolution 3450 on a vote of 234 to 200. The president used some chits he did not have to use to obtain the House victory. The Senate vote was never in doubt. Four days later, the Senate passed NAFTA with little debate.

Back home, we gathered in the meeting room next to my office to watch the House vote on the agreement. When the number of votes hit 217, cheers rang out and we popped a bottle of champagne to celebrate. The picture of our celebration made the New York Times. CBS News also covered it.

Three of our four congressmen supported NAFTA. Congressman Henry B. Gonzalez was the lone "no" vote. Democratic Congressman Frank Tejeda and Republicans Henry Bonilla and Lamar Smith voted in support of the treaty. Congressman Bonilla was an important leader for NAFTA on the Republican side.

The following evening, we held a celebration in the courtyard of the Spanish Governor's Palace. All those people who had worked so hard for NAFTA were invited. Consul General Haddad crushed a *cascaron* over my head. The picture made several newspapers around the country.

The efforts of Bentsen and Cisneros made the difference in galvanizing the support of President Clinton. The president had entered the game late and far behind, but pulled out an incredible victory. All of us who supported free trade became President Clinton's army. He was a great general in a difficult battle.

President Clinton had made the hardest decision a politician can make. To support NAFTA, he had gone against parts of his core constituencies — unions, environmentalists and the majority of congressional Democrats. He did what was right for our country and demonstrated true courage.

★★★

Lessons on the Battle for NAFTA

■ **Turn on your own international spotlight.**
San Antonio declared itself the leader in fighting for the passage of NAFTA. We fought hard and succeeded in landing the initialing ceremony. Other cities also claimed to be the major NAFTA city, but we got the jump and the media often played it our way.

■ **Friendship must precede business in Mexico.**
Our long history of relationships with Mexico made Mexican politicians and businessmen feel comfortable in San Antonio. Consequently, they supported the staging of international events here, as well as contributing to the city's large tourism industry.

■ **A low-cost trade office across the border can do wonders.**
The trade offices we set up in Guadalajara and Monterrey provided necessary assistance to small businesses. In turn, Mexico located trade offices in San Antonio, offsetting our costs and providing greater opportunities for trade.

15

"Go for the NADBank"

U.S. Representative Henry B. Gonzalez exemplifies the virtues of honesty, hard work and ideological purity more than any other politician to come out of San Antonio. He was elected city councilman in 1953, state senator in 1956, and then congressman in 1961. He is a Democrat who has never apologized for his liberal beliefs and strong ties to labor unions. While I disagree with many of his liberal views, I have always looked up to him as the politician to emulate in personal honesty and hard work.

Although he grew up at a time of discrimination against Hispanics, he never became involved in the more radical chicano groups such as La Raza Unida. To the contrary, on many occasions he battled against them. His strong streak of independence isolated him from power in Congress until 1989, his 28th year of tenure, when he was elected chairman of the Banking Committee.

While we were lobbying in Washington for the North American Free Trade Agreement, I ran into Gonzalez in the hallway of the building where he had his office. He had refused to give our group an appointment because he was opposed to NAFTA.

It had always been difficult to get an appointment with the congressman. He used the "old Mexican custom," as it was jokingly called, of expressing his power by forcing people to wait in order to see him. It served as a way to soften visitors up. But when I encountered him in the hallway he said he was glad to see me and the others. "Come by my office," he said.

We followed him and then gathered around as he stood behind his desk. He was in a mood to reminisce about local politics. He said, "We had a candidate run for City Council who only had one arm. He campaigned on the issue that he could not steal as much as a politician with two arms. We had another who said the only reason he was running was to get a street extended to his house." These were only two of some of the great stories he told.

Finally, he began to talk about NAFTA.

"I cannot support the treaty," he said. "I promised my labor friends I would vote against it. But I will not *work* against it because of one good provision." He reached over to pick up a stack of papers. "This was my legislation I introduced several years ago to create a bilateral bank between the United States and Mexico, but it failed. I gave a copy to Congressman (Esteban) Torres who was successful in implementing it as a part of the NAFTA agreement."

"Congressman, why didn't you carry it?" I asked. "It was your idea, your creation."

"I do not want anything to do with it. I tried and lost. Now it is up to Congressman Torres. Besides, I do not support the trade agreement."

He spoke for about an hour while standing behind his desk. He would remain true to his word. During the House debate on NAFTA, he did not speak out in opposition, but he voted "no" and simply delivered written remarks to the House.

The need for a bilateral bank between the United States and Mexico was evident to anyone who has traveled along the border that divides the two countries. The worst poverty and pollution in both seem to be concentrated along the border. The *maquiladora* industries (United States companies that assemble products tax free in Mexico) located their plants close to the border and contributed to the pollution.

In response to environmental concerns, NAFTA provided for the creation of the Border Environmental Cooperation Commission to identify water, sewer and landfill projects that needed financing. A bank was needed to provide that financing.

In anticipation of an affirmative vote on NAFTA, we had organized a committee to begin work to bring the headquarters of one of NAFTA's offspring agencies to San Antonio — the North American Development Bank, or one of the three secretariats of Labor, Environment, and Trade. Banker Tom Frost was chairman of our outreach committee.

The day after the NAFTA vote, Glenn Biggs, Jose Villarreal, Bartel Zachry, Frank Burney, Tom Frost and Bill Greehey met with Treasury Secretary Bentsen to give him a 52-page document presenting our arguments for locating one or all of the offices in San Antonio. After the meeting, Assistant Secretary Michael Levy told Tom Frost privately that the NADBank would be located in Washington and would never leave the capital.

Three days after the passage of NAFTA, I held a news conference to announce an expanded committee to be headed by Tom Frost and Bambi Cardenas to lobby for one or all of the NAFTA offices. I also said we were going to organize our international efforts under one umbrella organization. We took the San Antonio World Trade Association that had been spun off from Target '90 and formed the Free Trade Alliance. The alliance became a partnership of the Greater Chamber, the Economic Development Foundation, the Hispanic Chamber, and the city of San Antonio. Jose Martinez, a former aide to Senator John Tower, was named president.

Go for the Bank

In December, I led a delegation to Mexico City to meet with President Salinas. Our delegation gathered around tables arranged in a square as we waited for him. As a gesture of good will to San Antonio, Salinas invited members of the San Antonio media into the meeting. When he entered the room he took the seat next to me. He thanked us for the hard work we had done for NAFTA. We expressed our appreciation for his support of San Antonio.

After the meeting broke up, I stood next to Salinas in the hall-way. I said, "Mr. President, what should we work for, one of the secretariat offices or the North American Development Bank?"

"Go for the NADBank," he said without hesitation. This did not mean we had an inside track. It simply meant that the loca-tion of the three secretariat offices had already been decided. The bank was our only chance.

When I returned home we dropped all efforts to obtain one of the secretariats and concentrated on the NADBank. It was the big prize, anyway. The $3 billion bank would be funded equally by Mexico and the United States. It was expected to leverage another $20 to $30 billion from the private sector. It would fund infra-structure projects within 60 miles of the border. Ten percent of the bank's capital would be used for domestic purposes to help areas where employment was adversely affected by the trade agree-ment.

Early in February 1994, I met with Jose Villarreal; Andy Hernandez, director of the Southwest Voter Registration Educa-tion Project; and my assistant Beth Costello. Though only in his early 30s, Jose Villarreal knew the game of power politics well. He had joined the Clinton campaign and worked for more than eight months out of the Little Rock headquarters in an outreach program directed at Hispanic voters.

After the election, Jose worked for a short while in the White House and then resigned to return to private law practice. He knew all the key players in the White House, in addition to being a close friend of President Clinton.

Andy Hernandez was also in his early 30s. He had succeeded Willie Velasquez, the beloved founder of Southwest Voter Regis-tration. Willie had built Southwest Voter into a powerful national organization before his unfortunate early death. Andy was an exceedingly capable successor.

"The only chance we have for the bank is if President Clinton personally intervenes," Jose told us at our meeting. "Secretary Bentsen and the Treasury Department are not going to support us. They want the bank to be in Washington, under the thumb of the Inter-American Development Bank. Our local effort is doomed unless we expand our base. Andy has an idea of how to do this."

Andy Hernandez said that a coalition of national Hispanic organizations including the National Council of La Raza, Southwest Voter Registration, the Mexican American Legal Defense and Educational Fund, and the various Hispanic chambers of commerce were the key supporters of the NADBank. Without their support the bank would never have been created. He said we needed their active support to bring the bank to San Antonio. We would also need the support of Congressman Torres, the legislative sponsor of the bank.

"Tell me what to do and I'll do it," I said.

Andy said, "Support Jose in anything he needs to persuade President Clinton. Invite Congressman Torres to San Antonio and try to get his support." After the meeting with Andy and Jose, I put all my efforts into supporting their plan. I was convinced this was the only way we were going to get the bank.

Four days later, on February 6, I traveled with Jose to Houston for a fund-raiser for President Clinton. As the president and Secretary Bentsen greeted each of us, I mentioned that San Antonio wanted to be the site of the bank. I got nice smiles in return.

After the dinner, Jose saw President Clinton go into the men's room. Jose made a beeline for the bathroom and I followed him. He passed through security but I was stopped. Jose had clearance and I didn't.

In the men's room, Jose asked Clinton not to put the NADBank in Washington, where it would be buried in the bureaucracy. He urged him to put it close to the border where the projects would be. The president agreed that it would get lost in Washington, and said that he did not like everything being concentrated in the capital. He said he would not support placing it in Washington.

This "bathroom commitment" was extremely important. Getting the president to commit to locating the bank outside Washington gave us a clear shot at bringing it to San Antonio. The rest of the puzzle would have to be put together by Congressman Torres and the Hispanic coalition.

Less than two weeks later, Congressman Torres came to San Antonio at my invitation. He was up for re-election and the anti-NAFTA forces were out to beat him. I agreed to host a fund-raiser

President Bill Clinton joins Nelson and Tracy Wolff at a fund-raiser in Houston. (Wolff collection)

for him at my home. Prior to the event, he and I met with Andy Hernandez and Jose Villarreal.

"Congressman, we need your support to bring the bank to San Antonio," I said.

"I will support locating the bank close to the border of Mexico," he said. "I represent a congressional district in Los Angeles that may be adversely affected by the trade agreement. I want the domestic window to be located in my congressional district." The "domestic window" meant the office of the bank that would handle loans to neighborhoods and cities that lost jobs to the new foreign competition.

"We will support locating the domestic window in L.A.," I said.

Close to the Border

Now we had all the pieces of the puzzle together. Jose had convinced President Clinton to oppose putting the bank in Washington. Andy Hernandez had gotten the Hispanic coalition to support locating the bank close to the border.

"Close to the border" meant San Antonio. The decision to put the Border Environmental Cooperation Commission in Juarez, across the Rio Grande from El Paso, had precluded El Paso as a potential site for the bank. The only other major city close to the border that wanted the bank was San Diego, but Congressman Torres did not support San Diego. Our deal with him to spin off the domestic window to his district in Los Angeles tied up the whole package.

In mid-March, Dallas Congressman John Bryant announced that Dallas had been picked as the site for the Labor Secretariat. Immediate speculation began that San Antonio would not get the bank because another NAFTA plum could not be located in Texas. Some of our overly smart local academics said that we had set ourselves up for a fall. They said San Antonio's only future in international trade was trucking and warehousing.

After the Labor Secretariat announcement, San Diego put out a major effort to get the NADBank. Ironically, Assistant Treasury Secretary Michael Levy, who had told Tom Frost that the bank would not leave Washington, sent us a warning that San Diego was making headway with the White House. He called Albert Jacquez, chief of staff to Congressman Torres, with this information. Congressman Torres got several congressmen from the Los Angeles area to write the White House opposing San Diego. This was the knockout punch we needed.

At 4 p.m. on March 25, 1994, I received a call from Governor Richards. She said, "I just received a phone call from Secretary Bentsen. He is with President Clinton on Air Force One, headed for Dallas. He said the North American Development Bank will be located in San Antonio."

"That's great!" I replied. "What should I do now?"

"Call a press conference to announce that the bank is coming to San Antonio."

"You mean I should announce it instead of Secretary Bentsen or President Clinton?" I asked.

"Yes. Don't give them a chance to change their minds. Call the press conference right now."

I said, "Thanks, Governor. I love you." Within an hour, I held the news conference announcing that the bank would be located in San Antonio.

On June 17, Secretary Bentsen and Mexico's finance secretary, Pedro Aspe, convened the first board of directors meeting of the North American Development Bank in San Antonio. We held a luncheon for the directors attended by more than 500 business people.

Following the board meeting, City Manager Alex Briseño and I signed an agreement to provide space in a proposed International Center I wanted to be built on the grounds of HemisFair. The building would house the city's International Relations Department, the Mexico trade offices, the Free Trade Alliance, and the NADBank.

Tom Frost did a great job of organizing strong local support to get the NADBank. All elements of the community worked together. More than 70 individuals made calls to Washington officials regarding the location of the bank. San Antonio's strong local commitment was very important.

But without the leadership of Andy Hernandez, Jose Villarreal, and Congressman Torres, we simply would never have landed the bank. No matter how strong our local support was, we did not have the political muscle to pull off the victory by ourselves.

While there was jubilation over the passage of NAFTA and the decision to locate the NADBank in San Antonio, ominous signs in Mexico began to appear the day NAFTA went into effect. On New Year's Day 1994, a guerrilla uprising occurred in the Mexican state of Chiapas. The Zapatista National Liberation Army took the city of San Cristobal de las Casas. Although the uprising was contained in the jungles of Mexico's southernmost state, it raised fears about Mexico's stability. International investments in Mexico started to pull back.

Three months after the uprising, on March 23, 1994, PRI presidential candidate Donaldo Colosio was assassinated at a campaign rally in Tijuana. When Consul General Humberto Hernandez Haddad called me with the news, I could not believe it. Tracy and I had been so impressed with Colosio when we met him in July 1993. We were delighted when President Salinas designated him as the PRI candidate. It was a tragic loss both for Mexico and for the United States.

This was the first assassination of a major political figure in Mexico since presidential candidate Alvaro Obregon was killed in 1928. Mexico's foreign reserve accounts plunged. The Mexican government had to issue high-interest, short-term debt to attract foreign funds.

President Salinas quickly chose Ernesto Zedillo as the replacement candidate for Colosio. Zedillo, a Yale graduate, served as Colosio's campaign manager at the time of the assassination.

Zedillo was not prepared for the presidency. He did not have the charisma of Colosio nor did he know the key political leaders around the nation. But Salinas had few other choices. The key political leaders of PRI, including all the governors, acquiesced in his selection of Zedillo.

The PRI's political strength was put to the test in electing an unknown candidate. With a massive advertising campaign the PRI got out its supporters. On August 21, 1994, Zedillo was elected.

The election of President Zedillo seemed to assure most people that everything was back to normal. But not for long.

On September 28, Jose Franciso Ruiz Massieru, a former brother-in-law of President Salinas and the general secretary of PRI, was gunned down in his car outside the Casablanca Hotel in Mexico City. The assassin was caught and implicated several co-conspirators.

The revolt in Chiapas and two political assassinations had a negative impact on foreign investments. The economic miracle that President Salinas seemingly had brought to Mexico came to a screeching halt three weeks after the election of Ernesto Zedillo. Finance Minister Jaime Serra Puche announced a peso devaluation because Mexico could not pay its foreign debt.

A major financial disaster quickly developed. Billions of dollars in investment disappeared, inflation and interest rates soared, and thousands of jobs were lost. More than $34 billion in lost values on the Mexican stock market occurred within weeks. President Clinton put together a $50 billion international fund to stabilize the peso.

As of this writing, the peso has regained some of its strength and has stabilized. The Mexican stock market is rebounding and the Mexican economy is slowly coming back. After getting off to a shaky start, President Zedillo appears to have his feet solidly on the ground. Mexico repaid its debt to the United States at the end of 1996, years earlier than scheduled.

But former President Salinas became a man with no country when his brother, Raul, was indicted for murder in one of the political assassinations. Later it was discovered that Raul Salinas had more than $80 million in foreign bank accounts the origins of which he could not explain. Suspicions fell on his brother, the former president, although Carlos has been charged with no wrongdoing.

I believe that in the long run President Salinas will go down in history as the president who led Mexico into the modern era of free trade. Mexico will become much stronger as private enterprise and democracy grow there.

The North American Development Bank is up and operating. President Zedillo appointed former ambassador to Japan and Canada Alfredo Phillips Olmedo as director general of the bank. My friend Victor Miramontes was appointed deputy director by President Clinton. Victor was a founding partner of Cisneros Asset Management and holds a master's degree in economics and a law degree from Stanford University.

The capital funding for the bank is paid over a four-year period. Tom Frost has continued to be instrumental in supporting Congressman Torres' efforts to make sure the bank is funded fully. In its first year, the NADBank was the only international bank not to suffer cuts in funding. The next three years are important to assure full funding of the bank. There are seven financing projects pending before the bank. Two have been approved.

Even with all the major traumas in Mexico, our neighbor to the south is still our third-largest trading partner. Today in San Antonio, there are some 350 companies exporting approximately $685 million worth of goods and services annually. Retail trade and tourism with Mexico have picked up since the peso devaluation. Our close relationship with Mexico was one of the major reasons that Southwestern Bell moved its corporate headquarters to San Antonio in 1992. SBC Communications owns part of and manages the huge Telmex phone system in Mexico. Thirty Mexican companies are located in San Antonio.

The city of San Antonio continues to be a major player in developing international trade. The city has opened another trade office, this one in Mexico City. My former assistant, Beth Costello, now heads an International Relations Department of 15 people.

In September 1993, World Trade magazine ranked San Antonio among its Top Ten international cities. Conde Nast magazine ranks San Antonio as one of the Top Ten destination cities in the world for tourists. In April 1994, Hispanic Business magazine ranked San Antonio the most hospitable city for new Hispanic businesses.

The San Antonio economy is booming. We created more than 70,000 net new jobs from 1991 to 1995. Our unemployment rate as of this writing is 3.5 percent, down from 6.9 percent when I took office. Our international effort played a big part in creating these jobs.

★★★

Lessons on NADBank

■ **Find your international niche.**
San Antonio will never be able to compete directly with Houston and Dallas because of our lack of a port and a major airline hub. We found our niche in financial and information services as represented by the NADBank and the University of Mexico campus. We are a city of small businesses that can be effective in adding value by distribution and small manufacturing and assembly.

■ **Build alliances to support your efforts.**
The Hispanic alliance was the main reason that San Antonio got the North American Development Bank. We provided the local support and they provided the political muscle to persuade the White House to locate the bank in San Antonio.

■ **Strike while the news is hot.**
Governor Ann Richards gave me great advice when she told
me to call a news conference and announce that San Antonio
had the NADBank before President Clinton and his advisers
could change their minds. My news conference locked in the
deal.

■ **Organize one international trade alliance.**
In order to keep a clear focus on trade and not create an over-
lapping and confusing array of groups dealing with trade issues, we organized the Free Trade Alliance. The four partners
in the organization brought their respective strengths to the
confederation.

16

Downtown Rescue: Preserving Our History

Nobody in San Antonio gives a better embrace than Father Virgil Elizondo. The Mexican *abrazo* is a traditional greeting among friends, and Father Elizondo with his sincere, friendly manner is one of its premier practitioners.

Elizondo offered an *abrazo* when he came to see me at City Hall early in my term, on July 16, 1991. In my position as mayor, and his as pastor of San Fernando Cathedral, we were both temporary occupants of two historic buildings in the heart of the city.

The cathedral sits just across Flores Street from City Hall, facing historic Main Plaza, or "Plaza de las Islas," the original center of the city. The "islands" in the plaza's name are a reference to the Canary Islands, home of San Antonio's first Spanish civilian settlers, who arrived in 1731. Across the plaza and beyond Soledad Street is the flood bypass of the San Antonio River.

As is common with traditional settlements, the San Antonio settlers' parish church (now the cathedral) of San Fernando fronts one side of this plaza and the county courthouse occupies another. San Fernando, which was enlarged to its present size in the 19th century and restored in the 1970s, is the oldest "seat" of a Catholic bishop in the United States. Its cornerstone was laid by the Canary Islanders in 1734.

While Father Elizondo's temporary home faces one plaza, mine sits in the middle of another. City Hall was constructed in the "Plaza de Armas," or Military Plaza, the site of the presidio, or military garrison, founded in 1722.

Originally, our City Hall was a jewel box of a limestone building. An ornate little dome sat on top and alternating round and square turreted towers marked the corners. Unfortunately, the building was maimed in a 1920s "modernization" that removed the dome and the turrets, replacing them with a nondescript fourth floor. When I took office in 1991, the facade of City Hall was literally falling down around us.

After our warm *abrazo*, Father Elizondo said, "Mayor, I have a committee working on restoring San Fernando Cathedral. Andy Perez, our architect, has researched the records of the church as well as city records. He suggested we expand the work of the committee to include studying the area stretching from the San Antonio River to Market Square. The committee would like to visit with you."

The sector Father Elizondo was talking about stretches five blocks from the west bank of the San Antonio River to El Mercado, or Market Square, which backs up against an elevated interstate highway. Across the highway lies the Vista Verde Urban Renewal Area, which included the failed Fiesta Plaza shopping mall.

Many other historic buildings also occupy the west end of downtown. The Bexar County Courthouse is an imposing structure of red granite, built in the 1880s in Romanesque-revival style with towers at its two front corners. The white stucco Spanish Governor's Palace is located behind City Hall. Behind the Spanish Governor's Palace and across San Pedro Creek, the old Continental Hotel, once a favorite of expatriate Mexican revolutionaries as they planned their campaigns early in the century, has been converted into the offices of our city-county health department.

Just west of the extended City Hall complex is El Mercado, a one-time farmer's market transformed into a tourist center featuring Mexican arts and crafts. Milam Park is located between El

USAA Chairman Robert McDermott and Mayor Lila Cockrell attend a salute to Archbishop Patrick Flores to benefit the restoration of San Fernando Cathedral. (Gloria Ferniz, Express-News)

Mercado and Santa Rosa Hospital. On Houston Street, a block east, lies the Alameda Theater, the heart of Mexican culture from the 1950s through the 1970s. As this book goes to press, the Alameda is being restored. The home of Jose Antonio Navarro, one of the two native Texans among the signers of the Texas Declaration of Independence, is located just south of this area.

Father Elizondo understood that unless we took some steps to preserve our heritage we would lose it. At that time, City Hall was crumbling, as was the Alameda and the historic lobby of the Frost Bank Building. Trevino Street had become an ugly parking lot between the cathedral and the bank. Milam Park was unused green space, and the Farmer's Market had only a few tenants. And there was no access to west downtown from the San Antonio River, meaning most tourists never saw the historic areas of our city apart from the Alamo and the missions.

I told Father Elizondo that I was eager to meet with his committee. I told him that I had a few ideas of my own. I wanted to convert the Frost Bank lobby into a council chamber to replace the dark and crowded "bat cave" chamber we presently occupied. I also told him I wanted to restore the facade of City Hall, to renovate the Farmer's Market and adjacent Milam Park, and to tear down Fiesta Plaza and replace it with some worthy civic project.

Father Elizondo said he would arrange a meeting.

A few weeks later I met again with Father Elizondo, along with Lionel Sosa, Andy Perez and downtown City Councilman Roger Perez. Lionel said that if we could successfully revive the historic civic center of San Antonio, it could be a showplace of our cultural diversity and the history of our city. "This is where the city started and we should continuously celebrate it."

Andy Perez explained his plan to link activities in this area to the San Antonio River bypass, just east of the Plaza de las Islas. We needed an entryway to the river in order to do that.

Most of the east side of the plaza was a surface parking lot. Once, there had been an architecturally significant office building on the site, but it had been demolished over a weekend some years before, without benefit of a demolition permit. You could never have gotten a permit to tear the building down, but now that it was gone the opportunity existed to link the plaza directly to the river.

Andy suggested that a broad staircase linking the river and the plaza could be the starting point for a series of visual and pedestrian links extending past City Hall and the Spanish Governor's Palace all the way to Market Square.

I agreed to work with their committee as they continued to develop their plan. As they got up to leave I said, "One of the projects I mentioned may be coming up soon."

"Versailles West"

As Father Elizondo's committee worked on the overall historic civic center plan, I concentrated on one of the four projects I wanted to accomplish. Once a week during the summer of 1991 City Manager Alex Briseño, City Architect Tim Palomera and I would walk across Flores Street from City Hall to the old Frost Bank Building. We would enter the back door to the building and walk down a hallway into the building's abandoned lobby.

The 11-story building was constructed in 1922 across Trevino Street from San Fernando Cathedral. In 1973 Frost Bank put up a new 21-story building across Commerce Street, which it still occupies today. The Plaza Club, where I had lunch with Henry Cisneros when he asked me to take the helm of Target '90, is on the top floor of this new building.

In 1986, the year before I was elected to council, the city bought the bank building for $11.6 million. It was a controversial purchase because the city paid more than the appraised value.

Despite the controversy, Mayor Cisneros had forged ahead with the purchase. There simply were no other large buildings so close to City Hall that could house the many city agencies scattered in leased space all around the area.

The city renovated the top 10 floors of the building, and moved several city departments into this space. Officially we renamed it the Main Plaza Building, but everyone still referred to it as the Old Frost Bank Building.

At the time, Luby's Cafeteria had a lease on the lobby. In 1989 the lease expired and Luby's moved out, leaving the lobby and the mezzanine a mess. It looked as if vandals had torn it up.

Tim brought some old photos of the lobby as it looked on the opening day of the Frost Bank. The ornamental plaster ceiling featuring floral medallions was beautiful. It stood three stories above the floor of the lobby. The mezzanine that wrapped around the second story featured Tiffany lamps on marble railings. An Italian marble stairway led to the basement. Bronze pocket doors were at the entrance. We looked at these pictures envisioning a restoration.

The city had made no decision as to what the old lobby should be used for. I felt the best use of the space would be as the City Council chambers and a civic meeting hall.

By the fall of 1991, Alex and Tim had the plan and a budget ready. It called for restoring the original ornamental ceilings, replacing the damaged cast stone and marble finishes, and rewiring and restoring the historic light fixtures. The space would provide seating for 254 people and room to accommodate another 200 people in the mezzanine and aisles. The cost was estimated to be $1.5 million.

On October 10, council gave preliminary approval to the plan. There were only two "no" votes. This was going easier than I had first expected.

Then Express-News columnist Roddy Stinson decided to ignite a little fire. He wrote on October 16, "If you are a citizen of San Antonio and you are not outraged by the latest kingdom-building scheme at City Hall, you deserve whatever happens to your tax bill. This raw deal is as good as done unless taxpayers rise up and say: Enough is enough. We are sick of scams and schemes. We are tired of subterfuge and chicanery. We are fed up with politicians who work and play with their hands in our pockets. And we are not going to take it anymore ... If you have only one stamp, write Wolff. He is the chief slyboots behind this Versailles West Plan."

Stinson's blast sent me to the showers. The phone rang off the wall with calls from angry citizens. A full year would pass before we got back on track.

Meanwhile, at the urging of Father Elizondo, Councilman Roger Perez and I got council approval in July 1992 to appoint a seven-member committee to develop a comprehensive rescue plan for the historic civic center of San Antonio. June Reedy was appointed chairman.

In an interim report in the fall of 1992, one year after Roddy Stinson's ambush, the task force recommended the renovation of the old Frost Bank lobby into a new council chamber and the restoration of City Hall's facade. They also recommended closing Trevino Street between San Fernando Cathedral and the old Frost Bank Building. Converted into a plaza, the street would provide a visual link and pedestrian walkway from the Plaza de las Islas to City Hall.

During the time June Reedy's commission was working, Alex and I visited about the need to develop a comprehensive plan to address the space needs of several city departments. Alex put together a $9.6 million plan to renovate several city buildings.

I was now ready to go back to council with support from the task force as well as a financing package to restore City Hall and convert the bank lobby into a civic meeting hall, rather than a council chamber. When we revealed the plan in October, public reaction was positive. My confidence began to pick up. At one of the October council meetings, Weir Labatt told me, "Go for the whole enchilada."

"What do you mean?

"Let's use the space as a council chamber."

"Do you think we can get the votes?" I asked.

Weir assured me we could.

I began again to lobby each council member. They said they were ready to fade the heat.

In November 1992, the council unanimously approved the $9.6 million package and instructed staff to restore the old Frost Bank lobby into a new council chamber. San Antonio Light columnist Rick Casey called it "some foxy move."

Inell Schooler, president of the Conservation Society, told me, "I have something to show you that we have stored in a warehouse on the West Side of town."

What a surprise! There were 24 portraits of former mayors, including Antonio Menchaca (1838-39), Sam Maverick (1839-1840), Maury Maverick (1939-1941) and Bryan Callaghan (who spearheaded the construction of City Hall during his first term, 1885-92, and then served two more terms, 1897-99 and 1905-1912). The paintings had an estimated value as high as $10 million, and they had been in storage since 1959. The Conservation Society provided $10,000 to restore them and then gave them to the city to hang in the new council chamber lobby.

It was the crowning touch. The ceiling, paintings and Tiffany lights were restored. The marble stairway was installed to reach the mezzanine. A false wall was removed revealing the original arched stone windows facing San Fernando Cathedral.

On May 19, 1994, we held the grand opening of the new council chamber. Several hundred citizens came.

The Alameda, El Mercado, Milam Park and City Hall

With one battle out of the way, the historic civic center task force continued its restoration planning. Council approved the final plan, developed by architects Andrew Perez and Michael McChesney and landscape architect James Keeter, in October 1993.

It envisioned a restored historic civic center that would enable us to take the following walk:

Start from a river barge, at the point where the river crosses Commerce Street at Soledad. Walk up a staircase flanked on both sides by cascading water, and plants and trees.

Head west, crossing Soledad Street into a newly landscaped Plaza de las Islas. Walking through the park, you see across Main Avenue a courtyard between San Fernando Cathedral and the new City Council chambers. The courtyard frames a picture across Flores Street of the newly restored City Hall.

Meander through the courtyard, cross Flores Street, and on to the newly landscaped grounds of City Hall. Through City Hall and out the west door, you cross a new plaza between City Hall and the Spanish Governor's Palace.

Walk out the back of the Spanish Governor's Palace and cross a restored San Pedro Creek on a new footbridge that leads to the rear of the original Continental Hotel, now home to the city's health department.

Finally, cross Santa Rosa Street to El Mercado. See the newly restored Milam Park across Commerce Street north of El Mercado. Walk through El Mercado and cross another plaza to the newly restored Farmer's Market. Behind the Farmer's Market, cross another plaza under Interstate 35 to the new University of Texas downtown campus.

It's unusual for the city to get ahead of a final plan. Sometimes, though, momentum starts on a project and excitement carries the day. So it was with the historic civic center plan. Things really began to fall into place when Alex Briseño hired Becky Waldman in February 1992 to be in charge of "special projects" for downtown. She focused on the historic civic center plan and worked quickly to implement council policy.

By the end of 1994, we had completed the $4 million restoration of City Hall and enclosed the Farmer's Market, creating 96 retail spaces. Trevino Street became a courtyard between San Fernando Cathedral and the new City Council chambers, and the new plaza was named in honor of Father Virgil Elizondo, who first inspired me and the rest of council to proceed with the historic civic center plan.

The refurbishment of Milam Park, the original *campo santo,* or cemetery, of the Spanish Colonial settlement, was finished in early 1995. The bones of Texas revolutionary hero Ben Milam, which were found in the park, no doubt rest easier. The centerpiece is a kiosk given to the city by the Mexican state of Jalisco. Dr. Carlos Orozco, chairman of Friends of Milam Park, was instrumental in leading the effort to provide private funds for the project.

From the day Councilman Roger Perez was elected in 1991, he had a dream to complement the restored Majestic Theater with a restored Alameda Theater. The two theaters sit five blocks apart on Houston Street. The Majestic was a landmark of the Anglo culture of San Antonio and the Alameda of the Hispanic. When it opened in March 1949, the 2,500-seat Alameda was the premiere Spanish-language movie palace in the nation, featuring both films and live performances. Cantinflas and other Mexican stars performed there. A dramatic eight-story sign projects the Alameda name. It is made of porcelain, black iron and 4,000 feet of gas tubing using a cold-cathode lighting process. In December 1994, the council approved the purchase of the Alameda Theater and adjoining Casa de Mexico office building for $952,000.

Most of the architectural detail of the theater was in good condition. Pedro Teran's murals of Texas and Mexican history are rendered in a phosphorescent paint. The railings in the mezzanine are curved Plexiglas with drawings of plant life.

At the ceremonies celebrating the purchase, Henry Muñoz and Maria Elena Torralva were named to lead the newly created foundation to restore the Alameda.

Council approved plans and funding for a courtyard to link City Hall to the Spanish Governor's Palace, replacing the existing parking lot. We also purchased the parking lot at the corner of Soledad and Commerce that would become the stairway between Main Plaza and the River Walk. My friend Robert Braubach was instrumental in convincing Baron Theo Bracht to sell us the land. As of this writing, council has not found the funds to build the stairway to the River Walk.

While we moved quickly on implementing major elements of the plan, much more needs to be done. The entrance to the river needs to be built, San Pedro Creek has to be restored, a courtyard behind the old Continental Hotel needs to be built, the Alameda Theater needs restoration, Plaza de las Islas needs to be landscaped, and amenities such as trees, water features, and benches need to be located along the pedestrian walkways. Future councils and mayors will have to complete the plan in order to finish the restoration of our historic downtown area.

While the western edge of downtown is framed by the elevated Interstate 35, what happens on the other side of the highway plays a significant part in the success of the historic civic center. Across the freeway was the Vista Verde project that included the abandoned Fiesta Plaza when I took office. Some vision was needed to repair the area.

A Downtown Campus for UTSA

During the early evening hours of December 16, 1992, I walked into the Institute of Texan Cultures on the HemisFair grounds. I was there to attend a reception in honor of the recently installed chancellor of the University of Texas System, Dr. Bill Cunningham. As I walked in, a reporter for the San Antonio Light stopped me.

"Chancellor Cunningham told the editorial board at the paper today that he is not committed to the Fiesta Plaza site for a downtown university site," the reporter said. "In fact, he said he is not committed to any site downtown."

A flash of anger swept through me. "The community has been promised a downtown location by the university system for 20 years," I said. "If the university does not accept the land and does not make that commitment to a downtown campus, there's going to be a lot of disenchantment with the whole UT System. And I am going to lead that disenchantment."

After the reporter walked away, Dr. John Howe, president of the University of Texas Health Science Center at San Antonio, came up and said, "Would you join Chancellor Cunningham and me at the head table?"

I told him I wouldn't. "I have just been told that Chancellor Cunningham is not committed to the Fiesta Plaza site for a downtown campus, or for that matter to any other site downtown. The university has broken its word to me. In fact, John, I am going to walk out of this meeting right now." I turned and left the building.

The next day the San Antonio Light carried a headline that said, "UT not committed to downtown site." The paper quoted Chancellor Cunningham as saying, "I think we will decide at some point to build another campus within the San Antonio community." He did not say where or when.

To comprehend why I was so angry, we must go back to the university's first appearance in San Antonio. Decisions were made then that had a profound effect on the city's growth patterns and that carried symbolic importance for racial and ethnic relations in the city.

During the legislative sessions of 1971 and 1973, I was first a member of the Appropriations Committee in the Texas House and then a member of the Texas Senate and vice chairman of the Finance Committee. I had played a role in obtaining initial funding for construction of the University of Texas at San Antonio as well as funding for the University of Texas Medical School. The medical school is the centerpiece of a separate institution within the UT System, now known as the University of Texas Health Science Center at San Antonio.

UTSA and the Health Science Center were parts of the behemoth UT System that includes nine general academic universities and six health institutions with an annual budget exceeding $4 billion. The 1876 Texas Constitution established the Permanent University Fund through the appropriation of land grants. The University of Texas receives two-thirds of the generated funds and Texas A&M one-third. The funds grew into the billions of dollars when oil was discovered on the land grants in 1923.

While there was unanimous support in San Antonio in 1970 to locate a campus in our city, local opinion was divided over where to locate it. Many wanted the campus downtown. The more powerful players wanted it located far north of the city. Unfortunately, the University System's Board of Regents sided with those who wanted a northern campus. The regents picked a site closer to Boerne than to San Antonio, a location especially far from the less prosperous areas of the city, where transportation to a distant campus could prove a problem for some students and their families. The decision left an odor, because some of the regents' friends and associates owned extensive acreage in the area.

Today, more than 17,000 students attend the University of Texas at San Antonio and its four colleges: Business, Fine Arts and Humanities, Sciences and Engineering, and Social and Behavioral Studies. It offers 78 bachelor's, master's and doctoral degree programs, including 50 baccalaureate programs. Graduate programs include eight master's concentrations in the College of Business and doctoral programs in neurobiology and computer science. The vast majority of students are from San Antonio and South Texas. It is a commuter university with only a few students living on campus.

While UTSA grew faster than any other UT campus in the last two decades, it received the lowest level of funding increases. The university's funding was typical of other South Texas institutions. Funding inequities within the University of Texas System were alleged and challenged in a lawsuit filed by Al Kauffman, representing the Mexican American Legal Defense and Educational Fund, in 1989 on behalf of the League of United Latin American Citizens.

That lawsuit pressured the university system to address the inequities. As the 1993 legislative session drew near, the University of Texas System hoped to reach a compromise to settle the suit. With the potential for funding suddenly apparent, the issue of a downtown campus began to rise to the top of local concerns.

The desire for a downtown campus dates back to 1980 when the city traded six acres of land in HemisFair Plaza to the university for property across from the Alamo. A downtown campus was one of the goals of Target '90. Manuel Berriozabal, a UTSA faculty member and husband of City Councilwoman Maria Berriozabal, was the member of the Education Committee that made the recommendation for a downtown campus even though the idea was opposed by then-UTSA President James Wagener.

The university had promised to build a campus but somehow never seemed to find the funds. Now, because of MALDEF's lawsuit, there was an opportunity to acquire the funds. But you can't get funding without a location.

On June 29, 1991, Jude Valdez came to visit me. Jude was the vice president of downtown development for UTSA. He is a small man who wears large glasses. Behind the glasses is a never-yielding look of determination and seriousness. Over the next two years, Jude and I would develop a close working relationship while attempting to bring a university campus to downtown.

"I have been doing a lot of research on a location for a downtown campus for UTSA," Jude told me. "The HemisFair site is too small to accommodate a downtown campus. The Alamodome and the expansion of the convention center have made the location too crowded. I believe the campus should be located on the Fiesta Plaza site. Will you help me?"

Fiesta Plaza lies on 9.5 acres just west of Interstate 35. It is best known locally, and unfairly, as the site of Henry Cisneros' most spectacular failure in downtown redevelopment, hence the double entendre meaning of its nickname, the "Pepto-Bismol mall."

When Henry came into office as a councilman, the area known as Vista Verde had been one of obsolete industries and dilapidated housing.

Communities Organized for Public Service pushed through a plan to redevelop the area with new commercial development in the northern and eastern sectors, and new single-family houses for low-to-moderate income occupants in the southern and western portions. Although it was not particularly Henry's plan, he supported it all along and so he got most of the blame when parts of the plan went sour. The new housing and some businesses succeeded.

But the 280,000-square-foot, fully enclosed shopping mall clad in a garish pink stucco was an unmitigated disaster. Unlike Rivercenter Mall on the east end of downtown, which is supported by strong links to the convention center and the tourist industry, Fiesta Plaza was supposed to serve a local market. Unfortunately, that market simply did not exist amid the poverty of San Antonio's near West Side.

At the mall's opening in 1985, 60 tenants occupied just over half of the available space. It was never fully leased. The developer defaulted on his obligations, so in 1988 the place closed completely. The abandoned building soon deteriorated and became a hangout for bums. Other monikers were "the pink elephant" and "Fiasco Plaza." It was an albatross around Henry Cisneros' neck as mayor, a visible daily reminder of a government-funded project gone bad.

So I was positive in my response to Jude Valdez. I knew a downtown campus could transform the area into a vibrant part of the city. The Fiesta Plaza site was easily accessible to all parts of town and served by excellent bus lines. The university would be a great catalyst for the West Side, serving as a bridge to downtown in the same way the Alamodome would for the East Side. I asked Jude what he needed me to do.

"I need you to help me with the university's leadership," he said. "There is an element within the university that does not want a downtown campus. Second, I need you to help me with the Resolution Trust Corporation. I believe they will donate the site to the university if we clear up the tax problems."

The Resolution Trust Corporation was created by the federal government to dispose of the assets of failed thrift institutions. They had foreclosed on Fiesta Plaza in 1991. Every time I drove downtown I glanced out the window as I passed the "pink elephant." This daily reminder increased my resolve to solve the problem.

On August 18, I met with Sam Kirkpatrick, president of UTSA, and Jude, and pledged my support to acquire the property for the university. Seven months later, at a meeting with all the taxing authorities, we finally resolved the tax issues. We had a clear title.

But after the RTC obtained clear title, a new batch of RTC officials changed their minds, and decided to auction the property to the highest bidder on June 10.

Jude Valdez asked me to meet with him, President Sam Kirkpatrick, and UTSA finance chief Dan Williams. Alex Briseño and Assistant City Manager Rolando Bono joined us to discuss how the city could help.

After a series of meetings, we agreed to bid for the site at the minimum asking price of $980,000. We said we would also provide another $2.5 million to the University of Texas System in exchange for the return of a portion of the university's six-acre site in HemisFair. We were interested in the HemisFair land because of the convention center expansion.

Jude briefed Henry Cisneros on the issue and I called him for help. Henry and I met with Councilmen Juan Solis and Bill Thornton, President Kirkpatrick, Jude Valdez and Joe Krier, president of the Greater Chamber. The business community committed to support the purchase of the property for the University of Texas.

During the meeting, Solis mentioned he was extremely unhappy with the university. He was angry over the demotion of Vice President Leonard Valverde, the highest-ranking Hispanic at UTSA. An organization called Juntos was demanding Sam Kirkpatrick's resignation over the demotion of Valverde. Juan said he probably would not support our efforts.

Henry Cisneros got RTC President Albert Casey on the phone. We asked him to intervene and donate the land to the university. I followed up with a letter to Casey, writing, "We are creating a partnership between the city and UTSA to serve a heretofore unserved minority segment of our population. We need your intervention to make it happen." I asked for preference in our proposed bid and for a delay on the June 10 auction date.

On May 18, Henry arranged a meeting in Austin with the top leaders of the University of Texas System. Outgoing Chancellor Hans Mark and incoming Chancellor William Cunningham were both there. Henry presented all the arguments for the university to locate at the Fiesta Plaza site. I pledged to seek council approval.

Up to this point, I had kept all the meetings off my public calendar. But on May 20, 1992, the story leaked. The Express-News headline read, "UTSA may set up a downtown branch. Fiesta Plaza considered as site."

On May 28, I briefed the City Council on the plan in executive session. I got support to move forward. Then I went public.

Then, all hell broke loose. Juan Solis, whose district contained the Fiesta Plaza site, came out against the plan. COPS and the Metro Alliance supported him. They said it was a bad deal for the city. They felt the university should pay for the land if it wanted it.

The business community jumped in to help me. They not only supported the city purchase but also agreed to raise $1 million to reimburse the city for the purchase. Damaso Oliva got the Hispanic Chamber to pledge $1 million and Pat Legan backed that up with other business support.

The San Antonio Light launched an intensive campaign to kill the plan, criticizing us for buying back land in HemisFair Plaza that the editorial writers said we had given the university in 1980. Actually the land had been a trade. They said other downtown sites needed to be studied. Study and delay was what had been happening for the last 20 years! To study and delay is to kill.

I thought Councilman Solis and the San Antonio Light had taken a crazy pill. Financially it was a good deal for the city. The HemisFair land was very valuable.

Not only was the land transaction a benefit to the city, but getting rid of that eyesore on the West Side and replacing it with a university was a winner for everyone concerned. Many other cities have made outright gifts of land for a university. The city had a history of helping higher-education institutions. We had contributed $2.9 million to the building of Palo Alto College's Olympic swimming pool, and we had provided a building for the University of Mexico.

On the day before the council vote scheduled for June 4, Sam Kirkpatrick wrote a letter withdrawing the university's participation, stating "we couldn't deal with the business and legal details in a timely fashion." He expressed hope that the Fiesta Plaza deal would eventually work, but added that if it failed, then he doubted a downtown campus would be built anytime soon.

A well-placed source told us that what really happened: Sam had met with then-Board of Regents Chairman Louis Beecherl, who told him to drop the bid. Fortunately he was in the last year of his term and we knew Governor Ann Richards would appoint someone who believed in our cause. She did just that by appointing Bernard Rapoport, who had grown up in the neighborhood of the proposed site.

There's always another way to get a deal done. As mayor I served as chairman of the $414 million police and firefighters pension fund. The fund's board is made up of two council members, and two active and two retired officers. Weir Labatt was the other council member on the board.

I met with Carlos Resendez, the president of the fund, to persuade him to support the purchase of the site. He thought it was a good investment. Jude briefed the pension fund board on the issue. Weir agreed to carry the ball in convincing the board to bid for the Fiesta Plaza site. If the bid was high, the land would be held for one year for the benefit of UTSA. This would give the university time to do whatever study was needed. The board supported the proposed purchase with a unanimous vote on June 10, and submitted a bid of $1,000,100.

On June 12, the bids were open and a real estate agent who bid $1.8 million for the site was top bidder. He said his clients intended to build a retail center. What madness! I was sure his bid would fall through, so we decided to bide our time.

Sure enough, on September 15 the deal with the real estate agent did fall through. In addition to the pension fund bid, the Center for Health Care Services (formerly known as the Bexar County Mental Health-Mental Retardation agency) and Bill Miller's Bar-B-Q had submitted bids. Agents for Bill Miller told Jude they might use it for a headquarters or a Dolly Parton dinner theater, or they might give it to the university.

I called Balous Miller on September 15, the day the highest bid fell apart. He said he would definitely give the land to the university. I said I would get the pension fund to drop its bid. I called RTC President Alfred Casey and asked him to accept the Miller bid.

"We have an outstanding citizen with cash money who is ready to give the property to the university," I told Casey. "What else can you ask for?" He said he would try to help.

The second-highest bidder was the Center for Health Care Services, while Bill Miller was third. We launched an intensive lobbying effort to ask the center not to exercise its bid. We offered to help them find other space. Juan Solis came on board to help convince the agency to drop its bid. He had changed his mind and supported UTSA after the university resolved the dispute over the demotion of Leonard Valverde. On September 22, the Center for Health Care Services dropped its bid.

This made Bill Miller Bar-B-Q next in line. But our troubles were still not over. When it came to light that several old filling stations had been located on the property, environmental concerns were raised. I called RTC's President Casey again and asked for help in remediation of the environmental concerns while Jude lobbied the local RTC office. The RTC finally agreed to set aside $500,000 of the purchase price to clear up any environmental problems.

On November 6, the City Council drew up 20 legislative proposals we would support in the upcoming legislative session. We placed funding for the downtown university campus as our chief priority, and unanimously passed a resolution asking the UT System to accept the gift of the Fiesta Plaza site.

On November 11, the purchase agreement was signed between Miller and the RTC. We thought the battle was over. That is, until Chancellor William Cunningham came to San Antonio and said the UT System was *still* not committed.

This takes us back to the beginning of the story. I believe you can understand why after all our hard work I was so upset about Cunningham's remarks. It looked as if the university system was again playing San Antonio for a fool. More studies and more delays.

Based on inside information, I knew opinion at UTSA was divided. While officials there gave lip service to building a downtown campus, behind the scenes many were fighting the proposal. Professors complained about having to drive downtown from their homes on the North Side. To their way of thinking, it was better for a student to spend hours traveling by bus. Many did not like the idea that the university would be located in a poor area of the city.

The first two times Chancellor Cunningham tried to reach me after my walkout, I didn't take his calls. I had learned a few lessons from Henry B. about softening people up by making them

wait. I also wanted time to plan exactly what I was going to tell him.

When I took the third phone call, Cunningham said, "Mayor, I want you to know I am committed to a downtown campus. I like the Fiesta Plaza site. The newspaper misconstrued my remarks."

"I hope you understand that for the first time there is now unified support for the Fiesta Plaza site," I said. "Everybody is on board. It is not only the inner-city Hispanic community, but all of the business community and unanimous support of the council and our legislative delegation."

Officials representing the city, the Legislature and the University of Texas at San Antonio pose at the ground-breaking for the UTSA Downtown campus August 10, 1995. They include (left to right) Mayor Nelson Wolff, UT Regents chairman Bernard Rapoport, state Sen. Greg Luna, UT Regent Tom Loeffler, UTSA President Sam Kirkpatrick, state Rep. Leticia Van de Putte, state Rep. Robert Puente, UT Chancellor Bill Cunningham and state Rep. Ciro Rodriguez. (Wolff collection)

"We are going to make it happen," he said. "I will need the total support of San Antonio on the overall funding issues for the system, including a $254 million package for San Antonio and South Texas."

"You will have our total support if you hang with us on the downtown campus."

Chancellor Cunningham provided the key support. Despite the divided opinion at UTSA, he became the champion of the downtown site. Without his total support, the UT Board of Regents and the coordinating board would never have approved the downtown campus.

The council and our legislative delegation had dinner the night of December 15 at the Plaza San Antonio Hotel. We all agreed to work together for passage of the funding legislation. Senator Gregory Luna took the lead in the Senate and Representatives Christine Hernandez and Karyne Conley in the House. Our delegation, which was not well known in Austin for unity, provided bipartisan support.

On March 1, 1993, while the Legislature was in session, we held a news conference in the dilapidated Fiesta Plaza building.

"Out of these ashes will rise a university that will bring hope and opportunity to thousands of young men and women," I said. We then went outside and Balous Miller jumped on the bulldozer and took the first whack at demolishing the old building to make way for a new campus.

In early March, House Appropriations Chairman Rob Junell visited San Antonio to meet with UTSA President Sam Kirkpatrick and Representatives John Shields, Sylvia Romo and Hernandez. Kirkpatrick presented a list of three funding priorities with the downtown campus last. When Junell asked if these were the priorities, Kirkpatrick said yes.

Representative Hernandez said she was shocked and stunned. Senator Madla wrote a letter to Kirkpatrick saying he had reneged on a promise to make the downtown campus top priority. Lt. Governor Bob Bullock wrote a letter to Chancellor Cunningham. Ten days later, Kirkpatrick said the list was a misunderstanding and that the downtown campus was No. 1 on his priority list.

It seemed the problems would never end, but they finally did. Chancellor Cunningham stayed solidly behind the funding request, which the Legislature passed. Regents Tom Loeffler and Sam Barshop, both from San Antonio, became supportive.

On October 6, the university accepted the cleared land at a ceremony held at the Institute of Texan Cultures.

"I never had so much trouble giving away $1 million," Balous Miller said aptly. One and a half years had passed since Miller Bar-B-Q made its original bid on the property. No one has ever accused the University of Texas of being light on its feet.

On August 10, 1995, groundbreaking ceremonies were held. Chairman of the Board Bernard Rapoport gave an emotional speech. He spoke of the old neighborhood where he had grown up around the site. He was so proud of playing a role in bringing to the area a university campus that would act as a drawbridge out of poverty.

As of this writing, the first building in the downtown campus is almost complete, a 110,000-square-foot structure with 26 class-rooms and 1,000 seats. Classes will begin in the fall of 1997.

Groundbreaking for the second phase was held on January 24, 1997. State Senator Luna spoke of the time he patrolled nearby streets as a young policeman. The entire campus will be completed in the summer of 1998, and will accommodate 6,500 students. Maybe then a 25-year-old controversy that began when the original campus was placed too far north for many minority students will be put to rest.

On the other hand, some things never change, among them the arrogance of power.

If one person should be singled out for making the university live up to its word, it would be Jude Valdez. He never gave up.

On September 1, 1994, the position of vice president for downtown operations was eliminated, effectively removing Jude Valdez from any further responsibility for UTSA-Downtown. Jude still works for the university as vice president for extended education and economic development. He is engaged in a lawsuit over his removal.

★★★

Lessons from Rescuing Downtown

■ **Camouflage a controversial proposal.**
After I delayed the vote on the new council chamber in the lobby of the Frost Bank Building, I returned a year later and included the proposal in a financial package of downtown improvements. Although the council chamber proposal was out in the open, the other parts of the package helped give it cover.

■ **It's easier to win against concerted opposition with the help of an insider.**
I never could have overcome the opposition of the University of Texas System to a downtown campus had Jude Valdez not helped me with inside information.

■ **If one road is closed, find a detour.**
When my support for purchasing the Fiesta Plaza site for the university blew up, I turned to the police and firefighters pension fund for assistance. One can find a way around most roadblocks.

■ **A citizens' committee gives political cover.**
The recommendation of the historic civic center task force provided council with the citizens' support that was necessary to implement the historic civic center plan.

17

Growing Pains:
TriParty, the Convention Center,
and a Red Library

Central downtown, flanked by the tourist areas on the east and the historic centers of governance and religion on the west, contains office buildings, some hotels and apartments, and a few nondescript retail shops. When Henry Cisneros took office in 1981, most of the buildings were empty above the ground floor. Retail space at the ground level was being vacated or converted to "discount shops" at an alarming rate. The only action was below the street on the successful River Walk, where numerous cafes, bars, and shops were elbowing for position.

Henry Cisneros sought to strengthen the middle by linking the street level to the more prosperous east end of downtown. He forged an alliance of VIA Metropolitan Transit, the city, and downtown property owners to improve the infrastructure through a joint $48 million program. The idea was to make it more inviting as a pedestrian walkway by widening sidewalks and providing amenities such as trees, benches, and directional signs to encourage tourists to walk to the middle of downtown, and downtown office workers to get out during the lunch hour and stay after work.

The project became known as the "TriParty Downtown Improvement Project" after its three major participants. The key to the project, however, was the creation of a special tax assessment district in the area. Henry led an effort to convince the downtown property owners to tax themselves, with the city paying a proportionate share out of general revenues.

Henry had warned us that we would be under constant criticism during the construction phase of the project. He was right. Rebuilding the four major streets in every direction through the heart of downtown was a nightmare. Businesses suffered through traffic congestion and pedestrian inaccessibility that seemed endless. There were numerous technical glitches, such as placing traffic control boxes in the middle of crosswalks, and paving Alamo Street with quarried stones that complemented the Alamo's facade but had to be replaced over and over because they couldn't stand up to the traffic load.

Nevertheless, when the project was complete the central part of downtown was definitely improved. Better streets, improved traffic signal coordination, updated utilities, and wider sidewalks encouraged reinvestment in downtown.

The office space that was lagging when Henry took office now has a 90 percent occupancy rate.

In addition to leading the effort to improve the infrastructure downtown, Henry was also instrumental in laying the groundwork for downtown housing. He led the effort to create a $10 million trust fund for housing with part of the windfall the city received for approving the sale of our cable television franchise. The Towers at the Majestic apartments, the Exchange Building Apartments, the Maverick Apartments, and the Calcasieu Apartments all received partial funding from the trust fund.

Henry also took the lead in creating the San Antonio Performing Arts District in September 1988. In November, the city bought the historic Majestic Theater, built in 1929, and the adjacent Empire Theater, built in 1914, for a total cost of $10 million. The purchase price also included the Brady Building and the Majestic Towers, which would be converted into apartments.

The Las Casas Foundation was formed to raise money to renovate the two theaters. Joci Straus, who helped convince President Bush to bring the San Antonio Summit here, raised $5 million for the foundation to restore the Majestic to its original ornate beauty. The 2,500-seat theater is now home to the San Antonio Symphony.

The Empire Theater is under renovation as of this writing. In 1993, I persuaded council to contribute $1 million toward the restoration. The 900-seat theater will be used for small dance groups, repertory theater, and solo performances.

After I took office as mayor in 1991, I had the advantage of building on the groundwork that Henry laid through the TriParty Initiative. The city worked closely with two major central-city projects that affected both the streetscape and the river.

On May 2, 1991, during the mayoral campaign, I was invited by Tim Hixon to meet with members of his family. They had gathered from throughout the United States to meet at the Witte Museum to discuss proposed investments. Tim wanted to make a major investment in downtown and wanted me to talk about the revival. I spoke of the investments the city was making in downtown and encouraged the family to join in.

On December 15, 1993, we held groundbreaking ceremonies at the corner of Crockett and St. Mary's for a 50,000-square-foot complex, known as the South Bank, that the Hixon family would build. The center had river frontage, and replaced a parking lot along the river with a series of buildings housing restaurants and retail shops. Another link in the world-famous Hard Rock Cafe chain opened in January 1995 and became the anchor tenant for the South Bank.

Momentum was building for downtown development. Next up was my friend and prominent trial attorney Pat Maloney, who called on me to support the reconstruction of one block of Crockett Street that lies south of the river across from the historic La Mansion Hotel. Pat had plans to construct a 50,000-square-foot building next to his office in the old First National Bank Building. He also wanted the city's permission to tunnel under Crockett Street to give the building a river entrance. The city supported his project.

In 1995, Pat opened the multi-use Presidio Building, anchored by Planet Hollywood. During one of the opening ceremonies, a fund-raiser for the inner-city games for kids, actor Arnold Schwarzenegger gave my wife Tracy a big, fat kiss at a breakfast at Planet Hollywood. I thought about taking him out, but fortunately came to my senses and realized my limitations.

San Antonio was now a stop on the jet set itinerary since it had both a Planet Hollywood and a Hard Rock Cafe.

Karen Herrmann, wife of my then-partner in Sun Harvest, Ron Herrmann, also called on me in December 1993 to support a proposed children's museum on Houston Street. Her volunteer group had plans to renovate the Vance Building. I agreed to seek council support to give $300,000 to the project over a three-year period and to provide 100 free parking spaces in the Mid-City Parking Garage. Council supported the proposal. On September 9, 1995, the Children's Museum opened with more than 80 hands-on exhibits. More than 200,000 children attended the museum in its first year of operation.

Councilman Roger Perez took the lead in putting together a package of tax credits, federal funds, and other city assistance to help leverage private funds for the renovation of the 10-story Robert E. Lee Hotel. Built in 1923 as one of the city's first air-conditioned hotels, it was a handsome brick building, trimmed in glazed terra cotta. But for the last 20 years it had been vacant — a very visible eyesore. The giant rooftop sign that once so proudly announced the air-conditioned comfort inside became a civic bad joke, as it sat atop 10 stories of gutted window frames. But in March 1995, developer Milton Zaiontz began the renovation and conversion of the building into 72 apartments. As of this writing, construction is under way.

While we made major strides in bringing back downtown, Houston Street still has not reached its potential in retail space and more downtown housing is needed.

When I left office, there were more than 60 downtown projects at various stages of development. The most exciting central city project, however, lies at the northern edge of downtown.

The Central Library

Marie Swartz is a slender woman with delicate features, almost fragile in appearance. Looking at this seemingly sweet person, you wouldn't think she could swat a fly, but she can and does so quite frequently.

I first met Marie when I ran for the state Senate in 1972 and she supported my opponent. After that race we became close through our mutual friend, Lt. Governor Bill Hobby. In 1982, we teamed up with Republican activist Doug Harlan to start the World Affairs Council. I became chairman. Marie became the executive director until 1987.

After I became a councilman in 1987, Marie called me. She said she had been trying to do some research at the main library and found it impossible. She said our library was in the Dark Ages and I should do something about it. I did. I appointed her to the Library Board of Trustees on June 23, 1988, with her appointment to become effective October 1.

She lobbied council members to appoint business people to the board, knowing it would never have political stroke if it continued to be made up of librarians and school teachers. The coun-

Tracy Wolff reads to children at a story-telling session in the old Main Library prior to the construction of the new library. (Bob Owen, Express-News)

cil responded to Marie's requests by appointing Jerry Fuentes from Southwestern Bell, and Rachel Reynosa from the Federal Reserve.

Marie and I met to talk about improving the library system. We both believed that a new downtown library was needed. After Lila was elected mayor and bonds for a new library were approved in 1989, she appointed me chairman of a newly created nine-member Library Advisory Committee. Marie Swartz was one of the Library Board members on the new committee.

Our job was to act as a bridge between the Library Board and the City Council. It was critical we not make any mistakes in picking the site for a new downtown library, and also that the building provide for the library's long-term needs.

We recommended to the City Council and the Library Board that the city solicit consultants to develop a long-range plan addressing space needs.

Our committee worked through the tumultuous years of 1989 and 1990, the time when the city faced a budget shortfall in September 1989, a tax rollback in February 1990, and the selection of a new city manager in March 1990.

In July 1990, a consultant group headed by Cecil Beach of Fort Lauderdale, Fla., presented a long-range plan for the library. It proposed that the central library be at least 254,000 square feet with an expansion capacity to 500,000 square feet over a 20-year period. The existing central library was a mere 100,000 square feet. It suggested that four regional libraries be constructed, that the library's operating budget be tripled, that the library staff be doubled, and that a special library taxing district be created.

While I publicly praised the report for its long-range vision, I personally felt it was extremely unrealistic. Regional libraries, special taxing districts, and tripling the library budget were beyond our capacity. We laid these issues aside and concentrated on the space issue.

I publicly commented that I thought the future space suggestions for the main library were too high. I felt that with improved technology, future space requirements for the central library should be far less than 500,000 square feet. I did agree with the conclusion that the minimum space needs of any current library

Growing Pains ★ 273

should be 254,000 square feet. It was an old bargaining gambit: if you set your initial price higher than you really want, then the lower price seems like a bargain.

We now could see what locations in the downtown area would fit at least the minimum needs of 250,000 square feet while allowing for some expansion. Council approved the firm 3 D/M and architect Milton Babbitt as project manager for issues involving the downtown library.

The selection of Milton Babbitt was a critical decision. Milton knew the downtown area better than anyone. He could recite the history of each downtown building, and he also understood the needs of a central library.

The project management team received 16 proposed sites for a new central library. As the consultants studied these and other sites during the fall and winter of 1990, we were entering a very difficult time politically. Mayor Lila Cockrell, Councilwoman Maria Berriozabal (who also served on the joint advisory committee that I chaired), and I were in the middle of the mayoral race. There was potential for disaster if we three could not agree on a common site.

I became more and more convinced that we should build from scratch rather than expanding the existing library or trying to renovate a building. I was quoted in the press saying that I preferred a new facility. Slowly consensus began to develop that we should build a new facility rather than try to adapt an existing building.

Lynnell Burkett, then the Viewpoint editor of the San Antonio Light, followed the process closely and wrote a series of articles and editorials advocating a new building. Many of us felt that this would be a terrific opportunity to create a true landmark building in the downtown area. We also felt that if it were unique, the building itself could attract people to the library.

On Saturday, December 15, I toured the 16 sites along with Library Board members and Milton Babbitt. There were only two that I liked: a site on the south side of downtown on the corner of Durango and St. Mary's, and the Sears building across from Romana Plaza on the north side of downtown.

On December 17, we met for two hours with Milton Babbitt. Babbitt had narrowed the 16 sites down to four: the Sears site, the

Durango and St. Mary's site, the American Sports Building on Martin and St. Mary's, and the One Alamo Center bank building at Commerce and St. Mary's.

As I mentioned before, process is important in the political world. Thorough study, use of consultants and experts, time for review, and listening to advocates of different sites are all important. But sometimes process can get in the way of common sense. Political pressure naturally evolves in site selection and can sometimes lead to the wrong decision. While each site had its advocates and strong points, there was one site that was clearly the best in my mind.

Romana Plaza is close to institutions of learning. The main campus of the Alamo Community College District is less than a mile away. Fox Tech, Providence, and Central Catholic high schools are all within walking distance. It is across the street from Baptist Hospital and the historic Ursuline Academy where the Southwest Craft Center is located. Accessibility was easy with cross-city bus lines and a freeway only a few blocks away.

While it was unfortunate that property values had plunged in the late 1980s, it did provide us with an opportunity to buy the Sears site at an exceedingly good price. The price of the property in 1989 had been $7.5 million. Now it was owned by the Resolution Trust Corporation and could be bought for $3.8 million. The site also included a 475-car parking garage that would have cost $2.7 million to build elsewhere. The 4.1 acres were large enough to accommodate the long-term needs of the library.

I was careful not to get out in front of my committee. Marie Swartz worked the library board members of our committee to support the Romana Plaza site. Yolanda Vera and I worked hard on convincing our council colleagues on the Romana Plaza site.

Maria Berriozabal was the lone holdout. The Conservation Society pressed her to support the site close to their headquarters on Durango and St. Mary's. She spoke out in favor of that site.

On January 2, 1991, I told the media that our committee members had reached a consensus. I said we wanted to keep it confidential until the library board reviewed our recommendation.

On January 9, the San Antonio Light broke a story that the site recommended would be the Sears building site. The Durango and

St. Mary's site was ranked second. I confirmed the story the following day. It was a pre-emptive strike. The Library Board accepted our recommendation. The council set January 31 for a public hearing and a vote.

The Conservation Society began a lobbying campaign for the Durango and St. Mary's site. The property owners offered an $850,000 reduction in price, but at $4.5 million, the price was still higher than the $3.8 million for the Sears site. Jane Foster, president of the Conservation Society, testified for the Durango and St. Mary's site. She also tried persuading council that we could not demolish the old Sears building because it was historic!

Milton tore that argument apart. He said the building was built in 1929 and that in 1946 Sears had bought the building, doubled its size and removed all the original facade. It's too bad the Conservation Society used its reputation to try to protect what was clearly *not* a historic building.

The council voted 10 to 0 in favor of the Sears site. Mayor Cockrell was in Dallas in what would be a successful effort to bring the U.S. Olympic Festival to San Antonio.

With the site selection out of the way, the next major issue was what process should be used to select an architectural firm. Marie Swartz, after serving one year on the Library Board, had been elected chairwoman on October 17, 1990. She advocated having a design competition to select the architect. This process had never been used by the city. The picking of architects had always been the prerogative of the staff subject to ratification by council. To get council and staff to relinquish control would be an uphill battle.

Our committee responded to Marie's leadership and recommended a design competition. The Library Board and council agreed. The contest was on!

On July 9, 1991, a little over a month after I was elected mayor, the design teams presented their entries to a panel of architects, urban planners, and professional librarian consultants. It was a blind competition in that the panel did not know the identities of the designers.

Three days later, the panel chose Legorreta Arquitectos of Mexico City, in joint venture with two San Antonio firms, Johnson-Dempsey and Associates, and Davis Sprinkle, Architect. The choice was greeted with controversy from the day it was announced.

Ricardo Legorreta had designed a building that he felt expressed the cultural similarities between San Antonio and northern Mexico while at the same time preserving a link to San Antonio's past. It was a building of triangles, rectangles, spheres, and squares colored boldly in purple, yellow, and reddish pink. Narrow windows, a six-story atrium, courtyards on the first and second floors, and clever use of natural light made it a fun and people-friendly space. It was Mexican architecture at its best.

One of the most controversial elements of the design was the bold red paint that Legorreta proposed to use on most of the exterior surfaces. The precise shade of red, with its somewhat orange tint, defied most attempts at description. It became the lightning rod for critical and often sarcastic commentaries and letters to the editor. The Express-News sponsored a contest to name the color. It is now officially known as "enchilada red." Even its critics must concede that the color makes it easy to give directions to the building from any of numerous vantage points from which it can be seen.

The proposed building would contrast starkly with the other buildings in downtown San Antonio. Most of the historic buildings were constructed by German immigrants in the late 19th century and reflect European colonial architecture. While Legorreta's design was different, it did achieve his goal of reflecting our past. Our Hispanic heritage simply did not have buildings that glorified the new Mexican architecture.

Many of us had said we wanted a landmark building. Now we were going to get one. Milton and the library staff worked for more than a year with the Legorreta team in the building's final design.

Meanwhile, my wife Tracy began to work with Maria Cossio, the executive director of the Library Foundation, on building greater public support for the library system. They came up with the idea of a library telethon and called it a "Telefest."

Tracy called KENS-TV Community Affairs Director (now Congressman) Henry Bonilla to set up an appointment. After a meeting in January 1991, we had the OK for our Telefest.

As far as we know, the March 3, 1991, Telefest was the first public library telethon in the nation. Tracy chaired the two-hour event that raised more than $150,000. It has become the mainstay of the Library Foundation's annual fund-raising and community awareness efforts.

While there was great excitement over the building of the new central library, we knew the bond funds were insufficient to build a truly first-class library. To make it a state-of-the-art information center, we needed new computers, telecommunications equipment, more books, and a new library catalog system.

In early 1992, Maria Cossio began putting together a capital campaign for the central library. The foundation adopted a goal of raising $10 million.

George Ensley, a vice president at USAA and General Robert McDermott's right-hand man, marshaled USAA's human and financial resources to help the campaign. USAA pledged $1 million to the campaign and developed the campaign organization.

But the foundation soon came to the conclusion that they could raise only $5 million. Maria Cossio gave me a call.

In early November, she and Marie Swartz met with me, Alex Briseño, and Rolondo Bono. She said, "Mayor, we'll raise $5 million if the city will match it."

The second Maria, Marie Swartz, chimed in: "Give it to her."

I said, "It's OK with me if it's OK with Alex." I turned to Alex and said, "You have an extra $5 million?"

"I'll find it," he responded. "I'll have to spread it out over the next few budget years, though."

Alex and I are both pretty quick on our feet when we can get matching funds. Actually, Rolando and I had met with Alex before the visit and we knew what the request would be, so we were prepared to accept it.

On November 18, 1992, I publicly accepted the $5 million challenge from Library Foundation Chairwoman Debbie Proust. I went out on a limb in accepting this challenge because the council had not agreed to the pledge. But with Alex's support and with local property values rising, I felt confident we could provide the funds.

Henry, McDermott and I were named tri-chairmen of the campaign. The $5 million raised by the Library Foundation was by far the largest private sector contribution to the city for any cause.

The night before the May 20, 1995, grand opening, the Library Foundation held a "Food for Thought" fund-raising gala in the new building. More than 1,000 people donated $200 apiece to attend. Tracy prevailed on Dennis Nixon and Tom Travis of the International Bank of Commerce to underwrite $100,000 for the event.

It was a once-in-a-lifetime, elegant event for the library. Food was served on three floors as everyone traveled from floor to floor, amazed at the beauty and open space of the design. Tracy and I danced on the second-story patio until the early morning hours.

The next morning we began a "magical book parade" from the old library to the new. More than 30 groups wore historical costumes. The best dressed was Express-News columnist Susan Yerkes, who came as Robert Rehm's fabulous book worm. Tracy and I rode on a float with University of Mexico Rector Jose Sarukhan and the first lady of Texas, Laura Bush, who had been a librarian.

After we made our speeches in front of the library and cut the ribbon, a few of us walked over to Club Giraud on the Ursuline Academy and Southwest Craft Center grounds. Tracy and I sat with Ricardo Legorreta and his son Victor, an associate architect in his father's firm. Tracy and I had met Ricardo on several occasions, but this was the first time we were able to relax and visit privately.

In the first year after opening the new library, the number of visitors increased 30 percent to 783,269 people. It is worth noting that this is more people than attend Spurs basketball games.

A new branch library opened in the Great Northwest area on November 6, 1993. Two old branches, Bazan and Las Palmas, have been replaced by new buildings and six of the remaining 15 have been expanded or renovated. Four branches are now under construction and four others will be finished in 1997. The San Pedro branch will not be expanded because it is only a mile from the central library. Five literacy centers have been opened since 1989. The library budget has been increased substantially.

As this book goes to press, there is no building named after Mayor Henry Cisneros. Lila Cockrell has her theater, U.S. Representative Henry B. Gonzalez has his convention center, Walter McAllister has his freeway, Maury Maverick has his plaza, and I have my baseball park.

Henry Cisneros started the Library Foundation and led the effort to pass the bonds to build not only the new central library, but also learning centers, and improvements for the 17 branch libraries as well as adding one new branch library. He led the effort in the capital fund drive. I believe the Central Library should be named after Henry G. Cisneros.

East Downtown — The Convention Center

The Henry B. Gonzalez Convention Center was built in 1968, on the northwestern corner of the 92-acre HemisFair grounds in eastern downtown. Before HemisFair '68, our tourism industry hardly existed. Today it is a $2 billion industry supporting 50,000 jobs. The convention center gave rise to the building of several large hotels within immediate walking distance. It was during the fair that clubs, restaurants, and other commercial development first became a significant feature on the River Walk.

The convention center complex included a Theater for the Performing Arts (later renamed in honor of Lila Cockrell) and an arena, which became the home of the San Antonio Spurs before they moved to the Alamodome. A mosaic by Juan O'Gorman across the facade of the theater depicts the theme of the fair, "The Confluence of the Civilizations in the Americas." Much later, a Roland Rodriguez mural on the arena depicted major landmarks in the history of San Antonio. As part of the convention center's construction, the first artificial extension of the San Antonio River was dug from the center of the River Bend into a turning basin in front of the Lila Cockrell Theater.

In 1990, during Mayor Cockrell's term, we commissioned Arthur Anderson and Company to do a study of how our convention center measured up to others around the country. We also asked the firm to look at the possible need for future expansion of the convention center beyond what would be supplied by the Alamodome, which was then under construction.

A small expansion of the convention center had been completed in 1977. Under the leadership of Mayor Cisneros, a major expansion, enlarging the convention center to 240,000 square feet of contiguous exhibit space, was completed in 1988. And the Alamodome, already under construction, would add another 165,000 square feet of high ceiling exhibit space, fully equipped for any conceivable trade-show requirements.

Henry also provided the vision for development of the rest of the HemisFair grounds. Council adopted a plan to keep as much green space as possible in the park, preserve its historic character, and use the buildings in the park for education and children's activities.

In 1988, we took a walking tour of the park with Henry to view the results of his vision. On the west side of the park, facing Alamo Street, a large turreted, tivoli-lighted arch framed the entrance to Goliad Street that was resurfaced with concrete pavers. Goliad Street, although closed to vehicular traffic, has curbs and sidewalks framing the yards of several historic homes.

Goliad Street takes you past a playground of wooden tunnels, slides, platforms, swings, and stairs, built through a volunteer effort led by former Express-News publisher Charles Kilpatrick and his wife, Margie. At the end of Goliad Street lies Plaza Mexico, where the new building for the University of Mexico and the Mexican Cultural Institute (the original Mexico pavilion during HemisFair) are located. A tree-lined walkway with Victorian light poles and benches leads you past the new Texas A&M Engineering Building to a water garden park framing the Tower of the Americas.

The enlarged convention center and a parking garage flanked the western edge of the arena. The enlarged convention center included an International Conference Center wired for simultaneous translation in the style of the United Nations.

Henry added a final touch to our convention facilities when he built the Alamodome across the freeway from HemisFair Park. When finished, the Alamodome would be linked to the park by a walkway under the freeway.

During the campaign for the Dome in 1989, Henry stressed the convention assembly and trade show uses as one of the primary reasons to build it. Campaign literature said that the Dome was the next logical expansion of the convention center. It would be only an eight-minute walk from the convention center and could handle large conventions such as the Shriners (30,000 people) and the Southern Baptist Convention (35,000 people). The Dome could seat 65,000 people as well as provide 165,000 square feet of exhibit space and 30,000 square feet of meeting rooms.

So when we authorized the Arthur Anderson study I felt confident we had taken care of any need for expansion in the short term. If the study suggested another expansion, I thought it would be far off in the future. Consequently, when I took office as mayor in June 1991, I did not think that I would be faced with further expansion of convention facilities. I was wrong.

In December 1991, Arthur Anderson submitted its report. Much to my surprise, it suggested that we more than double the size of our exhibit space from 240,000 square feet to 500,000 square feet. This would be the largest expansion since the convention center was built in 1968.

The report said that our city had fallen out of the first tier of American cities that were now offering 500,000 square feet or more of contiguous exhibit space. In the last few years many cities had already expanded their convention facilities or had plans to do so.

I was skeptical of the report's findings. I thought it understated our position related to other cities. The report did not address the effect that the Dome would have on our convention facilities. I was also apprehensive about the proposal to finance the expansion by raising the hotel tax another two percent, bringing the total local and state tax to 15 percent. The only Texas city that high was Houston.

I was doubtful another hotel would be built if the proposed expansion came about. Large hotels were not springing up as they had been during the 1980s.

Then in early 1992, I greeted the American Association of Retired Persons at the convention center. I had to make my way through crowded hallways to the assembly hall to greet them. When I arrived, fire marshals were moving people out of the assembly hall because it was overcrowded.

I hung around after the address and talked to some of the conventioneers. They complained about not being able to attend the assembly and about the lack of sufficient meeting rooms. They said we needed a modern facility that had meeting rooms, assembly rooms, and banquet halls all under one roof. If we wanted them back, they said we needed to enlarge and improve our facilities.

My visit with those angry conventioneers was an eye-opener. I've learned in my own business that when a customer grabs you and says you are fouling up, it's best to listen carefully.

As the committee continued its work, I set in motion my own agenda. I began to meet with Steve Moore, the director of the Convention and Visitors Bureau, and leaders in the hotel industry. Steve was instrumental in gaining their support.

My friend Pat Kennedy, owner of La Mansion Hotel, set up meetings with Siegfried Richter, general manager of the Hilton Palacio del Rio, J.W. "Mac" McMillan, general manager of the Menger Hotel, and Ed Parradine, general manager of the Marriott Rivercenter.

They were unanimous in the opinion that we needed to move forward with expansion. I told them that they also needed to be unanimous in their support of raising the hotel tax. We would have to go to the Legislature for approval in 1993, and we had to present a united front. I also told them they had to help us build community support for the tourism industry. Many citizens were already beginning to complain that they voted for the Dome because they thought it would solve any need for extra convention space. The Dome campaign had contributed to that impression, and many people now felt they had been misled.

On October 22, Martin Weiss presented the committee's report to council. It substantiated the Arthur Anderson report that we were falling way behind in convention space compared to other major cities. Instead of being in the top 10 cities, we had fallen by 1991 to 22nd in convention space. With other cities already constructing more space, we would fall to 28th within five years if we failed to act.

The committee found that we were losing serious business in a way that could lead to a significant downturn in our tourism industry.

The report also found that the building of domed stadiums in other cities had increased the need to expand their convention space. They cited six cities that had built domes and then later expanded their convention centers. Domes brought more conventions that needed additional convention facilities beyond what the domes provided.

We would soon find that to be true with the Alamodome. In its first year of operation, 35 conventions used it, but they also needed more meeting rooms than the Dome could accommodate.

The report also emphasized the need for contiguous convention space. Buried in the report was a recommendation that we not expand the convention center south where historic houses were located. At the time of this recommendation we did not realize that a tremendous battle would develop over this issue.

The council voted unanimously to move forward with implementing the report.

We asked them to consider whether expansion should go underground, two or three stories above, or to the east or south. Alamo Street blocked expansion to the west and Market Street blocked expansion to the north. If we expanded east, the arena would be in the way, and if south, many historic buildings would be in the way.

I appeared at the committee's first meeting and asked them to think ahead. I wanted a plan that would include yet another expansion to carry us to the year 2020.

I also asked them to think boldly and reflect the heritage of HemisFair '68, which was an international fair. I advocated building an International Center to house our International Relations Department, the Mexican *casas*, the Mexican Cultural Institute, and the North American Development Bank. I thought this center should be built next to the UNAM building and the International Conference Center that was already located in the convention center. I asked the architects to be daring in their designs, as Legorreta had been in designing the new library.

The first order of business was to try to convince the Texas Legislature, which would begin its session within two months, to allow us to raise the hotel tax.

Carrying a tax bill is never popular, but the dean of our House delegation, State Representative Ciro Rodriguez, agreed to introduce it. On March 10, 1993, Alex Briseño and I testified before the House Ways and Means Committee in support of Ciro's bill.

The committee listened to our presentation and took no action. The following week Representative Karyne Conley delivered a bombshell, saying she would block the tax increase. If our local delegation was split on the tax issue, it simply would not pass.

I fired off a letter to all the members of our delegation saying how important the legislation was to San Antonio's tourism industry. I asked Ciro to meet with Karyne and me. I knew Karyne would want something for her district in return for support of Ciro's bill. Holding Ciro's bill hostage was an effective way to get what she wanted. That is, if the request was reasonable.

We met in my office on March 26. Karyne said she wanted support in developing a logistics center that would encompass warehousing and small manufacturing in her district. For several months we had been studying where to locate such a center in the city. One site we were considering was known as the Vaughan site in east Bexar County. It included Lancer Corporation's soda machine manufacturing plant owned by George Schroeder and his brother Jud.

I promised Karyne that I would support the Vaughan site for the logistics center and also support establishing an enterprise zone at the site. She agreed to back off in her opposition to the tax increase. Call it whatever you want: logrolling, horse trading, good or bad politics. In any case, it got the job done.

With the local delegation united, the Legislature passed the tax bill. Ciro Rodriguez's leadership was essential in providing us the means to finance the expansion. In October 1993, the City Council raised the rate from 13 percent to 15 percent. The tax would generate about $6.7 million a year to pay for the expansion.

But even with the tax increase, it was still necessary to have more hotel rooms to pay for the bonded indebtedness. As of this writing, Marriott Rivercenter plans a 1,000-room expansion, and the city is working to provide incentives for another large hotel to be built next to the convention center. Many smaller hotels have been built downtown since the announcement of the convention center expansion. We had fewer than 20,000 rooms citywide in 1990, but by 1996 the number of rooms was up to 25,583. With more than 7,000 additional rooms either planned or under construction, we will have 30,000 rooms by the year 2000.

As a result of the new construction, tax revenue to the city has increased substantially. The hotel tax produced $16 million in 1990 and $24 million in 1996, not including the increase of two percent in the tax rate. Sales tax collection went from $66 million in 1990 to $97 million in 1996.

Throughout 1993, I attended many of the meetings of the convention center expansion committee. I also met privately with the architects and city staff to review expansion plans. One plan called for an ultimate expansion to a million square feet, which would cover practically all of HemisFair Park. I thought that if the convention center ever got to that size it would overwhelm the capacity of the River Walk and surrounding area to handle the crowds. I urged them to suggest no more than one additional expansion beyond our current plan, which would limit the convention center to 750,000 square feet. They accepted that advice.

I was convinced that the added convention space had to be contiguous, and that the only logical way to expand was to go east. That meant the arena would have to be torn down. This kept faith with Henry's vision of retaining the historic nature of the park as well as open green space. Going east also gave future councils the space they would need to expand the convention center in the future.

The 25-year-old arena was in a sorry state. This was dramatically emphasized when a large part of the exterior facade fell off in the middle of one night. The rest had to be removed quickly to eliminate a safety hazard. It would cost $2.5 million to repair. Another $9 million was needed to bring the arena up to minimum standards, and another $30 million to meet handicapped access requirements and make it a first-class facility. The Dome was providing a home for the Spurs, with the arena being used infrequently. Excluding Spurs games, it had been used an average of only 36 times a year since 1989.

We had to decide on the demolition of the arena. I decided to bite the bullet and go public with my views. I thought there would be some opposition, but I felt it would not be significant. I was wrong again.

On January 16 the Express-News ran this headline: "HemisFair arena walls to come tumbling down." I was quoted as saying that "The arena has to come down. This is our only option."

Following the story, columnist Roddy Stinson delivered a stinging attack. He said that "the inmates at City Hall" were "unchecked and running amok." He said our "brains must be completely worn out." Columnist David Anthony Richelieu wrote, "But we can't know what's best until more options are on the table, not just the mayor's mystery plan picked behind closed doors."

Council opinion was split. Councilman Bill Thornton said he was not sure contiguous space was necessary. He said we should not "go through Georgia like Sherman" (i.e., not burn the arena) until we were certain. He then went on to suggest that we build a separate convention facility on a site at St. Mary's and Durango, three blocks away.

The timing of my announcement also threw a cloud over my pending proposal to call a $100 million bond election for parks, streets and drainage the following May. Pundits were predicting that the uproar over the demolition of the arena would jeopardize the bond election.

Jack Orbin, president of Stone City Attractions, which booked primarily rock concerts, began to organize opposition. Jack didn't like the idea of losing a concert venue. But the fact was that he booked the arena only twice in 1992 and once in 1993.

The decision was quickly becoming a political football. I clearly saw it was time to retreat and regroup. I said that we would step back and review all possible plans for expansion.

Councilman Howard Peak came to my rescue. An urban planner by profession, Howard suggested that we ask the Urban Land Institute to review all options. The institute had endorsed the recommendation to lower Montana Street in front of the Dome to avoid a conflict between pedestrians and traffic in that area.

Council readily agreed to Howard's suggestion. In July, the council approved a contract for 10 experts from the Urban Land Institute to come to San Antonio in September to review all alternatives.

But I knew that even if the land institute team agreed that the convention space had to be contiguous and that the arena needed to come down, I would still draw serious political opposition. Reason and a correct business decision would quickly evaporate unless I managed to marshal political support.

I spoke before the hotel association and warned members that unless they built political support for expanding on the present site and for the expansion to be contiguous, then they might very well get an expansion plan that did not meet their customers' needs. I told them if you have an idea of what is best, and if you've got any political muscle, you darn well better use it.

They later called a news conference and organized a campaign to fight a proposal to build a second convention site elsewhere. They specifically opposed Bill Thornton's plan to build three blocks away. They said their customers wanted contiguous space and that two separate locations would discourage large conventions. They prepared presentations they would make to the Urban Land Institute on how they thought the expansion should be accomplished.

Beating the Buzzer

As if I didn't have enough trouble already, the Spurs decided to complicate things even more. In September, President Jack Diller told me the Spurs were going to go public with a study on whether they would need a new arena sometime in the future.

Great timing, Jack! The conspiracy theory that we would tear down the arena so that we could build a new one was now worthy of an Oliver Stone film. I told Jack that I hope he made it clear that the existing arena would not fit the team's needs. I also said that the city could not take part in financing the study or building a new arena. He said he was not asking for city help and that the old arena could not work because they needed skyboxes.

As I expected, as soon as Jack went public with the study the conspiracy theorists went ballistic. The theories went like this: We built the Dome to get the Spurs to move out of the arena so we could tear it down. We knew the Spurs would not like the Alamodome, so we could then build them a new arena with tax money. Alamodome up, old arena down, new arena up. Many citizens were attributing to us long-range planning abilities with respect to the Dome and the arena that quite frankly never existed. They were simply overrating our capacity to think ahead. How quickly they had forgotten that the Dome was conceived without ever thinking the Spurs would play more than a few sold-out playoff games there, and that Red McCombs had stunned everybody by first asking to move his team there after the Dome was already well under construction.

On September 30, consultants from the Urban Land Institute presented their findings to council. They recommended that we demolish the arena, saying it was the only logical means of providing contiguous space. They said with the removal of the arena we could build the addition first and not affect existing convention business. After completing the addition, we then could remodel the old space.

I quickly scheduled a council vote for 4 p.m. October 13 to direct staff to implement the plan. More than 50 citizens spoke during the three-and-a-half-hour meeting, with opinions hotly divided. Former Mayor Charles Becker, speaking in favor of demolition, said the existing arena was "kind of like having a grain silo in your living room." Speaking in opposition Rosa Rosales said, "It takes many years to build something, but it takes one jackass to tear the barn down."

Although the vote carried 9 to 2, I knew a lot more trouble lay ahead because this was only the first vote. Another would have to come when we actually let a contract to tear the arena down. The problem was compounded on November 4 when Jack Orbin organized San Antonians to Save the Arena. With the backing of the Homeowner-Taxpayer Association, the new group launched a petition drive to force a public vote on the issue.

The hotel industry began to flex its political muscle in opposition to the petition drive. On November 8, a rally in front of the convention center supported the demolition of the arena.

On January 26, the council scheduled a vote on a contract that included a provision for plans to tear down the arena. I asked the hotel industry to show strength at the meeting. For the first time, the new council chamber was overcrowded as hundreds of workers showed up with signs and name tags stating, "Save my job — not the arena." Some speakers said that the council should put the issue on the ballot. I said that we were not elected to call referenda but rather to make tough decisions. The vote carried unanimously.

While the hotel industry organized opposition to the petition drive, I kept my distance so that I could keep a dialogue going with Jack. We met several times over the months trying to resolve his concern over a concert venue. I told him we would work to devise a plan to reconfigure the Dome for concert events that would accommodate crowds of 10,000 to 15,000.

Jack never told me he would back off the petition drive. But he did not collect enough signatures to force a referendum.

On April 13, we issued the contract to demolish the arena. Out of its dust will rise the new convention center that will be double the size of our existing center. We planned for the convention center to reflect the culture and architecture at the turn of the 21st century. The design reflects the stonework, plastered walls, vaults, skylights and heavy wooden doors of our Spanish missions.

Even after the convention center addition is complete, major problems lie ahead. Our major competitors, instead of having four times our space, will still have twice the space we will. Our plans provided for land space for another addition to be built between 2010 and 2020 that would bring the center to 750,000 square feet.

But there is a need to plan even beyond the next expansion. Any further expansion would have to extend south along the west side of Interstate 37. This means that the city would have to acquire the six acres of land in HemisFair Park that is presently being held by the University of Texas (not including the Institute of Texan Cultures). Victoria Courts should be acquired and the housing project located elsewhere.

Eventually, the river should be extended through HemisFair Park and then along Durango Street to join up with the main branch of the river south of downtown. The river would then make a full loop linking all the diverse elements of downtown, from the historic government centers to the new River Walk entertainment district to the renewed convention center and tourist areas.

★★★
Lessons from Growing Pains

■ **Good politicians need good appointees to institute change.**
My appointment of Marie Swartz to the Library Board made a huge difference in selling the idea of a new library to council and to the public. Good appointees do make a difference.

■ **As in all things, risks in architectural design can pay off.**
The delightfully extravagant design by Ricardo Legorreta stands out as nothing else does downtown. Yet it echoes the city's character. Breaking away from the everyday can have wonderful results.

■ **Keep talking; silence can never achieve compromise.**
I believe my continuing dialogue with Jack Orbin of Stone City Attractions helped quell a petition drive to stop the demolition of the arena.

18

Visions and Quests: Creating Small Businesses and a Skilled Work Force

I watched from the front row as Tommy Moore, publisher of a local African-American newspaper, the Informer, walked to the microphone. He was about to address the 175 people I had brought together for a conference on strategic economic development. It was Sunday, June 7, 1992, the last day of the three-day conference, and Tommy was ready to present a vision of the future.

An often vocal critic of City Hall, Tommy believed deeply that economic justice and opportunity would be the salvation of the black community. He did not think welfare was the answer. He wanted jobs that paid well.

"I envision a city that puts human development first, so that good jobs will follow," Tommy said. "I see a city with excellent education and job training institutions. I see a city that offers every parent the best child care, and one where every person has access to world-class health care facilities.

"I see a city that offers hope and opportunity to its small and minority and women-owned businesses; a city whose sustained economic growth is developed in harmony with our environment.

"Human capital will make us the city of commerce for all of North America and develop 50 Fortune 500 companies. And maybe my company will be one of them."

A burst of applause flooded the room when Tommy concluded. It was a rare thing, a speech that touched something deep inside, as Martin Luther King's 1963 address in the nation's capital had done.

I had assembled a diverse group for the conference, with only a small number from the business community. Developing and nurturing human capital would hardly have been the focus of discussion about economic development if only business leaders were in attendance.

When I went home that Sunday night, I felt buoyed with enthusiasm. The vision Tommy expressed was one we could all aspire to. But I was bothered by a nagging sense that all we had done was generate hope and excitement with no real notion of how to make it happen. It was the same thing I had felt when the conference was first proposed. How could one defeat the cynicism that seemed to envelop all aspirations in the '90s?

A year earlier, I had been introduced to Bob Gohlson by Jarret Jones, IBM's general manager for southwest Texas. Bob had led strategic-planning conferences for the states of Colorado, Utah and Oklahoma. He was a strategic-planning consultant who used the methodology described in "Strategic Choices: Supremacy, Survival or Sayonara," a book written by three IBM consultants in 1991. The theory is to develop a long-term vision and link existing assets to reach that vision.

At a meeting in my City Hall office, Bob had said, "We need to get your city to look ahead 25 years and develop a vision that has no limits. You must then develop a community consensus for this philosophical vision of the future and link community assets to reach it. This process looks at economic development in a totally different way."

"Bob, this all seems very utopian," I replied. "It has a good feeling, but I'm not sure what good the conference would do. Twenty-five years is a long way down the road."

"Maybe it sounds utopian ... but a city needs to have a long-term vision of what it hopes to achieve," Bob said.

I was searching for help to re-ignite our economy, and maybe Bob's message was what I was looking for. I decided to give it a try.

When I came into office in the summer of 1991, the city was in the doldrums. The unemployment rate was 6.9 percent. Tough economic times had taken their toll on the city budget, which had led to the tax rollback referendum. I was searching for ideas to pick up our spirits and get our economy rolling.

Even before Bob Gholson's visit, I had asked consultant Tom Brereton to head a group of volunteers to assess "the state of the city." He worked with civic activists who had organized a non-profit think tank called the Hemisphere Institute for Public Service. Dick Howe was chairman of the organization, and Walter Ague, a retired Air Force officer, was staff director.

The State of the City project was intended to pick up where Target '90 left off.

I presented the State of the City report with some fanfare at a City Hall press conference on November 1, 1991. But then I had a problem, one similar to the problem Henry Cisneros faced with Target '90: how to follow up on the report. Dick Howe's group proposed a plan and a budget for a new community planning effort, but I was not sure how to proceed. So I did what Henry did: I stalled for a few months. Now, I saw a possible solution through Bob's conference, with its offer of free planning services from IBM.

We spent several months preparing for the Vision 2020 conference. On June 5, 1992, we held our opening session. I told participants that we wanted to look at economic development in a new way. We were looking for the big picture — a vision of what we wanted to be and an inventory of the assets that would get us there.

We divided into 14 committees, each with a different issue. As each committee report came out, IBM computers assembled the information and narrowed our choices for solutions.

We reduced our goals to three, all intended to enhance "human capital." They were to place the highest priority on the elimination of poverty, the improvement of the educational system and the development of a family support system.

We then identified three key economic areas that would grow if we deployed our human capital wisely.

First was international trade and tourism, where we were already strong and still expanding.

Second was aerospace, where we could build on assets from the four Air Force bases in San Antonio.

Third was biomedical and scientific research and application, a field that could expand at the University of Texas Health Science Center and the Texas Research Park, as well as at established "R&D" companies such as the Southwest Foundation for Biomedical Research and the Southwest Research Institute.

After the conference we boiled down 600 pages of reports into a short summary. We decided not to create a follow-up organization but rather to rely on the many organizations represented at the conference. We sent them all copies of the report and encouraged them to buy into the vision of developing human capital.

So what did it all mean? The conference was a great pep rally. For a brief time, it instilled hope, vision and spirit in a large segment of our population. But without measurable goals and deadlines, it accomplished little else.

I'd like to think I'm wrong. Attitude and spirit certainly played a part in the creation of 60,000 new jobs during my term as mayor. I hope someday there will be a follow-up to the Vision 2020 conference. A new mayor may bring people together again to reaffirm the vision, to see what progress we have made and to develop more specific goals to reach that vision.

We'll have to wait and see.

In any case, the conference did inspire me to do my best to put pieces into place that would help the vision become a reality in the year 2020. The conference had a major effect on my yearly agendas. I focused on job training, child care and after-school care, small business development, educational issues, literacy and libraries. For the most part, these were exactly the kind of "soft" issues that had been on the "B list" for Henry Cisneros, with his major focus on brick-and-mortar projects.

Two of the major issues to come out of the conference were the need for greater opportunities for small businesses, and programs to encourage the pursuit of higher education and job training. The needs of small business were a natural for me because I'd been active all my adult life in our family businesses. But I would soon find out that, in the public arena, these issues aren't as easy to handle as they appear.

Small Business Development

Karyne Conley is a tall, personable African-American, gracious and charming in her relations with just about every political and business leader in San Antonio. But her allure in one-on-one encounters should not be mistaken for agreement with one's political views. Her comments about the views of others — unexpurgated from the news columns — can take a bite out of the hides of friends and foes alike.

Karyne and I were friends before I was elected mayor. As I said before, her parents were kind enough to host a reception during my campaign. At the time, Karyne was a state representative for the East Side district. Today she is a Washington-based lobbyist for SBC Communications Inc., the parent company of Southwestern Bell. We are still good friends, despite numerous confrontations.

Our political relationship during my four years as mayor tested two old political adages: "Watch out for your friends" and "Tension is needed to create progress." I believe very much in both, and Karyne tested me to the limit. We jousted over Dome dirt, water policy and economic discrimination.

On September 15, 1992, Karyne announced to the media that she had met with leaders of the Alamo City Chamber of Commerce and the San Antonio Business League (both largely African-American organizations) to plan a boycott by black athletes

State Representative Karyne Conley, shown here on her election night, threatened to lead a boycott of the Olympic Festival at the Alamodome if the city did not improve its minority contracting goals. (Charles Barksdale, Express-News)

of the upcoming U.S. Olympic Festival. The festival was to be the first major sporting event at the newly opened Alamodome in July 1993, and we were looking forward to the international media coverage it would bring.

But Karyne and other black leaders were ready to go to the national black media and publicize what they characterized as "economic enslavement" of African-Americans in San Antonio. They said the boycott would begin 10 days later unless action was taken to address their grievances.

After that unexpected announcement, I called Karyne and said angrily, "What are you doing? Why didn't you call me? If this gets out to the national media, everyone in San Antonio will be hurt and our tourism industry will really be damaged."

"Don't worry," she replied sweetly. "I gave you 10 days to come up with an answer to our demands. Now Nelson, don't waste time talking to me. Get to work."

"Thanks, Karyne," I said. Thanks a lot!

What led to this boycott threat? In July 1987, only two months after my election as a councilman, we created a committee to identify problems faced by small businesses.

In September 1988, we accepted the committee's report, which identified obstacles and recommended solutions. One of the major obstacles was the fact that small, minority and women-owned businesses did not get many local government contracts. Only three percent of city business went to such firms.

Under the leadership of Councilman Walter Martinez, we passed an ordinance creating a Small and Minority Business Advocacy Program in November 1988. We established goals for professional contracting with minority and women-owned businesses. The Hispanic Chamber took the lead in eliciting community support. Surprisingly, there was little controversy as we established the goals.

Then, in 1989, less than a year later, the U.S. Supreme Court ruled in "City of Richmond vs. J.A. Croson Company" that a city must establish proof of specific discrimination to justify a race or gender preference program.

The city of San Antonio would have to come up with such proof to make Councilman Martinez's plan lawful. In May 1989, the last month of Mayor Henry Cisneros' term, we passed a resolution to conduct a consultant's study.

The Richmond case put us in the position of either dropping the goals program or proving that we discriminated. Now, this may seem a little bizarre to you. Here we were spending taxpayers' money to investigate whether we discriminated against minorities. Not only were we paying money to investigate, but we also hoped we would be found guilty. If folks ever needed evidence to question government's sanity, this should be one of the best examples.

In July 1992, three years later, the report was delivered to City Council. As expected, the report found that there *was* evidence of discrimination against women and minority-owned businesses in construction, professional services and purchasing — the fields in which the city generally was required by state law to accept the lowest bid.

The report also showed that the city had made progress since we adopted Councilman Martinez's goals in 1988. We had gone from about two percent minority contract awards in 1988 to 14 percent in 1992. But more than 40 percent of the small businesses in San Antonio were minority owned. There was still a long way to go to reach equity.

Now that we had convicted ourselves of discrimination, there was ammunition to use against us. Karyne Conley quickly grabbed a few bullets and announced the threatened boycott. We certainly couldn't defend ourselves, since the report provided clear evidence of discrimination.

African-Americans had good reasons to threaten a boycott. In San Antonio, they are indeed the minority, representing about seven percent of the population. Hispanics constitute about 56 percent. Many African-Americans fear discrimination from Hispanics as much as from Anglos. They felt that unless they spoke out, all the benefits of the economic development goals would go to Hispanics.

The report showed that African-American businesses got a disproportionately small share of contracting and procurement business. Rubbing salt in the wound was the fact that they had received few contract awards at the Alamodome after being promised meaningful jobs and opportunities during the Dome campaign.

After my call to Karyne, I got a call from my East Side campaign manager and friend, Joe Scott. He offered to act as a back channel between me and the boycott organizers. "I've spoken with the leaders," he said. "The first thing you need to do is get Councilman Frank Wing involved. We have a Hispanic city manager, and he and his staff will need to be supportive of our demands. We know Frank is strong with the staff. He is also well respected on the East Side."

I called Frank and got him into "another fine mess," as he would characterize it. I said, "Frank, we have another hot potato. Will you work with me to come up with some solutions?"

"We'll fix the problem. Let's get started," he said.

Each day for the next six days the leaders of the boycott made renewed threats through the media that they were moving forward with the boycott unless we came up with answers to their demands. They announced they had a wealth of information on discrimination ready to send to the national media.

At the same time that the daily barrage of threats in the media was going on, Frank and I quietly met every day with the leaders delivering the threats, including Charles Andrews, president of Inner City Broadcasting, Tommy Moore (who two months earlier had given the closing remarks at the Vision 2020 conference) and Joe Linson, chairman of the Alamo City Chamber.

Frank Wing agreed to lead a 15-member inter-agency citizen board that I would appoint to promote African-American-owned businesses in contracting with local government. Clinton Bolden, an African-American and head of our economic development department, would take the staff lead. We included the county judge, the chairpersons of VIA, CPS and the San Antonio Water System, and several leaders of the threatened boycott.

I charged the board with addressing the demands of the black community. Among them were reducing bonding requirements, allowing other insurance in place of worker's compensation, breaking bid packages into smaller units, making it easier for small enterprises to do business with the city, and establishing specific contract goals for African-Americans. I agreed to attend all their meetings and follow up with action by the council on the board's recommendations.

With the formation of this board, the boycott was called off. Karyne Conley, who chose not to attend the meetings, told the media that the boycott was called off prematurely. She complained that the black leaders had given in to me. The San Antonio Light quoted her as calling them the "weenie brigade" — a kiss on the cheek and a slap through the media. I was determined to prove that the confidence the leaders had shown in Frank and me was not misplaced.

Within 30 days, the inter-agency board made 26 specific recommendations. Two months later, City Council adopted those
aimed at improving contracting opportunities for African-American businesses. Other government agencies signed up, too.

Karyne had created the tension, and progress was made. It
was a dangerous tension that easily could have gotten out of control. Clear heads and a willingness to work together stopped the
boycott and moved our city forward toward greater economic
fairness.

There are strong opinions within our community that goals
for minority- and women-owned businesses should not be set.
But most of the policies we adopted, such as breaking bids and
contracts into smaller packages, helped all small businesses.

As of the end of 1996, African-American businesses constitute 1.9 percent of the firms available to do business with the city,
but they have 2.7 percent of the city contracts. In 1992, that amount
was one quarter of one percent. Women and minority-owned
businesses have 33 percent of the city contracts, and small businesses have 53 percent. Had we not acted, I believe we would still
be awarding only three percent of city contracts to women and
minorities.

One of the inter-agency board's recommendations was to create a Bank Community Development Corporation. Other communities had created BCDCs to lend money or invest in projects
that traditional banks could not touch. Most loans were to assist
small businesses in meeting working capital requirements. The
BCDCs also were a viable option for banks to carry out their
responsibilities under the Community Reinvestment Act. Most
BCDCs were made up of banks that came together to pool their
funds.

On December 19, 1991, we approved funds for the hiring of a
consultant to develop a plan for such a bank. The City Council's
Small Business Committee, now headed by Councilman Frank
Pierce, set about the task right away.

The banking community wanted the city to provide some
funds to the bank and, more critically, to act as the bank's staff for
the first two years.

I told Frank Pierce that this would be a prescription for disaster. In the mid-1980s, the city had administered a small loan program in conjunction with the Small Business Administration. It became a political disaster when it was disclosed that the city had made loans to City Hall-"connected" people and the loans went belly up. I said, "Let's help financially, but keep the organization independent from City Hall."

In April 1993, City Council approved the creation of the San Antonio Business Development Corporation (SABDC). It would be a multi-bank institution and would function as an independent, nonprofit corporation. The city threw in money for administration, and the SABDC got off the ground with 12 banks committed to $500,000. We had promised $1 million.

Many banks were simply refusing to pony up. So I announced that I would start reading a list at each Thursday council meeting of banks that were taking money from, but not investing in, our community. This intimidation worked where persuasion had not. Within three months, we had 22 banks committed to $1 million. Today the bank is up and running and has made 23 loans totaling $898,900.

But we still were not reaching the very smallest entrepreneurs, the so-called "microenterprises," businesses so small that they were often run out of the home.

Al Martinez-Fonts Jr., vice president of Texas Commerce Bank, approached me with an idea to serve those businesses, a complementary organization to the SABDC. Al had been working with ACCION International, a recognized leader in the field in the Americas. Five other cities had created ACCION organizations in their communities. Al wanted to do it in San Antonio.

ACCION would make loans to these microenterprises in amounts generally smaller than $5,000. It was not economical for the SABDC and other banks to make such loans.

I helped Al attract investors. San Antonio ACCION organized in 1994. Today it has made 165 loans totaling $770,725 with an average loan size of $2,462.

Through 1993 and 1994, I held bimonthly luncheons with small business owners, in invited groups averaging about 25. The luncheons provided great feedback on issues large and small that we needed to address to foster small business development. Often the issues dealt with unnecessary city regulations. City staff was on hand to deal with each issue that was brought up.

From the minority and women business goals, to the SABDC, to ACCION, to eliminating unnecessary regulations, to lowering the threshold for tax abatement benefits, and in hundreds of other small ways I believe we made San Antonio a better place for small businesses to thrive.

Apparently Hispanic Business magazine agreed in 1994 when it ranked San Antonio No. 1 as the most hospitable city to new Hispanic businesses.

The Education Partnership

On October 1, 1991, during my first year as mayor, I attended a pep rally at South San Antonio High School. When I arrived I was greeted by members of the ROTC and escorted to the small gymnasium. Students were jammed together on portable risers along two sides of the gym. The band and cheerleaders were on the gymnasium floor facing a portable grandstand for invited guests. On the walls of the gym were the championship pennants of the baseball team.

"South San," as it's called, is a school with a proud tradition. Located in the southwest part of the city, it has approximately 1,800 students, 90 percent of whom are Hispanic. Over the years the school has won seven state baseball championships and has produced great players such as Raul Zamora, John Langerhans, and Juan Guerra, who went on to play either college or professional baseball. Coach Cliff Gustafson led South San to many of its state championships. When he left to coach the University of Texas baseball team, he became the "winningest" college baseball coach of all time.

As I joined the other guests on the platform, the South San band was playing an upbeat tune and the students were in a festive mood. But this was a different type of pep rally. It was not about sports. It was about the Education Partnership.

After the rally, a number of kids came up to ask for my autograph. Many said they were inspired to go on to college and were appreciative of the help being provided by the partnership. I was totally convinced that this program, which had been started by former Mayor Henry Cisneros, would be one of Henry's greatest legacies.

In 1988, COPS and Metro Alliance brought Henry a plan to target eight high schools that had the highest dropout rates and the smallest numbers of graduates going to college. The plan would offer scholarships to all students at those schools who had a 95 percent attendance record and a "B" average. The scholarships would pay costs at one of the six colleges and universities in San Antonio. If a student did not want to go to college, he or she would receive preference in employment by local businesses. The model for this program had been developed a few years before in Boston, and was known as the "Boston Compact."

The idea was to give hope to the average student. The bright students were going to get scholarships from any number of sources. Everyone recognizes their potential. Most are self-motivated and will go on to a successful life. But how do you motivate the average kid?

Henry succeeded in patching together a partnership among the city, the local colleges and universities, the business community, the public schools and COPS and Metro Alliance.

He then put his best fund-raising skills to the task. The only source of money for the scholarships was from private donations. Henry got some of the largest corporations to adopt schools. He convinced City Council to provide funds for staff support for the program, which included a counselor for each school. This enabled all of the private donations to go to scholarships.

The students were asked to sign a contract before the school year started. They agreed to work to comply with the requirement of a 95 percent attendance and a "B" average. The partnership signed the contract agreeing to fund a four-year scholarship.

Scholarship money was dependent on year-to-year fund raising. As long as Henry was mayor, there was no problem raising this money. But if later mayors were not committed to the program, the scholarship money could be in jeopardy.

When I decided to run for mayor, one of the issues Henry asked me to work on was the Education Partnership. He wanted to see it continue and grow. I told him I would be committed to helping the program.

I did make education an issue in my campaign. But although I told Henry I would make sure the Education Partnership was funded, I was also determined to approach the issue of education on a broader basis.

When I was elected in May 1991, President George Bush had moved education issues to a higher level of national interest. Six goals set by the nation's governors became President Bush's rallying cry to improve education. The goals for the year 2000 included preparing kids to start school, achieving a 90 percent graduation rate, making every adult literate, providing lifetime learning, making our students first in the world in math and science, and making schools violence- and drug-free. The atmosphere created by President Bush helped focus local interest on supporting education programs.

At the end of October 1991, Secretary of Education Lamar Alexander came to San Antonio to promote the goals. We had just recently created a partnership with the Greater Chamber, UTSA, Bexar County, and the city, called the San Antonio Education Coalition. We funded the effort with $300,000 for a three-year period. Working with General McDermott and Henry Cisneros, we persuaded the coalition to fund an organization we called San Antonio 2000 to reflect the national effort to achieve the six national goals by the year 2000.

During the visit Secretary Alexander recognized San Antonio as the first major city in the United States to adopt the goals and to form an organization to achieve them.

While San Antonio 2000 had some success in promoting the six national goals, Trinity University's Center for Education Leadership was the real leader for education reform. I served as a senior fellow for the center. John H. Moore, chairman of Trinity's Department of Education, was the driving force behind the organization. The center created 70 "Smart Schools," and Moore worked with them to develop core curriculums, acquire technology, extend the school year, create school-based governance, and make schools into community centers.

One of my wife Tracy's major concerns was child care. She had raised her two children, Paul and Rochelle, while working full time. She understood the link between quality child care and work in San Antonio, where more than half of our children are reared with either both parents or their only parent working outside the home. She wanted the city to take the lead in fostering better child care.

In July 1992, City Council created the Work/Family Commission and appointed Tracy chairwoman. The commission members were employees, mostly human resource professionals, of large firms. They drove right to the issue of why businesses had to concern themselves with child-care.

The commission's major recommendation was to create a Corporate Child Care Collaborative.

Tracy, along with Peggy Walker of NationsBank and Merle Lawrence of Levi Strauss, led the effort to establish the collaborative. A trust fund was created to be administered by an appointed board of collaborative members. They raised approximately $1 million to help child care facilities become nationally accredited, a step that raises the quality of care and increases educational activities.

To date the collaborative has assisted 67 child care centers and family home providers. It has produced its first 17 nationally accredited family child care homes and increased the number of these centers by 32 percent. It has positively affected more than 3,500 children. It has also provided scholarships to 15 child care leaders, who in turn provided training to 2,000 of their peers. In 1997, a media campaign, "Get Smart," encouraged more businesses to join.

Meanwhile, as mayor, I pushed the school districts to create additional magnet schools. The Health Careers and the Business Careers high schools operating out of Holmes High School were successful. Two more magnet schools were created during my term, a Foreign Language School at Tafolla Middle School and an International School at Lee High School.

Prior to being elected to City Council, I had served on the advisory board to the Texas Prefreshman Engineering Program, founded in 1979 by Manuel "Manny" Berriozabal, professor of mathematics at UTSA. Manny was inspired to start the program when he read an article in S.A. Magazine that quoted an anonymous member of the Texas Higher Education Coordinating Board saying that the Mexican-American community is not where engineers come from.

Each summer during my term as mayor I would visit the hundreds of students that Manny gathered from throughout the city for classes in science and mathematics. Since 1979, almost 7,000 students, 79 percent of them minorities, have gone through the summer program. In a follow-up survey of college-age students in 1996, 92 percent of students attending Manny's summer workshops went to college and 55 percent of those graduates received engineering and science degrees.

Today his program has spread throughout the state to 28 college campuses in 15 cities. Over the years, the number of minority students entering the fields of science and math has increased 50 percent. Manny Berriozabal, although he would accept no credit, is responsible for much of that increase.

All of these education activities helped set the right tone to raise funds for the Education Partnership. Because the partnership did not have an endowment or foundation, yearly fund raising was necessary to keep it going. Because of the economic slowdown that started in 1988, funds were slow in coming to the partnership.

Every year I served as mayor I attended each of the eight school rallies. I became totally committed to the program that Henry founded. Carol Bidus, executive director of the partnership scholarship fund, came up with the idea to obtain a five-year commitment from sponsoring companies to give stability to the funding. I worked hard with Mike De La Garza, head of public relations for Charles Butt's H-E-B Grocery Company, to raise money.

By the time I left office, we were able not only to provide five-year funding for the eight schools, but also to raise enough money to add an additional three schools to the partnership.

It's difficult to measure the effectiveness of many programs. But data on the Education Partnership left no doubt about its success. Prior to the partnership only 29 percent of students at the eight high schools went to college. After five years of the partnership, 60 percent went to college. More than $2 million in scholarships has been awarded to more than 2,000 students.

Project Quest

At 6:30 p.m. on September 3, 1991, Councilman Frank Wing joined me in my office to talk about a financial demand from Communities Organized for Public Service and the Metropolitan Congregational Alliance. "Frank, COPS and Metro are not going to accept what we've been offering them. In less than one hour I am going to have several hundred people on the front steps of City Hall ready to kick my butt unless I find them $2 million."

The events that led to the tension on that day began on January 8, 1990. The announcement of the closing of the Levi Strauss sewing plant and the layoffs of more than 1,000 people had awakened Metro Alliance leaders Father Al Jost and Father Will Wauters to the precarious position of many in their congregations.

Many of the people laid off had no skills for other jobs. And the deficiencies of the existing job training programs became painfully clear when the San Antonio Light revisited the laid-off workers months after the plant closed and found that only a few had found new jobs through city, county or state programs.

Ironically, the reporters and other workers at The Light would soon have personal experience with unemployment programs. In October 1992, the Hearst Corporation, which owned the San Antonio Light, announced it was buying the rival Express-News from Australian media magnate Rupert Murdoch. As part of the deal, Hearst would close The Light and lay off its 700-plus employees.

George Irish, publisher of The Light and a Hearst Corporation executive, had called me with the news before the public announcement. I greeted it with some sadness but little surprise; newspapers were closing all over the country. But San Antonio's century-long, rough-edged newspaper war was one of the city's sinful delights.

The Light had endorsed me for mayor, and more important, I thought the competition between two newspapers helped to keep the city and its public officials on their toes.

Two days after Hearst's public announcement, I delivered a state-of-the-city address to the Greater Chamber. I challenged the winner, the Express-News, to reach out and become "the voice of San Antonio and South Texas" in both the United States and Mexico. It has made great strides toward meeting that challenge, opening bureaus in Mexico City, Monterrey, and along the border.

The Hearst Corporation and its chief executive officer, Frank Bennack, also provided first-rate outplacement services for The Light's employees, services much better than those offered to workers laid off in other large company staff reductions.

But while many of The Light's employees had college degrees and could move to other jobs, most of the Levi Strauss employees were garment workers with no other job skills. Fathers Jost and Wauters went to COPS for help. The COPS leaders listened and then began to meet with their people to develop a plan.

At its May 1990 meeting, just months after the Levi's closing, COPS made job training and workforce development one of its top priorities. Through a series of followup meetings COPS developed a job training program that encompassed five major attributes: Training must be long enough to develop marketable skills; there must be a guaranteed private-sector job starting at a minimum salary of $7.50 an hour for the person in training; a stipend must be available to pay for books, tuition, and family bills while the person was being trained; a central intake agency must be created to direct the person to the proper job training organization; and an outreach program must be developed to reach potential trainees.

By the 1991 mayoral elections, COPS was demanding that the candidates pledge $5 million to implement their program. I said that I would work with them, but I refused to pledge $5 million. The city budget was tight and I did not want to pledge something I might not be able to deliver.

After I was elected, the first step I took was to force the existing board to resign. The new board and organization was named

San Antonio Works and it was charged with developing a quality job training program. The story of that successful effort is told in a previous chapter.

After appointing the new board, I began working with COPS to structure a new organization that could accomplish its goals. I met with COPS leaders Virginia Ramirez, Pat Ozuna, Ernie Cortes Jr. (who was by then Industrial Areas Foundation Southwest regional director), Metro leaders Father Will Wauters and Father Al Jost, banker Tom Frost, and Henry Cisneros. After a series of meetings we decided that the organization should be a stand-alone, nonprofit entity. We decided that it should be called Project Quest.

For Project Quest to be successful, COPS would have to obtain funding from three different sources: the newly created San Antonio Works board, Governor Ann Richards' discretionary funds for job training, and the City Council.

The money from City Council was the subject of the conversation Frank Wing and I were having. COPS needed money from the city because JTPA rules did not allow federal funds to be spent for a stipend. On the other hand, no city in the United States had used its general revenue funds for a stipend for job trainees. We were being asked to go first.

I had asked Frank to take the lead in working with COPS on this issue. Frank was the key supporter of COPS on the council. They always looked to him to take the lead on their issues. Frank and I had met with COPS on a number of occasions to identify funds for the stipend. Frank found an available $400,000 in Community Development Block Grant funds that could be used. He had also offered to provide part-time city jobs for those in training. But COPS was not buying the offer. They wanted $2 million.

In response to my statement that I was about to get my butt kicked, Frank said, "Well mayor, tell them that you will try to find the extra $1.6 million. I'll tell them that I will help you."

"Frank, I know you understand COPS better than anybody, but they have told me privately that they expect me to deliver. They are pointing the finger at me, not you. I have to make a decision in the next 45 minutes."

Frank smiled and replied, "A fine mess you've got us into."

"Come on, Frank. This is a great program that could have national implications if it works. The trainees will need the stipend to stay in a long-term job training program. They can't work, take care of their family and enter a job training program all at the same time. COPS doesn't need the money until the next budget year. It will be a year before they are able to start taking clients. I am going to tell them that I will put it in the next budget. Will you back me up?"

Frank replied, "You had better call Alex first. You'll need his help."

I walked over to the phone and buzzed Alex Briseño in his office. I told him what I was going to say and asked if he could help us find the funds in next year's budget. He said he would.

I said, "So, Frank, are we ready?"

"Yes."

We met briefly in the conference room with Ramirez, Ozuna, Wauters, and Jost. They told me they wanted a yes or no answer to the question, "Will you commit to $1.6 million in city funds for job training?" As we walked out onto the front porch of City Hall, Pat Ozuna gave me a stern look and said, "I hope you have the right answer." When we opened the door, we heard hundreds of COPS supporters shouting, "Invest in us."

As I looked out at the crowd, I thought how far ahead their thinking was on job development. The primary concern a company has in deciding where to locate is the local work force. Is the workforce trained and ready to work? If the answer is yes, a community has overcome the major hurdle in getting a company to locate in its city. The COPS' yell of "Invest in us" meant more jobs for San Antonio.

I felt really good about pledging the funds. I knew that I had to deliver and felt confident that I could. If I pledged, I knew that the other council members who accompanied me to the porch would also pledge their support.

After I made my pledge, a great roar went up from the crowd. Pat Ozuna then handed me a black marker to sign my name on a poster containing the pledge. I signed and then all of the council members who were with me signed their names.

On September 12, the City Council in a special work session voted unanimously to approve $400,000 for the pilot project, and to seek $1.6 million from other city sources.

Four days later I was able to help COPS persuade the new San Antonio Works board to set aside $2 million for Project Quest. Now there was only one piece of the puzzle left, Governor Ann Richards.

On November 17, at a major COPS accountability meeting, Governor Richards pledged $2.5 million as 1,500 people cheered. Then she turned the accountability issue back to COPS and said, "I now hold you accountable to make the program a success." Sharp lady. We had a total of $6.5 million for the project.

I followed the governor with my pledge. Tom Frost pledged that 650 jobs would be available for properly trained workers. Then began the arduous task of putting together the Quest organization.

COPS contacted the University of Texas Center for Study of Human Resources. Employment specialist Bob McPherson was employed to develop the job training program. He and his associate, Brian Deaton, spent the first two months of 1992 in San Antonio putting together the elements of a job training program that met the five criteria COPS had set out.

While the program was being designed, I called on several businesses with COPS to tie down job commitments. I knew COPS was right about its program when I found out that businesses such as hospitals were importing workers because they could not find people with the necessary skills in San Antonio.

On May 26, 1992, our steering committee hired former Air Force General Jack Salvadore, who had been in charge of Air Force training and recruitment. He was the ideal person to lead the effort.

We now had the task of making sure that actual job training courses met the criteria for the jobs that the private sector pledged. Texas A&M University provided some of the best job training courses through their excellent engineering school, which had an extension campus at HemisFair Park. We also persuaded the Alamo Community College District's new chancellor, Bob Ramsay, to take the lead in job training. He agreed to do so. COPS followed up by working with the college district to provide good training programs in medical, manufacturing, service technology, maintenance repair, and business systems.

By October 1992, Project Quest worked with COPS volunteers to recruit trainees out in their neighborhoods. In January 1993, 140 enrollees began classes. In September 1993, Cynthia Scott became Quest's first graduate from St. Philip's College and began work as a licensed vocational nurse at the Baptist Medical Center.

At the end of February 1996, nine months after I left office, I went to a Project Quest board meeting to hear an analysis of the program by Professor Paul Osterman of the Massachusetts Institute of Technology.

The key findings were:

1. Between 1993 and 1995, 825 participants entered training. Of those, 447 successfully finished and 196 were still in training, while 182 did not complete their training.

2. Even those who did not complete training reported increased pay. Annual earnings increased between $4,923 and $7,457 per year for both groups.

3. Gains were slightly lower for welfare recipients and for people with arrest records and slightly higher for people with some college education.

4. The average cost per participant was $10,077.

5. Project Quest had a significant impact on the Alamo Community College District in offering more and better job training programs.

6. The future of Project Quest is uncertain because of the lack of assured funding.

With the study in hand, COPS hopes to convince President Clinton and federal job training officials that the program should be a prototype for the nation's job training program. The Industrial Areas Foundation has been successful in getting Dallas, Fort Worth, Houston, and the Rio Grande Valley to begin implementing projects modeled on Project Quest.

Funding is the critical issue. Unless there is a change in federal policy that supports the five principles of Project Quest, it is doubtful the program can be expanded. While the cost is higher per participant, the job training program leads to better-paying jobs. It is better to train a smaller number of technicians than it is to train more hamburger flippers. Project Quest has provided hope and inspiration to its participants and, most important, better jobs with better pay. Let's hope our federal government wakes up.

★★★

Lessons on Economic Development

■ **A political "pep rally" can galvanize action.**
The Vision 2020 Conference created hope to reach a distant goal. The positive attitude created by the conference was instrumental in helping me push my agenda forward.

■ **Watch out for your friends.**
You know what your enemies want to do to you, but you never know about your friends. Representative Karyne Conley's call for a national boycott of the Olympic Festival caught me off guard.

■ **It takes tension to create political progress.**
The call for a national boycott created the tension necessary to pass meaningful incentives to help small and minority businesses. Many times during my term, community tensions created by environmental, neighborhood, and community activists led to progress. I used the same tactic myself in pushing the banks to invest in the Bank Community Development Corporation.

■ **Government must help "average" students to attend college or receive advanced training.**
The Education Partnership gave incentives to inner-city students with average grades to complete high school because they could see a pathway to college or better jobs. If the city had not provided funding for staffing the program, very little money would have gone for scholarships.

■ **Government must create quality job training.**
Project Quest proved that quality training for disadvantaged workers will produce a quality work force. But it could not have been done without City Council providing a stipend for job trainees. A well-trained local workforce ranks at the top of considerations for a business contemplating a move to your city.

19

Economic Challenges

In the earlier chapter on International Relations I mentioned a trip to Mexico City in September 1992 to meet with President Carlos Salinas de Gortari. It was at that meeting that President Salinas made it clear to me that the North American Free Trade Agreement would be initialed in San Antonio.

On our trip back, Dennis Nixon, president of the International Bank of Commerce, said, "Do you know what Fortune 500 company is thinking about moving to San Antonio?"

This was a tricky topic. The truth was we rarely knew the identities of the companies we were trying to attract until after they had reached a decision on whether to come to San Antonio. The companies used outside consultants to approach a city and lay out their requests for information, services, and tax incentives. The companies kept their names secret so they wouldn't be inundated by cities trying to muscle in on the action.

In the case of moving a large corporate headquarters, the contacts have to be supersensitive. A break in secrecy could very well stop the proposed move if local opposition back home has time to get organized.

"I've heard that it's a communications company," I told Dennis. "I'm not sure whether it's a possible corporate relocation or just a division. We've been contacted about the need for parking space downtown and for a tax abatement. We are meeting their needs."

"I've been contacted to provide a huge amount of office space," Dennis said. "In fact, they want virtually all of the building that we own."

Just a few days earlier, International Bank of Commerce had bought the Republic of Texas Plaza site downtown on the corner of St. Mary's and Houston Street. The site included two buildings, one containing 95,000 square feet and the other 275,000 square feet. Dennis was planning to move the San Antonio branch of his bank into the smaller building.

Dennis continued, "I think it's Southwestern Bell, and I think it is going to be a corporate relocation rather than a division relocation." Southwestern Bell's corporate headquarters was located in St. Louis, Missouri, their home since 1879. They were the 29th largest company in the United States and 63rd largest in the world, employing 60,000 people worldwide.

As one of the "Baby Bells" that had spun off from AT&T in 1983, they had a virtual monopoly in local phone service in a five-state area. Because Texas was the largest state they served, making up more than 50 percent of their business, it made sense for them to move to Texas. The company was also in the cellular phone, directory publishing, and equipment selling business.

There was another reason to come to Texas and specifically to San Antonio. Southwestern Bell had invested $935 million in Telefonos de Mexico, or Telmex, Mexico's phone system. San Antonio's strong ties to Mexico would be a plus in trying to manage this investment.

"If that happens," I told Dennis, "it will be the most important economic development event in San Antonio history. We have never had a Fortune 500 company move its headquarters to San Antonio. We have only four Fortune 500 companies in the city. You have got to make them an offer they can't refuse."

By a lucky coincidence, Dennis' purchase had removed the Republic of Texas Building from the clutches of the Resolution

Trust Corporation, a federal agency that took forever to do a deal. Dennis was ready to deal because the 13-story building he bought was virtually empty. What great timing!

Dennis said, "We'll make them a great offer."

Just a few months earlier, City Council had approved a new local franchise agreement Southwestern Bell had requested. Looking back I was glad we had handled that issue correctly. I knew Southwestern Bell, because of its investment in Mexico, looked favorably on our city's support for the North American Free Trade Agreement.

Back in St. Louis, Dick Gephardt, a local congressman and then House minority leader, opposed the NAFTA agreement. Ironically, Congressman Gephardt paid a visit to San Antonio on September 18, 1992, just days before the announcement of Southwestern Bell's move. I went to a breakfast meeting at the Barn Door restaurant to listen to his speech as he waffled on whether he would support NAFTA.

On September 28, 1992, only six days after we returned from Mexico, more than 500 people gathered in the International Bank of Commerce Plaza, as Governor Ann Richards, Chairman Ed Whitacre Jr., and I held up the Texas flag in celebration of Southwestern Bell's decision to move its corporate headquarters to San Antonio.

I met Ed Whitacre for the first time in a small gathering just before the announcement. Ed was born in Ennis, Texas. A graduate of Texas Tech University, he is a big, tall man in his early 50s. Although he has a dominating physical presence, he is soft-spoken, with the proper Texas drawl.

I told him about a number of investments the city was making in the downtown area, including the $40 million TriParty improvements, the Alamodome, the proposed expansion of the convention center, and the plans for the historic civic center. I told him I was really glad to see him locate downtown.

"Don't discount the role the Alamodome played in our decision," he said. "The Dome is a symbol that your city is willing to invest for the long term. I like a city that takes chances and invests in itself."

One of Henry's arguments for building the Dome was that it would give us greater visibility around the nation and would lead to other economic activity. I can't believe he foresaw that it would lead to something as major as Southwestern Bell's decision to relocate here, but who knows?

Governor Ann Richards had played a key role in luring Southwestern Bell to Texas when she had called on Ed the previous March, asking him to consider the move. Ed said he had never been called by a governor before. At the announcement ceremonies, she called the move an "Economic Super Bowl, the Oscar, and the gold medal."

Tom Frost also played a major role in the relocation decision. In addition to chairing Frost Bank, Tom serves on the board of directors of Southwestern Bell. It was he who made the motion to move to San Antonio at the board of directors meeting the previous week in Mexico City. Dennis Nixon's decision to quickly cement an office space agreement with Southwestern Bell was the final critical element.

Governor Ann Richards, SBC Communications Chairman Edward Whitacre Jr. and Mayor Nelson Wolff hold a Texas flag at a news conference announcing that Southwestern Bell would move its corporate headquarters from St. Louis to San Antonio. (Express-News)

After the decision, I led a delegation of 80 people organized by the Greater Chamber to St. Louis. We spent three days with 500 Southwestern Bell employees who were considering a move with their company. They were so impressed that 80 percent of them came here.

On the same day we announced the move by Southwestern Bell, the White House announced that the North American Free Trade Agreement would be initialed in San Antonio. One month later we hosted the second annual meeting of the Fortune 500 Forum. Tracy and I used the opportunity to lobby the chief executives of the nation's largest companies on the advantages of being in our city. A lot of good things were happening.

Earlier in the book, I discussed how Henry Cisneros instilled in the mayor's office the responsibility for creating jobs. Henry put San Antonio on the map with his relentless drive to create a modern city. Generally, the only names that anyone around the country recognized from San Antonio were the members of the San Antonio Spurs. The exception was Henry Cisneros. By the end of his term, every key leader around the country knew Henry.

Henry's national legacy provided enormous benefits to our city. As representatives of San Antonio's Economic Development Foundation knocked on doors to get businesses to locate in San Antonio, the executives of those companies knew through the previous work of Henry Cisneros that we were a city on the move.

During my term of office several major businesses moved to San Antonio, in large part because of Henry's legacy. They came also because of the groundwork laid by Mayor Lila Cockrell and General Robert McDermott when the Economic Development Foundation was created. McD, Lila, and Henry had planted the seeds and I would plow the fields and harvest the crop.

But plowing the fields requires crop rotation. Things never remain the same. During my term I pushed international relations to the top of the agenda with the strong efforts we made to support the North American Free Trade Agreement. This certainly played a role in attracting Southwestern Bell.

Mario Hernandez had become president of the Economic Development Foundation just before I was elected. He was very aggressive and effective, and he also forged strong relationships with both City Manager Alex Briseño and me. With the strong ties to the Economic Development Foundation we became more aggressive in using tax abatements to attract businesses.

When a business looks at opening a branch in another city or moving, its officers consider a number of things. They look at quality of life issues such as the arts, libraries, crime, transportation, local schools and child care and parks. But two issues rank at the top — the cost of doing business and the available trained work force in your city. Texas does not have an income tax and that is a plus in the eyes of most businesses. But offsetting the lack of an income tax are our high property taxes, particularly public school taxes. As a result, the Texas Legislature allows local communities to forego or gradually phase-in property taxes to a company willing to make a significant investment and create jobs.

The economic development agency of the city plays the lead in developing the policy for allowing tax abatements. The amount of the investment and the number of jobs to be created determines the amount and the number of years an abatement will be allowed. The city works with the county and the school districts so that each will develop a similar policy.

The tax abatement policy has become a key element in presentations made by the city and the Economic Development Foundation to prospective businesses. It is taken for granted as an incentive by nearly any business contemplating a move. San Antonio had to play the tax abatement "game" because competition is hot.

During my race for mayor, tax abatements became a key issue in the runoff. Teleservice Resources Corporation, a subsidiary of American Airlines, had decided to create up to 1,000 jobs in an airline reservation center in our city, based partly on the promise of a local tax abatement.

My opponent in the runoff, Maria Berriozabal, had voted against the tax abatement policy that we had recently established. I had voted for it. The policy provided for a tax abatement of up to 10 years if the company invested at least $4.5 million, created at least 100 jobs, and located in certain parts of the city. The American Airlines subsidiary had qualified for an "exceptional" category investment of at least $10 million and 200 jobs, which automatically qualified them for 10 years of abatement anywhere in the city. They more than qualified by agreeing to invest $24.5 million and to create up to 1,000 jobs.

Maria refused to say she would vote for the abatement if elected. I said I would vote for it.

After I won in June 1991, we approved the abatement the following month. Even during the 10 years of the phase-in, the city would receive $629,530 a year for property taxes. American Airlines made the investment and today 1,100 people work there.

In my second month in office, in July 1991, we worked with the Economic Development Foundation to land Citicorp, the nation's second largest bank. They agreed to invest $35 million and to employ 750 people in a customer service center. We also provided a tax abatement and today more than 1,500 people work in their financial service center.

The following November I met several times with officials from QVC Network Inc., the nation's largest home television shopping network. They invested $10 million and projected the creation of up to 2,000 jobs. We granted them a tax abatement in the form of an industrial district for five years.

When we landed the Southwestern Bell Corporation, I was in the middle of talking with a person by the name of "Bob Rich." I had no idea who he really was, but he said he was representing a company that was considering San Antonio for a major location. Bob was impressed that Southwestern Bell had chosen San Antonio.

I found out in February 1993 that "Bob Rich" was actually Rich Crane, representing Herbert Sandler, chairman, and Marion Sandler, president and chief executive officer, of Golden West Financial Corporation, the holding company for World Savings, a $25 billion company. We worked with World Savings to give them an abatement to build a $56 million, 275,000-square-foot service center. It would employ up to 900 people. They also agreed to donate 111 acres of land adjacent to their location to the Alamo Community College District for a northwest campus.

As our successes added up, we began to receive national publicity on our economic growth. After Governor Ann Richards, Austin Mayor Bruce Todd and I made a trip to California, the Los Angeles Times wrote a major story with the headline: "San Antonio is hot, Austin is hotter. They're selling salsa to Mexico and stealing jobs from the Silicon Valley." The article said, "Some economists argue that the two cities' burgeoning economies — based on high tech, entertainment, tourism, health care, and biomedicine — represent the future of Texas; Dallas and Houston — with their oil, banks, and real estate — represent its troubled past."

Building on our successes during my term, we widened the eligibility requirements to get a tax abatement, making it easier for smaller local firms to qualify. We also extended eligibility to downtown housing and aviation facilities.

Other companies that came during my tenure included: Mission Mexican Foods Inc., 200 jobs in a tortilla manufacturing plant; Reyes Industries Inc., 300 jobs in textile manufacturing; Kraft General Foods, 250 jobs in financial services; Pratt and Whitney, 100 jobs in manufacturing; Cessna Citation, 75 jobs in a regional service center; Integrated Cargo Management Systems, 100 jobs in cargo handling; West Telemarketing Corporation, 2,000 jobs in telemarketing inbound services; Caremark International, 800 jobs in the insurance industry; United Parcel Service, 600 jobs in an international call center; and Sitel Corporation, 500 jobs in outbound telemarketing.

But the use of tax abatements is controversial. Many people consider it "corporate welfare." It's popular to criticize tax abatements. But what is overlooked is that the city often gets a substantial stream of new revenue even during the abatement period, from sales taxes and hotel/motel taxes. The hard facts are that we are in competition with major cities throughout the world that provide incentives far beyond what we offer.

If you lived in Alabama, you would have cause to complain. Alabama provided more than $300 million in tax and infrastructure improvements to lure a Mercedes manufacturing plant. That amounted to $200,000 in tax subsidies for each job that Mercedes created in Vance, Alabama. Our cost per job in tax abatements for the three largest investments in San Antonio during my tenure was $5,000, or 2.5 percent of the Vance, Alabama, cost.

We would all be better served if Congress would prohibit tax abatements and other tax incentives. They are a "zero sum game" as far as domestic relocations go. But until lawmakers act, we must play the competitive game.

Regional Alliances

On July 9, 1991, I received Tony Sanchez, chairman of the International Bank of Commerce, in my office. Tony was accompanied by his business associates, Dennis Nixon and Jorge Haynes. Tony was in his 70s, 5'6" tall, silver hair, an immaculate dresser.

Tony was born in Laredo in 1916 to a hard-working family, poor but proud. He dropped out of high school and went from selling cars to Singer sewing machines to office machines. He started a small typewriter business that failed when IBM began to dominate the market.

He became a "land man" who leased oil and gas rights from local property owners, promising them that he would have an oil company drill on their land. Once he had the lease, he would then hustle an oil and gas company to drill. Then he decided to drill his own wells and hit it big-time, a huge gas field. He became one of Texas' richest men.

But Tony was not interested in just building his personal wealth. He wanted very much to unite the disparate voices of South Texas to work for economic development.

He wasted no time when he said, "Mayor, you need to pick up where Henry Cisneros left off. I am talking about Henry's 1986 Future of the Region conference. Henry developed some great initiatives for South Texas that need to be followed up on."

I responded, "Tony, I am very familiar with that conference. I attended it, and my wife Tracy was in charge of all the recorders at the conference. It was a great conference."

San Antonio has strong historical ties to South Texas. In a relationship dating back to the strong Mexican ranch society before Texas became an independent state, San Antonio has been the commercial trade center for this region.

But while San Antonio's economy has expanded tremendously in the last 20 years, South Texas continues to lag. It has the lowest per capita income and the highest unemployment in the state. It also has the lowest state funding for higher education per capita and the highest rate of high school dropouts. The people who suffer the most from these conditions are Hispanics who constitute more than half the population of most South Texas counties.

A major factor that contributed to the continuation of the region's poverty was our inability to work together at the state level. A gain by any community in the region was considered a loss by every other town. Thus Laredo envied San Antonio's growth, rather than positioning itself to benefit from it. The cities in the Lower Rio Grande Valley constantly undercut each other's efforts to gain highway and airport investments, with the result that none of them gained anything.

Tony continued, "I would like you to take the lead in forming a South Texas organization to work for the infrastructure and educational needs of our area. This would follow up on the program outlined in Henry's Future of the Region conference. I will put the resources of our bank behind such an effort."

Tony had founded International Bank of Commerce in 1966, in a small office in Laredo. In 1975, he hired Dennis Nixon as president and CEO. Nixon built the bank into a $3 billion operation that has numerous locations throughout South Texas.

I responded, "Well, Tony, I think the timing is right. We have always received the short end of the stick from the state, but now we have finally elected a governor who says she will correct the state neglect of our region. I really believe that Governor Richards will support us."

Tony said, "She will. I gave strong support to her campaign. It was the South Texas vote that got her elected." He was right about that.

I said, "OK, let's go to work and form this organization."

After our visit I pulled out my notes on the Future of the Region conference. Henry had used an outfit called the San Antonio Institute for American Studies to staff the conference. It was financed by a select group of his major contributors, led by developer Marty Wender.

The conference was held on August 15, 1986, only six days after Henry had won a major victory by defeating the Homeowner-Taxpayer Association's proposed "spending cap." Henry was very much at the height of his power. He was well known throughout the state, and everyone thought he would run for statewide office. Many of us thought that this was the underlying reason he called the conference, to begin solidifying his base beyond San Antonio. Henry attracted 400 leaders from throughout the region, and because of his stature the conference received great publicity throughout the state.

The initiatives that emerged from this process spanned a range as wide as the subject region itself. More important than the actual goals was a breakthrough in attitude. For the first time, San Antonio and the entire Texas border region were united in the stance that a gain for one was a gain for all.

The conference was a great success but one incident threw a damper on its impact. Henry became supersensitive to the whispered criticism that the conference was transparently intended to be a vehicle propelling him to greater statewide prominence. He announced that there would be no followup organized with his assistance. He ordered that his name should not appear a single time in the final published conference report.

A great set of initiatives had now lost the principal spokesman. All of the enthusiasm quickly evaporated.

So after Tony's visit, I dusted off the five-year-old report. I found that almost all the initiatives were still viable. I began to pick out those I thought we had a chance to accomplish.

On August 7, 1991, Tony and I announced the formation of ASTC, the Association of South Texas Communities. The International Bank of Commerce provided the staff and cities throughout the region hosted semi-annual meetings. We concentrated our efforts on supporting the NAFTA agreement and pushing our state and national governments to make needed infrastructure and education improvements in South Texas.

We worked with Texas Department of Transportation Commissioner Henry Muñoz to obtain increased funding for highways in South Texas. We worked with the University of Texas

System in 1993 to obtain the greatest increase in state spending on higher education ever achieved by South Texas. We made several NAFTA lobbying trips to Washington. In October 1994, we held a second Future of the Region Conference that updated the goals of Henry's 1986 conference.

Tony Sanchez did not live to see the work and accomplishments of the organization he helped create. He died on April 19, 1992, but left a strong legacy for South Texas.

Another major regional initiative started by Mayor Cisneros was the Greater Austin-San Antonio Corridor Council. In 1997 I was elected its chairman. My predecessor, former Austin city councilman and current University of Texas Regent Lowell Lebermann, began an initiative to enlarge the lanes on Interstate 35, build a parallel road (State Highway 130), and create rail passenger service along the corridor. I am presently working with Ross Milloy, the president of the corridor, to galvanize government and private support for the three projects.

Senator Jeff Wentworth has at the time of this writing introduced a bill in the Legislature to create a rail authority. Both VIA and Austin Metro are committed to the project and are helping fund it.

Funding for most of the Interstate 35 upgrade has been awarded by the Texas Department of Transportation. We have obtained partial funding for the engineering studies for the new Highway 130. We are presently lobbying for federal funds to help on all three projects.

The Military

On the night of June 21, 1995, three weeks after I had left office, I received a phone call from Mayor Bill Thornton. He said, "I'd like you to come to City Hall tomorrow morning. All of us who have worked to save Brooks Air Force Base and Kelly Air Force Base will be there to listen to the broadcast of the BRAC (Base Closure and Realignment Commission) decision on which bases they will recommend closing. I'd like to thank you and the rest of people who have worked so hard on this issue."

I replied, "How do you think we will come out?"

Thornton said, "I think we'll be OK, but I don't know for sure."
I said, "Thanks for the invitation. I will try to be there."

After I hung up, I told Tracy of my conversation. She said,
"Don't go. I think one of the bases will be closed, and they are
inviting you to share in the anguish. If they really wanted your
help, they should have invited you to be part of the reception
committee when the BRAC members came here two weeks ago,
and to the BRAC's regional hearings in Fort Worth on June 10.
Apparently, they decided they no longer needed your help, so I
hope you'll stay away."

The origins of this conversation went back two years. On May
21, 1993, the BRAC voted to add Kelly Air Force Base to the list of
bases it was considering for closure. The BRAC was created by
Congress to handle the difficult task of closing unneeded bases
after the collapse of communism and the breakup of the Warsaw
Pact. The purpose was to isolate the base-closing decisions from
politics as much as possible.

Six commissioners were appointed by the Democratic and
Republican congressional leadership. Two others were appointed
by the president for a total of eight. The secretary of defense would
first submit a list of possible closures to the commission. That
body could add or delete bases from the list if they believed the
secretary had significantly deviated from the criteria. The president had 30 days after the commission's recommendation to
either forward the recommendation to Congress or to return the
package to the commission for adjustment. Congress then had 45
days to disapprove the list, again without modification. If Congress did not vote to reject the list, then the closures became law.
The base closure process began in 1988 with the first round of
closures, followed by another round in 1991.

San Antonio is very much a military city. With five bases, we
depend on the military for the health of the city's economy. The
bases had a $4 billion impact on the area in 1994.

Kelly Air Force Base is the largest of the five bases. Opened in
1917, Kelly is one of five air logistics centers in the nation. Its major
mission is to maintain and upgrade very large aircraft such as the
C-5 Galaxy transport and the B-52 bomber and to overhaul jet

engines. Its 10,400 civilian employees and 4,998 military personnel had an $820 million economic impact in 1994.

Lackland Air Force Base opened in 1942 adjacent to Kelly. It is
called "The Gateway to the Air Force" because it is the Air Force's
only basic training facility. Lackland also houses Wilford Hall
Medical Center, the largest hospital in the Air Force.

Randolph Air Force base, which opened in 1930, is the headquarters of the Air Training Command, San Antonio's only "four
star" command and one of a handful of commands headed by
four-star generals outside of Washington. It trains pilot instruc-
tors — the people who train other people how to fly — at the
"West Point of the Air."

Brooks Air Force Base, opened in 1918, is home to the Arm-
strong Laboratory and the USAF School of Aerospace Medicine.
Its scientists conduct research on such topics as the ergonomics of
fighter plane cockpit design, to ensure that the pilot and the plane
become as one.

Fort Sam Houston is headquarters for the Fifth Army, which
is the Army Reserve in the middle third of the country. "Fort Sam"
has been an army base since 1878. The Apache chief Geronimo
was held prisoner there after his capture, and it was from there
that General John Pershing launched his raid into Mexico chas-
ing Pancho Villa. Today, it is better known as the home of the
Brooke Army Medical Center, the core of the largest health care
training center in the world and home of the world-famous "burn
unit" (formally, the Institute of Surgical Research).

San Antonio citizens have always supported the military, even
during the Vietnam War. With the leadership of the Greater Chamber, the city holds a week-long celebration each year to honor the
men and women in uniform, as well as the civilian workers who
contribute to the bases' various missions. Retired and active military personnel participate in all the major civic organizations in
San Antonio. It is a marriage that simply could not be broken up.

So when Kelly was added to the list of possible closures in
1993, nobody in San Antonio believed that the base would be
closed.

Kelly is the military's oldest continuously active air base. Its
most recent role was as a staging base for movements of troops

and supplies during the Desert Storm conflict. Its 12,000-foot runway is capable of accommodating the heaviest of aircraft. A favorite sight for locals and tourists alike is the occasional landing by a NASA Boeing 747 carrying a space shuttle from California to another launch in Florida.

Among the five air logistics centers, Kelly had the largest number of minority workers, with Hispanics making up 61 percent of its work force. They, in turn, made up 45 percent of all Hispanic civilians employed by the Air Force. Generations of Hispanic families had worked at the base over eight decades and their jobs had enabled them to climb the ladder to the middle class.

Kelly was part of the heart and soul of San Antonio. We were ready to do battle to save it from any threat.

After Kelly was added to "the list," I turned to the Greater Chamber to take the lead in fighting to keep the base open. I met with Joe Krier, chamber president, and Tullos Wells, chairman of the Military Affairs Committee. Joe recommended that Tullos lead a task force to be named "The Case for Kelly." I agreed.

We went to work full steam to protect Kelly from closure. On June 1, we held a rally with Governor Ann Richards. On June 5, one of the commissioners, Peter Bowman, came to visit the base. We greeted him at the airport and accompanied him on a bus to Kelly. More than 20,000 people lined the road entering Kelly.

The following day, we attended a public hearing before the commission in Corpus Christi. The COPS organization rallied 2,000 people to take buses provided by the chamber to the hearing.

On June 16, we flew to Washington to support our congressmen when they testified before the commission. And then on June 25, it was all over. The commission removed Kelly from the list.

In the midst of the celebrations, some of us knew that the battle was far from over. Through the hearings we learned that the greatest threat to Kelly was the fact that there was significant overcapacity, about 40 percent, at the nation's five air logistics centers. That meant that two ALCs could possibly be closed in the next round of base closures in 1995.

The pressure to close more bases began to mount as the reduction in personnel continued. Seventy military bases had been ordered closed in the 1988, 1991 and 1993 rounds of closure. That was only a 15 percent reduction of bases compared with a 30 percent reduction in the military's overall manpower. It was expected that the 1995 round would close more than the total number shut down during the first three rounds.

The Greater Chamber wasted no time in preparing for the 1995 round. On January 21, 1994, I announced the formation of "BRAC '95." A careful analysis showed that three of our bases were vulnerable: Kelly, Brooks because of a possibility of consolidating research lab facilities, and Fort Sam Houston because of a possible consolidation of medical services.

In October 1994, I accompanied the Greater Chamber on its annual trip to Washington, D.C., to buttonhole the Pentagon. We met with Navy Secretary John Dalton, Army Secretary Togo West, Air Force Under Secretary Rudy De Leon, and Defense Secretary William Perry.

At lunch I asked Rudy De Leon, "How important will the fact be that our workforce at Kelly Air Force Base is 61 percent minority?"

He said, "That is technically not a criterion to be taken into consideration .... I would not count on your minority employment saving your base."

We had always felt that the Hispanic work force at Kelly would somehow pull us through the threatened closure. If it were to be a significant factor it would have to be played as a political card. When I returned home I said to the media, "We're far from being safe."

On November 1, 1994, the Kelly union led an effort to hold a rally at Villita Assembly Hall. U.S. Representative Frank Tejeda, speaking to a half-filled room, said, "I didn't think there would be one chair left. Let's make this a wake-up call and get organized." I followed Frank and spoke of the need to take the threat of closure seriously.

Because of our successful effort to prevent closure in 1993, people just were not taking the threat seriously. People's attitude toward the possible closure was very much like the attitude I had experienced three months before the rally, when we had lost a referendum on reviving the Applewhite Reservoir project. People did not think we had a water problem, as they didn't think we had a problem with keeping Kelly open. They also could not see the relationship between water and Kelly. It would become clearer as time passed.

All of our bases were given the lowest ranking on environment because of the lack of a guaranteed water supply. This ranking couldn't have come at a worse moment because we were in the middle of a lawsuit filed by the Sierra Club to restrict pumping from the Edwards Aquifer.

In January 1995, the National Council of La Raza urged Secretary of Defense Perry and Air Force Secretary Sheila Widnall to spare Kelly Air Force Base from closure. BRAC co-chairman Jose Villarreal, with his close contacts in the White House, drove home the message of the importance of Hispanic voters to administration officials.

The political pressure seemed to be working. In January, Kelly was absent from the proposed list to be submitted to the BRAC. By late January, the decision was made by the Pentagon not to recommend closing any of the air logistics centers. They decided to downsize all five rather than close one or more.

This decision was not made public at the time because the list would not be submitted to the BRAC until March 1. But word began to leak out and our congressional delegation became confident that Kelly would not be on the list submitted by the Department of Defense. U.S. Representative Henry B. Gonzalez was quoted in the February 17 edition of La Prensa, a Spanish-language newspaper, saying, "Kelly is not going to close, and the workers at the air logistics center can move forward with their lives with the assurance of continued employment."

As the March 1 deadline neared, speculation surfaced that Brooks would be on the list instead of Kelly. On February 28, I received a phone call from Deputy Defense Secretary John Deutch. He said, "Mayor, I am sad to report that Brooks Air Force Base will be on the proposed closure list."

I responded, "Well, I am disappointed about Brooks but happy that Kelly was not put on the list. I thank you for the information, but I want you to know we will put on the best case possible to save Brooks."

"I understand that."

On March 1, 1995, Secretary of Defense Perry publicly submitted his list of 33 bases recommended for closure. It included Brooks Air Force Base and excluded all air logistic centers including Kelly. Things looked good for Kelly and bad for Brooks. But things are not always as they seem.

The following day, BRAC chairman Alan Dixon, a former Illinois senator, questioned Secretary Perry as to why none of the air logistics bases was included on the list. Perry said it was less expensive to keep them all open and downsize them. Chairman Dixon was not buying that argument. He asked the General Accounting Office to evaluate the closure of the air logistics centers.

Chairman Dixon's statement sent a tremor through many of us back home. We now knew that we had to prepare on two fronts. One was to articulate our arguments for Brooks and the second to defend Kelly.

Brooks is in the southeast part of San Antonio, where I grew up. I remember standing in front of our lumber business on Roosevelt Avenue on November 21, 1963, as President John F. Kennedy and his wife, Jackie, drove by on their way to the base. He was going there to dedicate four new buildings and the School of Aerospace Medicine. The following day, he would be assassinated in Dallas.

Although Brooks was not a large base it contained the highest paying jobs of all San Antonio bases. Its intellectual capital of 962 doctors, scientists, and engineers had a strong working relationship with other research institutions in San Antonio. If we lost Brooks, San Antonio would suffer a severe brain drain.

Rather than just arguing against the closure of Brooks, we came up with a plan that would actually save the military more money than if they closed the base completely. We developed a "cantonment" strategy that would close 75 percent of Brooks' 1,300 acres and cluster key missions in the remaining 25 percent to be administered by Kelly AFB.

As we were preparing our defense of Brooks, a Pentagon report was released to the commission that ranked Kelly and McClellan at the bottom of the five air logistics centers. One of the reasons for Kelly's low overall ranking was the lack of a guaranteed water supply.

The next shot came from the General Accounting Office. They said that the Pentagon acted on incomplete information when it decided to keep all the logistics centers open.

As the signs looked more and more ominous for Kelly, we still had to concentrate on our defense of Brooks. Brooks was already on the list and Kelly was not yet included. We began to prepare for a visit to Brooks from four of the commission members.

On the night of April 5, 1995, I joined hundreds of San Antonio citizens to greet commissioners Benjamin Montoya and Wendi Louise Steele at the airport. Montoya was a retired Navy rear admiral. Steele, who lived in Houston, was a former aide to Republican Senator Don Nichols of Oklahoma.

I took Montoya and Steele to a dinner party we had arranged on a decorative barge in the San Antonio River. Montoya enjoyed the ride so much that he asked if we could go around the river again. He sang with the mariachis as we rode the river again, with Councilwoman Lynda Billa Burke standing by his side, singing along with him.

After the barge trip, I took Steele and Montoya to their accommodations at Brooks Air Force Base. Montoya said, "I understand there is a large population of Hispanics employed at Brooks as well as Kelly."

I replied, "Yes, the military has provided the road to prosperity for many Hispanics." He seemed genuinely concerned about the workforce as I told him the story of the upward mobility of Hispanics in San Antonio.

Wendi Steele did not seem interested in much of anything. We already had concerns about her because of her connection to Oklahoma Senator Nichols. Tinker Air Force Base in Oklahoma was another of the air logistics centers. It would be happy for Kelly to close because that would mean more work might go there.

The next morning two more commissioners, Rebecca Cox of California and Joe Robles of San Antonio, joined us for the briefing at Brooks. Our arguments were so compelling I wondered how in the hell did Brooks get on the list to begin with? It crossed my mind that listing Brooks for possible closure may have been a diversionary tactic to take our focus off Kelly.

On April 19, we traveled to Dallas to present our arguments on Brooks to the full BRAC. More than 1,000 supporters made the bus trip to Dallas. Again we felt good about the presentation.

But while we felt confident about Brooks, we were increasingly fearful of what the commission would do next on Kelly. Congressman Frank Tejeda was instrumental in keeping us focused on Kelly. He insisted that the real threat was to Kelly. Senator Kay Bailey Hutchison told us in April that the BRAC staff was going to recommend reviewing all five air logistics center bases for closure.

Like every other community that has been threatened with a base closure, we employed lobbyists to represent us. We retained the 400-member law firm of Arter and Hadden, represented by former Congressman Tom Loeffler. It was interesting to have Tom, who had defeated me for Congress in 1978, now working for us. He was effective with the important Republican players in Washington. We also employed the law firm that Jose Villarreal then worked with, Hawkins, Delafield, and Wood.

After the hearing in Dallas, I received a phone call from Governor Richards. She said, "Mayor, you really need to hire Harry McPhearson's law firm. (Harry McPhearson was a commissioner on the 1993 BRAC.) They are very close to members of the commission. Take my word, you need them."

I replied, "OK, we'll do it."

I got on the phone right away and invited McPhearson to come to San Antonio. We reached a tentative agreement to employ his firm.

A few days later, I received a phone call saying they would not be able to work for us. Someone in the firm had already agreed to work for Tinker Air Force Base in Oklahoma. This was bad news. It looked as though they knew something we didn't.

On May 10, 1995, the commission added 35 military installations to the list, including Kelly and the other four air logistics centers.

Congressman Tejeda said, "This was not a surprise, and I believe that, in the end, Kelly will remain open and viable." All of us clung to that hope.

At a news conference after the Kelly announcement, I said that this was a real threat, more of a threat than two years earlier. We had already prepared our battle plan for arguing against Kelly closure.

One of the first arguments we used was the minority employment issue. The National Council of La Raza began lobbying again to save Kelly. But it seemed the BRAC was just not interested.

As if there were not enough problems already, another strong political voice spoke out for closure. Don Fuqua, president of the Aerospace Industries Association, said he doubted that downsizing all five air logistics centers would save money. He said the Air Force had too much infrastructure. Private enterprise wanted more of the Air Force maintenance work.

As we neared June 1, my time was running out. My last involvement was in planning for the June 6 visit of the BRAC to Kelly. After Bill Thornton became mayor on June 1, I was not asked to stay involved.

I thought it strange that I was not asked to continue helping. I thought that a show of continuity from one mayor to the next would have been helpful, particularly since I had gotten to know five of the eight commissioners. But the decision was not mine to make.

On June 6, the full commission visited Kelly. Thousands of people lined the streets to show their support, as they did in 1993. Mayor Thornton led a delegation to the BRAC hearings in Fort Worth on June 10.

For several months city staff and chamber leaders had been quietly doing some contingency planning in case the base was closed. But we kept this quiet for a number of reasons, not the least of which was the fear of sending out a capitulation statement to the people who worked at Kelly. We also did not want to send a message to the commission that we were ready for closure.

But a few days before the BRAC meeting date, the Express-News carried a banner headline that Mayor Thornton had a plan for the reuse of Kelly Air Force Base. Thornton's public remarks caused an uproar. The employees at Kelly felt they had been sold out. They were not interested in a plan for privatization. They wanted the base to remain open.

All this brings us back to the start of the story, on June 21, 1995, when I received a phone call from Mayor Thornton inviting me to City Hall to listen to the BRAC vote. Tracy's intuition was right. There would be bad news the next day.

The following morning, I listened to the commission report by myself on the radio in my office at Sun Harvest. When the vote to close Brooks failed, I was delighted. Our arguments were so compelling I had felt confident about that outcome.

When the vote was taken to close McClellan, I thought that maybe that would be enough to satisfy the commission. But it was not. On the next vote the commissioners voted to close Kelly Air Force Base. The commission went on to close a total of 243 military installations.

Powerful emotions swept through me. Although all of us knew the base was vulnerable, most of us believed it would survive. When I heard the vote taken, I found it hard to believe what I was hearing. The lives of 10,000 workers and their families would now be traumatized. There is hardly a family in San Antonio that does not have some connection to Kelly. I stayed in my office by myself for some time to gain control of my emotions.

On July 13, President Clinton approved the recommended closure list, but with an interesting flip. As a result of aggressive efforts by Mayor Thornton, community leaders, and our congressional delegation, he delayed the closing of Kelly and McClellan until 2001. He also gave some hope to saving jobs by announcing a plan for "privatization in place." This meant that although the facility would be closed as an Air Force facility, the same work would continue to be done there through contracting with the private sector.

There is no precedent for privatizing a workforce as large as Kelly's. Plans are moving forward for privatization at the Newark Air Force Base in Ohio, but Newark has only 1,000 workers compared to 10,000 at Kelly.

As of this writing, the privatization plan seems difficult to implement because a law known as the "60-40 rule" requires that no more than 40 percent of military maintenance work can be contracted out to private industry. The remaining work has to be done by federal employees.

The Air Force will decide in the summer of 1997 whether a private company or the air logistics center at Warner-Robins AFB in Georgia will get the $165 million a year contract for C-5 transport maintenance. If the private sector wins the bid, the work will be done in San Antonio and hopefully other commercial work will be done by the contractor. This works falls within the 40 percent allowance for outside contracting.

But as long as the 60-40 rule remains in place, only about 30 percent of Kelly's engine work can be contracted out. Congressmen who represent other military bases naturally do not want the 60-40 rule to be changed. On May 1, 1996, the House National Security Committee voted overwhelmingly to reject Congressman Tejeda's attempt to change 60-40. Senator Kay Bailey Hutchison tried but failed to convince the Senate Armed Services committee to change 60-40 to 50-50. Efforts to change the rule continue.

The American Federation of Government Employees Local 1617 has joined a lawsuit to stop privatization. Their members do not want to work for the private sector because they believe their pay and benefits will not be as good.

Mayor Thornton recovered quickly from the announced closure by organizing an Initial Base Adjustment Strategy Committee on July 20.

On October 14-15, more than 500 representatives from 200 companies participated in "Industry Days" at Kelly. In December, the mayor and council created the Greater Kelly Development Corporation to be run by a seven-member board of directors appointed by council. Retired Air Force General Paul Roberson was named executive director of the corporation.

During 1996, I chaired a committee for the Free Trade Alliance that developed "Inland Port S.A." The Free Trade Alliance is marketing San Antonio as an "inland port" for trade with Latin America, using Kelly as a primary area to locate. Kelly's long runway, good highway and railroad access, and ample warehouse facilities make it a good location for warehouse distribution and small manufacturing.

International trade, privatization of defense work, commercial aircraft maintenance and manufacturing offer several opportunities to San Antonio. Kelly got its first private tenant when Pratt and Whitney agreed to do its engine overhaul work at the base. We have an opportunity to create a large industrial complex that could pay lasting benefits to San Antonio. Mayor Thornton has announced a target of 21,000 jobs created at Kelly by the time the base is "closed." This would approximate the peak employment level that Kelly reached during the Vietnam War. It would leave San Antonio stronger economically than if Kelly had remained a downsized Air Force facility.

3.5 Percent and Falling

In other chapters I've discussed our tourism industry, international trade, and small business. I have not done justice to one other significant component of our economy: the health-care industry. Since the decision in the early 1970s to locate a medical school here, health-care services have taken on a life of their own — generating a $6 billion annual contribution to San Antonio's economy.

Dr. John Howe, president of the University of Texas Health Science Center in San Antonio, has pursued excellence at his institution, and we have all been rewarded with the results, as ancillary businesses and research projects have blossomed around the premier teaching facility. In the South Texas Medical Center — where the UT Health Science Center, its publicly funded teaching hospital, and the majority of the city's other major hospitals are located — 58 medical service companies with annual budgets totaling $1.6 billion are conducting business.

The industry includes a growing biotechnology component, medical equipment manufacturing, and a $500 million managed-care segment.

The city plays an active role in supporting this industry. I lobbied the Legislature to maintain funding levels and to award additional programs for San Antonio. The city has provided infrastructure improvements both in the Texas Research Park and in the South Texas Medical Center.

After the decision to shut down the air logistics center at Kelly, it became clear that we needed an all-out effort to diversify our economy so we could provide good job opportunities. Financial services, health care, tourism, the military, international trade, small manufacturing, and biotechnology will provide diversity and strength to our economy.

San Antonio's unemployment rate has dropped to its lowest level in 23 years, 3.5 percent. The William M. Mercers Inc. 1996 Texas Benchmark poll showed that wages and salaries in San Antonio's large companies have essentially caught up with the statewide average. They have gone from 11 percent below average in 1992 to one percent below average in 1996.

To keep providing job opportunities we need to continue our efforts to develop human capital. Even though we have made important strides, we are still a city with a large poor population. We have a long way to go to offer opportunities for all our citizens.

★★★

Lessons on Economic Challenges

■ **Local government must keep the cost of doing business low.**
When a business considers moving or locating a new branch, the most important criteria involve the cost of doing business. A low cost of municipal services, reasonable taxes, and a lack of unreasonable governmental regulations will pay big dividends in growing and obtaining more businesses.

■ **Tax abatements are a necessary evil.**
As long as cities compete with tax incentives, city governments must play the game if they want their economies to grow.

■ **Regional alliances strengthen a city.**
Our work with the Greater Austin-San Antonio Corridor Council and the Association of South Texas Communities is paying lasting economic dividends to our city.

■ **Addiction to federal jobs hinders private sector development.**
For years, San Antonio relied on the military as its top economic generator. Too many of our citizens thought those days would never end. For too long, this psychological dependence hampered the entrepreneurial spirit until Henry Cisneros altered our community when he was elected mayor in 1981. With the closing of Kelly, our whole community now understands the importance of our efforts to diversify our economy.

20

The Dome, The Spurs, and Baseball

We left the story of the Alamo-dome in May 1989. Henry Cisneros' term as mayor was ending, City Council had approved VIA's purchase of the Alamo Iron Works site, we had selected the project manager, the design team and the Dome Advisory Committee, and elected Henry as chairman.

The site selection should have been the end of a simple process, but it wasn't. The site hid several nasty surprises. It had been, after all, an industrial site for most of the past century. As Lila Cockrell assumed the mayor's office from Henry, she didn't realize the controversy that would bubble to the surface during her term and continue into mine.

Things began innocently enough. In late August 1990, VIA awarded a contract to remove five underground fuel storage tanks for the relatively modest cost of $149,037.50. By December, however, project managers had discovered more than a dozen additional underground tanks and sumps, the existence of which was either unknown or not revealed by the previous property owners. These contained contaminants such as cutting and processing oils, which had affected a shallow water table.

By June 1991, as I was becoming mayor, it became clear that the soil contamination was much worse than previously suspected. Soil from Southern Pacific Railroad property that lay immediately north of the Alamo Iron Works site was also tainted with hydrocarbons. Worse, the polluted soil had been mistakenly dumped at a site on Petroleum Drive that should have received only clean fill. This created a whole new disposal problem —102,000 cubic yards' worth of problem.

By April 1992, the total cost of contamination cleanup was approaching $2.5 million. VIA was preparing to seek $1 million from the Texas Water Commission's environmental cleanup fund, and vowing to pursue legal action against the former site owners.

More bad news surfaced in July. Testing revealed that 287,000 cubic yards excavated from the site was contaminated with lead. The project manager and consultants recommended that we dispose of as much as possible by building a landfill in an impermeable clay-lined pit under the parking lot to the south of the Dome structure. This would cost $2 million, and another $3 million if the remainder of the soil had to be transported to a certified hazardous waste disposal site.

However, since the lead contamination ran as deep as 20 feet below the surface, the Texas Water Commission eventually concluded that it was probably naturally occurring or "background" lead, rather than pollution left by industrial users. The commission approved the plan for construction of a clay-lined pit under the parking lots, with the remainder of the soil to be disposed of as "fill" for eroded areas in the city's old Pearsall Road landfill.

The decision to dispose of the contaminated soil in an underground pit on the Dome site was a serious error, both politically and environmentally. It triggered the formation of an environmental neighborhood group organized by David Arevalo and Ed Fanick and backed by State Representative Karyne Conley. Confronting City Council, the group claimed the city was subjecting residents around the Dome to a health hazard from the dust blowing off the exposed pile of contaminated dirt waiting to be moved.

The technical problem of how best to clean up the site now involved charges of "environmental racism," since the area's residents were predominantly poor blacks and Hispanics.

Throughout the next several months, protesters picketed the Dome site. They intermittently came to City Hall to protest. I began to meet with them on a monthly basis to try to resolve their concerns. Their bottom line was "move the landfill."

In November 1993, the Texas Natural Resource Conservation Commission reported that tests of the cap covering the landfill showed it to be very clean, and while some of the soil was "contaminated," none of it was hazardous or posed a health threat. I reminded people that the soil had been on that site for more than 100 years and nobody had complained or been hurt.

But that logic didn't fly. Strong pressure was kept on me — and the water commission — to remove the landfill. Eventually, the commission found other problems with the way the landfill was constructed, although we at the city thought they had agreed to the specifications. They gave us two choices: Cure the defects or remove the landfill. They also determined that the soil moved had been improperly classified, and instructed the city to remove all the soil from both the Petroleum Drive site and the Pearsall Road landfill.

It was cheaper to dig up the entire landfill under the Dome parking lot and transport the soil to a hazardous waste site in East Texas than to satisfy the state with on-site remediation. Just as important, moving the soil was also the bottom line demand of the neighborhood. I met with the neighborhood leaders and told them I would support removing the landfill.

My confidence in the consultants, engineers, and project manager had come to an end. I had followed their advice all along, and now not only was the landfill built improperly but improperly classified soil had been hauled to the wrong locations. I felt it was time to go to the courthouse.

On April 28, 1994, City Council authorized the filing of a lawsuit against Alamo Iron Works, project manager Day and Zimmermann, landfill builder American Ecology Services, and environmental consultants Raba-Kistner Consultants Inc.,

Malcolm Pirnie, and Fugro-McClelland (Southwest) Inc. We accused the defendants of breach of contract and negligence.

In the meantime, VIA was suing Alamo Iron Works, which filed a countersuit. The company also announced the layoff of 75 employees, blaming it on the costs of litigation.

Pretty soon, we were in the midst of a classic case of everybody suing everybody, the kind of case only lawyers could love. The consultants produced documents showing that they had repeatedly warned of possible problems, and that their warnings had gone unheeded. The legal bills were soon mounting toward levels exceeding the value of the disputes.

Eventually, in January 1996 — six months after I left office — two defendants settled. Malcolm Pirnie, which designed the on-site landfill, agreed to pay the city $2 million, and American Ecology, which had built the landfill, agreed to pay $250,000.

Four months later Day and Zimmermann, Fugro-McClelland and Raba-Kistner agreed to clean up the Petroleum Drive site. This would cost an estimated $2.9 million over two years. Alamo Iron Works agreed to $525,000 in cash payments, time payments, and discounts on products the city might buy from them in the future.

These settlements did not pay for all of the cleanup costs. The city had spent $9.4 million, of which $3 million was spent on legal fees.

To the credit of Mayor Bill Thornton and the council, the city made all the records of the lawsuit available to the public. They even asked staff to assist researchers in mining this mountain of paper. After an initial wave of curiosity, however, no one ever found much worth writing about, or a "smoking gun" that conclusively proved one side or the other "right."

"Four Telephone Poles on an Airplane Hangar"
While the "Dome dirt" sideshow dragged on through the years, the design and construction of the Dome proceeded. The structure had to be rectangular, its shape dictated by its intended uses, especially by the need to accommodate trade shows and other non-athletic events.

But this shape posed a problem: How to support a roof covering nine acres and spanning 600 feet without interior support columns. The solution? Hold the roof up from the outside.

In October 1989, the design team unveiled the most distinctive element of the Dome's design: a plan to suspend the roof from cables attached to four massive corner towers. Of course, this meant the "Dome" would not be a dome at all.

In typical San Antonio style, the design received mixed reviews. Supporters applauded the development of the world's first "third-generation" dome. In this view, the first generation was represented by the Astrodome and the Superdome — round buildings with rigid roofs, true domes in an architectural sense, but prohibitively expensive to build. The second generation had been the series of fabric-roof domes supported by air pressure inside the building and built from the mid-1970s through the mid-'80s. A series of failures had made them uninsurable, and they were regarded as obsolete. San Antonio would now pioneer a new approach that surely would be imitated worldwide.

Opponents simply thought the design was ugly. At various times in the debate, Councilwoman Helen Dutmer likened it to a cattle barn, a circus tent and an airplane hangar with four telephone poles on it. Council members and press commentators vied to invent the most colorful denunciations.

Personally, I like a design that is functional, but also breaks new ground in shape, texture and color. Councilman Bob Thompson probably summed it up best for most observers, though: "You have to help me develop some passion for this," he told his colleagues before finally voting his support. We approved it 9 to 1 on October 19, 1989.

The official groundbreaking occurred in a somewhat soggy field on November 5, 1990. Mayor Lila Cockrell, Henry Cisneros in his role as chairman of the Dome Advisory Committee, and VIA board Chairman Jim Dietzmann pushed the plunger of an "economic detonator" that set off silver sparklers around the 2,500-foot perimeter of the building's "footprint." A dynamite charge kicked up the earth at the center of the site, followed by a 21-shot fireworks salute.

Throughout construction, the news media and the public closely followed the Dome's progress. The newspapers recorded progress in a weekly "Dome boxscore" feature whose tone varied from upbeat to worried. Pictures tracked the work as the Dome continued to take shape.

Lowering Montana

In the legislation that allowed VIA to use a half-cent sales tax to build the Dome, the project was viewed as "a regional economic development facility" consisting of the Dome and an accompanying transit terminal north on Montana Street. The city would manage the Dome construction while VIA used a set amount of the total project budget to build the transit terminal. It seemed like a logical division of labor back in 1988. It wasn't.

The initial plan was for VIA to acquire and restore the old Southern Pacific "Sunset Depot" as the centerpiece of its terminal. This is a beautiful mission-style railroad station built in 1905, with a pink stucco exterior and a large stained-glass rose window lighting an elegant waiting room. It would be a sterling example of "adaptive reuse" of an important historic structure on the edge of the city's troubled St. Paul Square urban renewal area.

From the beginning, this plan began to go awry. Large crowds of Dome-bound pedestrians would have to cross lanes of heavy bus traffic loading and unloading at the terminal for every major event.

The solution was obvious: Depress Montana Street below ground level to separate bus and pedestrian traffic. This also had the virtue of allowing a grand entrance plaza to be developed at the north entrance of the Dome. The plaza would improve the connection with St. Paul Square.

The extra cost of lowering the street in front of the Dome wasn't in the project budget. The concept of lowering Montana Street and building an underground bus terminal beneath a formal entrance plaza was so attractive, however, that planning soon got out in front of financing.

Initially, in March 1990, the Dome Advisory Committee voted not to depress Montana Street unless VIA could find an extra $5 million needed to fund the $7.9 million plan. VIA Chairman Dietzmann quickly promised that VIA would try.

Mayor Cockrell made repeated but unsuccessful attempts to convince the state highway department to provide the funds through its Dome-related freeway ramp construction. The state wouldn't budge.

At the end of April, a revised projection of the sales-tax revenue indicated that an extra $2.6 million would be available for the project. This reduced the gap to $2.8 million. We pointed out that VIA would gain substantial revenues from the planned commercial uses at the Sunset Depot and thus should pay for the depression of Montana.

But Dietzmann said at a news conference the next day that a majority of his board would tell the city to pay for the Montana Street project itself. Board members were appointed by a variety of public agencies, ranging from San Antonio City Council to Bexar County Commissioners Court and the suburban governments. VIA made the situation worse by unveiling a plan to spend $3.4 million to renovate the old depot as a terminal for downtown buses and trolleys and a future light rail system.

The skirmishing dragged on throughout the summer and into the fall. Then things got really crazy. Without warning, at a VIA board meeting on November 27, 1990, a majority of the VIA trustees ousted Dietzmann as chairman and replaced him with former Mayor John Gatti, effective January 1.

Dietzmann had offended the board by repeatedly speaking out on issues before the board approved his position. The choice of Gatti to replace him, however, would only be the source of more problems. It would be kind to describe Gatti's manner of dealing with City Council as "high-handed." I believe he thought he was mayor again.

But if the VIA board really intended to declare war on the city, it suffered a self-inflicted fatal wound in its opening barrage. What made this bizarre was that it arose from a problem that had nothing to do with the Dome project. An opinion by the state attorney general's office had held that the four-year terms served by VIA's trustees were unconstitutional. Trustees of appointed bodies were limited to terms of two years.

In an attempt to comply with the law, the VIA trustees adopted a resolution asking the appointing agencies to reappoint all members to new two-year terms; all except Dietzmann.

The trustees should have realized that City Council members would leap at this unexpected opportunity to "clean house" at VIA. Council called for a briefing by the city manager on December 6.

On December 12, County Commissioners Court struck the first blow by summarily replacing one of its three appointees.

The next day, by a 6-to-5 vote, the City Council rejected Mayor Cockrell's plea for delay, and named four new members among the city's five appointees. The lone survivor was one who had spoken out in favor of the city's position. I voted with the majority because I felt this public squabbling had to end.

Council also instructed city negotiators to insist that VIA put $5.4 million of its own funds into the budget with no expectation of payback. This included the costs of acquiring the Sunset Depot and rehabilitating it.

On January 2, the Bexar County Council of Mayors also replaced both of its appointees. A total of seven of the 11 board members at VIA had been replaced within a period of three weeks. None remained among those who had voted in November to make Gatti chairman.

The "revolutionary" majority on VIA's board got to work quickly. They unanimously elected Arturo Sanchez, a reappointed county trustee who had supported the city's position, as the new chairman.

On February 11, the board finally voted to absorb the $4.5 million cost of the renovation of the Sunset Depot from the agency's capital reserves.

Finally, as this book goes to press and four years after the Dome opened, plans are under way for a "destination restaurant" in the old terminal and a 400-room hotel on a site immediately next door, on land acquired by VIA.

Another Run at Pro Football

As the new mayor in the fall of 1991, I took up the mantle of Henry Cisneros in trying to attract a National Football League team to play in the Alamodome. The NFL was in the process of listening to proposals for two expansion franchises. Larry Benson, whose brother Tom owned the New Orleans Saints, agreed to pony up the $100,000 entry fee required as a proposed owner of a new NFL franchise, and the city put together the details of its proposal for the team to play in the Dome.

Two weeks before our trip to New York to make our presentations to the league, Larry Benson threatened to withdraw his $100,000 entry fee unless the city guaranteed a level of attendance at the games. I refused, and asked B.J. "Red" McCombs, the owner of the San Antonio Spurs pro basketball team, to take Larry's place. Red agreed.

We made an excellent presentation to the NFL. Red told the league that if he got the franchise he would sell the Spurs. But one key element was missing in our package. Many cities were willing to guarantee the NFL as much as $10 million a year for 10 years if they received franchises. I refused to support using public funds for such a purpose. I felt offering the Alamodome for reasonable terms was about as far as the city should go.

On March 17, 1992, the league announced that San Antonio did not make the final cut of cities. Although league officials didn't say so directly, it was clear we didn't put enough bucks on the table. I also believe that the owners of the Dallas Cowboys and Houston Oilers did not want to see a franchise here, since a substantial portion of their fan support comes from San Antonio and South Texas.

This experience taught me that unless a city is willing to open its purse for the NFL to take all it wants, the city's chance of getting a franchise is nil. Other cities are very willing. And so long as they are, San Antonio won't get a team.

The NFL's action also convinced me that at best San Antonio can support only one major-league sports team. The city simply lacks enough large corporations to support two professional teams financially. Nor is the city willing to give taxpayers' money to wealthy owners.

The Spurs Lease

Sometimes *having* a professional sports team can be as much of a headache as *not* having one. Long before the National Football League gave us a thumbs down, the San Antonio Spurs were giving me a migraine as I positioned myself to run against Lila Cockrell for mayor.

The story begins on an upbeat note, with what might be described as a slam-dunk for the Dome. In June 1990, Red McCombs announced that he intended to move the Spurs out of the Convention Center Arena and into the Dome at the beginning of the 1993-94 season. The news electrified the city.

Previously, all projections of Dome "event days" had assumed that the Spurs would use the Dome only for a few sold-out play-off games. But as the anchor tenant, the Spurs would bring 45 home games to the Dome's calendar. The team would also create an instant market for high-dollar club suites. This would increase the Dome's expected profit over 10 years from $3 million to $10 million.

Red had discussed the move with Henry and Mayor Cockrell, both of whom approved. There was no danger of a conflict with some future pro football team, because the seasons of the two sports differed.

The arena, which had been home to the Spurs since they moved to San Antonio from Dallas in 1973, was outdated and inadequate. A renovation would cost upwards of $40 million, and even then it couldn't be redesigned to accommodate "skyboxes." These luxury suites have become an economic necessity to any major professional sports franchise.

I was impressed by the economic arguments in favor of the Spurs' move. Convention uses of the Dome would have to be subsidized by the hotel-motel tax. The city needed an anchor, a consistent revenue-producing user, to make the Dome profitable within three years, as voters had been promised during the campaign to pass the Dome tax.

It seemed we had to play ball with Red. But McCombs overplayed his hand. Beyond simply leasing the Dome as the Spurs' home court, he also proposed to manage the Dome and the arena together. His initial bargaining position was simply to continue the extremely favorable lease rates the Spurs enjoyed at the anti-quated arena when the team moved to the state-of-the-art Dome. Council didn't bite. We also wanted to consider the issues of managing and marketing the Dome more deliberately.

By early July, the Dome Advisory Committee voted unanimously for city staff to manage the Dome in conjunction with all of the city's other convention facilities. Council approved this recommendation, as well as marketing contracts with the San Antonio Sports Foundation and Spectacor.

Meanwhile, throughout the summer of 1990, the staff had been meeting with the Spurs to negotiate a Dome lease. In September, council returned to the issue. The Spurs were proposing a 10-year contract to lease the Dome and develop the concessions. The concession areas needed finishing out, with an estimated price tag of $5 million. The assumption was that a concessionaire would pay for these improvements and then recover the costs through a long-term contract.

There was concern, however, about giving this contract to the Spurs without an iron-clad guarantee that the team would remain in San Antonio. In those days, rumors that the team was for sale and might leave San Antonio at any moment were routine, hardly even newsworthy anymore. Without that guarantee, the city was at risk, since it would be tough to attract another professional team as a tenant without the lucrative concessions contract to offer as part of the deal. Worse, San Antonio fans might actually wind up subsidizing a team in another city.

Under the agreement staff had negotiated, the city would receive $5 million annually from the Spurs. It tripled our income and would make the Dome profitable by the second year of operation. The agreement included a penalty clause if the Spurs moved out of the Dome. I said I would support Alex Briseño's recommendation.

But when the issue came before council on September 14, Mayor Cockrell said she opposed the lease. She felt the Spurs should lose the concession lease if the team left the Dome before the expiration of its 10-year term. She felt that the financial penalty in the proposed lease was not strong enough.

McCombs argued that the lease and the concessions contract could not be linked. He said his lenders for the cost of finishing out the concessions insisted on an unqualified pledge of the concessions contract for security.

In fact, Lila had been influenced by a strong lobbying effort led by a few key business leaders including General McDermott. They did not support the Spurs' moving to the Dome because they felt basketball would conflict with possible convention business. They also thought the lease was too favorable to the Spurs.

The council voted 7 to 4 to reject the lease and to insert a "poison pill" in the new lease proposal that would return control of the concessions to the city if the Spurs ever left San Antonio.

I voted with the minority because I had already committed publicly to supporting the manager's recommendation.

As it turned out, after a month of huffing and puffing, we approved a lease not fundamentally different from the one we had rejected in September. The city manager and the Spurs had simply reworded it. Under the new lease, the city had the option to buy the Spurs out of the concession lease for the amount of the capital investment the team was putting up. Staff figures showed the Spurs could not recoup their investment until near the expiration of the 10-year lease, which essentially gave them the same deal called for in the first agreement. The financial penalty for moving the Spurs was dropped.

Lila played her cards very well in this incident. She made me look as though I was too eager to please the Spurs at the possible expense of city taxpayers.

"Show Me the Money"

Shortly before the NFL's announcement in March that San Antonio would not get a pro football franchise, Red told me that he needed either to sell the Spurs or find additional investors.

The cost of one individual's owning a major sports franchise was becoming prohibitive, and Red said he wanted to diversify his investment profile. He invited me to a meeting with the investment firm he had retained to market the Spurs. Their analysts said the team could be worth up to $125 million, depending on where it was to be located. Cities such as Toronto and Anaheim wanted a basketball team and might be willing to buy a franchise.

But Red also told me he really wanted to sell the Spurs to someone who would not move them. He asked me to see if there was any local interest in purchasing the team.

Initially, I was not sure how serious Red was about selling. I was worried, but I thought Red might just be fishing to see if he could get some additional investors. I started making calls to the few businessmen in San Antonio who were capable of buying or investing in the Spurs. The first person I alerted was General McDermott. McD was against the Spurs playing in the Dome. At the time he felt that Red was not serious about selling.

Three months later, on June 16, Red stated publicly that he was interested in selling a two-thirds or three-quarters interest in the Spurs. Soon after, I got a call from John Drossos, son of Angelo Drossos, the man who brought professional basketball to San Antonio when he bought Dallas' team in the old American Basketball Association and moved it here. Red had bought Angelo Drossos' 37 percent interest in the Spurs in 1988. Until then, Red had owned 35 percent of the team.

John, then a stockbroker in Dallas, told me he was interested in putting together an ownership group centered on a Dallas businessman named Bill Esping.

At my invitation, we all met in San Antonio, and I learned that Bill Esping had made a loan to the Spurs that would come due in June 1993. At that point, if the loan was not paid off he would receive an equity interest in the Spurs in addition to the collateral for his loan. He told me if the right partnership could be developed, he would be interested in buying the Spurs and keeping them in San Antonio.

I knew then we had one year to find a buyer for the Spurs. Red would either have to pay off Bill Esping's loan or lose additional equity in the team. Now I thought I understood part of the reason that Red wanted to sell or find additional investors.

During the next several months I visited with potential investors. John Drossos slipped in and out of town, meeting with me and potential investors such as Arturo Torres, who had sold his franchise chain of more than 200 Pizza Huts to Pepsi. I talked with other businessmen, including Charles Butt, CEO of the H-E-B supermarkets, Bartell Zachry of H.B. Zachry construction company, and Jim Leininger, CEO of Kinetic Concepts.

While I did discover some interest, no one really wanted to step out in front and lead a local investment group. John Drossos and Bill Esping never did make their position clear as to what they would be willing to invest and what sort of commitment they would make to San Antonio.

What we really needed was a group of local businessmen with controlling interest. The problem was we had only one strong horse in San Antonio and we needed at least two. The one strong horse we had was General McDermott.

The white knight we needed rode into town in September 1992. That was when Edward Whitacre Jr., chairman of Southwestern Bell Corporation, announced the move of the company's corporate headquarters to San Antonio. I did not say anything to Whitacre about the Spurs on the first day he arrived, but I didn't wait long to tell him of our problem. He said that Southwestern Bell had invested in the St. Louis Blues hockey team. He said he might be interested if a group were put together.

On an evening in January 1993, General McDermott turned on the 10 p.m. news to hear Leslie Alexander, a businessman from Florida, say he was in town to talk with Red McCombs about purchasing the Spurs. McD called him at the Hilton Hotel and asked whether he was interested in a local investor. Alexander said yes and McD invited him to dinner at the San Antonio Country Club on January 20, 1993.

At that dinner Alexander told McD that he wanted to buy the Spurs but that he would not commit to keeping the Spurs in San Antonio. McD left the meeting knowing the Spurs would probably move if Alexander bought the team.

So McD called Red the next day and asked for 30 days to put together a local ownership group. For more than a year, Red had waited patiently for a local group to step up to the free-throw line. He was doing everything in his power to keep the team in San Antonio. He gave McD a good price, $85 million. He said he could get $100 million or more if he dealt to a group interested in moving the team to a more lucrative market such as Toronto. He gave McDermott 30 days.

McD called me soon after his conversation with Red. He said he was going to convene a group to try to put together an offer to Red. He invited me to a meeting on January 29, 1993, in his office with Jim Dublin of the Dublin-McCarter public relations firm; Bartel Zachry; Jim Leininger; Ed Whitacre and Larry Alexander, the vice president for community relations at Southwestern Bell; Bill Greehey, the CEO of Valero Energy; investment banker Jimmy Rains; H.T. Johnson, a vice president at USAA; and Tim Fretthold, vice president at Diamond Shamrock.

McD and Ed Whitacre sat at the head of the table. McD asked me to say a few words. I told the group that the city was only four months away from opening the Dome and that it would be a major setback for the city and the Dome to lose the Spurs. I said the Spurs had been successful because of local ownership and only local ownership would guarantee keeping the Spurs in San Antonio. I said we would work with them to make the Spurs a success in the Dome.

Then McD took charge. He told the story of Leslie Alexander's desire to buy the team and possibly move it. He said Red had given him 30 days to organize a local group. He concluded that USAA would be willing to invest $10 million in cash and guarantee a loan to purchase the team.

Ed Whitacre then related how Southwestern Bell had put together a local ownership group to buy the St. Louis Blues. He said Southwestern Bell would match USAA's participation, but only if other local businesses would be part of the ownership group. This was the turning point. The deal simply could not have been put together without Ed Whitacre's support. With the second strong horse in harness, everyone else at the table also agreed to invest.

In an interesting side note to the meeting, the financial data on the Spurs showed that the team would gross more money on concessions in the Dome but make less profit than at the arena. McD asked how that could be? It was explained that the city would get 40 percent off the gross of the concessions, not 40 percent of the bottom-line profits.

I didn't say anything, but I felt vindicated that we had made a good deal for the city when we negotiated the contract to have the Spurs play in the Dome. Perhaps McD and the other businessmen discovered that day that the city was not as naive about contract negotiations as they had thought. As this book is written, the Spurs ownership is still trying to renegotiate that concessions contract.

After the meeting, McD continued to work on putting together other investors, including Bob Coleman, president of Texace Corporation, who was asked to serve as president of the Spurs.

On February 19, 1993, at a news conference I attended with Red and Bob Coleman, the sale was announced. Twenty-two local investors were named in the ownership group. This was a happy ending to the year-long struggle to keep the Spurs in San Antonio.

But as with most stories, there are always additional chapters. Bob Coleman was eventually replaced as president with General McDermott when McD retired from USAA. McD tried to run the Spurs as he did USAA, where he had total control. Too often he spoke out on issues without board approval. For example, in early 1996, he said that building the Dome was a mistake, that the Spurs should not play there, and that a new arena would have to be built to accommodate the team.

On June 19, 1996, McD came to my home to tell me that the Spurs were planning to remove him as chairman the following Tueday. I told McD to let go and enjoy life. Resign tomorrow morning rather than face an embarrassing vote.

Instead, McD fought the ouster, and gained enough support to stop the attempt to remove him. McD then came up with a proposal to sell the Spurs to yet another out-of-town family of investors. They said they would move here and keep the Spurs in San Antonio. But the board turned down the sale, and McD resigned as president after losing this vote.

Local businessman Peter Holt, president of Holt Machinery, bought a 30 percent ownership interest in the Spurs and vowed to keep them in San Antonio. Holt was soon installed in McD's place as chairman of the board.

This was a sad footnote to McD's three decades of exemplary service to San Antonio. No civic leader in the history of our city has had a greater impact. McDermott came to San Antonio in 1968 and took a small insurance company — USAA, sitting on the corner of Broadway and Hildebrand, serving the needs of military officers and their families — and turned it into one of the world's 10 largest insurance and financial services firms, employing more than 10,000 people in San Antonio alone. He also founded the Economic Development Foundation and was among the developers of the Texas Research Park. His company built Fiesta Texas and numerous other projects around our city.

McD was a close ally to both Henry and Lila. Many feared that General McDermott and his key associates were somewhat of a shadow government in San Antonio. When I became mayor in 1991, McD was nearing the end of his power. Before his retirement, his last major act was saving the Spurs in 1993. There will never be another McD.

And they will never make another Red McCombs. He shouldered the financial risk of owning the Spurs and held on until a local group could be put together to keep the team in San Antonio. Red could have made a lot more money selling the Spurs to an out-of-town group, but he sold for less instead and kept the Spurs in the city he loves.

Open for Business

By the spring of 1993, it was time to begin planning for the Dome's grand opening. I appointed Councilwoman Yolanda Vera to head the planning committee because of the excellent job she had done on the San Antonio Summit.

Initially, plans called for an opening celebration in conjunction with the Dome's first major event, the 1993 Olympic Festival. But the festival required a paid admission, so the city threw a free "open house" celebration on May 15, 1993.

Appropriately, it was proclaimed "Henry Cisneros Day." And there was the man himself, the creator of the Dome, responding to a hero's welcome at center stage with his familiar smile, coming home briefly from Washington, D.C., and his latest public service as President Clinton's secretary of housing and urban

Housing Secretary Henry Cisneros, the father of the Alamodome, chats with Mayor Nelson Wolff before the facility's opening celebration on May 15, 1993. (Express-News)

development. The demand for tickets was so great we had to extend the opening another day.

The Olympic Festival, the first major event in the Dome, was held two months later. This was also uniquely appropriate. This was the same festival we had sought unsuccessfully in our trip to Colorado Springs while the Dome bill was being considered in the 1987 session of the Legislature. It was Henry's "magic" that built the Dome and made it possible for San Antonio to host such a major event.

The Second Sacking of the VIA Board

Despite the good feelings surrounding the opening of the Dome, tensions soon rose again between the city and VIA. The trauma of replacing the VIA board in 1990 turned out to be just a dress rehearsal for another, equally traumatic housecleaning that now began to take shape.

Arturo Sanchez was a political insider and county appointee to the VIA board who was reappointed and then elected chairman after the first board purge. His hubris ultimately brought

VIA to its knees in 1995. Sanchez suffered a mortal, self-inflicted professional wound along the way.

Sanchez had worked for years as a campaign consultant for various candidates. At one time, he was acknowledged as a master at reading the tea leaves of the West Side Hispanic vote.

Once selected as VIA's chairman, he took over an office at VIA headquarters and set himself up as both a power broker and agency micro-manager. He had staff report to him outside the chain of command headed by John Milam, the agency's general manager.

Under his leadership, VIA threatened to discontinue bus service to the Dome unless the city provided a subsidy, refused to accept responsibility for the soil contamination problem, and arbitrarily dropped VIA out of the partnership for downtown development. Sanchez indulged in actions that led to the filing of a sexual harassment complaint and lawsuit.

On one of his conciliatory days, I was able to negotiate a deal that finally ended the impossibly awkward relationship between the city and VIA over ownership and management of the Dome. We agreed to divide the property along Montana Street, which formed the boundary between the Dome to the south and the transit terminal and Sunset Depot to the north. VIA sold the Dome and everything south of Montana to the city for $1. An entire file drawer's worth of paper that governed the landlord/tenant relationship between us became scrap. Thereafter, the city would have a free hand in running the Dome as it saw fit, and VIA could once again focus entirely on mass transit.

Meanwhile, Sanchez's actions continued to cause controversy. VIA's financial position deteriorated so radically that by 1995 it was hemorrhaging deficits of $1 million per month, and its once impressive cash reserves were rapidly vanishing.

The controversy at VIA was well known to political insiders long before it hit the front page of the Express-News, when his hand-picked director of public affairs, Diane Gonzalez, filed suit alleging sexual harassment. Another VIA employee, public relations spokeswoman Suzanne Detwiler, quietly settled a claim for $70,000.

Still, the majority of the VIA board continued to support Sanchez. He hung on to power by developing close relationships with most of his board members. He also personally managed the campaigns of key council members and legislators.

Eventually, I called for Sanchez's resignation and the resignations of every board member who supported him. I was pressured by his political friends to back off.

Finally a "smoking gun" surfaced: a tape recording in which Sanchez and another VIA trustee made crude racial remarks. Sanchez resigned. But it literally took an act of the Legislature to complete the job of cleaning house when some of the VIA trustees refused to comply with a council resolution officially demanding their resignations. Eventually Sanchez was convicted of "official oppression" for his conduct with Diana Gonzalez and fined $3,000.

In the year-and-a-half since then, VIA has regained stability under the chairmanships of T.J. Connolly and the Reverend Richard Tankerson. The new board cut the budget, obtained an overdue fare increase, and restored the general manager to a position of responsibility for staff operations. Staff morale has improved immensely. The damage to the agency, which could ultimately be traced back to the dispute over the Dome transit terminal, is finally being repaired.

For the record, the Dome has proven successful in spite of its critics. It has provided a venue for a host of events that could not otherwise have been staged in San Antonio, such as the NBA All-Star game in 1996 and the NCAA "Final Four" scheduled for 1998. And it has operated at a direct profit to the city treasury since its second year.

"Take Me Out to the Ball Game"

Since the summer of 1953, when I was 12, the chattering of professional baseball players has given me a lifetime of joy and learning. My brother George and I were bat boys for the Texas Consolidated Transporters. They were a semi-pro team that played first at Van Dale Stadium on the corner of Brazos and Laredo streets on the West Side, and then at Richter Field on Mission Road, across from Mission Stadium on the South Side.

The team included former major-league and minor-league players who still loved the game. Guys like Blas Monaco of the Cleveland Indians and Jack Crouch of the St. Louis Browns spun yarns about the "big show" while they chewed and spit their tobacco, cursed and drank beer in San Antonio.

They kidded my brother and me, let us shag baseballs and taught us the fundamentals of the game. The admonishments were many and the compliments few — all simple and direct: "Stay loose. Keep your eye on the ball. Hustle! How about a little chatter?" We learned about individual competitiveness, camaraderie, and love of the game. The toughness I learned has lasted a lifetime.

After the game, all us kids would dash onto the field to play a pick-up game until it got dark. Our parents joined the players on the patio to dance, drink a little beer and keep an eye on us.

Across from Richter Field, we could see the best minor-league ballpark in the country, Mission Stadium. It was built in 1947 by the St. Louis Browns at the height of minor-league attendance. Two mission towers, resembling the historical design of Mission Concepcion a block away, framed the entrance to the park. Fans flocked as they did to minor-league fields across the nation. In those days, more than 40 million fans a year attended minor-league games.

I was a member of the knothole gang. My dad and mother took us to Missions games almost every night. The stands and the sidelines were our playground. It was a simple time of Crackerjacks, soda pop, and hot dogs.

My dad was a truck driver but could still take our whole family because the cost was within what was jokingly called "the South Side price limit." The value of family togetherness reinforced at the baseball games stuck with me.

I went on to play baseball in high school, my freshman year at college, and then in the Spanish American League. As a pitcher for the Prospect Hill Yellow Jackets, coached by Fernando Arrellano, I had pitched at Mission Stadium in 1961. After a 30-year layoff, I began playing again in 1994 and am still playing today, at the age of 56, in the National Adult Baseball Association.

By the late 1960s, minor-league attendance had declined from 40 million to 10 million. Televised major-league baseball and other more exciting entertainment events drew people away.

The Missions left San Antonio in 1965. Mission Stadium was eventually torn down, as were Richter Field and Van Dale Stadium. The tradition of Texas League and San Antonio Missions baseball that began in San Antonio in 1888 came to an end.

As time swept away minor-league baseball and landmark Mission Stadium, it also swept away the values of that era. As a sad and ironic testament, the site of Mission Stadium is now the location of the Bexar County Juvenile Detention Center.

In 1968, three years after the Missions left, I helped organize a group of supporters to bring minor-league baseball back to San Antonio. We literally built the V.J. Keefe Field at St. Mary's University. Our family business at the time, Alamo Enterprises, provided the lumber for the stands. St. Mary's coach Elmer Kosub, Bill Sibera, Henry Christopher, Manuel Calderon, I and several other volunteers worked on the stadium every day.

After building the stadium, we ran the franchise as volunteers for three years until private ownership took over. Farm teams from Chicago, Cleveland, Milwaukee, Dallas and Los Angeles played at St. Mary's over the next 25 years. Many of the major-league teams played exhibition games in the early spring. Throughout most of the years, small crowds attended the games.

By the late 1980s, people across the country were coming back to minor-league baseball parks. They were looking for something they had lost: a way to slow down the pace of life, an affordable sport to share with their families, forgotten values and memories of their youth.

Communities began to respond by building family-friendly minor-league parks. Families flocked to the ballparks on hot summer nights to take part in a revival of family, friends, and values.

Ironically, just as minor-league baseball was making a comeback, San Antonio was about to lose it again. By the late 1980s, the stadium at St. Mary's could no longer hold the crowds. More than 180,000 people attended games in 1988. Many fans were turned away because there were not enough seats.

According to Major League Baseball guidelines, the park did not meet 23 standards set for minor-league parks. The clubhouse, restrooms, seats, concession stands and dugouts were all deemed inadequate. What wasn't?

In 1988, David Elmore bought the San Antonio Missions franchise. He said he wanted to work with the city to build a new stadium. He said he would have no choice but to move the franchise unless a stadium meeting the league's minimum standards could be built or renovated.

After Lila Cockrell was elected mayor in May 1989, she and I met with Elmore and Missions General Manager Burl Yarbrough. Lila ruled out the use of city funds, and rightly so because the city was in difficult financial shape at the time. However, she said she would work to try to find private financing.

In July 1989, City Council confirmed the decision to rule out baseball in the Dome. I supported this decision because I knew San Antonio did not have a chance to attract Major League Baseball. The major leagues play 81 home games a season and need an average attendance of 30,000 per game, while pro football plays only 10 home games and needs an average attendance of 60,000. Our city does not have the demographics to support Major League Baseball. Even if we did, Major League Baseball does not want to play in a dome. And baseball's season schedule would preclude the use of the Dome for too many convention events.

After that decision was made, I suggested we use part of the savings in Dome funds to build a new minor-league ballpark. It would cost only about $7 million.

Lila opposed using any Dome funds until the project was completed. She thought it was too risky. City staff concurred. We all worked at other failed attempts to build a ballpark.

Then, in December 1989, the Missions commissioned a feasibility study to investigate sites and potential funding sources for a ballpark.

In March 1990, the consultants evaluated potential sites at Sea World, UTSA and Harlandale Stadium, and recommended a site on the grounds of the county-owned Coliseum, home of the annual Stock Show and Rodeo. Estimated cost was $6 million.

I was excited — until we met with Mary Nan West, a wealthy independent rancher whose leadership had made the rodeo such a great success. She didn't think it was such a good idea to put baseball players in the same corral as cowboys, horses, and cows. Her posse of rodeo supporters ran the ballplayers out of town.

After I was elected mayor, I was determined to find a solution. I included the building of a new minor-league ballpark in my agenda. In June, I met with Councilmen Walter Martinez and Frank Wing, and David Elmore and Burl Yarbrough. The two council members and I committed to Burl and David that we would find a way to build a park. But we still had no idea how we would do it or where we would put it.

Then, while surveying some potential city park sites, we looked across a freeway to land that was owned by Levi Strauss. It was located on the corner of U.S. 90 West and Callaghan Road. We decided to contact Levi officials.

They agreed to talk to us provided we keep the talks strictly confidential. They said if the talks became public, they would break them off. They had a reason for demanding privacy.

Two years earlier, Levi Strauss had closed one of its three plants in San Antonio. After the closing, they donated $500,000 in community grants and spent more than $1 million training the laid-off workers. But the workers organized a group called "La Fuerza Unida" (The United Force) and used any occasion to take shots at the company.

Although I was not happy about the closing of the plant there were still 1,500 workers at two other Levi plants in San Antonio. I publicly supported the company through these difficult times. Despite my support, I got the runaround as we sought an answer on the land.

While talks continued with Levi, I explored other options. After Anheuser Busch bought Sea World, I thought August Busch would be interested in having a baseball park adjacent to the theme park. I also thought he cared about baseball because he owned the St. Louis Cardinals.

But one night at a fund-raising dinner for the Guadalupe Cultural Arts Center, I sat at the same table with August Busch. He was pompous and caught up in his own importance. I could not get him to talk about anything, let alone baseball. He sat with a scowl on his face even though everyone was drinking Budweiser to make him happy. I felt like pouring a Bud on his head and drinking my friend Dennis O'Malley's Miller beer.

Throughout the winter and spring of 1992, we continued to focus on the Levi Strauss site. We went to Dallas to assure secrecy as we met with the company's real estate people.

We were able to get a number they felt represented the land's market value: $1.3 million. We kept pressing them to sell to us below market or even to give the land to us.

But they remembered the controversy over building the Dome in San Antonio. They thought building a baseball stadium would lead to another flap. They were concerned about the reaction of the Levi workers.

By early summer 1992, interest rates had dropped to a point at which the city could refinance $300 million in general obligation bonds and give us some money to play with — best of all, without a tax increase. City Manager Alex Briseño had a few projects in mind; the baseball stadium occupied mine.

We had to move quickly before the rates changed. We presented a $20 million package of capital needs to City Council, including $6.5 million for the baseball stadium.

On the day before the council vote on the bond package, the San Antonio Light ran the results of a poll on whether the city of San Antonio should help finance a new stadium for the San Antonio Missions. The results were 804 for and 348 against. The poll results were not an accident.

Councilwoman Helen Ayala had been meeting with union members at Levi Strauss. She organized an effort among the employees to pressure Levi management to make the land deal with us. I called her and said, "Helen, ask the Levi employees to get on the phone and call The Light to support the park." They did.

While I worked the council for support, I also had to put some direct pressure on Levi Strauss.

I called Vice President Bob Dunn in San Francisco on the Wednesday before the council vote. I said, "Bob, I am tired of the runaround I have been given on your site. All I keep hearing is that you are concerned about the public relations aspect of the transaction. I am going to give you something to be a lot more concerned about. I have stood up for your company through the difficult times after the closing of your plant. If I do not get a favorable answer on the land, I am going to join your critics. If you think you have a problem now, you will really have one when I am finished."

"I will get you an answer," he said.

"I need it by tomorrow. The council will vote on the funding for the stadium and I need a site to get approval of the funding."

Later that day, I received a fax from Levi's real estate director offering to sell the 40-acre site for $650,000 (about half its market value), provided we built a baseball stadium there. If we did not build the stadium, the land would revert to Levi Strauss.

The next day, I briefed the council in executive session on the offer. A majority liked the site. In open session, council approved the $20 million bond package that included $6.5 million for the stadium. After the vote Councilman Roger Perez said, "Play ball!"

In less than two weeks, we had in place the financing for the stadium and a site. The political process can be exceedingly slow or exceedingly fast. Politics is a game of opportunity. You must strike quickly to take advantage. We did that with the baseball park.

I was one happy guy. I promised that we would build a family-friendly stadium that would be affordable for all the people of San Antonio. I wanted picnic areas, grass berms, a knothole-gang area and a design that reflected the original mission towers of the old Mission Stadium. I wanted something special.

Councilman Juan Solis and Councilwoman Helen Ayala made sure it was. Council approved Ford, Powell and Carson Inc. as the architects with the national architectural firm of Hellmuth, Obata and Kassabaum Inc. as consultants. Architect Ralph Bender designed the landscaping. Boone Powell became lead architect on the stadium.

Grass, plants and trees were planted around the periphery of the stadium, which faced southeast so the prevailing winds during the summer would cool the spectators. The sun set behind the stadium instead of in the faces of the fans. This made it a pitcher's park. I have always liked pitcher's parks.

By early 1994, everything was going smoothly. Construction of the 6,500-seat stadium was on time and under budget. We knew we would be ready for the 1994 season.

On April 18, 1994, we held the grand opening ceremonies. That night, 9,336 fans attended the game between San Antonio and El Paso. This was the largest attendance in Texas League history. In the first season, 411,959 fans attended games, breaking the Texas League season attendance record. They came whether the Missions won or lost to watch young men fighting to become part of the Big Show and making average salaries of about $20,000.

The following year, my last in office, I tried unsuccessfully to get a major-league exhibition game. The baseball strike killed my only chance. The greed of major league sports is unbelievable. All they seem to care about is making as much money as they can, players and owners alike.

The week before I left office, the City Council named the baseball park after me.

★★★

Lessons on the Dome, the Spurs and Baseball

■ **Bitter beginnings ensure continuing controversy.**
The long and bitter fight to get the Dome sales tax approved and the project built virtually guaranteed controversy. The media and the public scrutinized every aspect of the project. The Spurs lease, the Dome dirt fights, the VIA-city conflict, the design, the awarding of contracts, all provided grist for stories.

■ **Two agencies is one too many on a major project.**
Somehow, we endured the shotgun marriage of VIA and the city until the baby was successfully born. The relationship finally ended in a divorce when I gave $1 to VIA for alimony and finally got control of the Dome solely in the city's hands.

■ **Dishwashers shouldn't try to be chefs.**
VIA had no business building a domed stadium. It should have relinquished its tax revenue for five years to the city with no strings attached. Instead it got involved in building the Dome, which led to the VIA board's being disgraced and replaced.

■ **When you clean house, the dust sometimes falls back on the floor.**
When the city, the county, and the Council of Mayors replaced the VIA board of trustees in 1990, they created a new board that again brought discredit to VIA and had to be replaced in its turn in 1995.

■ **Approving a budget before designing a project is a gamble.**
The construction of a domed stadium was approved by the voters with a budget before it was designed. Unexpected increase in sales tax revenue covered unexpected cost. We were lucky.

■ **Deadlines and financial pressures cause mistakes.**
The Dome dirt controversy arose because of a rush to build using a limited budget. Shortcuts were taken.

■ **"Show me the money!"**
Pro sports never gets enough money. Between the high cost of players and the greed of the owners, a major-league football franchise is astronomically expensive. Cities must decide whether they can afford to play, and whether it's worth it.

■ **"Fields of dreams" still exist.**
Minor-league baseball brought "old-time" values that appealed to citizens of San Antonio. They in turn supported the building of a baseball park to capture those values for a lot less money than the cost of the Alamodome.

21

Water Wars — II

Dick Howe is tall and lanky, with boundless energy and a hint of irony in his constant smile.

As a young man, Dick served two of the most invaluable apprenticeships possible for a fellow growing up in America in the middle of the 20th century. He played basketball at the University of Kentucky in the late 1950s, and he cut his teeth on urban politics with the quintessential big-city ward boss, Mayor Richard Daley of Chicago. Howe spins fantastic stories of Daley, the man who allowed his police to "riot" and beat anti-war demonstrators on television during the 1968 National Democratic Party Convention. Two years after that memorable event, from 1970 to 1972, Dick Howe worked in the Daley administration as director of research and planning for the Department of Environmental Control, and later as deputy commissioner.

Dick came to San Antonio in 1976 as director of the Division of Environmental Studies at the University of Texas at San Antonio. He went on to propose an engineering school for the university, and with the help of Henry Cisneros and Lila Cockrell made it a reality. He became a professor at the school he helped create, and continues to teach there at the time of this writing. He was a key adviser during the administrations of both Cisneros and me.

After Lila Cockrell was elected for another term as mayor in 1989, Dick spoke with me about the need to consolidate the city's three water agencies. With Lila's support, we formed the Water Consolidation Study Panel in April 1990, and Dick was named chairman.

The first of the three water agencies was the City Water Board, the municipal water supply utility, run by a board of trustees with the mayor as a voting *ex officio* member and four other members appointed by the City Council.

Second was the San Antonio Wastewater Department, which ran our sewer system and sewage treatment plants. It operated as a regular city department.

The third was a relatively recent creation — the Alamo Water Reuse and Conservation District — set up to implement the "gray-water" reuse component of the 1988 Regional Water Plan. It was a semi-autonomous agency similar to the City Water Board.

In the summer of 1990, the panel under Dick recommended that the city consolidate all water-related activities into a single agency under a new board appointed by City Council. The plan had my support. But a majority of council opposed consolidation. Consequently, nothing was accomplished.

The next opportunity came a year later, when I took office as mayor. On the same ballot, a proposal to abandon the Applewhite project passed with 53 percent of the vote. The City Water Board promptly filed suit to overturn the result. The board had already spent $40 million on the project, and trustees felt they had a fiduciary responsibility to bondholders.

But the public was outraged at the picture of the city being named a defendant in a lawsuit by one of its own agencies seeking to overturn a popular vote.

Then Bill Thornton, who succeeded me as councilman from District 8, became the champion of consolidation. In that bulldog style that would soon become his trademark, Thornton stirred debate and caused tempers to flare, even attacking Councilman Labatt, our water point man. It was Thornton's first major issue, and he cooked it till it sizzled.

Council remained split. The leader of the opposition was Frank Wing, who said he feared that too much power would be vested in one agency.

After a council meeting in December, I told him, "Frank, we have to find common ground. I understand your concern about too much power being invested in an appointed board." I said I thought we could create a quasi-independent board which would consolidate all three agencies if it had a system of checks and balances through City Council. I suggested that council have power to review the water system's budget.

"Frank, this is a big one for me. There is no way that we can be successful in the next Legislature ... with the fighting between the city and its own agency. I cannot win this one without your support. I need you."

"Is this really that important to you?" Frank asked.

"There is nothing more important."

Frank smiled and said, "Put in the checks and balances and we've got a deal. Let's get it done, brother."

With Frank on board I knew that I would now win the vote. On December 19, 1991, council voted to begin the merger of the three water entities based on the plan I had outlined to Frank Wing. The new entity would be known as the San Antonio Water System (SAWS) and would have a combined workforce of 1,500 employees. It would serve 1.2 million customers with a $100 million operating budget and annual revenues of $150 million.

The vote was a major victory. The merger would result in significant savings and efficiency. It would lead to a successful effort to pass the Edwards Aquifer legislation, and would develop a strong conservation and reuse plan.

Next, we needed a leader to head the board. Cliff Morton was the Greater Chamber's point man on water. Cliff and I had not been friends before my election. He had supported my opponents in both my council and mayoral races. But I also knew that Cliff was a hard-working community leader. He was instrumental in Henry Cisneros' first election and helped Henry on all the bond votes and public referendums he faced. Now I needed Cliff's help.

Cliff made it clear he did not want to serve on the new board. He suggested several other people instead.

Under the ordinance I had the right to name the chairman. I wanted Cliff, but I had to play my cards right to get him. I didn't ask him until the day of the vote on appointments.

Sitting in the small room adjacent to the council chamber, I told him, "Cliff, you have to take the job. Nobody suggested to me has the experience and will devote the time and energy necessary to do it. You can't turn me down on this. I'm going out here to name you unless you force me not to."

Cliff hesitated, then smiled and responded, "You will get a lot of heat because I'm a developer."

"Out of the seven members there is only one other developer besides you. It will not be a problem."

"If you feel that strong about it, go ahead."

The board appointments with Cliff as chairman passed unanimously. On May 18, 1992, Cliff and I signed documents creating the agency.

At our first meeting the next day we hired our president and CEO: Joe Aceves, the city's director of public works and a professional engineer.

With the creation of the San Antonio Water System we could now turn our attention to other contentious issues. The Sierra Club lawsuit against the U.S. Fish and Wildlife Service was set for trial in early May 1992. The 1993 legislative session was looming and new legislation was desperately needed.

The 1993 Battle for the Edwards Aquifer Authority

The Southern-style, two-story Governor's Mansion in Austin sits across the street from the State Capitol, surrounded by beautiful landscaped lawns.

On June 11, 1993, as my son Matthew and I walked onto the mansion grounds we could see scores of television cameras on the lawn. Reporters were milling around waiting for Governor Ann Richards to sign a historic bill that would have a major effect on the 1.5 million people who live over the Edwards Aquifer, 90 percent of them in San Antonio.

As I was talking to a couple of reporters, I saw Governor Richards arrive at the back door of the mansion. She scanned the

Mayor Nelson Wolff discusses strategy with City Councilman Weir Labatt (right) as state Representative Robert Puente looks on during a meeting of the Texas Water Commission in Austin to discuss a commission plan to regulate pumping from the Edwards Aquifer. (Bob Owen, Express-News)

crowd, spotted me and waved, motioning me to come over. I grabbed Matthew's arm and said, "Come with me."

I kissed her on the cheek and then introduced her to my son. She said, "Come on upstairs. I want to show you where I live."

We walked up the narrow back flight of stairs that led to the private living quarters of the governor. She pointed out some of the historical artifacts and said, "I haven't changed much of anything. It really is a strange feeling living here where so many great governors of the past have lived."

By the time we walked back out the rear door of the mansion, everyone had arrived. Secretary of the Interior Bruce Babbitt had made a special trip for this event. State Senator Ken Armbrister, sponsor of Senate Bill 1477, and state Representative Robert Puente, the House sponsor, were waiting. Several other key legislators including Senators Jeff Wentworth and Frank Madla were there. Other key leaders from throughout the Edwards Aquifer region were also standing around.

As Governor Richards began to talk, I walked over to Cliff Morton. I said, "Cliff, you should have gotten here earlier. I have just been upstairs with the governor."

Cliff and Governor Richards had been friends since their college days at Baylor University. Cliff's close relationship with the governor had been instrumental in her support for the Edwards Aquifer legislation.

Cliff smiled and said, "She is a great lady. Hope you enjoyed your visit."

"I never thought we would see this day."

Cliff answered, "Neither did I." We were here to witness the signing of the bill creating the Edwards Aquifer Authority.

Recall that in January 1989 the Edwards Underground Water District had broken apart. In their rebellion against the pumping limits contained in the 1988 Regional Water Plan, the two western counties of Uvalde and Medina had voted overwhelmingly to withdraw from the district. Their irrigation was approaching the level of San Antonio's municipal water use, and more than half the aquifer's total annual recharge occurs in those two counties. They felt their needs were paramount. The truncated district that remained — including only the three counties of Bexar, Comal and Hays — was an impotent institution.

In 1989, the agricultural irrigators aroused their rural allies statewide to defeat any change in the traditional "right of capture" by the Legislature.

As we stood on the lawn waiting for the press conference to begin, I said to Cliff, "You should really feel good." Cliff had been the key leader in brokering an agreement.

A few minutes later, Secretary Babbitt, legislators, community leaders, and local officials flanked Governor Richards as she signed the bill creating the Edwards Aquifer Authority.

Secretary Babbitt delivered the most important message.

"By adopting this legislation, the state of Texas has shown that it is best to solve water problems at the local level rather than face federal government intervention," he said. "I am confident that now we can demonstrate to Judge Bunton that the federal court no longer needs to intervene in a Texas water problem."

Babbitt was referring to the Sierra Club lawsuit. A division of his agency, the U.S. Fish and Wildlife Service, was the defendant. The Sierra Club had felt obligated to file the lawsuit after voters stopped construction of the Applewhite Reservoir on May 5, 1991, and the Legislature failed to enact groundwater pumping limits.

The suit sought to force the secretary of the interior to protect several endangered species of invertebrates and plants that live in the Comal and San Marcos springs. The strategy was to ensure continuous spring flows by regulating the amount of water pumped from the aquifer by irrigators and municipal users alike.

The rejection of the Applewhite Reservoir by San Antonio voters had been a clear signal that they were as intractable as the western farmers about their rights to the aquifer's water. Further, San Antonio was obviously not willing to ease the pumping by developing a supplemental source of water.

Unrestricted pumping in the region had long ago virtually dried up San Pedro Springs in San Antonio's San Pedro Park, and the headwaters of the San Antonio River on the campus of Incarnate Word College. Much of the time, we relied on pumps to feed the rivers.

By filing suit in the U.S. District Court in Midland — which is hundreds of miles from the Edwards Aquifer — the Sierra Club was engaging in a classic case of venue shopping. Or perhaps it was coincidence that in the summer of 1991, the daughter of the general manager of the Guadalupe-Blanco River Authority, which was seeking pumping limits along with the Sierra Club, worked as a clerk for Judge Lucius Bunton.

The Sierra Club sought an order establishing minimum springflows. The levels proposed would require an immediate reduction in pumpage of 60 percent, which would kill San Antonio.

The effect of the Sierra Club lawsuit was to give greater urgency to the need to pass legislation creating a regional authority. As Secretary Babbitt said, we would be better off managing our own water problem rather than having a federal judge do it for us.

But the euphoria surrounding the signing of Senate Bill 1477 was short lived. Let me first tell you how we reached this day and then how it fell apart.

Over the years the Texas Water Commission had steered clear of the controversy surrounding the Edwards Aquifer. When Governor Ann Richards was elected in 1990 she named John Hall chairman of the commission. John was a former aide to Senator Lloyd Bentsen and he had later worked for the Lower Colorado River Authority. This tall, articulate African-American decided the Texas Water Commission would be the vehicle to make him a major political player.

In early 1992, Hall issued an ultimatum that either the region would develop a plan to manage the aquifer or the Texas Water Commission would do it for us. Cliff Morton, Joe Aceves and Jack Willome of Ray Ellison Industries began a contentious series of discussions with John on a proposed plan. We thought John was listening.

But in early April, Hall blindsided us. He released an interim plan and set an April 14 deadline for all parties to agree to it.

I was upset and publicly denounced the plan. I invited John to appear before the City Council to explain his action. On April 23 he came, and for two hours he presented his plan and answered council questions.

John promised to keep the lines of communication open and not act in an arbitrary manner. While the meeting was tense, it was conducted in a courteous and businesslike manner.

But Hall blindsided us again. On September 9, 1992, the Texas Water Commission suddenly declared the Edwards Aquifer to be an underground river subject to state allocation in the same manner as surface water. The rules would go into effect in June 1993 if the Legislature did not act to create a regional authority. Hall was determined to get atop the issue.

We joined others in a lawsuit in state court to overturn the ruling. We prevailed, establishing that the aquifer is groundwater, not a river.

While fighting in court, we continued to work with the Texas Water Commission to develop a plan for the Legislature to consider. John Hall became the key player in getting the feds to agree to allow use of up to 450,000 acre feet of aquifer water annually, the minimum volume needed to protect endangered species and the springs. This volume reflected historic use, and became the basis for the proposed legislation.

Over the next few months, Joe and Cliff hammered out a legislative plan with John Hall based on important goals for San Antonio.

On January 21, 1993, the proposed legislative bill drafted by the San Antonio Water System was approved by the City Council on a 9-to-2 vote. The anti-Applewhite leaders, including Kay Turner, testified before council against the legislation.

The proposed bill included the creation of a regional Edwards Aquifer Authority *appointed by the governor* to replace the existing elected Edwards Underground Water District.

The San Antonio Water System hired George Shipley as a consultant to work with the Legislature.

It was going to be one hell of a fight. The result would affect the lives of 1.5 million people living in the five counties over the Edwards Aquifer, as well as another million people living downstream along the Guadalupe River.

San Antonio was in a tough position. We were fighting for our economic lives against the Sierra Club. We were caught between two warring factions, irrigators to the west and people dependent on the Comal and San Marcos springs to the east. The giant in the middle, San Antonio with 90 percent of the population, had to provide the leadership to pass the necessary legislation.

On February 1, 1993, Judge Bunton ruled in favor of the Sierra Club. He gave the Texas Legislature until May 31, the last day of the biennial session, to enact a regional plan. We filed an immediate appeal.

In response to Judge Bunton's ruling, the Texas Water Commission said the required reduction would create unacceptable risks to public health and safety and devastate the region's economy. The water commission recommended only a 17 percent reduction during dry years.

Judge Bunton was quoted in the Express-News as saying the state commission's plan "conforms to the spirit" of his order. But the agricultural interests were not mollified. Rodney Reagan, president of the Uvalde County Underground Water District, was quoted in the Express-News calling the plan "a water hustler's boondoggle."

Nevertheless, bills were filed in the Legislature reflecting the state water commission's plans. But time was running out.

On March 13 Interior Secretary Babbitt came to San Antonio to visit me. He was dressed in khakis and hiking shoes. I said, "Mr. Secretary, we need your help with the Edwards legislation. Anything that you can say to encourage the passage of the Edwards Authority Act during the legislative battle would be very helpful." He agreed to help.

George Shipley kept in close communication with Secretary Babbitt's office. Periodic releases from Washington and pressure from Lt. Governor Bob Bullock and Speaker Pete Laney helped after rural interests tied the bill up in both the House and Senate.

It was a race to the finish.

With only 19 days left in the legislative session, it was now vital that the San Antonio business community turn up the heat. Cliff and I held a breakfast at the Barn Door attended by more than 100 business leaders and legislators.

I told the group that it was time to fish or cut bait. I said that our Senate delegation supported the measure unanimously, but our House delegation was split down the middle.

A few days later the Texas Senate passed the bill. Speaker Pete Laney referred the Senate bill to the House Natural Resources Committee, where it passed on May 19.

Then on Saturday, May 23, at 6:30 p.m., as the bill was called for consideration on the House floor, Karyne Conley raised a point of order to stop consideration of it. She argued that not enough members of our delegation were present. Laney reset the bill for House consideration the following Monday. That Monday I traveled to Austin for the House debate.

The pressure intensified as Governor Ann Richards visited the floor encouraging support of the bill. After four hours of debate, the House passed the bill on a voice vote.

Of our delegation of 11 members, eight supported the legislation. Representatives Conley, Ciro Rodriguez and Frank Corte did not. After the vote I congratulated each supporter.

We were still not through with the battle. The bill would have to be referred back to the Senate for concurrence with the amendments. The following day, May 26, the Senate refused, and a conference committee was appointed. We now had five days left.

In the conference, proposals were offered that further restricted San Antonio's rights. As the hour grew late, Cliff and I tired of compromises. At one point we told Frank Madla, "Tell them that we will withdraw support of the bill if they attach that provision. No bill is better than a bad bill." Senator Madla went on to defeat the provision.

The bill was passed out of the conference committee. The Senate passed the bill first, and then on May 30 the House passed it, one day before the end of the session. We were all elated.

This was the first legislative session in which San Antonio had stepped beyond its own delegation and forged strong links with key legislators from other areas.

The passage of the legislation brings us back to the start of this story, the signing of the bill by Governor Richards on the grounds of the Governor's Mansion. As I said, our feeling of elation at that moment would be short lived.

On June 24, 1993, the Mexican American Legal Defense and Educational Fund, representing the League of United Latin American Citizens, threatened to oppose clearance of the bill by the Justice Department under the Voting Rights Act. Their position was that an appointed board would dilute minority representation by replacing the elected board of the existing Edwards Underground Water District. On November 19, 1993, the Justice Department filed an objection to the bill.

Now we had one branch of the federal government (the Interior Department) supporting the legislation while another branch (the Justice Department) opposed it. I hope you can imagine the frustration I was feeling.

We tried with all our might to convince the Justice Department that it was wrong. We pointed out that many of the river authorities in Texas were appointed and that the appointed boards had better representation of minorities than elected boards. We enlisted the support of Housing Secretary Henry Cisneros and key Hispanic leaders. But the Justice Department would not budge.

The result was that the act became a dead letter. The EUWD continued in existence, with its limited powers and limited jurisdiction.

The State of Texas filed a suit in federal court to overturn the Justice Department ruling. As 1993 was coming to a close, the case was still pending in federal court. It looked as though the state would not prevail and we would have to return to the Legislature in 1995 to try again. But before the 1995 Legislature convened, I had to deal with two more local water issues.

The Second Battle Over Applewhite

In August 1993, while LULAC continued to oppose federal clearance of the Edwards Aquifer Authority, the Edwards Underground Water District staff released a technical report warning of increasing levels of contaminants in water samples from the Edwards Aquifer. They attributed this to the increased development over the recharge zone.

The circulation of the report led to increasing concern about the potential for aquifer pollution. I began to work with Councilman Howard Peak, who had demonstrated leadership on planning and environmental issues since being elected to City Council. We decided that the council as a whole should meet to discuss proposed new regulations for development over the recharge zone.

At the same time I felt it was also necessary to review what steps we should take to augment our water supply as well as protect it. As I explained in the chapter on our military bases, lack of a secure water supply was an important issue with the Department of Defense on keeping all our military bases open.

Because of the threats posed by the Sierra Club lawsuit and the upcoming 1995 round of base closures, I felt it essential to address the issue of an additional water supply.

On November 22, 1993, I appointed the 2050 Water Committee to develop a 50-year water plan.

The same day, I appointed the City Council, selected planning commissioners and water board representatives as a "committee of the whole" to review a menu of 33 water-quality initiatives proposed by the SAWS staff.

As both committees worked through the spring of 1994, I had to focus my attention on yet another major issue. Since the day I was elected, I had wanted to submit a bond issue on parks. There had not been a major bond issue to add and improve parks for 25 years. I also wanted to include streets and drainage. The last bond election for streets and drainage had been in 1987.

In February 1994, City Council voted to submit a $109 million bond package on May 7 that would include parks, streets, drainage and a central police substation.

Although I focused on campaigning for passage of the bond issue, I did keep up with the work of the 2050 Water Committee. After attending some of its meetings, I saw clearly that the committee would probably recommend a reconstituted Applewhite Reservoir. I did not want to complicate the bond election with such a controversial proposal, so I asked them to hold their report until after the bond election.

From January through May of 1994, the City Council met in numerous special sessions to review the staff recommendations for new regulations over the recharge zone and a comprehensive regional strategy for water-quality protection.

In addition to the 33 recommendations by staff, six others were submitted by a coalition of environmental organizations called Aquifer Guardians in Urban Areas. AGUA was a descendant of the Aquifer Protection Association that Fay Sinkin and others had founded in the early 1970s. The six measures proposed by AGUA were much broader in scope and much more stringent than the 33 recommendations from staff.

While Fay was an experienced hand and a former board member of the EUWD, other spokespersons for AGUA were newer to the scene. Danielle Milam, a young urban planner and a mother of four, stood out as both a strong environmentalist and a tough political infighter. She articulated the need for planned development that was environmentally sustainable.

On May 7, 1994, we won the bond election handily. I wasted no time in jumping back into the local water issue. I met with Howard Peak to select a citizens task force to work with staff on an aquifer protection ordinance. I balanced the representation between developers and environmentalists.

Also in May, the 2050 Committee made its report. It recommended a strategy of conservation and local reuse, revision of the act creating the Edwards Aquifer Authority, and leasing of agricultural irrigation rights during years of inadequate recharge.

Overshadowing all of this, however, was the committee's recommendation to develop Applewhite — not as a water supply for San Antonio, but as a storage reservoir for treated wastewater. To refresh your memory, the Applewhite Reservoir had been rejected by the voters in a referendum on May 5, 1991. Immediately after that vote, City Council instructed the City Water Board to summit a plan to abandon the project. But instead, on May 10, 1991, the water board voted to file suit to overturn the referendum and proceed with building the reservoir. City Council defended the results of the referendum we had submitted to the people.

After I took office as mayor in June 1991, I attacked the water board for acting in defiance of the council and the citizens' vote. I quickly called a meeting of key water board members and council members Labatt and Dutmer. We wrestled out an agreement that the water board would not proceed with any construction until the lawsuit was decided. We eventually settled the lawsuit by agreeing not to proceed with the construction of Applewhite unless voters approved it.

After that meeting I told the media I was considering the idea of resubmitting Applewhite for another vote. The Sierra Club lawsuit had changed our water situation by threatening our unlimited use of the aquifer. I also thought that if we changed the use of the reservoir from drinking water to non-drinking purposes such as irrigation and industrial use, some opponents might change their minds.

The anti-Applewhite forces immediately threatened to recall me and council members who might support a resubmitted vote.

Henry Cisneros and other Applewhite supporters advised me to let things cool off. So I dropped the idea.

So here we were two years later, reviewing the Applewhite issue again. Under the 2050 Water Committee's plan, Applewhite would collect both recycled water from our treatment plants and surface water from the Medina River. With both sources of water the reservoir would be a constant-level lake, full even during times of drought. The water would be used for non-drinking purposes, just like the existing Calaveras and Braunig lakes in southern Bexar County. We called this "the new Applewhite."

I was now faced with a decision of when to submit the vote. We needed the vote before the end of the year because the federal permit for Applewhite would expire in December.

On May 19, council approved the "2050 Plan" and called a referendum on August 13, 1994.

In June, we commissioned a poll. The results showed the issue would be defeated 50 percent to 41 percent. The same poll showed my own approval rating was at an all-time high of 82 percent. Even though the odds were against us, they were close enough to overcome.

But things got off to a bad start. Kay Turner appeared before council to say that she would organize a campaign to defeat the issue. She was in her best form: strident, loud, and abusive. She gave a great evening news sound bite.

With this early appearance, Turner managed to frame the issue before our side got our act together. She was using one of my key political rules, and had beaten me at my own game.

She said the building of the Applewhite was a conspiracy by developers that would allow them to build over the recharge zone of the aquifer and pollute it.

As Turner hammered away, I talked about the merits of the reservoir. I said that it would be a constant level lake that would be valuable as a recreational lake. I said it was crazy to give away our recycled water by letting it go downstream for nothing when we could capture it and have a full lake.

But my story was dull and boring, while Turner's was salacious and spicy. Turner was also a radio talk show's perfect guest. She was great at one-liners.

The Homeowner-Taxpayer Association ran an ad saying, "Applewhite is not new and improved. It is just a second try at allowing business interests to profit at taxpayers' expense." Our June poll showed that 25 percent of the people thought Applewhite was a real estate scam. An investigation by the Express-News found no business interests profiting from Applewhite other than the engineers and construction firms that would be picked to complete the lake.

Carl Wiglesworth, who ran one of the most notoriously vitriolic local talk shows on WOAI radio, had a field day giving anti-Applewhite spokespersons a forum.

As the hot summer days sped by, it was clear we were losing more and more ground. We then made some poor decisions within the campaign.

U.S. Representative Frank Tejeda cut a television commercial in which he said, "The Base Closure Commission is looking for any reason to close military bases, and we cannot afford to give them one. *My friends, this is not an idle threat — it is reality!*"

Tejeda certainly was proved right later.

But U.S. Representative Henry B. Gonzalez, who considered Kelly AFB his turf even though it was not in his district, contradicted Tejeda. In his newsletter to constituents, Gonzalez called concerns about the base-closing commission "fear mongering." Our opponents now had "evil developers" and "fear mongers" to use against us.

Then the church stepped in. The Reverend Mike DeGerolami, chairman of the Archdiocese's Justice and Peace Commission, called a news conference to announce that building Applewhite would be "a sin." Archbishop Flores approved putting this statement and other anti-Applewhite literature in all Catholic churches.

On July 26, banker Charlie Cheever and I met with Archbishop Flores at the Chancery and tried to persuade him to repudiate the statement. He refused, but did allow us to send pro-Applewhite literature to the churches. Very few churches accepted our literature. After this blow I knew we were going to lose.

On August 9, four days before the election, we got a wonderful rain after almost two months without a drop. We knew we were doomed now. Rain always seemed to come right when we were in a water crisis. People felt we could always count on rain to save us instead of investing in water projects.

Finally, almost mercifully, on August 13, the voters turned down the revised Applewhite Reservoir project by 7,100 votes, 55 percent to 45 percent. Only 18.4 percent of the eligible voters went to the polls. This was a worse defeat than the first vote on Applewhite, when it lost by 3,400 votes.

Protecting the Recharge Zone

After the loss on Applewhite II in August 1994, I was in deep trouble on the two remaining water issues: the proposed regulations of the recharge zone and the legislation needed to create an elected rather than appointed Edwards Aquifer Authority to satisfy the Justice Department.

The Applewhite defeat strengthened the hand of the forces that opposed the Edwards Aquifer Authority.

I had to strengthen my position before going to the Legislature. I had to win on the proposed regulations to protect the recharge zone. If we could successfully deal with this issue, I could regain leadership on the water problem before the start of the 1995 Legislature.

I began work right away to get the Applewhite issue behind us. I met with the editorial board of the Express-News. I said it is time to put Applewhite away and look ahead to seek other solutions.

On August 18, the City Council passed a resolution directing the San Antonio Water System to release the Applewhite water permit that was to expire in December. That possible solution to part of our water problem floated downstream.

After that vote, Tracy and I went to Santa Fe, New Mexico, for a much-needed rest. I had lost 15 pounds during the campaign and needed to regain my strength. I also needed time to think about how to move forward on the two controversial issues that I would face in my last few months in office.

On the same day council had voted to release our Applewhite permits, Councilwoman Ruth Jones McClendon brought up the issue of a possible moratorium on zoning and platting over the recharge zone, until the ordinances to protect the zone were passed. The next week, while Tracy and I were in Santa Fe, the council discussed the moratorium issue. Councilman Bill Thornton convinced the council not to adopt a moratorium and to instruct staff to get the rules in a proposed ordinance within two weeks.

From Santa Fe, I was in daily contact with the staff. The news I was receiving was not good. Just the mention of a moratorium caused a rash of permits to be filed. In just two days, 38 subdivision plat applications were received. Staff members also said it was impossible for the ordinances to be completed in two weeks. They said the task force was in the middle of a major battle over the proposed additional regulations that environmentalists had proposed, and it would take time to reach a consensus.

I knew when I got back home the following week I would have to really grab control of the issue or all would be lost. I had come to the conclusion that we needed to adopt some of the proposals that AGUA advocated. These primarily involved restricting the density of development over the aquifer. I knew my views would lead to a major fight with the development community.

When I got back home I met with Howard Peak and Ruth Jones McClendon. I told Ruth I would support her moratorium. On September 14, City Council voted to impose a moratorium on platting and zoning until the end of December. We gave the task force until the end of November to complete its work.

Howard Peak began to meet with the task force on almost a daily basis. I made it clear that Howard had my backing as he prodded, encouraged and sometimes threatened in order to reach a consensus.

Co-chairs Danielle Milam and Gene Dawson soon realized that the polarized dialogue on the commitee was an endless volley. They sought a "middle ground" that could be agreed to. Balancing complex issues of private property rights, the city's limited legal jurisdiction, and the imperative duty to protect our water supply now and in the future was not an easy task.

A hidden additional issue was that increased development was creating an enormous problem of life-threatening flooding downstream. The tools for water quality protection — preservation of natural floodplains, keeping sinkholes open, and using vegetation to filter urban pollutants — are the same as those that are effective for flood control.

The flooding issue brought North Side neighborhood associations to the table in support of tougher regulations. Now their neighborhoods, as well as the older neighborhoods of the inner city, were flooding. COPS and Metro Alliance now had a North Side ally in their cause to protect the recharge zone.

Finally on December 6, 1994, the committee reached a consensus. Both sides called it a history-making water-quality protection ordinance. The report was turned over to City Attorney Lloyd Garza to put into ordinance form. All seemed well until Garza ruled that several of the recommendations were not valid under state law. He drew up an ordinance that was considerably weaker than what the task force had agreed to.

Danielle Milam and the environmentalists felt they had been stabbed in the back. They suspected the developers on the committee, when they voted for the report, knew the city attorney would overrule the tougher regulations.

In any event, we now had an ordinance before us that was considerably weaker than what the task force had agreed on.

After the vote to extend the moratorium, Virginia Ramirez, COPS co-chair; Homer Bain, the spokesman for Metro Alliance; and Danielle Milam met with me to suggest that we hire Jim Blackburn, a noted Houston environmental lawyer. COPS and Metro Alliance had a long history of fights with developers.

Blackburn had represented the Sierra Club and other environmental groups on some major statewide pollution issues. He had represented the Audubon Society in preserving wetlands near Houston. I needed someone like Jim to counter the legal experts on the developers' side. At the meeting we got him on the phone and I struck a deal to bring him on board. I announced his selection on December 31.

The developers felt I had hired the devil himself. They did not want Jim Blackburn to have any input.

On January 2, 1995, the Express-News published an op-ed piece by Danielle Milam. She said that the city's legal department had been coached by local developer lawyers and the ordinance had been gutted. She wrote, "The public has been dealt some dirty blows in the 1994 round of water quality protection regulations ... Let's call this game what it is — greed. As a community we have been deceived. There is no deal."

The fight continued to escalate as we approached a January 5 council meeting. Developers made a major behind-the-scenes effort to secure six votes. They did not want any more delays by the council.

I worked on each council member to try to convince them to delay the vote another week, giving time for Jim Blackburn to review the ordinance. COPS and Metro Alliance worked with me. As the meeting began on January 5, I knew at best I would win by one vote.

I argued that the December 6 task force agreement was emasculated by the city attorney's draft. I said we needed another week to give us an opportunity to strengthen the ordinance that lay before us.

Bill Thornton led the charge to force a vote. He said he was against hiring Jim Blackburn. He called Danielle Milam to the podium and tore into her viciously. After this exchange, Juan Solis observed, "I wasn't alive at the Inquisition, but after hearing Mr. Thornton, I have a feeling of what it was like."

The debate went on for more than three hours. The tension was high in the council chamber as the city clerk called the roll. As each member voted, thoughts flew through my mind. I knew this vote would be the real test of whether the public would actually believe we could stand up to the developers. They had heard throughout the Applewhite campaign that developers controlled City Hall. They would soon see if that was true.

Council members Larson, Thornton, Ross, Ayala and Billa Burke voted to proceed and thereby accept the weakened ordinance. Council members Perez, Solis, Avila, McClendon, and Peak voted with me. We won by one vote.

After the vote we immediately swung into action. The moratorium would expire January 23, 1995. The deadline put pressure on all parties to work long hours to reach an agreement. The next day I went to meetings with Jim Blackburn, Lloyd Garza, Howard Peak, Danielle Milam and Gene Dawson. Blackburn had already prepared a six-page legal draft of proposed changes. I told them I wanted an ordinance as close as possible to the draft proposed by the task force on December 6.

Over the next five days, work continued around the clock. On Tuesday, January 10, I called a news conference with all the parties present and announced we had developed a 29-page ordinance that all groups would support. I said there would be a historic vote on the ordinance two days later. This was the last date we could vote on an ordinance and give it time to go into effect before the moratorium expired. I said we needed to nail down this agreement and get it passed. Both Danielle Milam and Gene Dawson spoke in favor of the compromise.

On the day of the vote Jim Blackburn was quoted in the Express-News as saying the draft that was accepted did an excellent job of protecting San Antonio's water.

January 12, 1995, was my finest day at City Hall. We passed the proposed ordinance on a unanimous vote of all 11 members.

Before the vote I said that Councilman Peak was the person who really made this happen. He received a long burst of applause. After the vote, the whole audience stood and applauded the council. We stood and applauded the audience back. I commented that I had never seen this happen in the eight years I had served as councilman and mayor.

On January 15, 1995, columnist Rick Casey wrote, "Unanimous passage by the City Council of regulations for growth over the Edwards Aquifer Recharge Zone this week is an extraordinary event in the political life of this city." He went on to say that my decision to include environmentalists was the first time that they had been given a solid seat at the table. He complimented them for being willing to work rather than just raise hell.

Before I left office, Councilman Peak and I worked hard to get the votes to appoint Danielle Milam to the San Antonio Water System board. She stills serves as of this writing.

Back to the Future: The 1995 Fight for the Edwards Authority

I had to hold at bay the troops who were anxious to prepare for the upcoming legislative session until the City Council completed work on the Edwards Aquifer Recharge Zone regulations.

Water System Chairman Cliff Morton had been pushing me to take action, saying we were way behind where we had been in 1993.

When that last session started, we had already approved the outline of the Edwards legislation and hired lobbyists. Here it was January 1995, the Legislature was in session, and we had done nothing.

So on January 26, two weeks after our council victory, I brought up the issue of the Edwards Aquifer Authority. The anti-Applewhite forces under Kay Turner's leadership complained bitterly during the campaign of their fear of pollution over the recharge zone. But when it came to enacting strong regulations, they sat out the battle. Now they emerged in strength to oppose our support of the necessary legislation to create the aquifer authority. Twenty-four of them spoke in opposition.

Joe Moore, the monitor appointed by Judge Bunton, testified that we must put in place some regulatory plan to limit pumping. We debated the issue for more than two hours. On a 9-to-2 vote we supported legislation to require an elected board for the authority. I do not believe that I could have won that vote without the victory on the aquifer protection ordinance.

All of the interested parties again geared up for the next legislative battle. Cliff and I had a much harder time gaining support from our delegation than we did in the 1993 Legislature. Some of the local legislators were angry with me for various reasons. They were getting strong pressure from the anti-Applewhite forces. Some were mad because I opposed casino gambling. I was quoted as saying that many legislators would vote for it because they did not have the backbone of a chicken. We were off to a bad start.

But one advantage we had was the passage of the Edwards Aquifer Authority bill in 1993. We only needed to amend the bill to include an elected board.

Representatives Ciro Rodriguez and Karyne Conley, who opposed the bill in 1993, would become the key leaders in structuring the size and makeup of the Edwards Aquifer board. We then met with Judith Sanders-Castro, who was the lawyer for MALDEF. She said she wanted a 23-member board, all elected from single-member districts.

We told her there was no way the Legislature would accept it. The Legislature was trying to balance too many competing interests.

One-man, one-vote did not work in trying to balance these separate interests because 90 percent of the people over the aquifer lived in San Antonio. We suggested a 15-member board with four from the west, seven from San Antonio and four from the east. She said she would think about it.

With the support of Ciro Rodriguez, I decided to call for a vote on City Council to make a recommendation on the size of the board. On March 10, 1995, the council voted to support the 15-member board that became known as 4-7-4.

But the Texas Senate passed a bill that kept the appointed board and also kept the existing elected EUWD board in existence in a contorted attempt to satisfy the Justice Department.

On April 6, Karyne Conley set up a meeting between Loretta King, deputy assistant attorney general in the Civil Rights Division, and key members of the Legislature. King told them that the *only* board that would approved would be the 15-member board.

On April 14, the House Natural Resources Committee passed the Senate bill that called for the appointed board and keeping the elected Edwards board alive. I said the Legislature was playing Russian roulette with the Justice Department and it was going to lose.

On April 28, the House Natural Resources Committee passed another House bill that called for a 17-member board, with two of the members from downstream on the Guadalupe River holding advisory positions. Representative Robert Puente supported the compromise. It passed out of committee 5 to 3. Both the Senate and the House bill moved to the calendar committee.

In a surprise move, Karyne Conley got nine members of our 11-member delegation to sign a letter to Calendar Committee Chairman Mark Stiles. The letter said they wanted him to hold both bills in committee. It said, "We are in the final stages of the 74th Legislature, Regular Session. We do not have the luxury of wasting any more time to further battle an already dead horse."

I called Karyne and said, "I know you are against the bill, but we should at least have a chance on the House floor."

She responded, "Nelson, I am trying to help you. This bill will not pass the Justice Department. The House leadership is refusing to listen to the Justice Department's demand for a 15-member board."

The next day Councilman Howard Peak and I went to Austin. Standing in the back of the House chamber, I sent messages to the floor asking for each member of our delegation to meet with me. Almost all of them gave me the opportunity to present my case for allowing the bill to come to the House floor. I promised the members that we would strongly support amending the bill to create a 15-member elected board. When I left, the majority of our delegation supported bringing the bill to the floor.

On May 10, 1995, the House took up the bill and amended it to include the 15-member elected board, based primarily on lobbying by Karyne Conley. I told the media that the passage of the bill was a life saver for our community.

The Senate went on to pass a similar bill, but it was necessary to appoint a conference committee to resolve the differences. The differences were resolved and the Legislature passed the bill. Governor George Bush signed it on May 31, 1995.

I announced the signing of the bill at my last City Council meeting. It was a nice way to end my term, but the battle over the legislation was not over.

On August 23, 1995, just five days before the new board was to take office, the Medina County Underground Water Conservation District filed a lawsuit saying the bill was unconstitutional. The following day state Judge Mickey Pennington issued a temporary restraining order prohibiting implementation of the legislation. On November 22, Pennington made the injunction permanent.

A week later, on November 29, Judge Bunton effectively took over the aquifer by directing the U.S. Fish and Wildlife Service to implement measures to curtail pumping. New Mayor Bill Thornton made a great show by flying to New Orleans with SAWS President Joe Aceves and our lead attorney Russ Johnson to personally file our appeal with the Fifth Circuit.

The appeal was successful when the Fifth Circuit stayed Bunton's order taking over the aquifer. Bunton referred to the ruling as "a tacky note" from his boss.

Almost a year later, on June 28, 1996, the Texas Supreme Court, by a 9-to-0 vote, upheld the constitutionality of the Edwards Aquifer Authority. The temporary appointed board was finally allowed to meet. In November, the first election of the Edwards Aquifer board was held. San Antonio businessman Mike Beldon was elected chairman. Finally, the battle to create the agency was over.

Looking Ahead

During the four years I served as mayor, we made significant headway in addressing water problems.

The Edwards Aquifer Authority is responsible for protecting and optimizing the use of the Edwards Aquifer in accordance with sound environmental policies. I hope studies will show that artificial springflow augmentation will work and that additional recharge dams can be built. But as a city we cannot rely on the hope that they will work. We must develop our own water resources.

The conservation plan we put in place has reduced San Antonio's usage dramatically even as the population continues to grow.

Under the leadership of Mayor Thornton, the San Antonio Water System has implemented a recycling plan. SAWS also gives rebates for installing low-flow water fixtures.

But if we had built the redesigned Applewhite, we could have recycled even more water — 65,000 acre feet — for the same cost. Applewhite would have stored 60,000 acre feet of water, of which 30,000 acre feet would have been recycled. The anti-Applewhite crowd led by Kay Turner prefers to see all of our treated wastewater go downstream for nothing.

The major remaining issue is that of creating another water source for San Antonio. At the time of this writing, debate is continuing about building another reservoir or piping in water from another water basin.

In 1996, Mayor Bill Thornton tried his hand at creating a new long-range water plan. He appointed a 34-member committee that included representatives of every viewpoint, including Kay Turner and dissidents Kirk and Carol Patterson.

In contrast to previous efforts by Henry Cisneros and me, Mayor Thornton kept his hands strictly off the committee process once the group was appointed. At the beginning, many doubted the committee could possibly succeed with so many strident spokespersons for such polarized views, but Thornton stood by his position.

The committee failed to meet its original deadline to report before the end of 1996, and by January 1997 it looked as if the whole effort was crashing and burning. A 58-page document failed to recognize that we had a water problem, ignored the legal and physical limitations affecting the aquifer and relegated the four cornerstones of a sound water policy (conservation, reuse, regional aquifer management, and an additional water supply) into the background.

The Greater Chamber quickly organized a committee appointed to intervene. Phil Barshop was appointed chairman and I served on the committee. I wrote a letter expressing my concerns to Bill Thornton and copied community leaders. Our committee circulated a paper outlining our position, and we met with some of the members of the water committee to let them know our concerns.

On Tuesday, January 21, the mayor's committee met for the 39th time. There was no consensus on the altered draft. In a last-minute effort, Air Force Colonel David Cannan, who represented the military on the committee, presented an outline which included all the key elements the chamber felt strongly about. The next day the committee approved a six-page summary report instead of the full draft report that had been circulated.

On January 23, City Council accepted the report and referred it to the SAWS board for a response and implementation.

While the committee broke no new ground, its report was widely praised as expressing a balanced and comprehensive strategy. It is still a bit short on specifics, but at least it has significantly broadened the understanding that we do have a long-range water problem and that complex trade-offs are required to solve it. It could be the basis of support to develop an alternative water supply. I hope they will find that elusive additional water source.

★★★

Lessons from Water Wars — II

■ **Battling bureaucrats is a long, hard fight.**
The battle to consolidate the city's three water agencies was difficult and prolonged because of the resistance of powerful entrenched interests. City Manager Alex Briseño had to rise above the bureaucratic infighting to support council policy.

■ **Sometimes you have to go out of town to find a friend.**
Local legislative delegations do not fare well in the face of a heavily controversial local issue such as the creation of the Edwards Aquifer Authority. It becomes necessary to turn to legislative leaders from other parts of the state.

■ **The "best" is the worst enemy of the "good."**
The Applewhite Reservoir was turned down because it was not the "best" project everyone could imagine. For decades, our leaders and citizens have turned down water projects, from Cibolo Reservoir and Canyon Lake to Applewhite. There is no universal, ultimate "best" water project.

■ **Opponents can sometimes prove to be friends.**
Even though Representative Karyne Conley opposed the Edwards Aquifer Authority, she provided the leadership to pass the key amendment calling for an elected board. Without this amendment the bill would have been dead.

■ **Environmentalists can win if they sit at the table instead of beating down the door.**
Under the leadership of Danielle Milam, the environmentalists won a major victory on the Edwards Aquifer protection ordinance because they kept up the pressure and stayed at the table. They did not pursue an all-or-nothing approach.

22

Growing with Grace

While following in Henry Cisneros' footsteps of economic development, I have also advocated my belief that San Antonio should "grow with grace," not in the Wild West style of cities such as Houston, where zoning is close to a mortal sin.

Even though San Antonio has a planning department and tools to tailor growth, the city had not written a new master plan since 1951, when the population was less than half its current level of more than a million residents.

Our rapid growth during the 1980s showed the shortcomings of local planning. New developments in the hills north of the city stripped ground cover and contributed to serious flooding in existing neighborhoods.

During my campaign for mayor, I called for a new master plan that would address environmental issues.

On June 12, 1991, one week after I was elected, I appeared before the Planning Commission to ask members to develop a new master plan. At the time Howard Peak was chairman of the commission. He was eager to begin.

The City Council held a public hearing and adopted the plan in December 1993. The plan's six sections set goals and objectives for neighborhoods, urban design, natural resources, economic development, growth management and community services. To achieve these goals, City Council would need to make policy decisions and adopt ordinances.

One of those issues was annexation. The master plan called for a systematic annexation process to promote orderly growth. In Texas, annexation is a very contentious process, as I discovered when I was still a councilman back in 1988.

"Growth with grace" is the phrase Nelson Wolff uses to describe his strategy of economic development while maintaining the city's quality of life, such as this city-sponsored race in November 1993 that included the mayor and Councilman Howard Peak (far left). (John Davenport, Express-News)

Annexation

The 600 people who had crowded into the auditorium at Zachry Middle School were in a mood to lynch City Council. We were proposing to annex them and almost 19,000 others into the city of San Antonio. The occasion was a public hearing on the proposal in October 1988.

Of all the members of City Council, I had the most at stake because these angry citizens would be annexed into my council district. It would be the largest annexation in the history of the city to come into a single council district.

Most of the people at the meeting lived in a neighborhood called the Great Northwest. Speaker after speaker complained about "taxation without representation." They were angry because the city could annex them without their consent and, they feared, spend their tax money in other parts of the city.

The people were about to lose the best of both worlds. Living in the unincorporated part of the county, they had access to city services without having to pay for them. Every day, they came into the city to work and play, using city streets, libraries, parks, museums and many other services. If I were among them I would not want to be annexed either.

After the meeting, I began to work with the leaders of the Great Northwest Community Improvement Association. This is a mandatory homeowners association, by far the largest of this type in the city. It has 4,000 members and a full-time paid staff of 15 employees, making it bigger than many of San Antonio's suburban municipalities.

The leaders of the Great Northwest knew annexation was inevitable. But they wanted it done in an orderly manner, with a plan that they helped develop. Their demands included the hiring of additional patrol officers, the city's purchase of a private water system that served their area, a new branch library, improved parks and participation in developing a zoning plan.

I agreed to all these demands and said I would seek support from the council to enter into a binding agreement to provide the services outlined. I also agreed to delay annexation for one year to give the citizens and the city time to plan.

It was not an easy task to get City Council support. The vote to annex prevailed with a bare majority of 6 to 5.

Before 1940, San Antonio had never expanded beyond the original city limits established by the king of Spain. This was a square six miles on a side, centered at Main Plaza. By 1950, the city had almost doubled in area. Continuing annexation along with internal population growth has made San Antonio the ninth-largest city in the nation, with a population of more than a million.

On February 4, 1993, five years after the confrontation over annexation I faced as a freshman councilman, we adopted the annexation policy that was the goal of the master plan. It established a rolling three-year annexation. The ordinance also suggested that the city consider annexing areas where development was expected to occur, instead of waiting until the area was fully developed. This would allow city zoning and building codes to apply to new construction.

As this book goes to press, the present City Council under the leadership of Mayor Thornton has continued the planned annexation policy. Despite strong opposition from the residents, even the exclusive gated community called The Dominion — popularly regarded as the wealthiest neighborhood in Bexar County — is scheduled to be annexed in 1998.

What to do with our garbage?

City Council in the late 1980s began to face an environmental crisis that didn't involve water. Our landfill, Nelson Gardens, was fast approaching capacity, and the city had been unable to reach a decision on another landfill.

As a councilman, I realized one program that could give us some breathing room was curbside recycling. It's the only effective means of getting widespread citizen participation in reducing waste.

I was able to convince the City Council in December 1989 to enter into a recycling contract with Garbage Gobbler. This became the city's first curbside recycling project.

By the summer of 1993, all of north central San Antonio was receiving curbside recycling service. City Council approved the purchase of 50 new trucks with state-of-the-art collection capability in early 1995. We now could offer the service to all 258,000 homes in San Antonio, and by year's end San Antonio had implemented the largest curbside recycling program in the country, collecting some 160 tons of recyclables each day and saving the city $2,000 a day in landfill costs.

But while the recycling made a dent in the garbage that was hauled to the landfill, it did not preclude the need to develop a new waste disposal site. Nelson Gardens was quickly reaching its limit, and council struggled to find a solution.

As Nelson Gardens approached capacity and the landfill time bomb continued to tick, the council remained deadlocked. Our problem was complicated by the fact that there are few areas in Bexar County geologically suitable for a landfill. Unfortunately, these areas are in a band across the southern part of the county, in predominately lower-income and Hispanic communities. This gives the issue overtones of environmental racism.

Every effort to locate a new landfill or expand our existing landfill in Bexar County was fought by the people who lived nearby, usually with the support of their council member or legislative representative.

After I became mayor, we began to develop a plan to extend the life of Nelson Gardens. The city had purchased the landfill in 1982 from Garbage Gobbler, a local company. As part of the agreement, Garbage Gobbler continued dumping all the garbage that it collected from its customers at a low cost.

The city should have seen what was going to happen. Garbage Gobbler sold to Waste Management Inc., a national company that operates landfills across the country. With the Nelson Gardens agreement, Waste Management then had a competitive advantage over other garbage haulers. It soon substantially increased the volume of garbage brought to Nelson Gardens for disposal, even bringing trash from other towns and industries. This cut the landfill's life by one-third, to only 10 years.

In order to extend the life of Nelson Gardens, we asked the Texas Water Commission to allow us to raise the landfill by 200 feet. This would give us five more years of capacity — still only a short-term relief.

But the Texas Water Commission raised objection after objection to our permit application. By the summer of 1992 we still did not have a permit for expansion and Nelson Gardens would be filled by December. As we worked for the extended permit, we began negotiations with Waste Management to sell Nelson Gardens back to that company and to contract with it to take our garbage. The company also owned land next to Nelson Gardens that was in the process of being permitted for a landfill.

As our time was running out at Nelson Gardens, Waste Management continued to load up Nelson Gardens with its garbage. Company officials became very demanding in pressing for terms for the proposed contract. They changed their proposals and raised the disposal price of garbage.

In my first meeting with Waste Management's top officials, they adopted a tough attitude. I felt as if I were meeting with movie-type tough-guys.

After the meeting I knew that we would be stuck with outrageous prices unless we got our state permit and unless we got other private sector landfills involved in competing for our business.

Two other major companies came forward: Browning-Ferris Industries, which owned a landfill in southeastern Bexar County, and Texas Disposal System, which owned a landfill in Buda, 60 miles northeast of San Antonio. We were already hauling part of our garbage to the BFI landfill, from collection routes where reduced travel time made it competitive with our own disposal facility.

On September 23, 1992, the week we were to decide on which private sector company to use, the Texas Water Commission gave us nine more months of life by allowing us to go 10 feet higher. Our permit to go 200 feet higher was still pending with the commission. The extra 10 feet wasn't much, but it gave us a little breathing room.

The next day I appointed a committee of four council members headed by Frank Wing to get public input and make recommendations on solving our landfill problem.

The committee recommended that our long-term solution should be to develop a landfill of 2,000 acres or more that would include a Regional Environmental Enterprise Zone (REEZ) and an industrial park for recycling and research facilities.

In January 1993, I appointed former Councilman Weir Labatt to head up a committee to plan for the regional landfill. At the same time we began to negotiate with three private companies for a five-year contract. They were BFI, Waste Management and Texas Disposal Systems.

In July, the City Council once again took up the issue of which private company to contract with. Waste Management made a major effort to get a long-term contract to take all the city's garbage.

In the end their hardball tactics did not work. Instead we awarded a $1 million contract to BFI for disposal of approximately one-third of our garbage. This relieved the pressure on Nelson Gardens as we sought to extend the permit.

Members of the Texas Water Commission assured us they would work with us in extending our permit. But they also continued to put roadblocks in our way.

On August 20, 1993, we found out they were lying to us. The Express-News got hold of an internal memo that recommended the denial of the extension of our permit. They were not supposed to rule on the permit until March 1995.

I was convinced that Waste Management was using all its power in Austin to stop approval of our permit expansion. Senator Madla had told me that he had good information on the lobbying efforts of Waste Management to do just that.

Public Works Director John German, Alex Briseño and I arranged for a meeting with TWC Executive Director Jesus Garza and Ron Bond, head of the landfill permit section. After a long, fruitless discussion I blew up and accused the commission staff of sabotaging our permit by succumbing to political pressure. I threatened legal action if I could gather enough evidence to prove inappropriate action on the part of state staff. Ron Bond sat like a stone and said nothing.

I was never able to come up with any proof to support my suspicion, but a year later another case showed that I might have been on the mark. An independent examiner for the Texas Water Commission, Linda Sorrells, said her supervisors repeatedly badgered her and suggested she would lose her job if she didn't change her findings in a case involving Waste Management's request to expand a landfill near Ferris. The FBI began an investigation.

After the meeting with the Texas Water Commission, I knew the game was over. On September 9, City Council ordered Nelson Gardens to be closed as soon as possible. It was important to close it before new EPA regulations went into effect that would have substantially raised the cost of disposing of garbage.

A week later, after an intense lobbying effort by all three firms, we awarded five-year contracts to BFI and Texas Disposal, leaving Waste Management out in the cold. The intense competition among the three firms helped bring the prices down.

On January 20, 1994, after six months of work, the Labatt committee recommended a 5,000-acre regional landfill near Moore, in Frio County, 43 miles southwest of San Antonio.

The master-plan goal of an environmental industrial park, with recycling, composting, tire-shredding and research facilities, could be developed at this site, with room left over for a buffer zone with a golf course and baseball and soccer fields.

Some 35 public officials and community leaders from Frio, Atascosa and Medina counties attended the meeting in support of the proposal. Their garbage was already going into San Antonio's two major landfills, and the new EPA regulations gave them no realistic alternative.

It sounded too good to be true. And it was. It did not take long for the private disposal companies to start bad-mouthing the deal. They hired local lawyers and community activists to kill it.

In July 1994, Councilman Henry Avila switched sides. Nelson Gardens was located in his district. Originally, he had opposed our permit expansion and said he would oppose any other landfill in his district. Now, he came out in opposition to the Frio County site, and said he wanted to give a contract to Waste Management.

Waste Management had gotten smart and backed off its hardball tactics. At the opening of its Covel Gardens landfill, adjacent to Nelson Gardens, in 1993, the company had presented a $5,000 check to Avila, to be used for youth and educational programs of his choice. They also gave funds to several other groups, including the Southwest School District that had previously opposed the landfill. This form of friendly persuasion was paying dividends.

Finally, the opposition to the Moore site proved too strong, and the financial and management demands by the Frio-Atacosa-Medina Solid Waste Agency became unreasonable. The deal fell apart.

Back home, Waste Management not only won the support of Councilman Avila, it also gained widespread community support. Even though I did not like Waste Management's tactics, I had to admit they had overcome a problem that had plagued council for years: the opposition of the council member in whose district a landfill would be located.

On April 14, 1995, Waste Management won unanimous approval from City Council of the zoning to expand Covel Gardens landfill from 215 acres to 700 acres. This would give them enough land for 75 years of big-dollar garbage dumping.

At that council meeting, Councilman Juan Solis, who once faulted Waste Management for "bullying, Northeastern-type of tactics," now praised them for changing leadership and adopting new policies. He went on to say, "While the city was not successful with the Texas Natural Resource Conservation Commission (the successor to the Texas Water Commission), Waste Management was very successful."

On May 30, 1995, at my last council meeting, we finally solved our long-term landfill problem. We approved 30-year contracts with Waste Management, BFI and Texas Disposal Systems for disposal of city garbage. This brought Waste Management back into the picture and gave the city three landfills to choose from, one in the southwest part of the city, another in the southeast, and a third in the north.

We also instructed the staff to continue negotiations with the three companies over proposals to develop a Regional Environmental Enterprise Zone. One year later the City Council designated Waste Management's Covel Gardens as the REEZ, with support from community groups and neighbors.

Today, San Antonio enjoys low disposal costs and competitive waste disposal operations for both the public and private sector. Our disposal cost in 1996 averages $13 per ton compared to $23 statewide.

A happy ending for trash.

Scenic Corridors, Landscaping and Trees

General Robert McDermott was concerned with haphazard development along Interstate 10 leading toward the Fiesta Texas theme park and USAA's La Cantera development. His temperature really began to rise when Motel 6 applied for a sign 120 feet high near Fiesta Texas.

The council had previously passed an ordinance regulating billboards, requiring that two signs come down for every new one erected. But there was no regulation regarding on-premise signs such as the one Motel 6 proposed to erect.

Councilman Bill Thornton, my successor in District 8, took the lead in responding to McD's concerns. He proposed a moratorium on sign permits until the City Council had time to address the issue.

Council enacted the moratorium. But we felt that what was good for McD and Interstate 10 would also be good for other corridors. We appointed an ad hoc committee with Robert Hunt as chairman to develop an urban scenic corridor ordinance.

From the start, the committee's work was difficult. Many developers were philosophically opposed to the idea of such an ordinance.

But Bill Thornton keep pushing the committee. He didn't mind pushing people a bit to make them come up with a compromise.

Committee members worked for more than a year to develop the ordinance. Eventually they proposed an amendment to the zoning code that authorized a series of overlay zoning districts with special standards for green space, driveways, building setbacks and screening, and sign height, size and spacing along street corridors that met certain criteria. Each corridor would have its own unique set of requirements.

On August 27, 1992, we passed the "Urban Corridor" ordinance unanimously. More than a dozen corridors were soon proposed to the Planning Commission. Bill Thornton again took the lead in pushing the designation of Interstate 10 West, Loop 1604 and two other arteries in the area as the first corridor, and the implementing ordinance for these roadways was adopted in mid-March 1993.

Since the first one, scenic corridors have been created along stretches of five more arterials and commercial streets, all in the inner city on the near North Side.

In June 1993, three months after we designated the first urban corridor, an incident occurred that galvanized a related effort to pass a landscape ordinance.

A "chain-saw massacre" of a grove of ancient oak trees occurred off U.S. 281, just north of the airport. The site was a new K-Mart that was to be built on an asphalt desert. It was the third incident of its kind in the area within two years. Express-News columnist Mike Greenberg, who is San Antonio's best analyst of urban planning issues, made it a *cause celebré*.

Until this incident, Councilman Howard Peak, elected in 1993 to represent the district, had been trying without success to convince council to consider a landscape ordinance.

But this case was so notorious that even many of the developers began to see the need for an ordinance. They began to work earnestly with environmentalists to reach a consensus.

As a result, in September council passed San Antonio's first landscape ordinance. It required developers of commercial buildings and apartments to retain or plant new trees and shrubs based on a point system. At the same time we instructed the Planning Commission to begin work on a tree preservation ordinance.

I called the landscape ordinance part of the plan to "grow with grace." This ordinance has resulted in thousands of trees being planted throughout the city.

The committee working on the tree preservation ordinance labored for more than two years. Howard Peak put together a committee that was equally divided between developers and environmentalists, but only stalemate resulted.

Eventually the committee did produce a recommended draft ordinance in the fall of 1996. It limited the number of trees that could be cut down when a site was developed, with emphasis on protection of old trees with large trunk diameters. It provided for both criminal and civil penalties, and it required the hiring of a city arborist to oversee enforcement of the ordinance.

Underground Power Lines

The policy of City Public Service, San Antonio's municipally owned gas and electric utility, had always been to supply power at the lowest cost to consumers without much regard for the surrounding environment.

But a major confrontation with CPS arising from this policy developed in September 1991, only a few months after I was elected mayor. CPS unveiled a plan to run two 138,000-volt power lines on 96-foot-high steel poles for 10 blocks along Hoefgen and Cherry streets in order to serve a new substation just south of the Alamodome. This was in accord with its standard policy that called for the cheapest possible utility extensions in order to hold down electric rates.

The ugliness of these poles, however, provoked immediate and intense opposition. City Councilman Frank Pierce, who served one term on council from that East Side district, pushed CPS to bury the line or reroute it along the Southern Pacific railroad tracks south of the Dome. City Council passed a resolution directing CPS to bury the line, except where it ran through an industrial area at its southern end. CPS grudgingly complied, but only after a statement that this would be a one-time exception.

This controversy inspired Express-News columnist David Anthony Richelieu to begin a personal crusade in the newspaper against overhead power lines. He attacked the ugly creosote poles that suspended power lines all over the city, in addition to the giant towers for major transmission lines. Then-Councilman Bill Thornton took up the cause of pushing CPS to put its power lines underground.

As a result of this pressure, CPS initiated a study to determine the cost of putting all new power lines underground and all existing ones within the next 25 years. This included high-voltage transmission lines that are rarely buried.

The study was completed in November 1992. It estimated the cost at a staggering $17 billion. As an ex-officio member of the

CPS board, I supported a proposal to instruct staff to go back and develop an underground conversion plan that was practical. In April 1993 the CPS staff suggested a politically brilliant solution. General Manager Arthur Von Rosenberg and Assistant General Manager Jamie Rochelle proposed we create a fund within the CPS budget to finance the conversion of overhead utility lines to an underground system. This fund would amount to one percent of retail sales of electricity, approximately $7 million a year.

City Council approved the program on April 8, 1993. We selected San Pedro Park as the first project in which to convert the overhead lines to underground. Then we directed staff to develop selection criteria and implementation procedures for future projects.

Technically, it was an easy process — from an engineering standpoint. But other issues were involved. Property owners would be required to make modifications on their own property in order to receive power from the new underground distribution system. Southwestern Bell and Paragon Cable obviously would have to bury their overhead lines at the same time. The utilities had joint-use agreements for the poles, and Southwestern Bell and Paragon were resistant to the added costs.

As this is written in early 1997, the ordinance establishing criteria and implementation procedures is on hold. But council has used the CPS fund successfully to finance underground utility conversion around San Pedro Park, around the UTSA downtown campus, and in an inner-city residential redevelopment project known as Villas de Esperanza, which was the site of the 1997 Parade of Homes. It has also set aside part of the available funds for an undefined project in the Mission Trails corridor, which will connect the Spanish Colonial missions on the South Side. Meantime, the money in the fund continues to accumulate.

Clean Up San Antonio

One day in January 1993, my old friend Ruben Munguia called me up to say, "Why don't you do a better job of cleaning up this city?" He complained of too many vacant lots where citizens were dumping their trash, and said we were not enforcing codes on building maintenance. He also complained about too much graffiti.

I said "Ruben, guess what? You are going to lead a commission to clean up San Antonio. I will take the issue to council right now if you are ready."

"I am ready," he replied.

So in February, council approved a Clean Up San Antonio Commission with a representative from each council district. I appointed Ruben chairman. Neighborhood leaders Rodrigo Garcia, David Carpenter and Jimmy Tucker became leaders in the effort.

The commission formulated a plan presented to council in August. It suggested a public awareness campaign, increasing the number of code violation inspectors, and measures to coordinate several city departments in a major clean-up effort.

The commission found that citizens in lower-income neighborhoods simply could not afford to haul large items such as furniture, refrigerators and tires to the far-off landfill and also pay a disposal fee. So they simply discarded these materials on abandoned lots, producing an estimated 800 illegal dump sites around the city.

The commission came up with the idea of a clean-up day. We formed a partnership of the city, the private landfill operators and Keep San Antonio Beautiful. In November 1993, we opened 30 locations around the city where citizens could bring their discarded items and dispose of them free of charge. The private landfill agreed to accept the trash collected on that day free of charge. Products that could be recycled were separated at the sites.

Citizens responded in overwhelming numbers. A thousand volunteers worked at the sites and collected 2,300 tons of trash. These programs continue today.

We have also worked on keeping our air clean. In mid-1994, I appointed a committee headed by Councilman Bob Ross to come up with a plan to keep San Antonio's air quality high. We are one of the largest cities in the United States that has not violated the federal standards for air quality. Once a city exceeds the ozone standards, its economic growth is restricted. We've come close to exceeding those standards a number of times. Although we've been a clean-air attainment city, I wanted to make sure we stayed that way. Councilman Ross' committee came up with a number of measures to keep San Antonio's air clean. They included converting all local governments' fleets to clean-burning fuels and advocating voluntary measures such as car-pooling.

The Parks Bond Issue

When I became mayor in 1991, San Antonio had 144 park sites of 6,536 acres. These figures placed the city nearly 40 percent below a conventional standard of 10 acres of park space per 1,000 people. In addition, many of our existing parks were in dire need of rehabilitation and capital improvements.

In early June 1991, I spoke to the "Neighbors for the '90's Conference" sponsored by the San Antonio Coalition of Neighborhood Associations, the city and the San Antonio Light. I told the 300 participants that I would call for a bond election for parks as soon as the economy recovered.

As I mentioned earlier, the most valuable lesson I learned from Henry Cisneros was to set an agenda. The most significant, and potentially the most difficult, agenda item is the timing of a bond issue and its contents.

While parks were my major objective, I also knew that streets and drainage would have to be addressed. Henry had passed the last streets and drainage bond issue in 1987.

But submitting a major bond package on parks along with streets and drainage would be a bit more difficult because there had never been a major parks bond issue. It had been more than 20 years since the voters approved a small package of $6.9 million in 1970. Since then there had been only a token $200,000 proposition in a 1980 bond issue. I wanted a parks bond package in the range of $40 to $50 million. I did not know what the public or council reaction would be.

I started advocating the idea of a parks bond issue early in my term so that I would have plenty of time to build community support. For more than two years, I talked about the issue on every occasion I could find.

Parks and Recreation Director Ron Darner was my partner in advocating more park space. Darner is quiet, unassuming, and among the most conscientious and hard working of city department heads. He started working with the city as a landscape architect in 1967, and because of a long battle with diabetes, he announced that he would retire in June 1997, just as a new city administration is taking office. He will be missed.

In July 1993, City Council agreed to call a bond election for May 1994 in an approximate amount of $100 million for parks, streets and drainage. This gave us time to get public input and time for me to work with Ron and my council colleagues in developing the bond package.

I reached an understanding with council that we would apportion the funds fairly equally among council districts. Council agreed to allow me to allocate roughly 20 percent of the bond issue for citywide projects. I told them I would allocate all of these funds for parks.

Salado Creek is one of the three major watersheds of San Antonio. It extends south from Camp Bullis, joining the San Antonio River seven miles south of Southeast Military Drive. San Antonio Express-News columnist Maury Maverick Jr. was a leading proponent of improving Salado Creek. With its springs, underbrush, bayous and cliffs, the creek was a wildlife treasure for birds and animals. Maverick wanted a series of parks, hiking trails and wildlife preserves along the creek.

Dixie Watkins, a local planning and design consultant, spearheaded the efforts of the Salado Creek Foundation (which I was member of before I was elected mayor) to enhance Salado Creek. We included in the bond package $500,000 to start on Maury Maverick's dream. The money would create an accessible greenbelt for hiking and picnicking in John James Park alongside Salado Creek.

Our two landmark parks, San Pedro and Brackenridge, received the most funds.

San Pedro Park is the second oldest in the United States. The 46-acre park was established in 1729 by command of the king of Spain. It originally had a natural lake fed by San Pedro Springs, the headwaters of San Pedro Creek, which flowed five miles south though downtown to join the San Antonio River. Today the springs and creek are dried up except in periods of extended heavy rainfall, and the lake has been replaced with a cement swimming pool.

Historian Mary Ann Noonan Guerra wrote me a letter stating that the restoration of San Pedro Park would be as historically significant as Mayor Maury Maverick's restoration of La Villita.

San Pedro Park became my priority. We included $5 million to renovate the San Pedro Playhouse located on the northeast side of the park, adding jogging trails, relocating parking to create more green space and landscaping. We planned to remove the concrete swimming pool and create a natural lake by recycling water from the springs.

Brackenridge Park, our most used park, includes the San Antonio Zoo, the Witte Museum, the Sunken Gardens and adjacent Sunken Gardens Theater, a miniature train, a skyride and several baseball fields. The San Antonio River runs through the park. We included $7.5 million in the bond package for a new entrance to the zoo, improved picnic facilities, hiking trails and several other improvements.

The bond package included $41.5 million for parks, providing funds to improve 88 existing parks and to acquire additional park land.

The bond issue also included $25.6 million for streets, $34.4 million for drainage and $8.1 million for a police substation and computer system. Some of the funds for streets and drainage also related to parks, such as the Mission Trails project.

On May 7, 1994, the voters overwhelmingly approved the bonds.

Government Canyon

The successful parks bond issue was matched by another important initiative during my terms as mayor. Between the two, we added almost as much park land as the city had accumulated over its long history.

In 1992, the Resolution Trust Corporation foreclosed on a 5,150-acre tract of land in northwestern Bexar County. The land is located over the recharge zone of the Edwards Aquifer and contains many sensitive recharge features.

Prior to the RTC foreclosure, Fay Sinkin, whom you met in the chapters on Water Wars, gathered several local citizens around her kitchen table to talk in general terms about acquiring land over the recharge zone. They organized the Edwards Aquifer Preservation Trust.

Out of Fay's effort new leadership developed to pursue a particular project. Danielle Milam, whom you also met in Water Wars, and Kyle Cunningham of the Helotes Creek Association, formed the Government Canyon Coalition.

The benefits of public acquisition of this tract were immense: Not only was the property important recharge land, but it is a rare and beautiful tract of canyons, creeks, meadows, endangered songbird habitat and "wild" open space only minutes from the heart of San Antonio.

The Government Canyon Coalition called on the Trust for Public Land, a non-profit organization based in San Francisco, for assistance. On March 19, 1993, the trust entered into a contract to buy the land. But it had no money. The trust had 120 days to come up with it. Trust Project Manager David Sutton came to San Antonio to raise the $2 million purchase price.

I encountered David at a meeting of the San Antonio Water System. Through Danielle Milam, David knew I was interested in acquiring more park land and in setting aside land over the Edwards Recharge Zone that could not be developed. David asked me for $500,000 from the city, one-fourth of the purchase price. The Edwards Underground Water District was considering giving $1 million and the Texas Parks and Wildlife Commission giving $500,000. I told him that I would try to get support for the project.

San Antonio was fortunate to have Tim Hixon serving on the Texas Parks and Wildlife Commission. Tim, a good friend and developer of the South Bank project on the San Antonio River, became the leading advocate in persuading the commission to support the project.

Together, Tim and I took two of his commission colleagues, Walter Umphrey from Port Arthur and Terry Hersey from Houston, along with the Texas Parks and Wildlife executive director, Andrew Sansom, to see the proposed park. We drove several miles up a rough gravel road, crossing what was originally a trail where Comanches and Apaches eluded government troops. We could see bat cave openings on the canyon walls, thickets of native brushes and grasses, and birds flying from one tree to another. The trail crossed a creek bed and faults from which 99 percent of the water that flowed over them would find its way down into the aquifer. After this trip no one had any doubts about the need to purchase this unique tract of land.

On May 4, the water system board, following the leadership of vice chairman Diane Rath and board member Victor Miramontes, voted to put up $500,000. One week later, the Edwards Underground Water District put up $1 million.

On May 20, the Texas Parks and Wildlife Commission agreed to put up the last portion of the purchase price.

This was government at its best: three governmental entities cooperating with each other to achieve a lasting benefit for future generations. In addition, County Judge Cyndi Krier committed the county to assist in operating the park.

Mitchell Lake Wetlands

While the acquisition of Government Canyon nearly doubled the acreage of park land in the city, another unique project that was assisted by the parks bonds was the Mitchell Lake Wetlands.

Growing up on the South Side of San Antonio in the 1940s and '50s, I could often smell the odor coming from Mitchell Lake. Until the 1930s, the lake was a sewage lagoon. But even after the city built its first modern sewage-treatment plant on Rilling Road, the lake continued to smell because it, along with the adjoining 589-acre Chavaneaux Gardens, was used as a place to store sludge.

When I took office as a councilman in 1987, the problem of the smell still had not been addressed. Council formed the Mitchell Lake Recovery Advisory Committee to develop a recovery plan for the area. In 1989, the committee presented a comprehensive plan that called for a permanent water-cap cover over the sludge sediments in the basins at the north end of the lake. But it was not until the City Council created the San Antonio Water System in 1992 that action finally began.

Soon after SAWS was created, Tim Darilek, project manager for Mitchell Lake, took us on a tour of the area. Since 1973 the area had been declared a refuge for shorebirds and waterfowl by the City Council. I was amazed at the number and variety. The lake had become an important stopping point on the migratory paths of many species, including the endangered whooping cranes.

Tim explained that if we flooded 200 acres of the 589-acre Chavaneaux Gardens site with treated wastewater, then the area would become a year-round haven for birds. We would create a wetlands from one to five feet deep that would entice more migratory birds. It would become one of the largest bird refuges in the United States.

The SAWS board approved the funding for the wetlands project. The Mitchell Lake Recovery Advisory Committee continues, under the leadership of urban planner Bob Ashcroft and microbiologist Dr. Ruth Lofgren, to push for the implementation of a plan to provide educational and environmental activities at the bird sanctuary. Roadway improvements, benches, restrooms and an educational center are planned, with some of the improvements funded in the 1997 SAWS budget. In the 1994 bond election, I included $500,000 for additional land acquisition. A Mitchell Lake Wetlands Society has also been started to study ways to better manage the area for wildlife, and the Audubon Society is playing a major role in these efforts.

What started out as an effort to cure a smell evolved into an internationally known bird sanctuary. Today nature lovers come from all over the world to visit the site.

Mission Trails

Another project on the South Side that was assisted by the parks bond was Mission Trails.

Henry Muñoz III is a man in his early 30s with the political skills that normally take a lifetime to acquire. I knew his father, Henry "The Fox" Muñoz Jr., a labor organizer and political activist who first worked at La Prensa for Congressman Henry B. Gonzalez's dad. Henry Muñoz III went to Loyola University and came back home to join the Kell-Wigodsky architecture firm in

1983. He did not enter politics until he attended the 1988 Democratic Convention and listened to Ann Richards' nominating speech for Michael Dukakis while sitting in Dukakis' box.

Afterward, Ann came up and told Henry she planned to run for governor. Henry signed on to the campaign and led the effort for Ann in Bexar County.

After her election, Ann appointed Henry to the Texas Transportation Commission in November 1991. One of Henry's most important legacies is the Mission Trails.

Everyone knows the crown jewel of San Antonio's historic treasures is the Alamo, but comparatively few people know that the Alamo is only the northernmost link in a necklace of five Spanish Colonial missions — more than any other city in North America. Extending south along the San Antonio River are Missions Concepcion, San Jose, San Juan, and Espada. To support these missions, the Spaniards built elaborate irrigation canal systems called *acequias,* the remains of which are still visible in many places in San Antonio. But these historic jewels are difficult to find unless you know the back streets of the South Side. Four million people a year visit the Alamo, but only one million visit any of the other four missions.

Efforts to link the Alamo with the other missions on the South Side go back at least to the 1930s. The city had tried several times to build a "Mission Parkway," but only scattered segments were ever completed. A major breakthrough occurred in the early 1970s, when Congress authorized the creation of the Missions National Historic Park, bringing the four southern missions under the administration and protection of the National Park Service. In a unique partnership of church and state, these missions also still continue in the service of the San Antonio Archdiocese. But the national park includes only the missions themselves and lands directly related to them. The problem of making them accessible remained, and it could only be solved by the San Antonio city government.

It was a project I really wanted to do. While growing up on the South Side I frequently visited these missions. I felt that the project would be an economic generator for the South Side and enhance the beauty of the area.

Henry told me that he thought he could persuade the Texas Transportation Commission to use "highway enhancement funds" for the project.

In May 1993, with Henry's help, the city was able to acquire a planning grant for $200,000 from the Federal Highway Administration. The study would focus on multiple routes to the missions, including bike and hiking trails, scenic corridors, pedestrian paths and greenways.

For Henry to be successful in funding the plan from the Transportation Enhancement Program, he needed local matching funds.

The Southside Chamber, under the leadership of Cindy Taylor and Bob Sanchez, and former state Rep. Tommy Adkisson, galvanized South Side support for the project.

In September 1993, the City Council agreed to allot $6.4 million in local funds to attract $25 million in state enhancement funds. With this united effort from San Antonio, in March 1994 Henry was able to secure $14 million over a three-year period from the Texas Transportation Commission. Two months later, San Antonio voters approved the bond package that included $3 million for the Mission Trails.

As designed, the trails would start at the Alamo and extend south 10 miles along two different routes with landscaping, antique-style benches, bus shelters and street lamps with Mission logo banners along them. One route largely followed the San Antonio River, but it would be flooded from time to time, so the other route was an all-weather route along city streets at a higher elevation.

Below Mission Concepcion, the scenic route following the west bank of the San Antonio River would provide picnic sites and parking where motorists could enjoy scenic views. Hike-and-bike trails would be included along the river. A six-mile stretch of the San Antonio River from East Guenther Street in the King William Historic District to Espada Dam near Southeast Military Drive would be improved.

Conclusion

The most controversial pending environmental issue is drainage. Current city policies allow new development to add to storm water runoff and to send the floodwaters downstream without provision for handling the increased volume of water. The uncontrolled downstream flow of storm water causes flooding and adds to pollution levels.

Ironically, the pollution itself may help us with a partial solution. During my term, council imposed a drainage fee to pay for testing for pesticides, gas, oil and other pollutants that may enter storm water runoff. The funds can be used for street cleaning and other measures to control pollutants entering the water.

On a related front, the parks bond issue also included $500,000 for the purchase of the old Vulcan Quarry. This encompasses approximately 141 acres of land close to the intersection of Huebner and De Zavala roads. The project is expected to be designed as a storm water detention pond with the surrounding land used for a park. This will help with the problem of flooding and pollution. At the time of this writing, that plan is still being studied.

In 1993, I appointed a committee led by Councilmen Howard Peak and Bob Ross to study our three major watersheds: the upper Olmos Creek, Leon Creek and Salado Creek. The study produced numerous suggestions for flood-retention facilities. The most controversial recommendation — which at this writing is in a draft ordinance form — is a requirement for on-site retention of increased storm water runoff caused by new development. This would add significant costs and will be opposed by developers, but it's necessary to stop the increased flow of storm water into our existing systems.

On the "visual environment" front, the council one year after I left office failed to pass an art ordinance that had been years in the making. The ordinance would have set aside one percent of funding for building projects for public art. Mayor Bill Thornton was absent on the day of the vote. I wrote a letter asking the council to reconsider. Bill came back home and took on the controversial issue. He and the council passed it over the objection of HTA and members of the media who had denigrated the plan.

The efforts we made to enhance our environment have paid off. In July 1994 the Green Metro Index, compiled annually from federal data by the World Resource Institute in Washington, D.C., ranked San Antonio first in the nation for environmental quality.

★★★

Lessons on Growing with Grace

■ **Annexation is the most important power to control growth.**
Without annexation powers, cities become encircled and lose control over their futures. City Councils must continue to plan ahead and vote for annexations.

■ **Dip your toe in the water to start a ripple.**
As a first-term councilman, I started the first curbside recycling program in a neighborhood of only 7,800 people. By the end of my term as mayor the service was offered citywide to 258,000 homes.

■ **The greed of private industry can sometimes lead to good policy.**
The overbearing push by Waste Management to get all the city's garbage for its landfill led for the first time to a council member supporting a landfill in his district. The "not in my backyard" syndrome was broken by astute maneuvering for private profit.

■ **Balancing interests can lead to breakthroughs.**
All the committees we appointed to address urban scenic corridors, landscaping, tree preservation and signs were balanced among business, environmentalist and neighborhood leaders. By keeping the pressure on all of them we were able to pass groundbreaking ordinances.

■ **You can create a diamond from coal.**
Putting some public funds into the old Mitchell Lake sewage treatment plant turned a smelly sewage lake into one of the best bird sanctuaries in the world.

Afterword

Henry Cisneros was the "agent of change" who set a vision for our city. The heart and soul of that vision was a strategy that sought to lift all boats on a rising tide of economic development. He not only created a new vision but he also showed us how to reach it. He forged a broad-based community consensus for his vision by elevating minorities to parity with Anglos and putting everyone at the table. He showed how power can be exercised in the mayor's office to move community consensus forward by melding together a coalition for progress.

While I shared Henry's vision of aggressive economic growth, I changed the tone of it with my message of "growth with grace." I learned from Henry how to exercise power and patch coalitions together to accomplish my objectives of enhancing our environment and developing our human potential along with job growth.

But will the policies and the visions that we articulated for our community have any lasting impact as we turn the corner into the next millennium? I believe so. The momentum is so strong that it will carry us far into the 21st century.

A last note on Henry and me. In January 1997, Henry completed four years of service as secretary of housing and urban development. He did an outstanding job in helping the homeless, replacing old, overcrowded public housing "ghettos" with subsidized housing where anyone would feel proud to live, and making public housing safe for its residents. He declined to be considered for reappointment by President Clinton.

Instead, Henry accepted the position of president and chief operating officer for Univision, the nation's largest Spanish-language television network. Henry called Tracy and me from Los Angeles, Univision's headquarters, as he sat in a hotel room overlooking the Pacific Ocean. He said he, Mary Alice and John Paul were looking for a home and a school. He seemed happy.

My two brothers, George and Gary, and I have bought out our partners in Sun Harvest. I am presently running our chain of eight natural foods grocery stores in San Antonio, Austin, Corpus Christi, McAllen, and El Paso. We are looking for other locations.

I stay active in San Antonio, serving as chairman-elect of the Greater San Antonio Chamber of Commerce, chairman of the Greater Austin-San Antonio Corridor Council, member of the board of directors of the San Antonio International Bank of Commerce, and City Public Service trustee.

I still play hardball for the Black Sox. My fastball has slowed down this year, but on good days it still hops.

Index